COMMUNITY PROPERTY
IN A NUTSHELL®

FIFTH EDITION

JO CARRILLO
Professor of Law,
University of California
College of the Law,
San Francisco

WEST ACADEMIC

860 Blue Gentian Road, Suite 350
Eagan, MN 55121
1-877-888-1330

Published in the United States of America

ISBN: 979-8-89209-252-4

For Max and Maddie,
with love.

PREFACE TO THE FIFTH EDITION

COMMUNITY PROPERTY IN A NUTSHELL, 5TH EDITION offers an updated roadmap to the law of the nine U.S. jurisdictions that maintain a community property system. Those states are Arizona, California, Idaho, Louisiana, Nevada, New Mexico, Texas, Washington, and Wisconsin. Also included, where relevant, is information about community property option states.

Family law covers a wide array of important legal issues, many of which are property related. This NUTSHELL introduces readers to the law of community property as a public institution for administering rights between married persons. The premise of a community property system is that spouses are partners, and as such they acquire property together during marriage. Nine U.S. states maintain a full-blown community property system; an expanding list of other states maintain statutory provisions that permit married persons in the jurisdiction to opt into community property contracts or trusts.

It is my hope that general readers who are motivated to learn about community property law will find useful information herein. I have made every effort to explain concepts within the realm of their legal context. Hyper-simplification, while useful to the general reader, can be misleading or noninformational to the professional reader. Thus, the idea here is to provide a springboard for further learning and research.

As for professional readers, it is also my hope that students, lawyers, and state legislators will find this work explanatorily useful. Students because they will be the lawyers and judges of the future. State legislators because the community property terrain is ever-changing, and law practice (which is often discretionary and oral) too often contradicts the written rules of legal doctrine and policy.

Each chapter is divided into three parts. Part A is an overview. Part B considers salient details. Part C excerpts statutory language and cites relevant cases from each of the nine U.S. community property states.

This is an original work of expository scholarship that I engage in as a public service.

In no way is this work intended as legal advice in a particular case. Property law is both complicated and contextual. Therefore, for assistance with an actual case, please consult a lawyer.

Any law school has multiple demands on faculty scholarship support funds. UC Law SF is no different. Therefore, I wish to extend a heartfelt thank you to Provost and Academic Dean Morris Ratner for his ongoing support of all faculty research, including my own.

I owe a special debt of gratitude to my professional research assistant, R.C. Vranesh.

I also wish to thank the librarians who helped us along the journey, both at my home institution and at the University of Michigan Law Library.

Last but never least, I thank my family for their support, their sense of humor, and their love.

JO CARRILLO
SAN FRANCISCO, CA

December 1, 2024

OUTLINE

PART 2. CHARACTERIZATION

PART 3. MANAGEMENT AND CONTROL

PART 5. SPECIAL PROBLEMS

TABLE OF CASES

References are to Pages

COMMUNITY PROPERTY
IN A NUTSHELL®

FIFTH EDITION

PART 1

PRELIMINARY MATTERS

CHAPTER 1

PRELIMINARY MATTERS

A. OVERVIEW AND HISTORY

A community property system is a default marital property system.

Community property system exists in nine jurisdictions of the United States: Arizona, California, Idaho, Louisiana, Nevada, New Mexico, Texas, Washington, and Wisconsin (by statute). Puerto Rico and Guam allow for community property as well. Two states, Alaska and Tennessee have long allowed married persons to opt into community property by contract or by trust; in these two states, a community property option can be exercised on an asset-by-asset basis or on an aggregate estate-wide basis. Florida and South Dakota more recently allow for use of a community property trust.

Under the traditional parent system—the Spanish ganancial system—the marriage itself is not a distinct juristic entity like a formal partnership or corporation. However, from the date of marriage forward, two people who are married to each other can acquire community property by default. For now, community property is loosely defined as property owned by the spouses, in undivided halves, as of the date it is acquired.

During marriage, each spouse has the right to own separate property. In the U.S., this right may be protected by the state constitution.

Each spouse also has the right to contract with each other over the property they acquire before or during marriage, just as they would have the right to do so with a third party.

Some U.S. community property states explicitly permit spouses to contract over personal rights and obligations so long as the contract provisions are not public policy or illegal. The right to petition for spousal support after divorce is one such personal right. The obligation to pay for spousal support after marriage is an example of a personal obligation.

No state allows parties to contract over child support rights in a way that negatively affects the rights of minor children of the marriage.

U.S. community property states allow for (only) two categories of property: community property and separate property.

Community property is property acquired by a married person while domiciled in the community property state.

Separate property is typically defined as property owned before marriage, property accepted during marriage as a gift, and property exchanged for or bought with separate property during marriage.

U.S. community property states split on how to characterize the rents, issues, and profits of separate property that are acquired during marriage. Some states adhere to the original civil law system and characterize separate property rents, issues, and profits as community property during marriage.

Other so-called American-rule states characterize the same as separate property during the marriage.

Common patterns and general principles are held in all community property jurisdictions.

- Ownership of community property during marriage is by undivided half shares.
- Record (paper) title does not necessarily control the character of an asset—community or separate—because the community property interest arises automatically upon acquisition of the asset.
- The character of an asset—community or separate—determines corollary rights related to management and control, disposition at dissolution and death, and federal income tax liability.
- The Internal Revenue Service, where relevant, calculates and collects tax by the taxpayer's community property domicile.

Differences among systems exist on important points depending on whether and how the state has changed the traditional parent system of community property by statute. In the U.S. community property states, early legislatures adopted the English common law but kept the earlier civil law ganancial system for marriage. Over time, hybrid civil-common law marital property systems have come into existence in the U.S. States. See Chapter 1, Section 3.

Two broad categorical state law differences in community property systems are:

- Separate property rents, issues, and profits acquired during marriage:
    - Under the traditional civil law, separate property rents, issues, and profits received during marriage are community property. A minority of U.S. community property states continue this approach.
    - Most U.S. community property states follow the so-called American-rule, under which separate property rents, issues, and profits received during marriage are themselves separate property.
- Properties for which special asset-specific community property presumptions apply.
    - All states apply an evidentiary presumption that property acquired by a person during the marriage while domiciled in the state is community property. This presumption is a general presumption. that can be superseded by a special presumption. See Chapter 4 for more on the general community property presumption.
    - Some states have adopted special statutory community property presumptions for certain classes of assets. See Chapter 4 and Chapter 7 for more on special community property presumptions.

- All community property presumptions start the analysis with a rebuttable conclusion that the asset in question is community property. How each presumption may differ lies in the type of factual proof needed for rebuttal. The separate property claimant carries the burden to rebut. Most often the standard of rebuttal is preponderance of the evidence. See Chapter 4 and 7 for more on community property rebuttal.

THE COMMUNITY PROPERTY STATES

By default: Arizona, California, Idaho, Louisiana, Nevada, New Mexico, Texas, Washington, and Wisconsin.

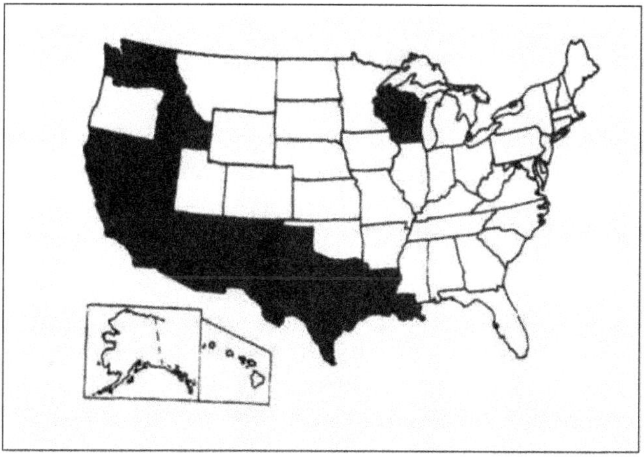

By option only: Alaska, Florida, South Dakota, and Tennessee.

1. DEFINITIONS

Characterization describes the process by which property is classified as *community property* or *separate property* within a community property system. *Community property* is property acquired by a person during marriage while domiciled in the state. Because of modern day mobility and mistakes in the contracting of a marriage, other sub-categories of community property such as quasi-community property and quasi-marital property are useful sub-categories of community property.

Quasi-community property is a labeling system that allows a court to identify property that would have been community property in the state, for purposes of a dissolution or probate proceeding, had the property been acquired while the parties were domiciled in the state.

Illustration 1.1: Assume H and W are domiciled in a non-community property state where they both have jobs and acquire assets. Assume further that the couple re-establish their domicile in a community property state where they also work and acquire assets. Eventually, they petition to dissolve their marriage.

For purposes of the dissolution process, the property acquired in the former domicile is quasi-community property for three reasons. First, the parties have changed their domicile. Second, the parties have filed a petition for dissolution in their new domicile, thus giving their consent that the laws of that state apply to their divorce. And third, any property acquired by the parties in their previous domicile that would have been community property had it been acquired in the new domicile will be characterized (for labeling purposes) as quasi-community property.

Quasi-marital property is property acquired by parties during a time when at least one of them can be adjudged a putative spouse, meaning a person who mistakenly and in good faith believed they were validly married under state law when in fact they were not. The property acquired when the parties believed themselves to be married can be treated as if it had been acquired during a valid marriage. For more on quasi-marital property, see Chapter 12, Sec. B.

Terminology varies from state to state.

The more popular term *community property* is used in this Nutshell, however, Wisconsin uses the term *marital property* to describe property owned by a married couple (as opposed to a larger community, such as the entire family).

Separate property is owned by a spouse as individual property. The term separate property is used in this Nutshell. Wisconsin uses the term individual property, a usage that derives from the adoption of the Uniform Marital Property Act. Washington cases occasionally use the term individually owned property.

During marriage in a community property state, parties acquire community property or separate property as marital property. Mostly the property is referred to with one of these labels. Aggregated marital holdings are sometimes called *an estate.* California courts and statutes use the phrase *community estate* to refer to aggregated community property holdings. In Texas, the phrase used to refer to aggregated holdings of any character is *marital estate.*

From an atmospheric point of view, once assets are identified they can be characterized as community property or as separate property.

From a property perspective, however, the analytic difficulty can be in the detail. This book addresses the atmospheric and the ground level perspectives. The text assumes a legally trained reader. It is accessible to motivated readers as well. The purpose of the text is educational. For legal advice, please consult an attorney.

The first step to better understanding community property law is to define the key words in the community property principle:

Community property is property acquired by a person who is married and domiciled in a community property state.

Separate property is property that does not fall into or is statutorily excluded from the community property principle.

a. Property

Community property law is at its core a sub-field of property law.

Property is a multi-faceted right that can be defended in court.

Property can be a thing of value. Value is a complex word. It can mean market value, sentimental value, or symbolic value. Anything capable of legal transfer can be property. Property can be a thing, but it is not always a thing. Property rights can be in tangible or intangible sources of value. Property rights can be in land (real property) or anything else (personal property). A property right can be vested (possessory or certain to become possessory) or contingent (not yet possessory and not certain to become possessory).

Understanding property as a right is what unifies the legal field of property. At its core, a property right is subject to transfer, whether by sale or gift. The full property right includes the right to sell on a state sponsored market (title) and the right to use (possession). Title is superior to possession, but without rights to use the property (manage and control), title and possession become rights in name only. The right to manage and control property includes the right to exclude or invite others to use the property. The property right can be unified in one person, disaggregated for a time, then reaggregated. (Think Legos.) If a building owner, for example, rents a building to a tenant, the owner transfers possession to the tenant by the lease but retains a future interest that allows the owner to retake possession of the building when the lease ends. Possession is itself a significant property right. Absent a contract, possession is transferable.

Community property is thus anything capable of being owned and divided if a marriage ends. All marriages end, either by dissolution (divorce) or by the death of one of the spouses.

Employment earnings, real estate, contract rights, shares of stock, stock dividends, stock profits, sums on deposit in a bank account, investment accounts, computer hardware, software, data, vehicles, a patent, a copyright, a trademark, a professional practice, business goodwill, celebrity identity: Each of these are "things" that can bring a benefit to their "owner" and, as such, each "thing" can be "owned" and even "titled" as community property during marriage.

Some assets, because they are not transferable, may be exempt from the community property system by statute or by case law. Professional degrees are one example. So too is raw talent that has not been transmuted into earnings or creations. Generally, professional degrees and raw talent are considered personal to their holders. An unfiled personal injury claim is another example of something not transferable; however, money and property received in settlement of litigated personal injury claim are transferable.

An expectancy—called in property law a *mere* expectancy to drive home the point—is only a potential property interest, a generalized dream, the hope of ownership in the future. Hope and expectation have their place in law, but a mere expectancy cannot be defended as a property right in a court of law.

By contrast, a contingent interest can be community property. A contingent interest may or may not vest if a condition set by the grantor and known to the grantee happens (or does not). Nevertheless, once the condition is met, the contingency lifts, and the property right vests in the grantee. Speaking metaphorically, a contingent interest is less solid than a vested right but more solid than a mere expectancy. Because lifting the condition on title passing is in the hands of the grantee, a contingent interest can be protected in court and, therefore, it is a property right.

A valid marriage is not a form of property, nor does it create a legal entity. Marriage, in the property sense, at least in a community property state, allows for the automatic acquisition of concurrently owned, undivided community property. But a marriage itself is not an entity like a corporation, or a nonprofit, or a limited partnership. A marriage does not own property in its own fictitious entity name, nor does it pay obligations as a fictitious entity. (Louisiana is an exception.) Nevertheless, more community property states are making explicit that spouses are joint venturers in transactions between them.

b. Acquisition

To *acquire* property means to obtain a legal right to the asset. An asset can be legally acquired, by purchase, gift or otherwise. In a community property state, the inception of title rule holds that the character of an asset is determined when the owner's legal rights to it comes into existence. Each state may have a presumption that assists with characterization of the asset when the acquisition facts are unclear.

Property acquired during marriage is generally presumed to be community property in character.

Onerous title is property acquired by labor, industry, time, or toil. Earnings and accumulations are derived from the exercise of time, toil, labor, and industry. So too are created properties such as copyrights, patents, and adverse possession titles.

Property acquired before marriage, at least in a ganancial system, comes into the marriage as the owning spouses' s separate property.

Lucrative title is property acquired by gift, windfall, or the conferral of a benefit. In a ganancial system, gifts and other lucrative titles received during marriage are characterized as separate property.

A conferred benefit is like a gift in that it is a gratuitous, transfer, but it is unlike a gift in that the party conferring the benefit expects reciprocity. Often community property law allows the spouse who conferred the benefit to be reimbursed by the community. Restitution is a remedy for preventing unjust enrichment.

Commingled property is a mixture of community and separate property. An asset can be co-owned between the community property estate and one or both spouses' separate property estates.

Transmuted property is property whose character has been changed, as when community property becomes separate property or vice versa.

c. Marriage

Marriage is a fundamental right guaranteed by the Fourteenth Amendment and the Due Process clause of the U.S. Constitution. A corollary of the right to marry is the right to divorce. See Chapter 10 for more on divorce.

Two individuals regardless of gender or gender identity have the right to obtain a marriage license and to have their licensed marriage recognized across states and for all federal purposes. *Obergefell v. Hodges*, 576 U.S. 644, 135 S. Ct. 2584, 192 L.Ed.2d 609 (2015).

The Respect for Marriage Act (the RMA for short) repeals prior inconsistent legislation and gives full faith and credit to a valid same-sex marriage. RMA § 5.3 and 5.4

Under the RMA: **"For purposes of a federal law, rule, or regulation in which marital status is a factor, an individual shall be considered married if that individual's marriage is between 2 individuals and is valid in the State where the marriage was entered into or, in the case of a marriage entered into outside of any State, if the marriage is between 2 individuals and is valid in the place where entered into and the marriage could have been entered into in a State."** RMA § 5.7.

For federal purposes, a lawful marriage comes into existence when statutory formalities are met under state law. RMA § 5.5(c). See Chapter 13 for more on federal law issues.

State law sets forth formalities for contracting a valid marriage and for becoming domiciled therein. See Chapter 12, Sec. A for more on marriage validity.

Among the nine U.S. community property states, informal marriage (so-called "common law marriage") is allowed in only one state: Texas. An informal marriage contracted in Texas is a lawful valid marriage, in Texas. If the informally married Texas spouses were to move to California, their marriage would be recognized as valid for purposes of California law. But if this couple divorced and later decided, while still domiciled in California, to attempt a second informal marriage, that marriage would not be valid because California does not allow informal marriage.

No state, not even Texas, allows informal dissolution (divorce).

Registered Domestic Partners [RDPs for short] status requires proof of registration with the state. RDP status is offered in several states. In those states, RDPs enjoy rights and obligations as counted under state law. Most states equate RDP with marriage.

A void marriage never comes into legal existence. It is a marriage subject to a defect that cannot be cured either because the spouses are too closely related by blood or because one of the spouses is still married to one or more third parties. Nevertheless, to provide notice to creditors and other third parties in the market (like real estate purchasers), states either require or allow a party to a void marriage to file for an annulment by court judgment. The death of one of the parties to a void marriage does not make that void marriage valid.

A voidable marriage is presumed valid. It is a marriage subject to a defective that can be cured by the parties. When the defect is cured, the marriage becomes valid. If the defect is not cured, the parties have a choice to either annul the marriage or seek dissolution. If the parties decide to annul their voidable marriage, they dissolve their property holdings under general law. If they decide to dissolve their voidable marriage, they affirm that the defect was cured and proceed to dissolve their property under state community property laws. The death of one of the parties to a voidable marriage, does make that marriage valid.

A putative marriage is one in which one or both partners believe, in good faith, that their otherwise void or voidable marriage is valid. Many states adopt an equitable doctrine called the putative spouse doctrine. This doctrine confers the benefit of marriage on the person who petitions and is awarded putative spouse status. An analogous form of marital property rights and obligations then flow, not from marriage since the marriage is defective, but from the court's decision to exercise its discretionary powers in favor of the putative spouse. A putative marriage acquires quasi-*marital* property, not community property or quasi-community property.

Nonmarried cohabitants are two people who live together in what courts have called a marriage-like relationship. Nonmarried cohabitants do not owe each other spousal obligations because they are not validly married to each other, by their choice. But neither do they enjoy spousal rights. Nonmarriage can lead to different outcomes at break-up or at death, depending on state law. Washington, for example, adopts the committed relationship doctrine so that nonmarried persons in certain cases can use the state community property and spousal support laws. Other states like California allow no such adjustment out of concern over various issues including forced marriage. See Chapter 11 for more on nonmarital partners.

d. Domicile

Domicile is a legal conclusion based on presence in a state for personal legal matters. A person chooses their legal domicile by an intentional act that makes the state home.

Spouses are permitted to have different domiciles in most states. This is a reversal of the outdated gender-based rule that automatically used the husband's domicile to name the wife's domicile.

Domicile is a key concept in community property law. It decides if a marriage is valid. It defines how property is characterized. It is important for spousal support rights (as when a party moves to another state), domestic violence orders, and the filing of dissolution petitions. Domicile is discussed further in Chapter 11.

e. Apportionment

Apportionment means to split property into fractional shares.

A person must be married to acquire community property. However, not all property of a married person must be or is community property. That said, when a marriage ends there is often property and obligation in the form of contracts, court judgments or court orders. The existence of these assets and obligations means there must be an accounting.

Community property ownership of a single asset means that the asset is concurrently owned in undivided one-half shares. Depending on state law community property shares are either 50-50 or equitably determined by the court at the end of marriage.

Separate property ownership of a single asset means that the asset is owned by one spouse.

Commingled property ownership of a single asset means that the asset is owned *pro rata* by the community and by one or both spouses as individuals.

At dissolution, parties are encouraged to divide their property by a marriage settlement agreement (MSA). If the parties reach a bargained for exchange, a court can incorporate their MSA into the final judgment.

Statutes guide the court on how to exercise its jurisdiction if the parties cannot agree on an MSA. In some states, the authority of the court extends only to community property. If so, the court would be limited to issuing rulings and orders about the parties' community property assets and their commingled assets.

In some states, if the parties cannot agree on how to divide their property, the court is mandated by statute to divide the property in equal shares. Equal means an arithmetic 50-50 split. In other states the statutory mandate is for the court to divide the property equitably between the parties. Equitable means any split (50-50, 70-30, or even 90-10) that the court deems fair considering the evidence.

Statutes mandate how to analyze the case. In some states, if the parties cannot reach an MSA, the court is mandated to characterize inventoried property on an asset-by-asset basis. In other states the court is allowed to lump community property assets together in a hotchpot, or aggregate, estate

Considering statutory mandates like these, marital property law in a community property state incentivizes the use of marital settlement agreements. Additional incentives are created around mediation and collaborative lawyering.

2. IMPLICATIONS OF CHARACTERIZATION

In a community property system, issues routinely arise over acquisition, apportionment, control, dissolution, succession, and taxation.

Some such issues include:

- Management and control rights to sell, lease, encumber, gift, confer, and transfer community property.
- Disclosure and financial transparency rights related to obligations arising from the use of community property.
- The rights of creditors to reach or to satisfy claims against community property.
- The characterization and assignment of money and property received in settlement of a tort claim that arose during marriage.
- Tax determinations and liens.

A final judgment of dissolution (a divorce decree) terminates a marriage. Divorce automatically ends a party's legal ability to acquire community property. Dissolution divides the assets.

The death of a spouse terminates a marriage. Death triggers the transfer of property to the decedent spouse's intestate heirs or will beneficiaries. Since no person has the right to devise property belonging to another, each spouse's testamentary rights extend only to the decedent's one-half interest in the (former) community property.

As to community property of the marriage, a surviving spouse has an exalted status relative to the decedent's consanguineous intestate heirs. Thus, by statute, if one spouse dies intestate, the surviving spouse is entitled to the decedent's one-half share of the (former) community property, leaving the surviving spouse with a 100% individual interest in that property. Otherwise, most states require the surviving spouse to share the decedent spouse's separate property with the decedent's other eligible heirs. For more on intestacy see Chapter 12.

See Chapter 13 for end of marriage issues that can involve conflicts of law.

3. RATIONALE FOR THE COMMUNITY PROPERTY SYSTEM

The community property system favors the family by allowing spouses to automatically acquire property in undivided, vested, equal shares during the marriage.

This system conclusively presumes that each spouse's labor contributes to the acquisition of family wealth in the form of community property. For example, if only one spouse earns wages, those wages and anything they might be used to purchase belong to the community, not solely to the earning spouse. Likewise, if one spouse detracts from the process of property acquisition, that spouse is nevertheless entitled to their one-half undivided share of the community property.

The language of equality of interest in community property preceded actual legal equality in many cases. For example, California used the term "community property" as early as 1849, but under the ruling in *Van Maren v. Johnson*, 15 Cal. 308 (1860), a wife had (only) a contingent interest in community property that vested, if it did, (only) at divorce or the death of the husband. It was not until 1927, following *Stewart v. Stewart*, 199 Cal. 318, 249 P. 197 (1926), which held that a trial court had erred in calling community property a vested right, that the state legislature passed a statute to abrogate the case and make community property a vested right. Today that statute appears at Cal.Fam.Code § 751: **"the respective interests of each spouse in community property during continuance of the marriage relation are *present, existing, and equal*."** (Italics added.)

The transition from understanding community property as a contingent right to a vested right that is present (possessory), existing (vested), and equal (undivided one-half share) was massively important to recognizing the property rights of married women in U.S. community property states. For background see, *Arnett v. Reade*, 220 U.S. 311, 31 S. Ct. 425, 55 L.Ed. 477 (1911) and *McDonald v. Senn*, 53 N.M. 198, 204 P.2d 990 (1949), discussed below.

Additionally, until the mid-1970s, community property states followed a gender-biased rule called male management. This rule gave husbands the *legal right* of management and control of community personal property by default. Today, states have transitioned to a gender-neutral equal management and control rule. Either spouse acting alone can manage the community personal property in matters non testamentary. See Chapter 7 for more on management and control rights and duties.

4. TYPES OF COMMUNITY PROPERTY SYSTEMS

There is no single community property system. There are several systems, each with its commonalities and differences.

Here are some frequent questions that come up about community property.

Is a valid marriage an entity like a partnership or a corporation? Most states do not treat a marriage as a juristic entity, as noted above. However, the term *matrimonial regime* shows how a marriage can be a juristic entity for certain purposes. Louisiana, and in some parts of the Commonwealth of Puerto Rico, the marital regime system lives. In California, by comparison, marriage is a personal and public contract that allows spouses to own, manage and control property as individuals, within policy parameters set by state law.

The difference matters. In both types of community property systems creditors can reach community property. In a marital regime state, however, once the community property is exhausted, the creditor is prevented from reaching one or both spouses' separate property holdings. By contrast, in a state where marriage is not a juristic entity, a creditor can marshal the property so that community property is reached first, the separate property of the obligor spouse second, and sometimes the separate property of the non-obligor spouse third.

Does property owned before marriage become community property upon marriage?

No, not in a ganancial community property system.

The universal, or Roman-Dutch, form of community property changes all premarital property into community property upon marriage. This marital property system was carried by the Dutch to southern Africa, the East Indies, and the West Indies. It is still today used in the Netherlands.

Among middle approaches the dividing issue is whether all premarital property comes into marriage as community property (or not). In France between 1804 and 1965, all movable property (personal property in the common law system) became community property upon marriage (as in the universal system), but all immovable property (real property in the common law system) did not. Modifications were also made for dowry and for gifts to the married couple. In 1965, however, France adopted a ganancial system.

The ganancial system is the parent form of U.S. community property systems. The ganancial system derives from the Visigoths, the Germanic tribes that came to rule Spain in the Middle Ages.

In a ganancial system, all premarital property remains the separate property (called in Spanish bienes propios) of its individual owner, while property acquired during marriage by labor, while domiciled in the jurisdiction is characterized as community property (called in Spanish bienes gananciales).

Today the ganancial system or a variant thereof operates in the U.S. (Arizona, California, Idaho, Louisiana, Nevada, New Mexico, Texas, and Washington, Puerto Rico, Guam), the civil law systems of Central and South America, the Virgin Islands, The Philippines, to name but a few jurisdictions.

U.S., ganancial systems also divide along how much they lean toward common law concepts. Louisiana is closer to its civil law origins than are the other U.S. community property states. California has had strong ties to the common law tradition since early statehood, for reasons discussed below. New Mexico relied on California statutes in setting up its community property system, but then looked to the law of Spain and of Mexico to define and interpret those statutes.

Finally, just as an introductory tidbit about U.S. community property systems. Louisiana alone uses usufruct (discussed below) as a rationale for why separate property rents, issues, and profits acquired during marriage are community property. Texas treats separate property rents, issues, and profits acquired during marriage identically to Louisiana, but uses the rationale of its state constitution rather than usufruct. Texas relies on the common law of unjust enrichment far more heavily than California does.

B. CIVIL LAW VERSUS COMMON LAW INFLUENCES

This section speaks to the legal historical origins of community property.

The first written recognition of community property appeared in the year 693 CE in the Visigothic Code and it was restated in the Fuero Juzgo of 1241 CE. The Visigoths, nomadic Germanic tribes in the North Atlantic, crossed the Danube River into the Roman Empire in 376 CE. In their migrations first south and then west and even north, the Visigoths left a legal heritage that includes the community property system. For example, the community system appeared in Sweden as early as 1200 C.E. in the Law of West Goths, according to the Manuscript of Aeskil or Eskil.

The historical community property ganancial system pre-dates the English common law system. In the community property system, a married woman kept her legal identity during marriage. The result was that she could own property and contract with third parties over property, even if her husband had the legal rights of management. Partly the reason for this was necessity, not proto feminism, as in early times Visigoth men were mercenaries for the Romans, a highly dangerous occupation.

By contrast, under the historical English common law system, upon marriage, a married woman's legal identity merged into that of her husband's. A married woman could not acquire, manage, or control property during marriage because from the date of her marriage forward, she no longer possessed a legal identity of her own. Indeed, before the passage of the Married Woman's Property Act, an unmarried woman (*feme sole*) could own property, while a married woman (*feme covert*) was required to assume her husband's legal identity during marriage (*coverture*).

Moreover, the married woman under common law did not acquire a share in her husband's earnings, accumulations, or property, as did her counterpart in the ganancial community property system. The married woman had common law dower rights. She was however excluded from intestate succession under the law of primogeniture, which favored her husband's eldest male heir, and his male heirs generally over any surviving wife and daughters. Dower gave the surviving wife (only) a life estate in one-third of the realty that her husband died owning in fee simple absolute during the marriage.

In the common law system, a married woman was effectively barred from the institution of property. The husband had legal dominion over the property of the marriage, and he had all legal rights of management and control over that property as well. His legal dominion gave him financial and physical dominion (control) over the person of the wife. A husband was the married woman's legal guardian, and she his legal ward.

In the U.S., community property doctrines were adopted for reasons outlined in the next section. Still U.S. states adopted the common law method of reasoning. This makes sense as American lawyers were and still are trained in the common law method of reasoning. These 19th century legal actors employed logic that reflected their knowledge of English common law unmodified by the Married Women's Property Act. In this way, the law of U.S. community property states grafted onto itself aspects of the English common law. What was different, of course, is that many of the European newcomers to the U.S., and especially those who went west, were not the high-born male aristocrats that the common law of marriage privileged.

In the last half of the 20th century, separate property states began to move in the direction of community property states in the name of divorce reform. These states passed statutes to achieve equitable partition between marital partners at the end of marriage.

The Uniform Martial Property Act was promulgated in 1983 (UMPA 1983) (see also the Model Marital Property Act of 2009 (MMPA)). UMPA 1983) was adopted by Wisconsin in 1986, shifting that state from a separate property state to a community property state. See Chapter 4 for more on UMPA 1983.

The Uniform Marriage and Divorce Act of 1970 (the UMDA 1970 for short), which creates community property-results, depending on what provisions are included, was adopted by some states as well. Among community property states Arizona and Washington enacted UMDA 1970 provisions in 1973, when they shifted from fault-based to no-fault divorce.

Despite these trends toward divorce reform in the U.S., misunderstandings about the community property system are widespread and continue to persist.

Prior to 1948, for example, acquirers and possessors of community property had federal income, and estate and gift tax advantages that did not exist for a domiciliary of common law (separate property title) states. To gain those same advantages, the states of Michigan, Nebraska, Oklahoma, Oregon, and Pennsylvania and the (then) Territory of Hawaii adopted community property systems. In Pennsylvania, the community property statute was declared unconstitutional. In the other states and in Hawaii the community property system was repealed shortly after the 1948 amendments to the Internal Revenue Code (I.R.C.) eliminated the tax advantages that the adoption of community property had meant to address by permitting joint income tax returns, a marital deduction for both gift and estate taxes, and the gift-splitting provisions of the gift tax.

Property casebooks tend to minimize community property systems as something of a backwater. Considering that community property systems appear all around the world, nothing could be further from the truth.

C. U.S. COMMUNITY PROPERTY SYSTEMS

1. COMMON THREADS

The common threads of the community property systems rest in a major premise and its underlying principles.

Broadly told, the premise of any community property system is that marriage creates something like a joint venture or a partnership (although not a juristic entity) between the spouses.

Three principles are common to community property jurisdictions. They are

- the contractual modification principle,
- the equality of interest principle, and
- the tracing principle.

The contractual modification principle holds that the spouses can alter some or all default community property rules by an enforceable private contract. See Chapters 2 and 3 for more on contractual modification.

The *equality of interest principle* recognizes that, during marriage, spouses acquire equal vested shares in community property as of the date of acquisition or accumulation. See Chapter 4.

The *tracing principle* characterizes an asset acquired during marriage identically with the labor, funds, or property that were used to acquire the legal right to it. The character of an asset is set or determined—depending on the state—at the inception of title, meaning the date that the legal right to the property comes into existence. Tracing, an equitable remedy, can then be used to identify pro rata (fractional) ownership shares in the property See Chapters 7 for more on tracing.

These three principles—contract modification, equality of interest, and tracing—are the foundation of a default U.S. community property system.

The benefit of such a system is that it is strong enough to offer financial protections to the spouses within marriage and yet flexible enough to allow them to modify the system by contract as they see fit. The downside of the system tends to be technical and straightforwardly addressable.

Although the community property system is said to better protect the non-earning spouse's contribution to family wealth, those protections have not been and sometimes are still not fail safe.

For example, prior to 1975, state statutes named the husband (the male spouse) as the spouse who was legally entitled to manage and control community property. This form of gender bias incentivized banks (including those issuing credit cards) not to extend credit to a married women without her husband's signature. The consequence was that a married woman's right to obtain credit in her own name was compromised.

Today, case holdings that support legally enforced gender bias are constitutionally impermissible. In California, for example, this could invalidate case holdings that predate 1927, insofar as those holdings are based on the premise that the community property right is contingent during marriage. Likewise, cases that predate 1975 are called into question because of the transition from male-management to equal management. Most of these cases have been superseded by statute, but even today bar preparation materials might sometimes refer to rules that once supported male management as if those rules are still current law.

2. SOME (CURRENT) UNCOMMON THREADS

Each state balances the above three common principles differently. This could create instances of what might be called local peculiarities were it not for the fact that each state's system is one of local peculiarities.

State law differs as to:

- Premarital contracting: Some states, like Arizona and Texas have adopted the Uniform Premarital Agreement Act (the UPAA 1983 for short). Louisiana and Washington have not. California has adopted and so significantly amended the UPAA 1983 that its statute—the California Premarital Agreement Act—is considered sui generis.
- Marriage validity issues: Among U.S. community property states, only Texas continues to allow informal, so-called "common-law", marriage. Idaho recognizes as valid only those informal marriages that were contracted in the state before January 1, 1996.

All community property states define a bigamous marriage as void. The federal Respect for Marriage Act (RMA 2022) defines a marriage for federal purposes as a union between two people, thus indicating that "**[n]othing in this Act, or any amendment made by this Act, shall be construed to require or authorize Federal recognition of marriages between two or more individuals**." RMA § 7(b).

- Usufruct versus property right: Some states characterize the rents, issues, and profits of separate property as community property, in line with the civil law usufruct approach. Other states recognize the same as separate property, in line with a California innovation grafted onto the community property system in the 19th century by common law trained lawyers influenced by English law of trusts.

- All states follow the inception of title rule, in line with the civil law approach, but they do not follow it in the same way. See Chapter 7 for more on the uses of the inception of title rule.

    - Texas leads the way in applying the inception of title rule to *determine* the character of an asset during and through to dissolution. This is in line with traditional civil law.

    - California leads the way in applying the inception of title rule to *set* the character of an asset at acquisition, understanding that the asset's character can change over the course of the marriage.

Legislatures are respectful of due process rights which might be implicated by a retroactive change to vested community property rights. In states where community property is protected by the state constitution, legislative changes may affect vested property rights. Moreover, in states where the community property system is entirely or primarily legislative, retroactive changes can cause characterization disputes between the spouses and between the spouses and third-party purchasers and creditors.

The practical result of retroactive change is that each change in the definition of community property may create a new category of community property that gets added on to preexisting categories. Too many changes can overcomplicate the system. Thus, historical analysis is a useful tool in community property law, especially when its use incentivizes keeping the system detailed enough to protect property rights, yet straightforward enough to lighten court case loads.

3. HISTORICAL DIFFERENCES

The history of statehood and adoption of the community property system in each of the U.S. states also has both common threads and individual variations:

Arizona, California, Nevada, and part of New Mexico were acquired by the U.S. in 1848 by the Treaty of Guadalupe Hidalgo, which officially ended the Mexican American War. Mexico followed the ganancial community property system. These states adopted the community property system, as was required by the Treaty provision that called for the protection of Mexican property owners' rights during the transition from Mexican to U.S. governance.

Utah and parts of Colorado and Wyoming were also ceded by Mexico to the U.S. by the Treaty of Guadalupe Hidalgo, but none of these states undertook to protect the rights of Mexican property owners by adopting community property principles. Pre-statehood Utah was polygamous, raising obvious questions about how community property might be readily applicable in the state. Likewise, Idaho was a state with a distinct Church of Latter-Day Saints (Mormon) history.

From at least since 1865, the Arizona Territory recognized the community property system. THE RECORDS OF THE ARIZONA CONSTITUTIONAL CONVENTION OF 1910 (John S. Goff ed.) confirm that the delegates voted to indefinitely postpone including a restatement of community property law in the state constitution. They regarded community property as purely legislative in character, not as a system whose adoption was required by international treaty. Moreover, they did not mention, much less enshrine, community property principles in the state constitution. Since statehood, Arizona has tended to follow California and Texas community property law, with some early leanings towards the laws of Washington, which itself has looked somewhat to California.

State constitutions and statutory developments have created state-specific U.S. community property systems.

In 1849, California adopted a territorial constitution that continued, but hardly enshrined, the Spanish community property system. After statehood, the 1850 Organic Act brought in changes that further pushed the already anemic constitutional recognition of community property towards common law property principles and decision-making processes. Marriages were certified as a matter of public right, not canonical law, as had been the case under Mexican rule. Married Catholics could continue to seek canonical divorces, but marital property division became the sole province of the civil state. The husband was given legal management and control over community property, with absolute power of disposition. A married woman was understood to have a conditional community property right until the end of the marriage.

The 1879 California constitution enshrined the right to own separate property during marriage, not the right to acquire community property during marriage. This led to the development of a robust jurisprudence on how to identify separate property rights at the end of a marriage.

Until 1969, the state Family Act was included within the California Civil Code, but effective 1970, the state adopted a standalone Family Code.

Today, the California Family Code includes customized uniform and model codes alongside original provisions. For example, the Uniform Premarital Agreement Act 1983 (UPAA 1983) was adopted and customized to such an extent that it is now called the California Premarital Agreement Act (CPAA 1985, amended in 2001). Similar changes have been made to other uniform or model codes such as the Revised Uniform Partnership Act, the Uniform Fraudulent Transfer Act, the Uniform Parentage Act, the Uniform Multiple-Party Accounts Law, and others.

California Community Property Law is a distinct field of law, and it continues to be tested on the state bar exam. Yet it is an undervalued field among law school academics, perhaps because it is a technical sub-field of property law. As to its property provisions, most law schools teach this subject directly to the bar exam, which makes for a crash course of distortedly undertheorized and simplistic rules.

This is unfortunate considering that California community property law influences the law of all U.S. states and a considerable number of countries in the world. It is more than the sum of its parts. Consequently, the California system can be fairly characterized as a sui generis hybrid common law slash civil law system. One kept current by the

California Legislature, aided by the courts of appeal, and the state supreme court.

Idaho is unique in that when Idaho became a state in 1890 it had already developed twenty-three years of its own body of community property law, one not heavily influenced by a Spanish or Mexican heritage. This is because Idaho was originally included in the Oregon Territory and was added to the Washington Territory in two parts, one in 1853 and the other in 1859. Idaho existed from 1863 until 1867 as a territory without a community property system. The community property system was added in 1867. It has continued into the present.

Louisiana is recognized as the state that has most closely nurtured the legal traditions of the parent civil law system, primarily by its reliance on the matrimonial regime. The present state of Louisiana bears only a slight resemblance to the vast territory which was named after Louis XIV of France. The shifting ownership of the mouth of the Mississippi River during the 17th and 18th centuries is a history in miniature of alternating Spanish and French colonial influence. The Custom of Paris prevailed in Louisiana until 1769; after which the Spanish ganancial system took effect. When Napoleon terminated the alternating ownerships by selling the Louisiana Territory to the U.S. in 1803, the community property system was already well established in the territory. Of all the territory the U.S. acquired in that vast purchase, only the land south of the 33d parallel (called by Congress the Territory of Orleans, and now the state of Louisiana) retained the community property system. The balance of the states which were formed from the Louisiana Purchase (like the territory of East and West Florida) did not continue the community property system even though it is part of their legal history.

Nevada, acquired from Mexico along with California, was originally part of the Utah Territory. Since admission to the Union in 1864, Nevada has had a constitutional provision recognizing community property. Nevada tends to look to California or Washington law in developing its law.

New Mexico, consisting partly of land from the Republic of Texas and partly of land acquired by the U.S. via the Treaty of Guadalupe Hidalgo, included the present state of Arizona until 1863. New Mexico's borders between Texas and California were subject to change from time to time. Historians differ as to whether Spanish to Mexican to New Mexican community property rules continued in an unbroken chain, although case law in the state holds that it does. See for example *McDonald v. Senn*, supra.

In 1876, the common law was adopted in the New Mexico Territory; consequently, the civil law was repealed, except when adopted by statute or required by treaty. Otherwise, a military code (the Kearny Code) was in effect. In 1907, the New Mexico Act was passed. That Act largely adopted California community property statutes. *McDonald v. Senn,* supra at 205. In 1912, New Mexico become a state. New Mexico courts, reflecting the multicultural origins of the state, began to look to the law of Spain and Mexico to interpret the state community property system. Id. at 201. In so doing, the courts and the legislature officially recognized the civil law origin of rules detailing property rights between spouses. Today, effective 2024, New Mexico is beginning to incorporate Indigenous tribal law into its community property system.

Texas, an independent republic from 1836, joined the Union on December 29, 1845. An original Texas Constitution of 1869 was formed, but it was replaced in its entirety with the Texas Constitution of 1876, which still is the organic law of Texas. Texas was formerly a part of Mexico and subject to the laws of Spain. When the state became a Republic and later joined the Union it carried over a Spanish and Mexican heritage of the earlier community property system. The basic elements of that system were enshrined in the Constitution of 1876, placing them above the reach of any particular Texas legislature. It should also be noted that part of the legal history of Texas is the low regard in which decisions of the post-Civil War Reconstruction period courts are held. For more on the Texas community property system, see Jean A. Stuntz, HERS, HIS, AND THEIRS: COMMUNITY PROPERTY LAW IN SPAIN AND EARLY TEXAS (2005).

Washington, originally part of the Oregon Territory, entered the union as a constitutional dependency in 1853. Much like Idaho, discussed above, Washington did not have a strong French, Spanish, or Mexican legal tradition; and the English common law was prevalent through the 1870s. But

Washington had a progressive start as a territory where distinctly non-aristocratic European settlers (individually and collectively) homesteaded geographies divided by the sometimes-impassable Cascade Mountains. Washington adopted its first community property statute in 1869, by a statute modeled on the community property provision in the 1850 California Organic Act. The statute was updated in 1873 and codified in 1881 in a form that remained in force up to and after statehood in 1889. For more on early Washington legal history, see Sandra F. VanBurkleo, GENDER REMADE: CITIZENSHIP, SUFFRAGE, AND PUBLIC POWER IN THE NEW NORTHWEST, 1879–1912 (2015).

Wisconsin attained statehood in 1848 and had a common law regime through 1985. On January 1, 1986, Wisconsin became the first U.S. state to adopt a shared marital property system, the Uniform Marital Property Act (called WUMPA for short). The W in WUMPA is for Wisconsin.

Alaska and Tennessee are separate property states that allow a community property option.

Alaska adopted the Alaska Community Property Act in 1998. The Alaska community property system is an elective (optional) system modeled on Wisconsin's UMPA approach. The legislation permits married persons to opt into community property by use of a contract or an Alaska trust. The trust may be settled by persons who are not domiciled in the state so long as the trustee is an Alaskan domiciliary. Requirements for validly settling a community property trust are enumerated in the statute. The community property option can be exercised on an asset-by-asset or an estate-wide (aggregate) basis. See, ALASKA STAT. ANN. § 34.77.010 (West 2016).

Tennessee enables use of a private contract for married residents of the state who wish to opt into community property. See, TENN. CODE. ANN § 35–17–101 (West 2016).

Florida and South Dakota allow married couples to settle a community property trust. 736.1501

Scholarship proposals have been made for New Hampshire to enable a community property option. See Calvin Massey, *Why New Hampshire Should Permit Married Couples to Choose Community Property*, 13 U.N.H. L. REV. 35 (2015) and Jo Carrillo, *Liberty and Community in Marriage: Expanding on Massey's Proposal for a Community Property Option in New Hampshire,* 15 U.N.H. L. REV. 289 (2017).

CHAPTER 2

PREMARITAL CONTRACTS

A. OVERVIEW

A premarital contract is a written agreement signed by prospective spouses before marriage. The contract comes into legal existence on the date of the marriage.

Premarital contracting supports two broad policies. Freedom of contract and legal protection for vulnerable parties. Freedom of contract protects a person's right to change the default rules of a marital property system. The legal protection of a vulnerable spouse supports the recognition of marriage as a public institution.

A few states inquire into the relative financial resources that are available to a party when they sign a premarital contract, but most do not. It is more accurate to say that the concern of the state is not the relative wealth of the parties. Rather, the state is concerned with enacting systemic benefits in favor of preventing undue influence, coercion, and unjust enrichment, especially in arm's length transactions between intimate partners. The theory is that such legal mechanisms protect the vulnerable partner from unintentionally contracting away important rights. From this perspective, one can see that in a sense the vulnerable spouse stands in the stead of the public fisc.

The traditional English common law and the civil law parted ways on whether married persons could change their marital rights and duties by a private contract signed before marriage. Under the common law, the right of a married woman to enter a contract was severely restricted, hence so too was her right to own property. The traditional civil law by comparison, allowed a married woman, to contract over property ownership and settlements with her spouse as well as with a third party.

Forty-one U.S. states base their marital property law on the English common law. In that legal context, marriage is a private contract that changes the parties' personal status from single to married. In marriage, each spouse owns their earnings and whatever they may purchase with those earnings, unless they affirmatively opt into sharing with their spouse. This sounds fair, but as a default rule, it obviously favors the higher earning spouse in day-to-day life.

Nine U.S. community property states base their law on a civil law ganancial community property model. In these nine states, marriage is a contract that changes a person's status from single to married. Marriage is also, by virtue of the marital property laws, a public contract that incorporates the community property laws. Prospective spouses can modify or even reject marital property laws in whole or part by premarital contract.

However, premarital contracts are not risk free and in fact there is a high likelihood is any dissolution that one party or the other will challenge the premarital contract in court at the end of the marriage.

The party who wants the court to enforce the contract is called the contract proponent. The party who wants the court to dismiss the contract is either called the contract opponent or the party against whom contract enforcement is sought. Statutes often use the latter terminology—*the party against whom enforcement is sought*—to reflect that prior to the filing of a lawsuit, either party could potentially seek to enforce the contract against the other. Therefore, I use the phrase in this Nutshell as well.

Here is a list of issues raised by premarital contracts.

Timing. Parties enter a premarital agreement in contemplation of marriage. They sign the contract when they are single, before they are married, but in reasonable expectation of their future marriage. The contract becomes enforceable on the date of their marriage. The date the contract is signed, rather than the date of the marriage, will, however, decide the governing law in the event of a legal challenge.

Parties enter a cohabitation agreement when they are not married. Cohabiting partners are intentionally not married when they sign the contract, and perhaps more importantly, they do not expect to marriage. Rather they expect the contract to come into legal existence on the date they sign it. Of course, the parties might change their minds and decide to get married. But if they do, the cohabitation agreement they signed will terminate on the date of their valid marriage.

Parties enter a martial contract during their marriage to each other. A marital contract is a transaction between spouses who, because of their marriage, are in a confidential relationship with each other, as a matter of law.

Parties who are still married to each other enter a marriage settlement agreement after a date of separation but prior to the final judgment that dissolves their marriage. A marriage settlement agreement (MSA) is a private contract that can be incorporated by reference into the final divorce decree.

Formalities. The most common contract formalities are a writing signed by the parties who plan to marry each other. States can add to these basic formalities by adding witnessing and acknowledgement (notarization) requirements.

Formalities make proof of a contract easier and more certain, and pre-marital contract formalities help guide the parties through the contracting process. Later in time, formalities help prove the existence of the contract. Under the law of equity, proof of part performance or reliance can be the basis for enforcing an oral or a tacit contract. However, when it comes to premarital contracts, the clear and obvious arc of the law is to dismiss, not enforce, oral premarital agreements.

Consideration is not a requirement for proving a premarital contract. The idea here is to discourage any argument that the promise to marry is support for the contract.

Processes to insure fairness. Add-on formalities to the writing requirement are two: fairness and voluntariness. Fairness means financial disclosure. Voluntariness means having enough time to review a final draft of the contract before signing it. Rushing an intimate partner into signing a premarital contract, for example, can later be deemed coercive. Misrepresentations about financial facts can later be deemed unconscionable.

Public policy. With a premarital contract, parties can make decisions about statutorily enumerated property rights and personal obligations.

There are, however, some topics parties cannot contract over.

Parties cannot waive the basic duty of support during marriage, neither can they contract over rights that affect minor children. Moreover, any term that violates public policy or that violates the criminal law is void. Depending on state law, the court can either strike a void term, leaving the rest of the contract to stand, or else dismiss the contract entirely because of the void clause.

Before marriage, prospective spouses are not in a confidential relationship as a matter of law. Thus, the rules against taking substantive advantage of the other's property disadvantage generally do not apply prior to marriage. Yet, some states, like Wisconsin by statute, do require fair substantive terms. But what does fair mean in this context? Does it mean acknowledging the parties' "disparate property status," as stated in *Button v. Button*, 131 Wis.2d 84, 388 N.W.2d 546 (1986), a landmark Wisconsin case?

The date of marriage signals the clear start date of a confidential relationship as a matter of law. Where the parties had no duties to each other before marriage, once married they do. And where there are duties, there are rights. For these reasons, courts decide whether personal rights and obligations are waivable at the end of a marriage, even if the parties agreed at the start of the marriage to waive those rights by a premarital contract. Spousal support rights, intended to protect vulnerable parties, are a good example of this point.

- *During marriage*, the right to receive support by a spouse is a public right not waivable by contract.

- *After a date of separation*, the right to petition a court for temporary support (alimony *pendente lite*) is a public right left to judicial discretion.

- *After divorce*, the right to petition a court for postdissolution spousal support leans more toward a private right. However, the public interest can be implicated if denying the right to petition for spousal support will likely make the party against whom enforcement is sought eligible for public assistance.

During marriage, the right to receive support from a spouse is a key component of the institution of marriage. That said, the right to receive support after a marriage is not a key component of the institution of divorce.

Views about premarital contracts have changed over time in response to changing public mores about marriage and divorce. Therefore, understanding how the law has developed can help us understand what the law is today.

B. DETAIL

1. PREMARITAL AGREEMENTS BEFORE 1983

Under the Spanish ganancial system, premarital contracts were enforceable from the date of the marriage forward. Mutual consent to the marriage was sufficient consideration to support the contract. Proof of mistake, duress, or fraud at the start of the contract provided a basis for arguing that the contract was unenforceable.

Spanish law provided that prospective spouses were in a confidential relationship with each other from their engagement forward. The consequence of this rule was that even before marriage, prospective spouses had a *legal duty* to act in good faith toward each other. Despite these protections contract enforcement often resulted in exacerbated financial disparities between the parties.

In early 20th century U.S. law, general contract law governed premarital agreements. In most states, prospective spouses contracted at arm's length. But a minority of states viewed an engagement to marry as the start of a confidential relationship. The law gradually changed, not on the confidential relationship split, but on the necessity of formalities. To that end, most states eventually enacted a requirement that the contract be in writing and signed by the parties to be married, not their cultural agents (parents for example).

A midcentury case in the community property context is *Friedlander v. Friedlander*, 80 Wash.2d 293, 301 494 P.2d 208, 214 (1972) (*en banc*), where the court adopted what it called a well-recognized "common sense rule" meant to prevent overreaching by a prospective spouse in the context of premarital contract negotiations.

In *Friedlander,* the parties began a 5-year affair while the prospective husband was ending his 27-year long marriage. During that time, the prospective spouses "discussed marriage" with each other. The plaintiff (the prospective husband who was still married to his first wife) suggested that he and the defendant (the prospective second wife) enter a written premarital agreement. He wanted to prevent the (so-called) problems he was encountering in his first divorce. The prospective second wife agreed with her still married prospective husband that his problems required her to agree to a premarital contract that would identify and protect his separate property. The prospective husband provided his new bride with a contract two days before their wedding. She obviously had no time to consult an attorney. Once married, the parties lived off the husband's community property income. At dissolution, by the terms of the contract, the wife's share of community property turned out to be minuscule ($32,000) compared to the husband's share ($1,300,000). Id. at 294, 210.

The *Friedlander* court ruled that the confidential relationship began on the date the parties signed the contract. At that time, the parties were not yet married.

Was the parties' 5-year relationship before marriage the basis for finding a confidential relationship *in fact*?

Or was the court applying the original Spanish rule that an engagement brings parties into a confidential relationship *as a matter of law*? And if so, should this rule apply even if one of the engaged parties is still married to another person?

Or was the court *legislating from the bench*?

Differences in rationale matter. Whether the confidential relationship is a product of fact, law, or legislation from the bench can decide how a court steps in, if it does, to assist a party who finds themselves adversely affected at divorce by a contract they signed with their spouse before marriage.

If the confidential relationship is a question of fact, then the dicta of *Friedlander* can be set aside.

Alternatively, if the ruling signaled reliance on the Spanish law (engagement brings parties into a confidential relationship), doctrinal issues aside, that would be a new turn in a state, Washington, which does not claim Spanish or Mexican legal history as a precursor to its own legal history.

But if the court was legislating from the bench, what was it communicating? The husband was in a confidential relationship with his first wife (by marriage), but was he also in a confidential relationship with his prospective spouse? Was this because he was confiding in her? Was this because they were engaged? Was the husband's confidential relationship with his soon to be second wife in conflict with the confidential relationship he was still in with his first wife?

Friedlander claimed to invoke a commonsense rule, but was it really that commonsense considering the legal questions it raised?

One could argue that the problem with using the confidential relationship rubric to settle actual disputes is that the parties' understanding about whether they are engaged (or not) may be vague or situational. From this view, engagement is not so much a fact as it is a proxy for proving intent to sign a contract before marriage that will take legal effect upon the date of the marriage. Without a showing of this specific kind of intent, the contract is at best a cohabitation agreement.

That said, the start date of the parties' confidential relationship does more than just decide what kind of contract the parties are signing. It can also be the legal rationale for applying procedural protections.

At the start of a confidential relationship, whether in fact or by law, the parties may bargain for an exchange between them. But, given the confidential relationship, each party has an obligation not to take any unfair advantage of the other in that exchange. When facts show that a premarital contract has enriched one party ($1,300,000) at the expense of the other party ($32,000), the next obvious question is whether the contract was fair and voluntary.

One selling point of the Uniform Premarital Agreement Act (the UPAA 1983 for short) 1983 is that it offers definitional provisions. Note however that the UPAA 1983 Prefatory Note concedes that as uniform legislation the UPAA 1983 is "relatively limited in scope."

The UPAA 1983 defines a premarital agreement as an agreement between prospective spouses that is in writing and signed by the parties to be married with the intention that the agreement take effect on the date of their marriage. The UPAA 1983's definitions and provisions establish parameters to make clear that the UPAA 1983 covers only premarital agreements, not cohabitation agreements, unsigned premarital agreements, marital agreements, or marriage settlement agreements. The UPAA 1983 does not explicitly address contract amendments.

Once it is determined that the contract in question is categorically a premarital contract, the UPAA 1983 then makes clear that prospective spouses are *not* in a confidential relationship. Only a valid marriage creates a confidential relationship as a matter of law, an engagement does not. The legal effect of this bright line rule aids in the first purpose of the UPAA 1983, namely, definitional clarity. Parties negotiate and sign a premarital contract before the date of their valid marriage. Therefore, the contract is at arm's length. Once married, if the spouses want to amend the contract, they can do so within the framework of their confidential relationship.

Moreover, a model law like the UPAA 1983 can cast light on two important public policies of the institution of marriage. The first policy is that prospective spouses have freedom of contract rights as to financial matters of their upcoming marriage. The second policy is a recognition that contract terms that allow spouses to waive financial duties and rights to each other can negatively impact the public fisc.

In *Friedlander*, supra, the court characterized what happens when one party takes advantage of another party as overreaching. This happens, for example, when "a pre-nuptial contract makes provision for a wife that is disproportionate to the means of the intended husband." Id. At 301, 214. The idea, wrote the court, was to place the burden on "the intended husband and those claiming under him" to prove that the wife "had full knowledge of all the facts and circumstances that materially affected the contract." Id. at 301, 214. Considering the above, what was it that the court was reaching for when it asserted that parties to a premarital contract "do not deal at arm's length [as] their relationship is one of mutual confidence and trust which calls for the exercise of good faith, candor and sincerity in all matters bearing upon the proposed agreement." Id.

at 301, 213. Was the court searching for proof of disclosure of financial information?

Friedlander, supra, is a good illustration of one attempt to help the vulnerable party in a state that has not adopted the UPAA 1983. One can value the courts effort to achieve fairness between the parties, but still have concern for the complexity of the approach.

Clear law helps prospective spouses plan. Clear law helps predict contract enforceability at dissolution, as well as the validity of all transactions that were taken by the parties in reliance on the contract.

For this and other reasons, adoption of the UPAA 1983 can be critically important to clarifying issues of timing, formalities, spousal support waiver enforceability, fairness, and issues of undue influence.

2. THE UNIFORM PREMARITAL AGREEMENT ACT OF 1983

In 1983, the National Conference of Commissioners on Uniform State Laws promulgated the Uniform Premarital Agreement Act (the UPAA 1983 for short). As of this printing, the UPAA 1983 twenty-six U.S. states and the District of Columbia have enacted a version of this uniform law. This includes Arizona, California, Idaho, Nevada, New Mexico, Texas, and Wisconsin.

Louisiana and Washington have not adopted the UPAA 1983.

California adopted the UPAA in 1985, but then amplified and modified it into the California Premarital Agreement Act (the CPAA 1985 for short), a sui generis statute.

New Mexico adopted UPAA 1983 formalities for contract enforceability (a writing signed by both parties), but then added the additional requirement of formal acknowledgment (witnesses).

Wisconsin premarital agreement law departed from the original UPAA 1983. Of interest in Wisconsin is that it enacted legislation for automatically terminable premarital agreements (the STMPA for short). A STMPA terminates after a statutorily determined period to protect against stale premarital contracts.

Louisiana has state-specific statutory provisions.

Washington relies on judge-made law by referring to general civil law statutes.

UPAA 1983 §§ 1 and 4 define a premarital agreement as **"an agreement between prospective spouses made in contemplation of marriage and to be effective upon marriage."**

The UPAA 1983 defines property as **"an interest, present or future, legal or equitable, vested or contingent, in real or personal property, including income and earnings."** Id.

Enforceability of any premarital agreement depends on the presentation of a stand-alone **"writing . . . signed by both parties."** UPAA 1983 § 2. Consideration is not a requirement for enforcement as it was under a prior law that defined a premarital contract as one made in consideration of marriage. Dropping the consideration requirement underscores that a premarital contract is a proposed property settlement between people who plan to marry; it is not in exchange for a promise to marry or for the marriage itself. Id.

The UPAA 1983 § 3(a) permits parties to contract over a broad scope of property matters, including **"the modification or elimination of spousal support[,]"** choice of law to govern the construction of the agreement, and **"any other matter, including personal rights and obligations, not in violation of public policy or a statute imposing a criminal penalty."** UPAA 1983 § 3(a)(8) 1985 (1983).

Whether property terms are enforceable is a function of voluntariness and financial disclosure. UPAA 1983 § 6(a). The burden of proof falls on the party against whom contract enforcement is sought. Courts can easily distinguish between property terms and spousal support terms.

An earlier act, the Uniform Marriage and Divorce Act (the UMDA 1970 for short) first linked spousal support provisions with eligibility for public assistance. Following suit, the UPAA 1983 § 6(b) does as well. It says that a court may require the financially more able spouse to support their less financially able spouse to avoid eligibility for public assistance. The goal is to alleviate pressure on the public fisc.

Contract unconscionability is a question of law.

Economic circumstances drive the test for unconscionability in UMDA 1970 § 306 . According to that law, the terms of a separation agreement are legally binding on a court "unless it finds, after considering the economic circumstances of the parties and any other relevant evidence produced by the parties . . . that the separation agreement is unconscionable."

Under UPAA 1983 § 6(c), by comparison, provides that a property term or a spousal support provision is unconscionable if disclosure was lacking or inadequate at the time the parties signed the contract. Financial disclosure for the purpose of understanding the contract terms suggests a narrower inquiry than does a party's general economic circumstances.

UPAA 1983 § 9 clearly states that rebuttal rests "with the party against whom enforcement is sought," meaning the party who is challenging the contract or any provision in it. The Legislative Note following this section restates this burden with an italicized declarative sentence: "*Section 9(a) places the burden of proof on the party challenging a premarital agreement or marital agreement.*" An adopter that wants the burden placed differently can amend this statement.

Once the contract proponent proves contract formalities, the party challenging the contract has an opportunity to prove any one of the following points listed in UPAA 1983:

- That party's consent was "involuntary or the result of duress" (UPAA 1983 § 9 (a)(1)).
- That party "did not have access to independent legal representation" (UPAA 1983 § 9(a)(2)).
- That party signed an agreement that "did not include a waiver of notice . . . or an explanation in plain language of the marital rights or obligations being modified or waived by the agreement" (UPAA 1983 § 9(a)(3)).
- That party, before signing the agreement, "did not receive adequate financial disclosure" (UPAA 1983 § 9(a)(4)).

Does the UPAA 1983 § 6. cover fraud, deceit, or coercion, all of which are questions of fact?

Deceit can be difficult to prove under general law. The UPAA 1983 attempts to address this issue by linking the concept of deceit to unconscionability, thereby making deceit definable by the absence of meaningful financial disclosure.

Likewise, the term coercion can be difficult to prove under general law. The UPAA 1983 links the concept of coercion to the idea of the absence of voluntariness in the negotiation and execution (signing) process. California has done a great deal of work to enact code provisions that help define the otherwise amorphous concepts of fairness (and its opposite unconscionability) and voluntariness (and its opposite coercion) in the context of premarital contracting. See Sec. C. California below.

In the absence of legislation to the contrary, a U.S. community property state could potentially adopt a common law or the civil law approach for fraud, deceit, and concealment in a premarital contract case.

3. THE UNIFORM PREMARITAL AND MARITAL AGREEMENT ACT OF 2012

In 2012, the National Conference of Commissioners of Uniform State Laws promulgated the Uniform Premarital and Marital Agreement Act (the UPMAA 2012 for short).

Colorado and North Dakota have adopted the UPMAA 2012. But no community property state has done so.

The UPMAA 2012 § 6 expands the UPAA 1983 definition of a premarital agreement from an agreement made in contemplation of marriage to an agreement that is **"between individuals who intend to marry which affirms, modifies, or waives a marital right or obligation during marriage or at separation, marital dissolution, death of one of the spouses, or the occurrence or nonoccurrence of any other event.**" UPMAA 2012 § 2(5).

The Comment to the UPMAA 2012 indicates that the model language was promulgated in part to make clear that premarital and marital agreements are different from cohabitation agreements, separation agreements, or "conventional day-to-day commercial transactions between spouses." Id.

For premarital agreements, the parties intend to marry. Moreover, they intend the contract to become enforceable on the date of marriage, not on the date when they sign the contract.

By contrast, a couple sign a cohabitation agreement expecting that it will become enforceable immediately. If they also expect their cohabitation agreement to continue in force after the date of their valid marriage, the statute makes clear that this would not be a reasonable expectation. It suggests that the couple instead consider using a premarital agreement.

The UPMAA Comment expresses concern that premarital agreements may contain fragments that violate public policy. The example given is "Islamic marriage contracts with their deferred Mahr payment provisions." UPMAA 2012 § 2, Comment. The National Conference of Commissioners gives no further clarification on this point. If case law is a guide, this may be because the Islamic marriage contract provides that the bride will keep the mahr payment in the event of divorce, regardless of who initiates the divorce. In the context of a U.S. state, an automatic cash payment at divorce could raise concerns about violating the state public policy against encouraging divorce.

C. INDIVIDUAL STATES

1. ARIZONA

Arizona adopted the UPAA 1983, effective September 21, 1991, approved on March 25, 1991. Ariz.Rev.Stat.Ann. § 25–201 to § 25–205.

From that date forward, proof of a premarital agreement **"must be in writing and signed by both parties. The agreement is enforceable without consideration."** Ariz.Rev.Stat. § 25–202(A) and (B). The phrase "both parties" means both parties to the marriage. The agreement becomes effective on the date of a valid marriage between the parties.

A premarital contract is eligible for enforcement unless **"the party against whom enforcement is sought proves either of the following: (1) the person did not execute the agreement voluntarily, (2) the agreement was unconscionable when it was executed . . ."** Before execution, financial disclosure is necessary to provide sufficient information about the exchange the contract proposes. Ariz.Rev.Stat. § 25–202(C). Unconscionability is **"decided by the court as a matter of law."** Ariz.Rev.Stat. § 25–202(E).

The statute allows parties to contract over property rights, and personal rights and responsibilities. Ariz.Rev.Stat. § 25–203. The statute allows the waiver of spousal support rights, a phrase that likely means the right to petition for postdissolution spousal support. But if a modification or elimination of spousal support **"causes one party to the agreement to be eligible for support under a program of public assistance at the time of separation or marital dissolution, a court, notwithstanding the terms of the agreement, may require the other party to provide support to the extent necessary to avoid that eligibility."** Ariz.Rev.Stat. § 25–202(D). In disputes about spousal support modifications or waivers, case law shows that the standard of proof is the highest clear and convincing evidence standard. *Hrudka v. Hrudka*, 186 Ariz. 84, 919 P.2d 179 (Ariz. App. 1995), citing *Williams v. Williams*, 166 Ariz. 260, 801 P.2d 495, 497 (Ariz. App. 1990), superseded by statute on other grounds.

By delineating the time of spousal support on the face of Ariz.Rev.Stat. § 2–202(D), the Arizona statute addresses ambiguities that are also raised by California law. In Arizona, parties can use a contract to waive spousal support rights from the date of separation forward, but a court has discretion to modify the waiver up to the amount of support needed to avoid eligibility for public assistance. Left ambiguous is the timing issue. The courts in California are approximating this same outcome by a statute that grants the court discretion to award temporary spousal support during a period of separation (alimony *pendente lite*) even if the parties have signed a premarital contract that includes general language that waives "spousal support." See Section C. California for more on this point.

The Arizona Uniform Premarital Agreement Act places the burden of proof on **"the person against whom enforcement is sought . . ."** Ariz.Rev.Stat. § 25–202(C)(1) and (2)(a)–(c). It is up to that party—the party who is challenging the contract—to show that there was a lack of meaningful financial disclosure at the time the parties signed the contract.

Placing the burden of proof on the person who claims that the premarital agreement is unconscionable, as the statute does on its face, is in line with Arizona law. First, proof of financial disclosure is not a contract formality. Second, case law holds that the party who challenges the contract bears the burden of proving unconscionability. The court does not have the power to raise the issue of unconscionability sua sponte (on its own initiative). *Schlaefer v. Financial Management Service*, 196 Ariz. 336, 996 P.2d 745 (Ariz. App. 2000).

Likewise, a spouse claiming fraud must prove fraud. *Bender v. Bender*, 123 Ariz. 90, 597 P.2d 993, 997 (1979), citing *Hunt v. Campbell*, 19 Ariz. 254, 169 P.596 (1917) as to fraud, and *Fruth v. Divito*, 26 Ariz.App. 154, 546 P.2d 1163 (1976) as to mistake. These cases discuss the absence of an evidentiary presumption to facilitate the litigation of an interspousal fraud claim. In other words, in Arizona, suing a spouse for fraud is procedurally like suing a third party for fraud.

For a premarital agreement executed *before* 1991 (the effective date of Arizona's UPAA 1985), the burden of proving premarital contract formalities is on the spouse who seeks to enforce the contract. The statute continues this approach. Once established, the burden shifts to the contract opponent, as stated above, to raise issues of unconscionability, coercion or even fraud.

2. CALIFORNIA

California originally passed the California Premarital Agreement Act in 1985, effective January 1, 1986 (the CPAA 1985 for short).

The CPAA 1985 is modeled on the UPAA 1983, with differences discussed below.

The CPAA 2001, effective January 1, 2002, expanded the original CPAA 1985. The CPAA 2001 appears at Cal.Fam.Code §§ 1500 through 1620.

Recent amendments to CPAA 2001 §§ 1615(c)(1) and (2) took effect on January 1, 2020.

Premarital contract enforceability is determined by the law in force when the premarital contract is signed by the parties. The rationale is that vested property interests may be at stake. Adding a writing requirement where one did not exist before can affect vested property rights. Adding an evidentiary presumption by statute, however, does not. See Chapter 3, California for more on this topic in the context of newly enacted writing requirements and evidentiary presumptions.

Because the date the parties sign the contract determines the governing law, the following is true.

- California Civil Code and case law govern premarital agreements signed prior to December 31, 1985.
- The CPAA 1985 and cases decided between 1985 and 2001 govern contracts signed between January 1, 1986, and December 31, 2001.
- The CPAA 2001 and cases decided from 2002 forward govern contracts signed on or after January 1, 2002.
- Recent amendments to CPAA 2001 § 1615, as noted above, govern after January 1, 2020.

Proving the contract: Like the UPAA 1983, the CPAA 1985, and the CPAA 2001 the contract proponent carries the burden of proving the existence of the contract.

To that end, the CPAA 1985 and the CPAA 2001 require that premarital agreements be in writing and signed by the parties to be married. Neither CPAA 1985 nor the CPAA 2001 require consideration to support a contract, a rule that discourages arguments over whether the marriage is itself consideration for the contract,

The law also requires the contract proponent to prove substantive and procedural formalities. Substantive formalities primarily concern processes around financial disclosure before and on the date the parties to the marriage sign the contract. Procedural formalities go to the issue of voluntariness in both the contract negotiation and signing process. Once the contract proponent proves the contract, the burden of proof shifts to the contract opponent—called in the statute **"the party against whom enforcement is sought."**

The quantum of proof required to show that a premarital contract exists is the low preponderance of the evidence standard. For a discussion of burdens of proof see *Marriage of Bonds*, 24 Cal.4th 1, 99 Cal. Rptr 2d 252, 5 P.3d 815 (2000), which has been superseded by Cal.Fam.Code § 1615(c), which was most recently amended effective January 1, 2020.

Once established, a court decides the issue of enforceability. Default community property rules control if the court deems the contract unenforceable.

Enforceability: Generally, California law applies. As to property terms, Cal.Fam.Code § 1612(a)(1) through (a)(5) lists an inclusive list of property rights that the prospective spouses can contract over.

For choice of law issues raised by the contract language, Cal.Fam.Code § 1612(a)(6) allows parties to opt for another state's rules of contract construction, but not for another state's substantive marital property law.

As to personal rights and obligations, Cal.Fam.Code § 1612(a)(1)–(7) and (b) permit parties to contract over terms **"not in violation of public policy or a statute imposing a criminal penalty . . . ."** § 1612(a)(7).

As to child support, the **"right of a child to support may not be adversely affected by a premarital agreement."** § 1612(b).

Disclosure: Reasonable financial disclosure is a requirement both parties must meet.

As for unconscionability, the litigation of that term has a long legal history in the state. Here again, the date the parties sign the contract determines the governing law.

Unconscionability: The word unconscionability has two definitions in the CPAA 2001. The first definition applies to spousal support waivers. The second definition applies to the contracting process more generally.

Unconscionability as applied to spousal support waivers:

<u>Prior to December 31, 1985</u>, spousal support rights waivers were void as against public policy.

<u>From January 1, 1986, to December 31, 2001</u>, Prospective spouses could contract over **"personal rights and obligations, *not in violation of public policy* . . . ."** See Cal.Fam.Code § 1612(a)(7). The law was unclear, however, for how it omitted the UPAA 1983 language § 3 provision that expressly permitted prospective spouses to contract over *postdissolution* spousal support rights and obligations.

In *Marriage of Pendleton & Fireman*, 24 Cal.4th 39, 99 Cal. Rptr.2d 278, 5 P.3d 839 (2000), the California Supreme Court held that postdissolution spousal support waivers in a premarital agreement executed after January 1, 1986 (and thus governed by the CPAA 1983) are not per se unenforceable.

The court reasoned that the right to petition for postdissolution spousal support is a private right, not a public right. Private rights are **"personal rights and obligations"** included in the CPAA 1985 § 1612(a)(7) and, therefore, enforceable as long to do so is ***"not in violation of public policy . . . ."*** Id. In this case, the waiver of postdissolution spousal support rights was not in violation of public policy because at the time the parties signed the premarital contract they were (a) mature, (b) self-sufficient in property, (c) relatively equal in education, and (d) each represented by independent counsel. Moreover, the contract opponent argued that she needed postdissolution spousal support to maintain her marital standard of living, not to avoid becoming eligible for public aid. At the time of the divorce, she had access to the same financial resources she had enjoyed at the beginning of the marriage ($2.5 million in invested assets plus other sources of income). See *Marriage of Howell*, 195 Cal.App. 4th 1062, 126 Cal Rptr.3d 539 (2011) and See *Marriage of Melissa*, 212 Cal.App.4th 598, 151 Cal. Rptr.3d 608 (2012) for a continuation of the public policy discussion in the CPAA 2001 era.

Pendleton & Fireman, supra, led to the passage of Cal.Fam.Code § 1612(c), a CPAA 2001 addition that took effect on January 1, 2002.

From January 1, 2002, to the present, the newly added Cal.Fam.Code § 1612(c) governs spousal support terms. That section says **"[a]ny provision**

in a premarital agreement regarding spousal support, including, but not limited to, a waiver of it, is not enforceable if the party against whom enforcement ... is sought was not represented by independent counsel at the time the agreement ... was signed, or if the provision regarding spousal support is unconscionable at the time of enforcement. An otherwise unenforceable provision ... may not become enforceable solely because the party against whom enforcement is sought was represented by independent counsel."

The language of Cal.Fam.Code § 1612(c) permits contracting over private right of spousal support. At the time the contract is signed the waiving party must be represented by independent counsel. At the time of enforcement, the waiving party must not be likely eligible for public services.

If parties use general language ("we waive spousal support"), then when do they intend the waiver to apply? During the marriage? After a date of separation but before the final marriage settlement agreement or judgment of dissolution? Or only after divorce?

During marriage, the right to support a spouse is an obligation, and the right to receive support from a spouse a public right.

Likewise, after a date of separation, the duty to support a spouse continues even if in pared down form. See Chapter 9 for more on liabilities. Specifically, during the pendency of a dissolution proceeding, Cal.Fam.Code § 3600 authorizes judicial discretion to grant temporary spousal support (alimony *pendente lite*) when necessary. See *Last v. Superior Court*, 94 Cal. App. 5th 30 (2023).

But after divorce, the right to petition for spousal support is a private right. That right can however begin to impinge on the public right if judicial enforcement of the premarital contract waiver would leave the party against whom enforcement is sought eligible for public aid. In such a case, the court shall deem the spousal support waiver unconscionable and strike it from the contract.

Relative to CPAA 2001 § 1612(c), and especially considering the timing issues just discussed, an obvious lesson emerges to challenge the textbook description of marriage. Marriage is a contract, yes. But marriage is also a public institution. For that reason, with contracting over support modification or waiver terms, it is prudent for the parties to identify which period of marriage they intend the waiver to apply to. Whether the support right is primarily private or public during that period may lend insight into whether the waiver is likely to be deemed enforceable.

Public rights are an expression of state public policy that define the institution of marriage. Public rights include the right to support during marriage and the right to temporary support (alimony *pendente* lite) after a date of separation. Public rights protect the public from having to support a former spouse when private funds are available to do so.

Thus, CPAA 2001 § 1612(c) relies on the concept of financial need to define the concept of unconscionability. This CPAA section is based on the UPAA 1983 § 6(b). For that reason, CPAA 2001 § 1612(c) unconscionability mirrors the UPAA 1983 eligibility by its use of a public assistance yardstick.

Spousal support waivers found unconscionable by the court are stricken from the contract, not modified as under the UPAA 1983 § 6(b). Once stricken, default family code rules govern.

Unconscionability as applied to the contract more generally:

The original UPAA 1983 treats unconscionability as a question of law, as does California law.

The word unconscionability under CPAA 2001 § 1615 has a different definition than it does under CPAA 2001 § 1612(c), as discussed above. A definition of unconscionability appears in Cal.Fam.Code § 1615(a)(1) and (2)(A)–(C), which went into effect on January 1, 1986. These three provisions center around financial disclosure.

Cal.Fam.Code § 1615(a) provides that: **A premarital agreement is not enforceable if the party against whom enforcement is sought proves either of the following: (1) That party did not execute the agreement voluntarily. (2) The agreement was unconscionable when it was executed and, before execution of the agreement, all of the following applied to that party.**

Cal.Fam.Code § 1615(b) clearly states [u]nconscionability **"shall be decided by the court as a matter of law."** In theory this section limits judicial discretion.

Stepping back to the legal definition of unconscionability for general contracting purposes, what facts prove sufficient disclosure?

Cal.Fam.Code § 1615(a)(1) provides: **"The agreement was unconscionable when it was executed and, before execution of the agreement, *all* of the following applied to that party."** (Italics added.)

- **"That party was not provided a fair, reasonable, and full disclosure of the property or financial obligations of the other party."** Cal.Fam.Code § 1615(a)(2)(A).
- **"That party did not voluntarily and expressly waive, in writing, any right to disclosure of the property or financial obligations of the other party beyond the disclosure provided."** Cal.Fam.Code § 1615(a)(2)(B).
- **"That party did not have, or reasonably could not have had, an adequate knowledge of the property or financial obligations of the other party."** Cal.Fam.Code § 1615(a)(2)(C).

The question of whether the contract was entered into voluntarily, on the other hand, is one over which the judge has considerable discretion, at least within the parameters set out at Cal.Fam.Code § 1615(c).

In *Marriage of Bonds*, supra, the California Supreme Court upheld the placement of the burden of on the **"the party against whom enforcement is sought."** In that case, the parties signed a premarital agreement that all property earned during the marriage would be the separate property of the earning spouse. Prospective husband Barry Bonds, who was not at his earning peak when he signed a premarital contract making all his earnings his separate property, went on to become a high earning baseball star. Prospective wife Sun Bonds was a beautician. After a decade of marriage, the parties divorced. Wife Sun Bonds alleged, among other things, that she did not sign the premarital contract voluntarily because she was not represented by counsel, nor did she have time to hire counsel given the immanent wedding date. She also argued that the contract was in English, not her language of proficiency.

The legislature enacted CPAA 2001 § 1615(c) after the decision in *Bonds*, supra.

CPAA 2001 § 1615(c)—with its five subsections—took effect on January 1, 2002. The legislature updated Sections 1615(c)(1) and (2) in 2019, effective January 1, 2020.

Here is an interpretive heading (in italics) followed by the statutory language (in bold) of CPAA 2001 § 1615(c):

"For the purposes of subdivision (a), it shall be deemed that a premarital agreement was not executed voluntarily unless the court finds in writing or on the record all of the following:"

- *The party who seeks to enforce the contract presented the final contract* <u>*and*</u> *advised the other party to seek counsel* <u>*and*</u> *allowed that party at least 7 calendar days to review the final contract draft.* **"For an agreement executed between January 1, 2002, and January 1, 2020, the party against whom the enforcement is sought had *not less than seven calendar days* between the time that party was first presented with the final agreement and advised to seek independent legal counsel *and* the time the agreement was signed. This requirement does not apply to nonsubstantive amendments that do not change the terms of the agreement."** Cal.Fam.Code § 1615(c)(2)(A). (Italics added.)

- *If a party to the contract decides not to seek counsel, the party who seeks to enforce the contract must prove that the unrepresented party had at least 7 calendar days to review the contract.* **"For an agreement executed on or after January 1, 2020, the party against whom enforcement is sought had not less than seven calendar days between the time that party was first presented with the final agreement and the time the agreement was signed,**

regardless of whether the party is represented by legal counsel. This requirement does not apply to nonsubstantive amendments that do not change the terms of the agreement." Cal.Fam.Code § 1615(c)(2)(B).

- *If a party decides not to seek counsel, the party who seeks to enforce the contract must prove that their counsel compiled a record of proof on the issue of voluntariness.* **"The party against whom enforcement is sought, if unrepresented by legal counsel, was fully informed of the terms and basic effect of the agreement as well as the rights and obligations the party was giving up by signing the agreement and was proficient in the language in which the explanation of the party's rights was conducted and in which the agreement was written. The explanation of the rights and obligations relinquished shall be memorialized in writing and delivered to the party prior to signing the agreement. The unrepresented party shall, on or before the signing of the premarital agreement, execute a document declaring that the party received the information required by this paragraph and indicating who provided that information."** Cal.Fam.Code. § 1615(c)(3).

- *If a party decides not to seek counsel, the party who seeks to enforce the contract must prove that their counsel compiled a record of proof on the other party's capacity to enter the premarital contract, and proof that all documents required for the premarital contracting process were voluntarily signed.* **"The agreement and the writings executed pursuant to paragraphs (1) and (3) were not executed under duress, fraud, or undue influence, and the parties did not lack capacity to enter into the agreement."** (§ 1615(c)(4)); and
- *The judge has discretion to address all other factors, including circumstantial factors outside the contracting process.* **"Any other factors the court deems relevant."** (§ 1615(c)(5)).

Summing up: The contract proponent proves the existence of the contract by showing that the contracting parties met all formalities. The contract must be in writing and signed by the parties to be married.

Disclosure, defined in financial terms, is necessary to the contracting process. So too is voluntariness, which is defined in procedural terms.

If the parties have waived the right to petition for postdissolution spousal support rights, a two-part analysis is necessary: the party against whom enforcement is sought (the party who will be barred from petitioning for spousal support) was represented by independent counsel when the contract was signed; and at the time of enforcement, the court deems the waiver unconscionable.

The contract proponent bears the burden of proving the contract. This is because the contract proponent is the party who seeks to modify the state community property laws affected by the contract.

The legislation does not go so far to create a presumption of involuntariness. See e.g., *Last v. Superior Court of Orange County*, 94 Cal. App. 5th 30, 39 (2023) (the court asserts there is "a default presumption that a premarital agreement was not executed voluntarily"). Prospective spouses are not in a confidential relationship when they sign a premarital contract. But that said, the legal terrain can be difficult terrain, especially for the party who seeks to enforce the contract.

Partly, the terrain is difficult because to negotiate and sign a contract requires an understanding of the law at the time of signing.

Partly the terrain is difficult because the parties are hopeful at the start of marriage that they will never end their marriage by divorce. Neither spouse anticipates a break-up. Although even for marriages that do not end in divorce one must also consider termination by death.

Partly the terrain is difficult because premarital contracts often contain mutual terms that (at least in theory) will benefit and burden spouses in (seemingly) identical ways. Mutual terms look fair on their face, but this is why financial disclosure becomes important. Only by looking at financial facts can one see how it is that a mutual property term, that looks like it will apply equally to both parties, can operate in an unfair way given the parties' disparate resources at the start of the marriage.

For that reason, the CPAA 2001 provides technical provisions that help a court balance freedom of contract rights with the default protections.

CPAA 2001 § 1615 specifically lays out the parameters of proof on the issues of unconscionability and voluntariness. The statute helps the party who seeks to establish the contract. Likewise, the statute helps the party who seeks to attack the enforceability of the contract.

The CPAA lightens the burden for the judge as well by providing a standard that disincentivizes legislating from the bench. Otherwise, the Jenga-like placements of burdens and benefits at contrasting times (execution versus enforcement) can collapse into a heap of unintelligible sentences.

Premarital contract amendments and revocations:

Amendments and revocations complicate matters. When the parties amend a premarital agreement, they sign documents during marriage when the parties are in a confidential relationship as a matter of law.

3. IDAHO

Idaho adopted the Uniform Premarital Agreement Act (UPAA 2003) in Idaho Code §§ 32–921 to 32–929, effective July 1, 1986. Idaho Code § 32–922 was added in 1995; this statute provides that a premarital agreement **"must be in writing signed by both parties."** Consideration is not required.

Enforceability of the written contract also requires compliance with Idaho Code §§ 32–917 et. seq., which mandates, in addition to the writing and signature requirement of § 32–922, that such contracts must be **"executed and acknowledged or proved"** in the same way that conveyances of land require.

Does the law require that the parties acknowledge a premarital contract?

Dunagan v. Dunagan, 147 Idaho 599, 213 P.3d 384 (2009) reiterated the acknowledgment requirement in dicta. There, the parties orally agreed, prior to marriage, that they would keep their finances segregated during the marriage. The judge refused to consider financial conduct as evidence of a contract, and in so doing rejected the use of the part performance doctrine to prove the existence of the contract. The court made an analogy to a written contract left unsigned.

On appeal the Supreme Court of Idaho upheld the trial court's decision saying that Idaho courts will recognize and enforce only those premarital agreements that comply with Idaho Code §§ 32–917 (the signature and the acknowledgment requirement). Meeting formalities, in other words, is a key prerequisite to enforcement of a premarital contract that supersedes contract-relevant community property law. Formalities requiring writing and acknowledgment also underscore the general requirement that a premarital agreement be in writing, and not otherwise illegal.

Acknowledgment of a premarital contract occurs at signing. For a premarital agreement signing (execution) and acknowledgement must occur prior to marriage. A contract that is signed before marriage but not acknowledged until after their marriage is not a premarital contract. Likewise, a contract that is signed and acknowledged during the parties' marriage is not a premarital contract. Id. at 387.

In terms of the scope of what parties can contract over, Idaho Code § 32–923(d) explicitly permits the modification or elimination of postdissolution spousal support.

Idaho Code § 32–925(2) provides that a spousal support provision is **"not enforceable"** if it **"causes one party to the agreement to be eligible for support under a program for public assistance at the time of separation or marital dissolution."** Upon proof of causation **"a court, notwithstanding the terms of the agreement, may require the other party to provide support to the extent necessary to avoid [public assistance] eligibility."** The burden of proof is on the party against whom enforcement is sought, meaning the contract opponent who, by executing the premarital contract in the first place, agreed to waive those important rights. Id.

4. LOUISIANA

Louisiana has not adopted the Uniform Premarital Agreement Act.

The Louisiana Civil Code relies on the concept of the matrimonial regime, and how it distinguishes between legal and contractual matrimonial regimes. LSA-C.C. Art. 1734 and 1755 deal with matrimonial agreements made in contemplation of marriage.

"A matrimonial regime is a system of principles and rules governing the ownership and management of the property of married persons as between themselves and toward third persons." LSA-C.C. Art.2325. By statute, a matrimonial regime may be legal (referred to as a community of **"acquets and gains"** as established by LSA-C.C., Book 3, Title VI), contractual (the result of the parties' agreement to waive default statutory rules of the community property system), or hybrid (a modified regime that is partly legal and partly contractual). LSA-C.C. Art. 2326.

If the parties opt for a contractual matrimonial regime, they do so by a matrimonial agreement. **"A matrimonial agreement is a contract establishing a regime of separation of property or modifying or terminating the legal regime . . . as provided by law."** LSA-C.C. Art. 2328. The provisions of the marital agreement control, but provisions of the legal regime that "have not been excluded, limited, or modified by contract retain their force and effect." Revision Comments, 1979, LSA-C.C. Art. 2325.

Married persons choose to abide by the community property system without court approval, and no doubt many married persons do opt for a matrimonial regime (the default community property system) unmodified. But for those who do establish a legal matrimonial regime between them, court approval is a prerequisite to enforceability for a contract that seeks to modify and terminate that matrimonial regime, and that, if enforced, seeks to govern the characterization of future acquisitions. *In re Succession of Faget*, 53 So.3d 414 (2010).

LSA-C.C. Art. 2329 states a mandatory court approval process that requires a **"joint petition and a finding by the court that [the agreement] serves their best interests and that they understand the governing principles and rules."**

LSA-C.C. Art. 2329 explicitly states a strong legislative policy against signing away community property rights during marriage without court approval. Courts uphold this policy repeatedly. See e.g., *Shaheen v. Khan*, 142 So.3d 257 (2014); *In re Succession of O'Krepki*, 193 So.3d 574 (2016). *Acurio v. Acurio*, 224 So.3d 935 states the policy in the positive: "the legal regime of community property is presumed, and the state has a long legislative policy favoring community rights."

Courts interpret statutes governing matrimonial agreements strictly (or not), and this heightens unpredictability. See e.g., *Muller v. Muller*, 72 So.3d 364, 367 (2011), distinguished by *Benedetto v. Benedetto*, 182 So.3d 344 (2015); and *Deshotels v.*

Deshotels, 150 So.3d 541 (2014), which is disagreed with by *Acurio*, supra.

At the same time LSA-C.C. Art. 2329 recognizes a freedom of contract policy by how it removes incapacities to contract based on marital status that were part of the 1870 Code. Today, married persons in Louisiana have the right to enter a contractual matrimonial regime with each other **"before or during marriage as to all matters that are not prohibited by public policy."** They may contract with each other, sell or lease property to each other, employ each other, enter into compromise agreements with each other, and otherwise transact with each other as either could with a third party.

New Louisiana residents are exempt from the matrimonial agreement court approval requirement **"[d]uring the first year after moving into and acquiring a domicile in [Louisiana], spouses may enter into a matrimonial agreement without court approval."** LSA-C.C. Art. 2329.

Otherwise, LSA-C.C. Art. 2331 prescribes mandatory formalities.

A matrimonial contract **"shall be made by authentic act *or* by an act under private signature duly acknowledged by the spouses."** [Italics added.] An authentic act requires that each party sign (execute) the agreement before two persons who witness each prospective spouse sign, and before a notary public. An act under private signature duly acknowledged requires that the parties sign the document in the presence of a notary public. Thus, the parties can have the matrimonial agreement privately witnessed and notarized; or they can sign the agreement more privately before a notary public. Each option is acceptable for meeting the formalities in LSA-C.C. 1836.

When should due acknowledgment (signing in the presence of a notary public) take place? Before or during marriage? LSA-C.C. 2331 places no explicit time requirement on notarization. But case law, in this and other states, makes clear why this statutory ambiguity can lead to litigation.

In *Acurio v. Acurio*, 197 So.3d 253 (Ct. App. 2016), for example, the state supreme court reversed a trial court decision that invalidated a matrimonial agreement that was signed before marriage, but not duly acknowledged (notarized) until after the marriage.

LSA-C.C. 2329 suggests that a marital agreement negotiated before marriage and executed after the date of the marriage can still be valid as a legal document, but there was a split on this point among the appellate courts.

The Louisiana Supreme Court resolved the split by reading LSA-C.C. 2331 (**"shall be made by authentic act *or* by an act under private signature duly acknowledged by the spouses"**) against the backdrop of LSA-C.C. 2329, which articulates a strong legislative policy against signing away community property rights during marriage without court approval. In so doing, the Louisiana Court interpreted LSA-C.C. 2331 to require signatures plus due acknowledgment as formalities to meet prior to marriage.

To sum up, LSA-C.C. 2329 requires court approval for a matrimonial agreement, and LSA-C.C. 2331 sets out the formalities (signing and due acknowledgment). If the parties do not comply with these applicable statutes, the risk is an unenforceable contract that also voids all resulting contract-initiated property effects. *Deshotels*, supra at 544 and *Acurio*, supra. In the absence of an enforceable matrimonial agreement, the default matrimonial regime (meaning the state's default community property system) comes into effect by operation of law. LSA-C.C. Art.2325, Revision Comments, 1979.

In terms of the scope of a matrimonial agreement, prospective spouses and spouses have the right to agree "as to all matters that are not prohibited by public policy." *Barber v. Barber,* 38 So.3d 1046 (La.App. 2010), citing Louisiana legislative policy expressly prohibits, as a matter of public policy, agreements that **"renounce or alter the marital portion or the established order of succession."** Any attempt to alter, by contract, rights of devise and succession (the right to take by state intestacy statute) is void ab initio, the justification being that testamentary rights are rules of public order. LSA-C.C. Art. 7 and LSA-C.C. Art. 2330.

Louisiana legislative and case law specifically prohibit modifications and waivers of spousal support during marriage. Marriage includes any period of separation. *Barber*, supra at 1049, citing

LSA-C.C. Art. 98. Case law defines the start and end date of a period of separation. The case of *Aufrichtig v. Aufrichtig*, 796 So.2d 57 (2001) reviews relevant cases on the difference between marriage, separation, and termination.

Alimony *pendente lite* is spousal support during a period of separation. It covers temporary maintenance (basic living expenses) and suit money (attorney fees to litigate the divorce). As an historical matter, the court could award *pendente lite* only upon proof of an irretrievably broken-down marriage. Otherwise, the public policy that spouses support each other during marriage is in full force.

The rationale for drawing a line before and after an irretrievable breakdown in a marriage also relates back to how the law distinguishes between public and private rights of support. The parties cannot waive a public right during marriage by private contract. However, they can attempt to waive postdissolution spousal support, as that is a private right.

So, for example, LSA-C.C. Art. 98 provides that **"[m]arried persons owe each other fidelity, support, and assistance."** Comment (e) explains that **"[t]he spouses' duties under this Article, as a general rule, are matters of public order from which they may not derogate by contract."** *Barber*, supra at 1049, citing *Holliday v. Holliday*, 358 So.2d 618, 620 (La. 1978). Therefore, a spousal support provision that modifies or waives the duty of support during marriage is unenforceable; likewise, a provision that does the same after a date of separation. LSC-C.C. Art. 2034. See also, *Boudreaux* *v. Boudreaux*, 745 So.2d 61, 62 (1999), *Williams v. Williams,* 760 So.2d 469, 474 (2000).

Contracts that attempt to modify or eliminate permanent alimony (postdissolution spousal support rights) are not per se against public policy. The Louisiana Supreme Court decided as much in the rehearing decision of *McAlpine v. McAlpine*, 679 So.2d 85, 90 (La. 1996). The court reasoned that the right to petition for permanent postdissolution alimony is a private right and thus it is not against public policy to modify or waive it by contract. *McAlpine*, supra at 90, citing *Holliday*, supra, 620. See also, LSC-C.C. Art. 2034. Offending clauses are null (stricken), potentially leaving the remainder of the contract enforceable.

Matrimonial agreements can affect the rights of third parties as well as the rights of the spouses. Therefore, a statute permits a creditor to challenge the enforceability of a matrimonial agreement that may be in fraud of that creditor's rights. See LSA-C.C. Art. 2036–2044. To protect creditors' rights, Louisiana law advises recording matrimonial agreements as one would a deed. A matrimonial contract is **"effective toward third persons as to immovable property, when filed for registry in the conveyance records of the parish in which the property is situated and as to movables when filed for registry in the parish or parishes in which the spouses are domiciled."** LSA-C.C. Art. 2332.

5. NEVADA

Nevada adopted the UPAA 1983 in 1989; it applies to all premarital contracts executed on or after Oct. 1, 1989. See Nev.Rev.Stat. § 123A.010 through § 123A.100.

Statutory law requires that premarital contracts be in writing and signed by both parties. Nev.Rev.Stat. § 123A.040. Consideration is not necessary. Nev.Rev.Stat. § 123A.050.

A premarital contract is enforceable unless the party against whom enforcement is sought proves that, at the time of signing the contract (execution), he or she did not enter the agreement voluntarily or that disclosure was lacking. Nev.Rev.Stat. § 123A.080(1).

The statute also permits the parties to contract for **"[t]he modification or elimination of alimony or support or maintenance of a spouse; . . . ."** Nev.Rev.Stat. § 123A.050.1.(d). But Nev.Rev.Stat. § 123A.080.2. provides: if a premarital agreement modifies or eliminates **"alimony or support maintenance of a spouse, and that modification or elimination causes one party to the agreement to be eligible for support under a program of public assistance at the time of separation or marital dissolution, a court, notwithstanding the terms of the agreement, may require the other party to provide support to the extent necessary to avoid that eligibility."**

Unconscionability is a question of law, and the definition of that word conforms to the definition used in the UPAA 1983 discussed in Section B above.

If a pre-1989 agreement complies with the Nevada UPAA, the court has discretion to find it enforceable "if it either conforms to the requirements of the UPAA or if it conforms to the common law, as interpreted by the courts of Nevada prior to the enactment of the UPAA." *Sogg v. Nevada State Bank*, 832 P.2d 781, 783. (Nev. 1992). The Nevada Supreme Court has the power to review the existence of a premarital contract de novo. Id.

6. NEW MEXICO

New Mexico passed the UPAA 1983 effective July 1, 1995. See N.M.Stat.Ann. § 40–3A–1 to § 40–3A–10 (1978).

In that adoption, the New Mexico legislature amplified formalities so that a premarital agreement now must be in a writing, signed by both parties *and* duly acknowledged while in the state of New Mexico. N.M.Stat.Ann. § 40–3A–4B (1978).

The same code section amplifies the uniform law in yet another way. The UPAA 1983 disallows only provisions that affect the right of a child to support, whereas the New Mexico version of the UPAA disallows any provisions that **"adversely affect the right of a child *or spouse* to support, ..."**

Both unconscionability and voluntariness are issues of law in New Mexico (unlike, for example, in

California, where unconscionability is a question of law, but voluntariness is one of fact).

Rivera v. Rivera, 149 N.M. 66, 243 P.3d 1148 (Ct. App. 2010), adjudicated the relationship between general contract enforceability and a potentially severable waiver of spousal support rights. In that case, the parties signed a premarital agreement with a postdissolution spousal support rights waiver. The record showed that the contract proponent did not provide disclosure to the party against whom enforcement of the contract was sought. Also, the contract lacked a severability clause. When the issue of contract enforceability went up on appeal, the appellate ruled that in the absence of disclosure, the waiver of the right to petition for spousal support is unconscionable as against New Mexico public policy. Moreover, the omission of a severability clause raised questions about whether "the waiver of spousal support [was] in exchange for other benefits or concessions." Id. at 1154. The court found the contract unenforceable on the ground that it was "unable to conclude that any portion of the agreement is valid without the unconscionable provisions."

7. TEXAS

Texas adopted the UPAA 1983 effective April 17, 1997. The Texas provisions appear at V.T.C.A. Fam.Code §§ 4.001–4.010. Texas law follows the UPAA 1983 on the issue of formalities. Premarital agreements must be in writing and signed by both prospective spouses. As in other states, a premarital agreement is enforceable without consideration. V.T.C.A. Fam.Code § 4.002.

Parties may contract for the modification or elimination of postdissolution spousal support per V.T.C.A. Fam.Code § 4.003(4). Like California, Texas omitted the UPAA 1983 language granting a court the authority to modify an unconscionable spousal support provision at enforcement. The omission is significant because V.T.C.A.Fam.Code § 4.006(C)(c) provides: **"[t]he remedies and defenses in this section are the exclusive remedies or defenses, including common law remedies or defenses."**

The Texas Constitution of 1876, Art XVI § 15 Separate and Community Property of Spouses was last amended on Nov. 2, 1999. That Section enshrines a person's right to **"by written instrument . . . partition between themselves all of part of their property, then existing or to be acquired, or exchange between themselves the community interest of one spouse or *future spouse* in any property . . . ."** Italics added.

This section also directs the legislature that: **"laws shall be passed more clearly defining the rights of the spouses, in relation to separate and community property . . . ."** The section speaks of "persons about to marry" and of "future spouses." Id.

8. WASHINGTON

Washington has not adopted the UPAA 1983. Instead, Washington refers to general civil law statutes.

Washington case law raises salient premarital contracting issues, two of relevance here. At what point does a confidential relationship arise between intimate partners? And what standards of proof apply to what issues?

In Washington, as briefly discussed in Sections A and B above, the law on when a confidential relationship arises is unclear. Does a confidential relationship arise on the date the parties are engaged? How is engagement proved? If this is the rule, what is the explanation for the rule? Is it that on the date of engagement the parties are in a confidential relationship as a matter of law? Or is it that engagement gives rise to the confidential relationship as a matter of fact?

There is not legislation disallowing premarital agreements. There is, however, legislation that allows separate property agreements. This suggests that Washington does allow written premarital contracts.

A premarital agreement is a contract signed before marriage.

A separate property agreement, by comparison, is a marital contract that is signed (executed) by the parties during their marriage. Such a contract validly determines ownership rights upon the death of either spouse. Statutory law requires that the separate property agreement be in writing and acknowledged. Wash.Rev.Code § 26.16.120. But the rationale for labeling a separate property agreement a nontestamentary instrument is that the agreement works as a nonprobate device by how it automatically conveys property to the surviving spouse at the decedent spouse's death. By contrast, a will becomes irrevocable at death but does not otherwise result in an automatic conveyance of title at death, since rules of probate govern.

The legislation that allows separate property agreements, along with the absence of legislation that disallows premarital agreements, therefore, adds to support for the idea that Washington allows written premarital contracts if they meet the same requirements as separate property agreements, which is to say if they are in writing, signed, and duly acknowledged (notarized).

A court can deem a premarital contract substantively fair if it makes a meaningful provision for the spouse against whom enforcement is sought. A meaningful provision is the consequence of full disclosure as to the amount, character and value of the property involved.

A contract is voluntarily entered if it is procedurally fair. *Friedlander v. Friedlander*, 80 Wash.2d 293, 494 P.2d 208 (1972) and *Marriage of Matson*, 107 Wash.2d 479, 730 P.2d 668 (1986) set forth the basic doctrine. *Marriage of Zier*, 136 Wash.App. 40, 147 P.3d 624 (App.Div. 3 2006) and

Marriage of Bolster, 146 Wash.App. 1042 (App.Div. 1 2008) split on how the doctrine applies if it does.

The adversely affected party should have sufficient time to review the final contract, most preferably with independent legal counsel. See e.g., *Marriage of Bernard*, 165 Wash. 2d 895, 204 P.3d 907, 910–913 (2009), which found an agreement unenforceable due to involuntariness when a significantly revised version of a premarital agreement was presented by the contract proponent to the party against whom enforcement was later sought three days before the wedding.

In a general contract case, the burden of proof lies with the party who seeks to prove the existence of a valid contract. Only when the defendant raises fraud as an affirmative defense might the burden shift.

In a premarital agreement case, whether the burden shifts will depend upon whether the state allows a presumption of undue influence. Given that the parties are in a confidential relationship as of the date of their engagement, the adversely affected party could rely on the confidential relationship and related facts to argue that the presumption of undue influence ought to be raised. Once raised, the premarital agreement would be nonconclusively presumed to be a product of undue influence. The contract proponent would have the burden of rebuttal. The procedural benefit of a presumption of undue influence goes to the party against whom enforcement is sought (the language used by states that have enacted the UPAA 1983), who is also the party adversely affected by the contract.

9. WISCONSIN (WUMPA)

Wisconsin adopted the Uniform Marital Property Act (1983), referred to as WUMPA, effective January 1, 1986. Legislative Counsel Committee Notes appear at the start of Chapter 766. "Nontax Provisions." W.S.A. 2009, Chapter 766, at 39–40 discusses premarital and marital agreements in general terms.

Generally, marital property agreements are made between the spouses and comply with Wis.Stat. § 766.58(6). This code section includes provisions on procedural and substantive fairness. It indicates that three elements of proof are necessary for a marital property agreement to be established and eventually deemed equitable: (i) the agreement was voluntarily signed; (ii) the agreement was entered into based on fair and reasonable disclosure given by each spouse of his or her financial information; and (iii) the substantive provisions dividing the property are fair to each party. The statute does not define "fair." See e.g., *Greenwald v. Greenwald*, 154 Wis.2d 767, 779–80, 454 N.W.2d 34, 38 (Ct. App. 1990), disagreed with by *Meyer v. Meyer*, 239 Wis.2d 231, 620 N.W.2d 382 (2000) on a different issue.

Additionally, spouses owe each other a duty of good faith in matters involving **"marital property or other property of the other spouse. This obligation may not be varied by a marital property agreement."** Wis.Stat. § 766.15.

"Agreements executed before marriage" (called premarital agreements in other states) if

"intended to apply only after [the parties'] determination date" are marital property agreements per Wis.Stat. § 766.585. The parties' determination date is the last to occur of marriage; or domicile in the state; or the date that WUMPA became effective (12:01 a.m., January 1, 1986).

This same statute does not govern agreements signed *before* the determination date **"except as provided otherwise in a marital property agreement made after the determination date."** Wis.Stat. § 766.58(12). But Wis.Stat. § 766.588, discussed below, does apply.

Finally, the law on the date that the agreement applies (meaning the date that the agreement comes into legal existence) governs by the authority of Wis.Stat. § 766.585. As in other states, a contract becomes enforceable on the date of marriage.

Spousal support modification and waiver provisions are known as "elimination." A clause for elimination is enforceable so long as it does not result **"in a spouse having less than necessary and adequate support, taking into consideration all sources of support."** Wis.Stat. § 766.58(9)(a). If a spousal support provision makes **"one spouse eligible for public assistance at the time of dissolution of the marriage or termination of the marriage by death, the court may require the other spouse or the other spouse's estate to provide support necessary to avoid that eligibility, notwithstanding the marital property agreement."** Wis.Stat. § 766.58(9)(b).

Here, the statutory remedy is not severance but judicial modification.

To affect a marital agreement, parties may use a statutory terminable marital property classification agreement form (STMPCA for short), details for which are set out at Wis.Stat. § 766.588. A STMPCA is a terminable agreement. It is terminable because a STMPCA either automatically ends 3 years after the date of signing (in the absence of disclosure) or 30-days after one spouse delivers a signed notice of termination to the other spouse (with adequate disclosure). The 30-day notice termination is unilateral, meaning that one spouse acting alone can set the termination of a STMPCA into motion. A spouse can personally deliver a signed notice of termination to the other spouse or send it by certified mail to a last known address.

Wis.Stat. § 766.588, Schedule A is a form that lists general asset and liability categories that, if disclosed, could avoid an automatic termination of the STMPCA after three years.

STMPCA termination is prospective only, not retrospective, as to property rights. STMPCA does not reclassify property rights. Ordinary contract defenses are not ruled out when it comes to a STMPCA; the rationale being that a sole owner uses a STMPCA to reclassify sole property as marital property, and therefore, contract defenses (such as the defense of lack of consideration) should remain available to this sole owner as the adversely affected party. Legislative Counsel Committee Notes—1987 Act 393, W.S.A. 2009 at 111.

Like separate property agreements, also discussed in Chapter 3, a STMPCA is only effective against those creditors who obtained a copy of the STMPCA document before extending credit.

Otherwise, marital property agreements are presumptively equitable. A party who challenges the agreement at the end of the marriage bears the burden of rebuttal *Gardner v. Gardner*, 527 N.W.2d 701, 190 Wis.2d 216 (1994), rev. denied 531 N.W.2d 327 (1995).

CHAPTER 3
TRANSMUTATIONS

A. OVERVIEW

A transmutation is a change in the character of an asset during marriage.

In terms of possibilities, a transmutation can be of community property to separate property; separate property to community property; or the separate property of one spouse to the separate property of the other spouse. Logically, all three options make sense, but legally all three options may not be permitted by state law.

A transmutation is consequential for at least four reasons.

- *Confidential relationship*: A transmutation occurs between spouses who are in a confidential relationship with each other as a matter of law.
- *Impact on net worth:* A transmutation adversely affects one spouse's interest in the transmuted asset or property, whereas it benefits the other spouse's interest.
- *Impact on legal rights*: A transmutation changes the spouses' legal rights, relative to each other as to the transmuted asset or property.

- *Impact on rights of third parties:* A transmutation can negatively impact the rights of third parties such as creditors.

In terms of formalities, most states require that a transmutation be in writing. The writing can be in any form. A contract, a gift deed, a deed, a holiday card, possibly even an email or a text will suffice.

A transmutation *by contractual agreement* is classifiable as a bargained for exchange between the spouses.

A transmutation by gift or donation is classifiable as a gratuitous exchange between the spouses.

A transmutation *by valid deed* adds or subtracts the name of a spouse from a deed, thus potentially changing beneficial title to the asset.

A transmutation *by the sole action of a spouse who manages a community property business* can change the character of property in any number of ways (by contract, gift, deed, sale, hypothecation, to name a few). If the transmutation is part of the ordinary course of a community property business, then the managing spouse may have statutory authority to engage in transmutations within the ordinary scope of business.

Transmutations that meet statutory formalities are:

- Valid on the date they are made.
- Subject to challenge for fraud.
- Subject to challenge for undue influence.

- Subject to challenge for unfairness, as discussed below.

A valid transmutation can only be reversed by a subsequent (also valid) transmutation. Once a transmutation has been affected by a written document, the physical destruction of that document does not and cannot invalidate a prior transaction.

Any property interest—present or future, legal or equitable, vested or contingent, real or personal, including contractual benefits like royalties or rents—that can be characterized within the state marital property system may be the subject of a transmutation.

A transmutation may be made on an asset-by-asset basis or on an estate wide basis.

For most types of property state transmutation formalities are mandatory. Any transmutation that does not meet the state's statutory formalities is void. If there is uncertainty as to whether the transmutation formalities were met, then the transmutation is voidable.

In some states certain categories of assets are exempt from transmutation formalities. Interspousal tangible gifts of a personal nature are an example of an asset category that can be transmuted with few or no formalities. If exempt, interspousal gifts are transmuted upon proof of legal delivery, subject, in some jurisdictions, to a value limitation to protect the rights of creditors. The policy reason for value limitations is to avoid dissipation of the community estate by changing the character of personal property. Value limitations are consistent with the modern Uniform Fraudulent Transfer Act of 1984 (UFTA 1984) was amended by the Uniform Law Commission to address a few narrowly defined issues. The new act is called the Uniform Voidable Transactions (plural) Act of 2014 (the UVTA 2014 for short) and protect the interests of creditors. The Uniform Law Commission Enactment Map shows that California, Idaho, New Mexico, Washington, and Wisconsin have adopted the UVTA 2014; Arizona, Nevada, and Texas adopted the UFTA 1984; Louisiana is the sole holdout.)

A gift of real estate must meet transmutation formalities. A transfer deed must comply with the statute of frauds to be valid. The elements of the statute of frauds are a writing, with essential information, signed by the party to be charged (typically the grantor). For this reason, a deed itself can be offered as proof of a written express declaration of the grantor's present intent to change the character of an asset.

Transmutation by operation of law occurs when assets of different characters (community and separate) are commingled to such a degree that their component parts became untraceable. The rationale here is based on a theory of gift or, depending on the facts, donation: the spouse who allows their separate property to be intermixed with community property to the point of confusion delivers that property to the community with donative intent.

B. DETAIL

Prior to the 1980s, U.S. community property states permitted oral and even tacit transmutations.

Today, most jurisdictions require that a transmutation be proved by writing.

1. FORMALITIES: THE WRITING AND EXPRESS DECLARATION REQUIREMENT

Since the 1980s, transmutation formalities require that transmutations be in writing unless the property being transmuted is exempt either by a statute or by a court ruling. For example, California enacted legislation, effective on January 1, 1985, requiring that a transmutation, to be valid, must be **"made in writing by an express declaration that is made, joined in, consented to, or accepted by the spouse whose interest in the property is adversely affected."** Cal.Fam.Code § 852(a).

The concept of the *express declaration* ensures that the adversely affected spouse's present intent to change the character of the asset (or assets) in question appears on the face of a written document . Declarations are statements of present intent (*I hereby transmute this asset*) not of future intent (*I want to transmute this asset in the future*). The express declaration is also evidence that the spouse understands that their interest in the property will be adversely affected by the transmutation. *Estate of MacDonald*, 51 Cal.3d 262, 272 Cal.Rptr. 153, 794 P.2d 911 (1990).

An express declaration can be made by any written document. It can take the form of an attorney prepared transmutation document, or of an informal writing, like a card, a letter, a text, or email. If it takes the form of a contractual agreement, the express declaration can appear in a contract term or fragment, in a document signed by both parties. Some states have acknowledgement and recordation requirements as well. Whether a deed alone can transmute an asset depends on a close reading of state law, of the deed itself, and of the facts of the case.

2. TRANSMUTATIONS BY DEED

Every U.S. community property state relies on community property presumptions that are raised depending on whether and, if so, how the asset is titled. The key issue in determining the character of an asset, is time of acquisition. For a titled asset, the date of acquisition appears in the title itself. See Chapter 4 for more on community property presumptions

In U.S. community property states, an asset acquired by a person during marriage while domiciled in a community property state—no matter whether it is titled in both spouses' names, titled in one spouse's name alone, or untitled—is nonconclusively presumed to be community property in character. For a titled asset, changing the form of title by deed (for example, from joint title to sole title or vice versa), without more, may not necessarily be a transmutation, depending on state law.

Illustration 2.1: Assume B and C buy a house during marriage and take title in joint tenancy with right of survivorship (JTWROS). The house is acquired while B and C are married, making it presumptively community in character. Assume further that during marriage, B and C use a quitclaim deed to convey the house to B in B's name alone. The change in title from concurrent title (a JTWROS in the names of B and C) to sole title (title in the name of B alone) may not meet the express declaration requirement for a valid transmutation. The deed is in writing, but the fact that a quitclaim deed was used may cast doubt on whether the grantor had the present intent to change the character of the asset from community property to the separate property of B at the time the quitclaim deed was signed.

More evidence is needed than just the quitclaim deed. However, if the law of the jurisdiction allows transmutation by deed, then the issue becomes whether the word "grant" or the phrase "hereby grants" in the deed constitutes an express declaration of intent to change the character of the asset from community property to the separate property of B.

In some states, a deed between spouses is sufficient to affect a transmutation unless the adversely affected spouse has proactively sought out other protections, like filing a separate property inventory or a community property claim.

In still other states, whether a deed constitutes a transmutation depends on whether it meets certain requirements such as having been duly acknowledged or recorded. In these states, the rights of a subsequent bona fide purchaser are balanced against the rights of a spouse whose name was removed from title. See for example Sec. C, Washington.

Still in other states where Interspousal Transfer Deeds are available, a quitclaim deed may be considered too bare in its recitations to prove a present intent to transmute the asset.

Despite the differences in state laws about whether a deed can effect a valid transmutation, if B and C petition for dissolution, how will the problem be addressed?

First, the house in Illustration 2.1 above likely will be inventoried as a presumptively community property asset—since it was acquired during marriage—as the first title clearly shows. See Chapter 6 for more on a special community property presumption for concurrent titles.

Second, if B wants to claim that the delivery of the deed in B's name alone transmuted the house from community property to B's separate property, then the burden of proof will fall on B, as the benefitted party, to establish the validity of the transmutation.

Illustration 2.2: Assume that before marriage B owns a house with a mortgage. Title is in B's name alone. During marriage, B conveys title to B and to C as joint tenants with the right of survivorship (JTWROS). B's intention for this title change is to use C's income to get a new mortgage loan. Before marriage, the house is titled in B's name alone; upon the date of marriage, it becomes characterised as B's separate property. Did B's conveyance to "*B and C as joint tenants with the right of survivorship*" during marriage change the character of the house from B's separate property to community property?

Here, the answer is likely yes. Some states presume that joint form titles are community property, especially for purposes of a dissolution proceeding. Other states treat the deed, with its granting language as an express declaration of B's intent to transmute the house from separate property to community property. Still other states consider both the conveyance and its purpose. Here, at least one purpose of the new deed was to signal to the lender that either spouse or both spouses would be personally liable for a newly originated mortgage loan, as it brought the lender into privity of contract with both spouses.

With *Illustration 2.2* (as with *Illustration 2.1*) if B and C petition for dissolution the house will be inventoried as presumptively community property—either because it is in joint title when the parties seek dissolution, or because the community of B and C can be said to have acquired an interest in the house on the day B changed the title from sole title to joint title. Either rationale relies on a rebuttable presumption to place the house in the community property column of assets. If B wants to claim that the house is separate property, then B bears the burden of rebutting the community property presumption by challenging the validity of the transmutation.

In the case of a deed, one issue might be whether B merely intended to refinance a loan, not affect a change in the character of the house. However, whenever a deed is clear or deemed unambiguous by the court, California, Arizona, and Idaho exclude extrinsic evidence on the issue of the grantor's intent for purposes of conveyance or, more specifically, transmutation by conveyance. In such a situation, the general rule is that a court may look only to the deed language for the evidence of the grantor's intent.

Estate of Bibb, 87 Cal.App.4th 461, 104 Cal.Rptr.2d 415 (2001) illustrates this point. In *Bibb*, supra, the single word "*grant*" in a deed was held to meet the express declaration requirement for a valid transmutation. There, the grantor owned the property in sole title before marriage. He subsequently conveyed the property to himself and his wife during marriage in order to refinance the purchase loan. The court found that the grantor's intent was to transmute the asset by the conveyance. (the facts of *Illustration 2.2* above).

By contrast, in *Bender v. Bender*, 123 Ariz. 90, 597 P.2d 993, 997 (1979), discussed in Section C, Arizona below, the husband asked the wife to sign a rather lengthy "disclaimer deed." The court found that the disclaimer deed met the requirement of a written express declaration, made by the wife, to transmute any one-half community property interest she might own in the property. The court explained in dicta that had the wife, as the spouse whose interest in the real estate was adversely affected, signed a quitclaim deed rather than a disclaimer deed, the quitclaim would have been too bare in its recitations to prove her present intent to transmute the property.

A statement in the valid will of a still-living testator will not transmute an asset because it is a declaration of future intent, and as such it is ambulatory (subject to change or revocation during the testator's lifetime). For this reason, the wills of living persons are inadmissible on the issue of the present intent to change the character of an asset. See e.g. Cal.Fam.Code § 853.

Federal law prohibits or restricts the transmutation of a federal obligation from separate property into community property. In such a case, a transmutation might comply with state law, clearly contain an express declaration, and yet still be invalid for federal law purposes. See Chapter 13 for more on federal law.

Relatedly, efforts to transmute property can be effective between the spouses but ineffective against third parties, like creditors. See, for example, *Lucas v. Earl*, 281 U.S. 111, 50 S.Ct. 241, 74 L.Ed. 731 (1930), a case in which a transmutation agreement was valid as between the spouses under state law, but void for purposes of shifting an income tax burden under federal law.

3. VOLUNTARINESS AND ADVERSE FINANCIAL AFFECT

Colonial Spanish law provided that a wife's renunciation of existing property was voidable in cases of fraud, deceit, duress, or undue influence. If a husband gained any advantage in a transaction with the wife, the law presumed a constructive fraud. The husband bore the burden of rebutting the presumption with evidence of "full and fair disclosure or explanation to the wife. . . that she understood fully the effect [of the transmutation] upon her." deFuniak and Vaughn, PRINCIPLES OF COMMUNITY PROPERTY (2nd ed. 1971), § 138.

California legislation parallels the Spanish concept. As discussed in Chapter 2, a transmutation is a voluntary transaction for which fraud is actionable, as is undue influence.

Moreover, since the parties are married and in a confidential relationship, some states (like California) incorporate nonmarital business partnership rules into the family code. See Cal.Fam.Code § 721(b), which provides that spouses occupy **"confidential relations with each other"** and, therefore, ***"any unfair advantage"*** that one spouse obtains in a transaction with the other spouse gives rise to an evidentiary presumption of undue influence. (Italics added.) The initial burden is on the spouse whose is adversely affected by the transaction to prove any unfair advantage. (The adversely affected spouse is the spouse whose net worth is diminished by the transmutation.) Once the presumption of undue influence is raised, the burden shifts to the benefited spouse to disprove the presumption with factual proof of disclosure and voluntariness.

If the transaction is gratuitous the presumption of undue influence is raised as a matter of law. The rationale here is that the donor spouse's net worth is negatively affected by making a gift to the other spouse.

If the transaction is a bargained for exchange the presumption of undue influence is raised upon proof of any unfair advantage taken by one spouse against the other. The idea here is that fraud and coercion might be present even in a bargained for exchange between spouses, and so evidence of any unfair advantage ought to raise the presumption of undue influence to protect the adversely affected spouse.

Depending on the state, it is may or may not necessary to acknowledge and record the written document that contains the express declaration. However, because recording can decide priority issues between a spouse and a subsequent bona fide purchaser or encumbrancer, recording is likely best practice. When a transmutation affects the rights of a third party, most states require that the spouses give the third parties at least constructive notice of the change in character. Constructive notice is imparted by recordation of the written transmutation in the public record in the county where the property in question sits or is located. Recording implicates acknowledgment (notarization) in any jurisdiction, and thus recording makes acknowledgement a prerequisite for recording, whether that prerequisite appears in the family code or not. Failure to record a written transmutation leaves the third party's rights unchanged as to the transmuted asset. See e.g., Cal.Fam.Code § 852(b).

A transmutation of personal property generally need not be recorded. But here again, if the rights of a third party are affected by the transmutation, then recording may be necessary to preserve a spouse's rights relative to a third party, like a bona fide purchaser or a creditor.

All transmutations are potentially subject to the laws governing fraudulent transfers. Eight community property states have adopted either the original version of the Uniform Fraudulent Transfer Act of 1984 (the UFTA 1984 for short) or its Voidable Transactions (plural) Act of 2014 amendments, as listed above.

The Uniform Law Commission promulgated the UFTA 1984, but it is not new law. Rather, it is derived from the 1571 Statute of 13 Elizabeth c. 5. Recently, the UFTA 1984 was amended by the UFTA 2014.

At this time, California, Idaho, New Mexico, Washington, and Wisconsin repealed the UFTA 1984 and replaced it the UVTA 2014. See e.g., Cal.Fam.Code § 851, Cal.Civ.Code § 3439, effective January 1, 2016.

Arizona, Nevada, and Texas continue with the UFTA 1984.

Louisiana remains a holdout.

See Chapter 9 for more on liabilities and the rights of third-party creditors.

4. EXEMPTIONS

Certain types of property may be categorically exempt from the written express declaration requirement discussed above.

Cal.Fam.Code § 852(c), for example, exempts interspousal gifts of a tangible, personal nature that are intended to be used solely or primarily by the donee spouse and that are not **"substantial in value taking into account the circumstances of the marriage."**

Exempt property is transmuted upon the date of legal delivery by the donor to the donee.

5. TRANSMUTATION BY OPERATION OF LAW

Transmutation by operation of law occurs when property is commingled to the point of confusion, as mentioned above. The doctrine of confusion is sometimes codified or alluded to as the rationale for this outcome. See for example, Cal.Fam.Code § 852(d).

C. INDIVIDUAL STATES

1. ARIZONA

Arizona has no statutory transmutation provision. Instead, for proof of transmutation, Arizona relies on the inception of title rule as modified by an agreement between the spouses. Inception of title refers to the time the property right comes into existence. *Potthoff v. Potthoff*, 128 Ariz. 557, 627 P.2d 708 (1981). The inception of title rule determines the initial character—community or separate—of the property. See *Musker v. Gil Haskins Auto Leasing, Inc.*, 18 Ariz.App. 104, 500 P.2d 635 (Ariz. App. 1972); see also inception of title cases tracing back to *Horton v. Horton*, 35 Ariz. 378, 278 P. 370 (1929).

Under the inception of title rule, once the character of an asset is determined, it does not change except (i) by agreement between the spouses or (ii) by operation of law. *Bender,* supra, *Porter v. Porter*, 67 Ariz. 273, 195 P.2d 132 (1948). If a relevant community property presumption should be raised, the separate property proponent bears the burden of rebuttal, which requires clear and convincing evidence of a transmutation. *Neely v. Neely*, 115 Ariz. 47, 563 P.2d 302 (1977).

To affect a valid transfer of interest, a writing is required; and a written contract or deed will suffice for this element. (See above for more on deeds.) Additionally, there must be evidence of conduct undertaken contemporaneously with the written instrument that indicates a *present intent* on the adversely affected spouse's part to benefit the other spouse with rights to the property. *In re Sims' Estate,* 13 Ariz. App. 215, 475 P.2d 505 (Ariz. App. 1970). *Bender,* supra, at 996, applies this present intent test to a deed.

In *Bender*, supra, the wife signed a writing labeled a "disclaimer deed" for an Arizona trailer park (real estate) that had been purchased by the husband with funds that he earned during marriage while domiciled in Canada (a noncommunity property jurisdiction). The disclaimer deed recited the source and character of the real estate purchase funds as the husband's separate property. The deed read: "[*t]he undersigned [wife] has no past or present right, title, interest, claim or lien of any kind or nature whatsoever in, to or against said property.*"

As the disclaiming spouse, the wife was the adversely affected party. *Bender*, supra, at 996. The court said the disclaimer deed was clear and unambiguous on its face, thus excluding the introduction of extrinsic evidence on the issue of how the deed came to be executed. On the issue of the wife's intent to transmute her interest in the property on the date she signed the disclaimer deed, the court also found the recitation in the deed sufficient to prove the wife's present intent to release any interest she had or might have in the Arizona trailer park.

Bender, supra, distinguishes, in dicta, between the use of a disclaimer deed versus a quitclaim deed. The court called the deed in *Bender* a disclaimer deed because it contained abundant recitations that the court recognized as and called contractual. By contrast, said the court, a quitclaim deed is "solely the relinquishment (or gift) of any *possible* interest one has in certain property." Id. 997 (italics added). Certainly a fine line in some cases, but in this case the label (disclaimer deed) and the contractual language in the disclaimer deed itself elevated the writing signed by the wife to something above a bare quitclaim. Id.

This leads to the question of transmutation by gift. Ariz.Rev.Stat.Ann. 25–211, discussed in Chapter 5, presumptively excludes from the definition of community property any asset acquired during marriage by one spouse by gift, devise, or descent. It is only when property is acquired during marriage by both spouses from a third-party donor that the property is presumptively community property. Likewise, when property is acquired during marriage as a gift by one spouse from the other spouse, the property is presumed to be community property, but a rebuttal is possible with clear and convincing evidence. *Hrudka*, supra at 186.

For personal items such as jewelry, one spouse's possession or sole use of a personal item that was purchased with community property funds is not sufficient evidence to prove that the item was transmuted from community property to the separate property of the spouse who is in possession. Possession alone is not indicia of title in the context of marriage, even if it often is in the commercial context. Instead, the recipient must prove (i) donative intent on the part of the donor spouse with the intent to effect a valid transmutation, (ii) delivery of the gifted property, and (iii) acceptance of the gift by the donee spouse. *Armer v. Armer*, 105 Ariz. 284, 289, 463 P.2d 818, 823 (1970)(in banc).

There does not appear to be an explicitly followed value limitation in Arizona law for interspousal gifts. However, it bears noting that the equities are with the community and with protecting the rights of creditors. Id.

Generally, changes in form are not enough to transmute property. Neither is the act of commingling one character of property with another character, so long as tracing is possible.

Arizona follows the general rule that when community and separate property are commingled, they retain their character to the point of confusion. The doctrine of confusion holds that when the separate property component of an asset can no longer be identified, the entire property becomes community property by operation of law. Here, the rationale is gift-based: the donor who allows their separate property to become confused with the community property makes a gift from their separate property estate to the community estate. Allowing the separate property to become confused is proof of delivery with donative intent. *Potthoff*, supra, at 711.

2. CALIFORNIA

A transmutation is a transaction between the spouses. Cal.Fam.Code § 852 governs.

During marriage, the spouses are in a confidential relationship with each other as a matter of law. As such, the spouses, in a transaction between themselves, are held to fiduciary duties set forth in Cal.Fam.Code § 721(b), discussed briefly below and again in more detail in Chapter 3.

A transmutation can effect a change in character by agreement or by gift. Transmutation also be by operation of law.

A valid transmutation complies with statutory formalities: **"A transmutation of real or personal property is not valid unless made *in writing by an express declaration* that is made, joined in, consented to, or accepted by the spouse whose interest in the property is adversely affected."** Cal.Fam.Code § 852(a)(italics added).

The writing requirement does not require a formal instrument. Whatever the form the writing takes, however, it must include an express declaration to change the character of the asset.

The phrase "express declaration" has been the source of much litigation.

A declaration is a unilateral statement. An *express* declaration is a clearly visible statement, on the face of the document offered to prove the adversely affected spouse's present intent is to change the character of the property at issue. The standard of proof is the lowest preponderance of the evidence standard. A signature on the declaration is not required so long as the spouse whose property interests will be diminished by the transmutation makes, joins in, consents to, or otherwise accepts the change. Thus, the statute is at once narrow and broad. It is narrow in the sense that a writing and an express declaration are required for the transmutation to be valid, but it is broad in the sense that there are several ways for the adversely affected spouse to indicate their consent to the change in character.

Only one exemption to statutory requirements exists under state law, and that is for tangible interspousal gifts of a personal nature within a certain value limit. For an eligible interspousal gift, the change in character occurs when the property is delivered with donative intent. See Cal.Fam.Code § 852(c), which carves out an interspousal gift exemption from the written transmutation formalities of § 852(a).

The Cal.Fam.Code § 852(c) exemption reads like this: **"This section does not apply to a gift between the spouses of clothing, wearing apparel, jewelry, or other tangible articles of a personal nature that is used solely or principally by the spouse to whom the gift is made and that is not substantial in value taking into account the circumstances of the marriage."**

A transmutation effects the change in character when it is made, which can impact valuations. But often the transmutation does not get presented for inspection until it is offered as proof to rebut one or more of the general community property presumptions. At that point, whatever is offered is subject to legal scrutiny.

A transmutation that negatively impacts a creditor also can be challenged at dissolution. In 2015, California, repealed the Uniform Fraudulent Tranfer Act and replaced it the Uniform Voidable

Transactions Act, effective January 1, 2016. See e.g., Cal.Fam.Code § 851, and Cal.Civ.Code § 3439. The key to the operation of the UVTA is in the word "voidable" which means presumptively good but subject to challenge.

A transmutation, in the words of 852(a) is **"not valid unless"** it meets the prescribed formalities. A transmutation can be valid as between the spouses, for example, in a dissolution or probate proceeding. But it might still be challengeable by a general creditor for being made "with actual intent to hinder, delay, or defraud any creditor of the debtor." Cal.Civ.Code 3439.04(a). Proof of actual intent can take the form of a value assessment or an appraisal of the property. This means that a transmutation valid between the spouses might still be subject to set aside by a creditor as fraudulent, especially if it involves "substantially all the debtor's assets." See e.g., Cal.Civ.Code 3439.04(B)(5). See Chapter 9 for more on liabilities and the rights of third-party creditors.

As noted above, spouses have full statutory authorization to transact with each other as they could if they were unmarried. Cal.Fam.Code § 721(a). Thus, a spouse can change community property to separate property, separate property to community property, or separate property of one spouse to separate property of another spouse.

However, when spouses transact with each other they enjoy rights while being held to duties. This is because, once married, spouses are in a confidential relationship with each other as a matter of law. As such they do not deal with each other at arm's length, rather they deal with each other—in the transaction—as nonmarital business partners. See Chapter 8 for more on management and control issues.

Cal.Fam.Code § 721(b) is the relevant statute: "**. . . *in transactions between themselves*, spouses are subject to the general rules governing fiduciary relationships that control the actions of persons occupying confidential relations with each other. This confidential relationship imposes a duty of the highest good faith and fair dealing on each spouse, and neither shall take *any unfair advantage* of the other. This confidential relationship is a fiduciary relationship subject to the same rights and duties of *nonmarital business partners*, as provided in . . . . the [state] Corporations Code** . . . ." (Italics added)

The word "transaction" is broad in meaning. A transaction can be gratuitous (a gift), or the conferral of a benefit (something like a loan), or it can be a bargained for exchange (a contract). Transmutations of certain tangible gifts may or may not be exempt, depending on the facts of the case. Only a gift that falls within the interspousal gift exemption qualifies as a transmutation that is exempt from statutory formalities. Otherwise, to validly transmute an asset the adversely affected spouse must follow the transmutation formalities set out in the governing statute above.

If the transmutation is successfully challenged, then the transmutation is void. Even a transmutation by interspousal gift can be adjudged void if it does not fall within the exempt category of property or if it exceeds the value limitation set out under 852(c). The value limitation tracks Cal.Civ.Code § 3439.04(b)(5) **"substantially all the debtor's assets"** language.

Despite the use of the words "not valid" in the transmutation legislation, it is useful to think of transmutations as generally voidable due to the interaction between the transmutation formalities and the legislative protections found in Cal.Fam.Code § 721(b). Given the confidential nature of the marriage relationship, a presumption of undue influence arises or can arise to protect the spouse who is adversely affected by the transmutation. If so, even a transmutation that meet all statutory formalities, can be deemed void if it was the result of undue influence.

A presumption of undue influence is *automatically* raised when the validity of a gratuitous (gift) transaction is challenged. The presumption protects the donor spouse (the gift giver). The donor is the adversely affected spouse. The benefited party bears the burden to rebut the presumption. The donee spouse (the recipient) can do so with evidence that the adversely affected spouse voluntarily made, joined in, consented to or accepted the transmutation.

A presumption of undue influence *may be* raised if the transmutation is the result of a bargained for exchange. Upon proof that the benefited spouse took "any unfair advantage" of the adversely affected spouse, the court has discretion to raise the presumption of undue influence as to the transaction. This leaves it to the benefited party to rebut the presumption with proof that the adversely affected spouse voluntarily made, joined in, consented to, or accepted the transmutation. The evidentiary standard is preponderance of the evidence. In other states (Arizona for example) rebuttal is by the evidentiary standard is the higher clear and convincing standard. See Arizona, Sec. C.1.

What about the phrase "any unfair advantage" in the context of a bargained for exchange? Does it mean the transmutation must leave both spouses in an equal financial position? No. *Marriage of Burkle*, 139 Cal.App.4th 712, 43 Cal.Rptr.3d 181 (2006) held no in a case where both parties were represented by their own team of attorneys when they negotiated the transmutation contract. *Burkle*, supra. The court reasoned that because it is the duty of an attorney to ensure that any contract entered is done so voluntarily and with the necessary disclosure, representation by independent counsel is its own proof of voluntariness and fairness.

What about the down-stream financial consequences of the transmutation? If the benefited party takes property that does not appreciate as robustly as the adversely affected party's remaining property appreciates, does it mean that the now wealthier-party took any unfair advantage of the now less-wealthier party? Again, that depends on the facts of the case. The nature of the exchange (depreciating assets exchanged for appreciating assets) could constitute unfair advantage at the time of the transmutation. Whether the adversely affected spouse was represented by independent counsel is a material fact. But the value of the exchanged assets on the date of dissolution or the death of a spouse might not be material to the issue of undue influence when the transmutation was made. *Burkle*, supra.

3. IDAHO

In Idaho, spouses can change community property to separate property, separate property to community property, or the separate property of one spouse to the separate property of the other spouse. And they can transmute property any time during marriage. However, to be deemed valid, a transmutation, whether of personal or real property, must comply with the statutory formalities of a written and notarized instrument. *Stockdale v. Stockdale*, 102 Idaho 870, 643 P.2d 82 (1982), *Reed v. Reed*, 137 Idaho 53, 44 P.3d 1108, 1114 (2002), citing *Wolford v. Wolford*, 117 Idaho 61, 785 P.2d 625, 630 (1990). The party alleging the validity of the transmutation bears the burden of proof. *Wolford*, supra at 630.

Idaho permits transmutations by deed with no additional writing requirement. Under Idaho Code § 32–906(2) provides that "**[p]roperty conveyed by one spouse to the other shall be presumed to be the sole and separate estate of the grantee and only the grantor spouse need execute and**

acknowledge the deed or other instrument of conveyance . . ." notwithstanding the provisions on equal management and control of community property found at Idaho Code 32–912. The transmutation is limited to the base property, not to any rents, issues, and profits derived therefrom. If the parties seek to transmute both the base property and its rents, issues, and profits, the grantor must specifically state that additional intention in the instrument of conveyance.

Although conveyances typically involve a deed, a conveyance could arguably by effected by an agreement or another type of written instrument such as a will or a trust. Idaho Code § 32–912, at the very least, presumes the admission of a written and duly acknowledged instrument into evidence, but there is no explicit language otherwise limiting the form that the conveying instrument must take. Nevertheless, when the conveyance is by deed, case law conflicts on whether parol evidence should be admissible for purposes of explaining a deed that the judge deems clear on its face. See e.g., *Hall v. Hall*, 116 Idaho 483, 777 P.2 255 (1989) and *Barrett v. Barrett*, 149 Idaho 21, 232 P.3d 799 (2010). See also Stockdale, supra.

Idaho Code § 32–916 says generally that statutory law governing domestic relations (Idaho Code, Title 32), which is to say the state community property system, applies unless there is **"a marriage settlement agreement entered into during marriage containing stipulations contrary thereto."** Idaho Code § 32–917, discussed above applies. such that the agreement **"must be in writing, and executed and acknowledged or proved in like manner as conveyances of land are required to be executed and acknowledged or proved."** Relatedly, agreements concerning rights and obligations during marriage, whether executed before or during marriage, are enforceable only if they are in writing and not against public policy or illegal. *Wolford*, supra, *Stevens v. Stevens*, 135 Idaho 224, 16 P.3d 900 (2000), *Dunagan,* supra.

An illegal contract is void for public policy. In *Quiring v. Quiring*, 130 Idaho 560, 944 P.2d 695 (1997), wife induced husband to sign a quitclaim deed of his interest in the community property home in exchange for two promises: a promise to refrain from informing law enforcement about alleged acts of sexual abuse by husband against the wife's minor child; and a promise not to inform husband's employer about a criminal indictment against him for which charges had later been dropped. The family court awarded the house to the wife as her sole property on the basis of the quitclaim deed. On appeal, the Idaho Supreme Court reversed, calling the underlying agreement that resulted in the delivery of the quitclaim deed to the wife illegal and void because (i) a party cannot contract to refrain from reporting sexual abuse of a child, and (ii) obtaining a contract benefit (in this case the quitclaim deed) by threat of "arrest or exposure to hatred, contempt or ridicule is theft by extortion and violates Idaho criminal law." Id. at 702.

4. LOUISIANA

Matrimonial agreements can impact the rights of third parties as well as the rights the spouses themselves. For that reason, a creditor is permitted to challenge the enforceability of a matrimonial agreement that is in fraud of the creditor's rights. See LSA-C.C. Art. 2036–2044. To protect creditors' rights, Louisiana law advises that matrimonial agreements be recorded. A matrimonial contract is **"effective toward third persons as to immovable property, when filed for registry in the conveyance records of the parish in which the property is situated and as to movables when filed for registry in the parish or parishes in which the spouses are domiciled."** LSA-C.C. Art. 2332.

A gift of community property by one spouse to the other is called a donation. Community property donations are governed by LSA-C.C. Art. 1744. LSA-C.C. Art. 2343. The rule is that **"[t]he donation by a spouse to the other spouse"** of an undivided community property interest **"transforms that interest into separate property of the donee . . . [and] an equal interest of the donee is also transformed into separate property. . . ."**

Likewise, a gift of separate property made by one spouse to the community is also called a donation. The rule for separate property donations is LSA-C.C. Art. 2343.1: **"[t]he transfer by a spouse to the other . . ."** of separate property **"with the stipulation that it shall be part of the**

community, transforms the thing into community property."

Louisiana statutory law incorporates the civil law distinction between onerous (effort based) and gratuitous (lucrative) title. This is a clearer statutory adoption of the onerous/lucrative distinction than found in other states like, for example, California where the distinction appears in case law only. A donation can straddle the line between gratuitous and onerous. Gifts from employers are remunerative, which makes them onerous. Under LSA-C.C. Art. 2343.1 **"a transfer by *onerous* title must be made in writing and a transfer by *gratuitous* title must be made by authentic act."** As discussed in Chapter 2, in Louisiana, authentic act generally means that the legal document in question is duly acknowledged, in the presence of two witnesses, and signed by the parties involved. Formalities are how Louisiana protects the adversely affected party.

5. NEVADA

Nevada law covers interspousal gifts by reference to the general definition of separate property found at Nev.Rev.Stats. § 123, 130. Thus, when one spouse obtains property by gift from the other spouse during marriage, that property falls outside of the community property presumption; it is initially characterized as separate property absent clear and convincing evidence to the contrary. *Kerley v. Kerley*, 112 Nev. 36, 910 P.2d 279 (1996). Contrarily when one spouse conveys or places separate property in joint title during marriage, the presumption is that the change in title is a gift to the community absent clear and convincing evidence to the contrary. *Schmanksi v. Schmanski*, 115 Nev. 247, 984 P.2d 752 (1999), citing *Gorden v. Gorden*, 93 Nev. 494, 569 P.2d 397, 398 (1977).

This rule is broad enough to cover spouse to spouse conveyances of real property, so long as they are gifts (gratuitous transfers) made to the donee spouse alone. In *Kerley*, supra, for example, husband conveyed property to himself and wife as joint tenants, and later the husband and wife jointly reconveyed by quitclaim deed to the husband alone. At dissolution, the district court applied the community property presumption to the conveyed property. Husband appealed. The Supreme Court of Nevada granted a rehearing and remanded with instructions to presume that the spouses' delivery of the second-in-time quitclaim deed to the husband alone was a gift from the wife to the husband of her interest in the property. Here, the burden of proof fell to the community property proponent to prove by clear and convincing evidence that the second-in-time quitclaim conveyance was not a gift from the community to the husband. Id. at 280.

By contrast, in *Schmanksi*, supra, a case involving the transfer of funds into a joint tenancy investment account, the Nevada Supreme Court clarified that the act of transferring separate property from a sole account into joint tenancy investment account is presumed to be a gift from the grantor (the donor spouse) to the community (the donee).

As for a transmutation that is the result of a bargained for exchange, a host of Nevada statutes (bullet pointed below) explicitly contemplate or outright require that *agreements* between spouses be in writing to be enforceable. And yet, none of the statutes listed below specifically address the question of whether a *transmutation* positively must be in writing to be valid under Nevada law. This statutory gap leaves open the possibility that an oral transmutation may still be valid in Nevada.

- *Separate property asset inventory:* Nev.Rev.Stat. §§ 123.140, 123.150 and § 123.160 contemplate a written inventory of separate property assets. The inventory is required by Nev.Rev.Stat. § 123.140 to be **"made out and signed . . . acknowledged or proved in the manner required for the acknowledgment of proof of a conveyance of real property, and may be recorded, if such person is a resident of this State . . . ."**

- *Joint titled asset:* Nev. Rev.Stat. § 125.150.2 mandates a court to dispose of property held, at divorce, by the spouses in a joint tenancy deed form in equal shares unless justice requires otherwise. This rule leaves open the question of whether and to what extent a deed form can matter in a transmutation dispute.

- *Separation agreement:* Nev.Rev.Stat. § 123.220, the general definition of community property, permits spouses to exclude assets from that definition by **"[a]n**

agreement in writing between the spouses." This same provision does not explicitly refer to transmutations made during marriage.

- Nev.Rev.Stat. § 123.270 speaks to marriage settlement agreements executed near or at dissolution. (It is unclear whether this statute imports an implicit requirement that the parties have already separated.) The statute mandates that "**[a]ll marriage contracts or settlements must be in writing, and executed and acknowledged or proved in like manner as a conveyance of land is required to be executed and acknowledged or proved.**"

In *Anderson v. Anderson*, 107 Nev. 570, 816 P.2d 463 (1991), the spouses signed the requisite withdrawal slips, and closed a community property joint bank account. At that time they signed the withdrawal slips, they divided what were community property funds between them in unequal shares. The husband later challenged the unequal division, relying on *Schreiber v. Schreiber*, 99 Nev. 453, 663 P.2d 1189 (1983), which upheld an oral transmutation agreement already performed. The Nevada Supreme Court ruled that, even if part performance were available as a defense (the oral contract performed theory), the husband was equitably estopped from challenging the unequal distribution of account funds. The court declined to rule on the peripheral question of whether a transmutation must be in writing, preferring to leave it instead to the Nevada legislature to clarify. In the opinion of the court: "The important principle to be gleaned from the California experience is that the task of creating requirements that depart from prevailing common-law norms is one better left to the legislature." Id. at 574.

Nevada case law confirms that common law contract defenses are available, including those of part performance and estoppel. See for example, *Schreiber*, supra.

As between the spouses and a third party (like for instance the Internal Revenue Service and other creditors), however, a transmutation must be in writing to be valid.

6. NEW MEXICO

New Mexico permits transmutations per N.M.Stat.Ann. § 40–2–2 (1978). 2024 NM H.B. 242, Feb. 8, 2024, will amend this statute so that it reads gender neutrally: **"Either spouse may enter into any engagement or transaction with the other, or with any other person with respect to property that either enter into if unmarried; subject, in transactions between themselves, to the general rules of common law that control the actions of persons occupying confidential relations with each other."**

In New Mexico, as in Nevada, the code section is silent about whether any such "engagement or transaction" must be in writing.

The validity of an oral transmutation contract between married persons appears to remain unsettled. One early case says that joinder (meaning both spouses' signature on a written instrument) is required to transmute community real estate. See *McDonald v. Senn*, 53 N.M. 198, 204 P.2d 990 (1949), discussed in Chapter 1. But that same case makes no mention of an historical writing requirement for transmutations of community personal property. Of course, the mid-twentieth century was generally an easy-transmutation era, meaning that even oral transmutations were generally enforceable if proved. But since the court itself drew the line between real and personal property, the decision not to complete the analysis resulted in incoherence in the law.

Instead of a bright line rule imposing a writing requirement for any transmutation, whether of real estate or personal property, any gap in the above statute (N.M. STAT.ANN. § 40–2–2 (1978) is filled by cases that invoke the law of confidential relationships, as discussed below.

N.M.Stat.Ann. § 40–3–14, the management and control statute discussed in Chapter 8, creates exceptions to the equal management and control rule for community personal property titled in one spouse's name alone or that the spouses have **"designated in a written agreement"** to be under the sole authority of one spouse. (Title documents are written documents.)

This statute (N.M. Stat. Ann. § 40–3–14) arguably could be interpreted to transmute the titled asset by operation of law, especially considering case law indicating that an asset title in one spouse's name alone raises a *presumption of separate property* as to that asset. *Sanchez v. Sanchez*, 106 N.M. 648, 748 P.2d 21 (Ct. App.), cert. denied, 106 N.M. 627, 747 P.2d 922 (1987). But at least three strong policy arguments push hard against such an interpretation. One, community property codes most typically contain themselves to employing community property presumptions, not separate property presumptions. Two, community property states generally require that transmutations be intentional, not accidental. Three, community property systems and the community property presumptions they allow serve the purpose of protecting the community. For the above reasons, New Mexico would be well served by enacting a clear statutory provision specific to transmutations.

New Mexico case law on confidential relationships includes at least four widely followed lines of precedent with which to analyze a contested transmutation. Any one line could be applied depending on the facts of the case. For this reason, much of the precedent is yellow flagged.

Here are four reported options that have been the basis for analyzing undue influence within the confidential relationship of marriage:

- Option one invokes a high standard of proof per the *Trimble* Rule, which holds that a "transmutation must be established by clear, strong and convincing proof—more than a mere preponderance of evidence" so as to "preserve the virility of our indigenous form of marital property ownership." *In re Trimble's Estate*, 57 N.M. 51, 253 P.2d 805 (1953). A clear, strong, and convincing proof standard might not require a transmutation to be in writing, but it would certainly privilege a written transmutation document relative to any circumstantial evidence offered to prove an oral transmutation.

- Option two raises a presumption of undue influence to protect the adversely affected spouse. *Hughes v. Hughes*, 96 N.M. 719, 634 P.2d 1271 (1981).
- Option three relies on the common law of fraud and the remedy of the equitable trust. *Beals v. Ares*, 25 N.M. 459, 185 P. 780 (1919)(fraud), discussed in *McDonald*, supra, at 201; and *Curtis v. Curtis*, 56 N.M. 695, 248 P.2d 683 (1952)(presumptive fraud).
- Option four mandates full and fair disclosure as to the property that is the subject of the transmutation. *Beals*, supra.

7. TEXAS

The Texas Constitution of 1876 was silent on the issue of the right to transmute. Nevertheless, the constitution does enshrine a married person's right to partition or exchange community property for separate property, which is essentially the definition of the right to transmute. In 1949, Tex. Const Art. XVI § 15 was amended in 1999 to permit spouses to **"partition between themselves all or part of**

their property, then existing to be acquired, or exchange between themselves the community interest of one spouse or future spouse in any property for the community interest of the other spouse in other community property, then existing or to be acquired, whereupon the portion or interest set aside to each spouse shall be and constitute a part of the separate property . . . ." The amendment enabled the legislature to pass statutes governing formalities for the partition and exchange process.

Among those legislative formalities passed under the authority of the 1949 constitution is, V.T.C.A.Fam.Code § 4.102. This statute clarifies the formalities required for enforcing **"partition or exchange."**

A partition and exchange maneuver requires what is known as the "Texas two-step" (a transmutation strategy discussed in Chapter 6). Partition and exchange agreements must be in writing and signed by both parties. V.T.C.A.Fam.Code § 4.104. They presumably can be challenged on the same grounds as premarital contracts, which is to say for failure to meet formalities or for lack of voluntariness or disclosure. *McClary v. Thompson*, 65 S.W.3d 829 (2002).

Amendments to Tex. Const. Art. XVI § 15 in the 1949, 1980, 1987 and 1999 constitution were necessary to allow for spouses to convert separate property to community property. Texas law now provides that **"[a]t any time, spouses may agree that all or part of the separate property owned**

by either or both spouses is converted to community property." V.T.C.A.Fam.Code § 4.202. Statutory provisions further require that such agreement **"(a) . . . to convert separate property to community property: (1) must be in writing and: (A) be signed by the spouses; (B) identify the property being converted; and (C) specify that the property is being converted to the spouses' community property; . . . .**" Importantly: **"(b) The mere transfer of a spouse's separate property to the name of the other spouse or to the name of both spouses is not sufficient to convert the property to community property . . . .**" V.T.C.A.Fam.Code § 4.203. This provision supports the constitutional protection of the right to own separate property during marriage.

Further protection comes in the form of V.T.C.A.Fam.Code § 4.205(b). This section offers example language that if **"prominently displayed in bold-faced type, capital letters, or underlined, is rebuttably presumed to provide a fair and reasonable disclosure of the legal effect of converting property to community property: . . ."**

Texas follows **"the rule of inception of title"** which is statutorily said to **"determine"** the character of property **"at the time the right to own or claim the property arises."** V.T.C.A. § 3.404 (effective Sept. 1, 2023). As with Arizona, once character is determined by the inception of title rule, it holds through to the dissolution unless there is a valid transmutation. But whereas in Arizona, a contract or a deed that meets judge made formalities can affect the transmutation, in Texas, the constitution controls what formalities are acceptable to effect a change in character.

Texas follows the civil law rule that characterizes the rents, issues, and profits of separate property as community property during the continuance of the marriage. The Texas approach can be inferred from Tex. Const. Art. XVI § 15: **"spouses also may from time to time, by written instrument, agree between themselves that the income or property from all or part of the separate property then owned or which thereafter might be acquired by only one of them, shall be the separate property of that spouse."**

Statutory law gives spouses the right to opt for the American rule, which automatically makes rents, issues and profits separate property during the continuance of the marriage. V.T.C.A.Fam.Code § 4.103 provides that **"At any time, the spouses may agree that the income or property arising from the separate property that is then owned by one of them, or that may thereafter be acquired, shall be the separate property of the owner."** The statutory rule applies to income earned from the date of the agreement forward, not to the base property itself, or to income earned from the base property prior to the agreement.

8. WASHINGTON

A separate property agreement, defined as a contract not a will, can be used to determine ownership rights upon the death of either spouse. Wash.Rev.Code § 26.16.120. Separate property agreements must meet statutory requirements (writing and acknowledgment) to be valid. The rationale for labeling separate property agreements as nontestamentary instruments is that the agreement automatically conveys property to the surviving spouse outside of probate, and hence it is a nonprobate device. By contrast a will becomes irrevocable at death of the testator but does not otherwise result in an automatic conveyance of title at death (rather than at probate, which is a legal event that occurs after death).

Community real property can be transmuted by one spouse's gift, by conveyance, or by sale to the other spouse. Wash.Rev.Code § 26.16.050 allows spouses and registered domestic partners to **"give, grant, sell or convey directly to the other spouse or other domestic partner his or her community right, title, interest or estate in all or any portion of their community real property. . . ."** Statutory formalities serve as proof of the grantor-spouse's intent to transfer an interest in the community property described in the deed. Those formalities provide that the grantor-spouse (meaning the spouse who is releasing their community property interest in the property) **"shall sign, seal, execute and acknowledge the deed as a single person . . . ."** The benefited spouse need not also sign the deed. Noncompliance with statutory formalities supports a legal conclusion that the grantor's intent was not to release his, her or their community property interest.

When a release of one spouse's community property interest in community property real estate affects the rights of a third-party grantee or transferee. Wash.Rev.Code § 26.16.095 comes into play. The statute deems as a bona fide purchaser any third party who can prove that (i) the purchase was for value, and (ii) title to the asset, on the date of purchase, was clear on its face.

The spouse who continues to claim a community property interest in the disputed property bears the burden of proof for purposes of rebuttal.

What can a spouse do to protect their community property interest in real estate relative to third parties? This is potential trap for the unwary since married persons can and do take title to community property in one spouse's name alone.

Wash.Rev.Code § 26.16.100 gives a spouse whose name is not on a deed ninety (90) days after the original deed to the property has been recorded to set forth the nature of his or her claim to the property in a subsequent instrument. That instrument must be recorded in the auditor's office in the county where the land is to affect the rights of third-party conveyees. Recordation presumes the instrument is duly acknowledged as well. Only recordation imparts subsequent conveyees with constructive notice of the existence of a marital relationship between the spouse in whose name title appears to be vested (the spouse whose name is on title) and the spouse whose name does not appear on the deed (but whose marital claim is nevertheless recorded in the chain of title).

Wash. Rev. Code § 26.16.100 asl reads that failure to record a statement of claim in the allotted time results in a mandate to the court to find that the bona fide purchaser **"shall be deemed and held to have received the full legal and equitable title to such real estate free and clear of all claim of the other spouse or other domestic partner."** In such a case, the bona fide purchaser for value would walk away with the whole of the property; the bona fide purchaser would take the grantor-spouse's community property interest by conveyance and the other spouse's community property interest by operation of law. Wash.Rev.Code § 26.16.100.

Recordation of an instrument claiming a community poprerty interest inconsistent with the face of the title document gives third parties constructive notice of the marital relationship, but it also acts as a cloud on title for the bona fide purchaser. The cloud on title can be released by (i) the party who complied with Wash.Rev.Code § 26.16.100 to protect their property interest or (ii) with proof that the property is **"the separate property of the person in whose name the title to the said real estate, or any part thereof. . . ."** Proof can be found by examination of the public record, specifically meaning the **"conveyances on record in the office of the auditor of the county . . ."** where the land is located. Wash.Rev.Code § 26.16.110.

Wash.Rev.Code § 26.16.100 protects the bona fide purchaser for value. Washington case law supports this reading of the statute by a long history of cases that hold that a third party who buys real estate from a married person who holds sole title is deserving of bona fide purchaser status. However, the statute does not necessarily protect a purchaser from the claims of the grantor's spouse. Protection will depend on whether the third party exercised reasonable diligence to obtain knowledge of the existence of a marital relationship within the state of Washington. This is the issue that will be litigated if the grantor's spouse files a timely claim of interest. See *Campbell v. Sandy*, 190 Wash. 528, 69 P.2d 808 (1937).

9. WISCONSIN (WUMPA)

Among the permitted methods of transmutation (called classification or reclassification under WUMPA) are deeds signed by both spouses, gifts, bilateral written marital property agreements, and written consents regarding life insurance premiums and proceeds.

Wisconsin allows parties to identify separate property by use of an individual property classification agreement. Wis.Stat. § 766.587. Separate property agreements determine the property rights of the parties at the end of the marriage, but in relation to creditors, they are only effective against those creditors who were given a copy of the document before the credit was extended, meaning at origination of the loan. *Matter of Geise*, 132 B.R. 908 (Bkrtcy. E.D. Wis. 1991), citing Wis.Stat. § 766.587.

Parties can reclassify separate property so that it becomes marital property on the date of marriage. To affect such an agreement, parties are directed to use a statutory terminable marital property classification agreement form (STMPCA for short). Details are set out at Wis.Stat. § 766.588. See Chapter 2 for more on the STMPCA.

PART 2

CHARACTERIZATION

CHAPTER 4
COMMUNITY PROPERTY

A. OVERVIEW

There are two categories of marital property in a community property system: community property and separate property.

Every U.S. community property jurisdiction defines community property by a broad principle according to which property acquired by a married person while domiciled in the state is community property.

State evidence codes also can be used to recognize a general community property presumption upon proof of a group of facts. If the parties can prove they were married and domiciled in the state when they acquired the asset in question, then that asset is presumed to be community property unless rebutted by factual proof that the asset is separate property.

Contemporary legal systems attempt to streamline dissolution by the enactment of special community property presumptions that apply to specific categories of asset. General and specific community property presumptions lead to a community property characterization. Where the presumptions differ is in the type of factual proof required for rebuttal.

B. DETAIL

A community property system is many things. For our analysis it can be called a default marital property system. Community property is acquired by a person during marriage, owned during marriage, and dissolved at the end of marriage.

Not every U.S. state is a community property state, but every U.S., state employs traditional ganancial community property principles if not during marriage then at dissolution or probate.

In U.S. community property states, community property is owned during marriage in undivided halves. At dissolution, community property is dissolved (apportioned, split). Depending on the state, and not considering offsets and private agreements between the parties, the split by law is either an arithmetic fifty-fifty split or an equitable split. In every community property state, the split results in an individual property right.

In common law title states (non-community property U.S. states) title controls the ownership of property during marriage. An asset acquired by a married person with their own earnings, if titled in their name alone, will be the individual property of the earning spouse. The title holding spouse can subsequently decide to bring the other spouse on title by use of a joint form title. At dissolution, absent a joint form title, these states impose equitable division by force of statutory law. If the marriage ends by death, a forced share statute controls to give a court discretion to take a share of the decedent's property and divide it equitably. Equitable does not necessarily mean equal fifty-fifty shares. Key is that under the terms of an equitable division statute, the non-owning spouse exits a marriage with property because of the court's exercise of discretion, not because of a property right. Equitable division statutes apply at divorce. Forced share statutes apply at death.

1. TYPES OF COMMUNITY PROPERTY SYSTEMS

Forty-one U.S. states are common law separate property title states; and four of these—Alaska, Florida, South Dakota, and Tennessee—are community property option states.

Nine U.S. states are ganancial community property states. This is so even if the state does not claim a Spanish or Mexican legal heritage (as Washington and Idaho do not) or even if the state bases its community property system on the Uniform Marital Property Act (as Wisconsin does).

A *ganancial* system allows for the acquisition of community property during marriage but defines some categories of property as separate property. See Chapter 5 for more on separate property.

A *universal* marital property system characterizes all property no matter how or when acquired as community property. Wisconsin tends toward this direction without going all the way. See this chapter, Section 3, Wisconsin.

A *deferred* community property system relies on title as evidence of ownership even during marriage, but at the end of the marriage (divorce or the death of a spouse) mandates by statute that the court identify what is essentially a community property estate, as authorized by statute or decisional law.

An *equitable division* state is a U.S. common law title state that replicates community property outcomes at dissolution or death. At divorce, common law equitable division states follow the equitable division doctrine. At death, the forced share doctrine. Of the forty-one U.S. common law equitable division states, forty have adopted equitable division and forced shares statutes; one, Mississippi, relies on a judge made law.

One meaningful difference between the forty-one separate title states and the nine community property states has to do with vesting. In the nine U.S. community property states, community property rights in an asset vest upon acquisition. Whereas in the forty-one U.S. common law states, vesting first requires the exercise of court discretion in the claimant's favor.

2. THE COMMUNITY PROPERTY SHARING PRINCIPLE

One cornerstone of any community property system is the sharing principle. All U.S. community property statutes employ it, most typically in an "all property except separate property" form.

According to the sharing principle, all property acquired by a person during marriage while domiciled in the state is community property.

Marriage is a required element of proof. Only a person who is validly married can acquire community property by default with their spouse. See Chapter 12 for more on marriage validity.

Domicile is a required element of proof. Only property acquired while the person is domiciled in the state can be community property by default within that state's community property system. Location of the asset does not matter. It is important to underscore here that California community property, for example, might be very different than Idaho community property law. Therefore, domicile in the state identifies which community property laws—California or Idaho in the example here—apply in a dissolution or probate proceeding.

Manner of acquisition is a required element of proof. Manner refers to whether the property was acquired onerously (by work or effort) or lucratively (by gift or windfall). Onerous acquisition involves labor, toil, time, creation, or any other nonmonetary way of acquiring property by work. Lucrative acquisition involves no more than accepting a gift, donation, or windfall.

Acquisition means the date when the formal legal property right or interest comes into existence. Proof of date of date of acquisition can be established by title documents, receipts, or any other credible method.

Unpaid housekeeping is a form of labor that has been historically left unaccounted for in divorce and probate.

Every U.S. community property system relies on a housekeeper's presumption as a matter of state policy. A spouse's labor, whether paid or unpaid, is conclusively presumed to be of value to the community. Therefore, any asset acquired during marriage by the effort of one or both spouses (whether that effort is treated as paid work or not) results, for both spouses, in a vested community property right or interest in the asset acquired. The spouse who works without pay to keep the home or care for the children is thus understood, as a matter of law, to make an economic contribution to the acquisition of community property.

3. THE GENERAL COMMUNITY PROPERTY PRESUMPTION

When written forms of proof are not available or not credible, an evidentiary presumption can be used. If an evidence statute provides that a group of facts (*property acquired by a married person while domiciled in the state*) is presumed to establish another fact (*community property*), then proof of the group of facts gives rise to a presumption of community property.

This evidentiary presumption is known as the general community property presumption. It is acquisition-based. It is rebutted by facts showing that the property is not community property.

In some community property states, the standard for rebutting the general community property presumption is the low preponderance of the evidence standard. In other states, rebuttal is by the higher clear and convincing evidence standard. One reason for using the low evidentiary standard is to spread the risk of judicial error in a dissolution proceeding equally between the spouses. See Cal.Fam.Code § 760 and N.M.Stat.Ann. § 40–3–8 (1978). Another reason is that it guards against inadvertently creating a fault-based property division.

Divorce in all U.S. community property states is either pure no-fault or no-fault by option of the petitioner. Hence when a community property jurisdiction commits to no-fault dissolution, evidence about whose conduct led to the end of the marriage is inadmissible for purposes of dividing community property. A community property right is acquired as a *vested* right, not one conditional upon absence of fault.

Louisiana and Texas have enacted, in addition to their acquisition-based general community property presumption, a possession-based general community property presumption. Here, the mere fact of possession at the end of the marriage results in a community property characterization. Because proof of acquisition is more precise an indicator than proof of possession, Texas requires clear and convincing evidence to rebut the possession-based presumption. See LSA-C.C. Art. 2340 and V.C.T.A. Fam.Code § 3.003.

Differences exist among the nine U.S. community property states as to what type of evidence rebuts the general community property presumption.

Rebuttal confirms that the disputed asset is all or some separate property in character. Proportional (pro rata) ownership between the community estate and one spouse's or both spouses' separate property estates is permitted.

The following illustrations apply a general community property presumption to the facts in question.

Illustrations 3.1 through 3.4 below involve an untitled asset. Illustration 3.5 and 3.6 involve an asset titled in one spouse's name alone.

Illustration 3.1: Assume a person *purchases* an untitled work of art while married and domiciled in a community property state. A dated receipt can prove acquisition during marriage. But if there is no such receipt, then the general community presumption can be raised upon proof that on the date of acquisition, the purchaser of the artwork was married and domiciled in the state.

Illustration 3.2: Same facts as Illustration 3.1 except that the purchasing spouse wants to rebut the general community property presumption. The rebutting spouse—called the separate property proponent—can introduce facts proving that the artwork was purchased during marriage, but it was purchased with a provable source of separate property funds. Alternatively, the separate property proponent can produce an enforceable agreement between the spouses that the artwork is not to be community property.

Illustration 3.3: Assume a married person *possesses* an untitled artwork but cannot prove its date of acquisition. In a state with only an acquisition-based community property presumption, possession alone is not evidence of acquisition. The court may decide not to raise the general community property presumption as to the artwork. In a state with a possession-based community property presumption, however, proof of possession is enough to raise the community property presumption as to the artwork.

Illustration 3.4: Same facts as Illustration 3.3 except that the purchasing spouse wants to rebut the possession-based community property presumption as to the artwork. When the evidentiary standard for rebuttal is clear and convincing evidence, then specific, irrefutable, clear proof is required as to why the possession-based community property presumption should be rebutted.

Fidelity & Casualty Co. v. Mahoney, 161 P.2d 944 (Cal. Ct. App. 1945) helps distinguish between the concept of acquisition and possession. The case also gives insight into the discretion available to the court in deciding whether to raise the general community property presumption in the first place.

In *Fidelity*, before boarding a plane a newlywed spouse used out-of-pocket cash (which the court deemed to be $1) to buy an airplane accident insurance policy. The insured named his son from a prior marriage as the sole pay-on-death (POD) beneficiary. The plane crashed. The insured was killed. The insurer sought to pay the $5,000 insurance proceeds to the rightful owner. The insured's son argued that proceeds were purchased with his father's separate property and, therefore, the payout belonged entirely to him by contractual designation (the insurance POD). The insured's surviving spouse contended that the proceeds were paid for with community property, and therefore that she was entitled to at least her one-half share ($2,500) of the contract payout. The legal basis of the surviving spouse's argument was that the decedent spouse was in possession of the $1 that he used to buy the accident policy. She asked the court to draw the inference that possession and acquisition were the same in this case. The court declined to do so and ruled in favor of the decedent's son, the separate property proponent, for the entire $5,000.

The court of appeal affirmed the trial court's decision, explaining that California presumes that property is community property if it is shown to have been *acquired* by a person during the marriage while domiciled in the state. The court went so far as to suggest that had the wife introduced evidence about the decedent's financial information (like "whether [the decedent's] bank account was large or small or whether the bank account had been in existence a long or short time . . . [or] whether his monthly salary was large or small") there would have been a legal basis to rule that the husband acquired the $1 he used to buy the accident policy during marriage.

Had *Fidelity* been decided in Texas, the possession-based general community presumption (rather than the acquisition-based community property presumption) could have been raised by the mere fact that the decedent spouse possessed the $1 he used to buy the accident policy. It would then be up to the separate property claimant, the decedent's son, to rebut that presumption by clear and convincing evidence. V.T.C.A.Fam.Code § 3.003.

The difference between the two outcomes is procedural as well as practical. With an acquisition-based community property presumption, the community property proponent bears the burden of proving that the person acquired legal rights to the asset while married and domiciled in the state. By comparison, in a state with both an acquisition-based and a possession-based community property presumption, such as Texas, the party can prove either that they acquired legal rights to the asset while married and domiciled in the state or that they possessed the asset while married and domiciled in the state.

Here is an example of how the general community property presumption applies to an asset that is titled in one spouse's name alone.

Illustration 3.5: Driver and Passenger are married to each other and domiciled in the relevant state. Assume that Driver purchases a $50,000 collectible (appreciating) sports car with $25,000 of provable separate property funds and $25,000 of community property funds. Driver takes title to the car in Driver's name alone. There are no agreements between the spouses with respect to ownership of this car. Applying the inception of title rule, the vehicle title record proves that Driver acquired rights to the car during marriage. Applying the evidentiary presumption, Driver was married and domiciled in the state thus making the car presumptively community property in character.

Illustration 3.6: Same facts as Illustration 3.5 except that Driver seeks to confirm a separate property interest in the sports car, Driver can rebut the general community property presumption by 50%. To do this, Driver will need to prove that $25,000 of Driver's separate property was used to make the $50,000 purchase.

4. SPECIAL COMMUNITY PROPERTY PRESUMPTIONS

A special community property presumption supersedes the general community property presumption.

In a few states (California being one), a special community property presumption provides, within the context of the statute that enables the presumption itself, the exact parameters for its rebuttal. In most states, however, the statute that enables a special community property presumption might not include rebuttal instructions.

The legal (as opposed to the policy or social) rationale for enabling a special presumption is key to how that presumption functions. For example, when it comes to joint titles, some states explain the presumption by reference to contract law. If so, then the only way to rebut the presumption would be with a second contract.

a. The Special Joint Form Title Community Property Presumption

In the context of marriage, title in "joint form" refers to a title instrument in both spouses' names. With a joint title, both spouses' names appear as grantees on the face of the title instrument: "*Spouse Bip and Spouse Bop*" or even just "*Bip and Bop*". Joint form titles are discussed in more detail in Chapter 6.

Some states have enacted a special community property presumption for joint form titles. Some states limit the use of this presumption to a dissolution proceeding only. California follows this approach. Other states allow its use in dissolution and probate proceedings.

Some states explain the use of the joint title presumption using contract theory, as noted above. Here, the idea is that a joint title represents a first agreement between the spouses to characterize the titled asset as community property in the event of dissolution. Rebuttal then must be upon proof of a second agreement that amends the first agreement. The second agreement can appear in the title document itself or in a stand-alone written agreement. The content of the second agreement should communicate that the property is to be all or part separate property in the event of a dissolution.

Some states, New Mexico is the example, have enacted a special joint form title community property presumption without tying it to contract theory. In these states, rebuttal can be by a second contract or by tracing.

Still other states divide joint titles at dissolution as if they were community property. In these states, no special presumption is involved. Rebuttal evidence of an intention to hold a separate property interest can come from any number of sources. Washington and Arizona follow this approach.

When a special presumption is enacted, issues of retroactively can come up. In California, for example, retroactive application of the special joint form title community property *presumption* is constitutionally permissible. The rationale is that the use of an evidentiary presumption merely starts the analysis; it does not disrupt either party's vested property rights.

However, when rebuttal requirements are heightened constitutional concerns may be raised for how the statute impacts vested property interests if it does. See Chapters 6 and 13 for more on constitutional issues.

Illustration 3.7: Aay and Bee purchase a house during marriage. At that time, Aay and Bee take title in both of their names as joint tenants. Aay and Bee reach no other agreements as to the character of the house. Later Aay files for dissolution. Assume that the community property state has enacted a special joint form title community property presumption that applies in a dissolution proceeding only. For purposes of the dissolution proceeding the house is community property in character.

Illustration 3.8: Same facts as Illustration 3.7 except that Bee seeks to rebut the joint form title community property presumption. In this jurisdiction, Bee's rebuttal will fail for lack of a second written contract that the house was not to be community property at dissolution.

Illustration 3.9: Same facts as Illustration 3.7 above except that the jurisdiction has not enacted a statutory joint form title community property presumption. Instead, it treats property in joint title as community property for purposes of division in a dissolution proceeding. In this jurisdiction, the house was acquired during marriage and will be presumed to be community property. Bee can rebut the presumption using any relevant evidence. See Section C, Nevada, and Washington.

Illustration 3.10: Same facts as Illustration 3.7 except that the marriage ends by Aay's death. When a marriage ends by death, the joint form title operates as designed. Since Aay and Bee took a joint tenancy with the right of survivorship title, at Aay's death, Aay's interest is extinguished, and Bee becomes the sole owner of the house.

b. Multiple-Persons Accounts Acts in General

A minority of states have adopted multiple persons accounts acts. This legislation addresses beneficial ownership rights between account depositors to sums on deposit in the account.

Two multiple-parties-accounts acts are discussed here. They are the National Conference of

Commissioner's Uniform Multiple-Persons Accounts Act of 1989 (UMPAA 1989 for short)) and the California Multiple-Parties Accounts Law (CAMPAL 1990 for short). Multiple-parties accounts laws are generally categorized as both consumer protection law and as nonprobate transfer law.

First some background information on bank accounts. Every bank account is made up of two distinct assets: (i) the account contract and (ii) the sums on deposit in the account on any given day. The bank account contract is the account "title" that determines who has legal access to the account. Importantly, ownership of the account does not necessarily determine ownership of the sums on deposit in the bank account. Yet, because the account owner has access to the account, that person alone can access sums on deposit in the account. Therefore, in a dissolution, questions about who owns sums on deposit in a bank account can arise.

If the bank account can be analogized to a jewelry box, the sums on deposit are like items of jewelry in the box. The owner of the jewelry box has access to the box, and access gives that box owner the practical ability to remove jewels from the box. But just because a box owner can remove jewels from a box does not mean they own the jewels. Ownership of the box does not necessarily determine ownership of the jewels in the box, as the box and each of the jewels are distinct assets.

A *sole bank account* is an account for which the bank deposit contract (the account title) is between the bank and the depositor in the depositor's name alone. A sole bank account gives only the depositor named on the contract access to the account or the authority to name other users who might get limited access to the account.

A *joint bank account* is an account for which the deposit contract (the account title) is between the bank and two or more depositors in all depositors' names. A joint account gives all named depositors access to the account.

When depositors are married to each other, a sole bank account in one spouse's name alone gives that spouse access to the account, whereas a joint account in both spouses' names gives both spouses access to the account.

What about the money in the account? In the context of this legislation, money is too vague a term. Instead, the money in the account is referred to as the *sums on deposit* in the account.

The net deposit rule provides that absent proof otherwise, beneficial ownership of the sums on deposit in a bank account are owned by the account owner's net contributions to the account. If more than one depositor contributes to the account, sums on deposit are owned by all the depositors' net contributions.

In a community property jurisdiction where contributions can be of different characters, the net deposit rule may be modified by the net *character* deposit rule: beneficial ownership of the sums on deposit in any bank account of a married person are determined by the net *character* of the deposits.

The difference between the "net contribution" language and the "net character deposits" language is that the latter more specifically references the community property context. A spouse can contribute a deposit to a bank account, but if that deposit is community property, then the contribution belongs to both the spouses. To add this important context, states that use the "net contribution" language also tend to add language that presumes the contributions are community property. Alternatively, the statute might use language indicating that the spouses have contributed an "equal amount" to net contributions.

If a state has not enacted multiple-persons accounts legislation, ownership outcomes, in a community property state, might be as follows.

The first outcome might stem from a line of cases that holds that sums on deposit in the account of a married person are presumed to be entirely community property. All U.S. community property systems acknowledge as much, especially when it comes to joint accounts, meaning accounts to which both spouses have contractual rights to access the account. This is only a partial resolution to a problem involving beneficial ownership of sums on deposit in the account, however, because this line of cases often does not address common situations that arise when one spouse deposits separate property sums into the account (commingling). Nor do the cases lend guidance on how a spouse might prove beneficial ownership of different characters of sums on deposit in the account (community or separate). More broadly, this approach may result in a violation of any state constitutional provision protecting the right to own separate property during marriage.

The second outcome might stem from a line of precedent that the title to the account (sole or joint) determines the character (community or separate) of the sums on deposit in the account. This rule would extend beneficial ownership of the account itself to the sums on deposit in the account. Using the box analogy, it makes the owner of the box the owner of the jewels in the box by operation of law. This rule has a few problems. It conflates the account (the jewelry box) with the sums on deposit in the account (the jewels). And it divests the spouse whose name is not on the bank contract of their one-half share of community property sums on deposit in the account and of any separate property sums on deposit they may have on deposit in the account. It also creates a situation in which one spouse's rights of survivorship, devise, and descent can be defeated by the simple movement of money from one bank account to another.

The third outcome might stem from a line of precedent that traces the sums on deposit to their source (not to the account title) to ultimately determine the character of the sums on deposit. Unless this line of precedent addresses the character of the sums on deposit in the account before the process of tracing is undertaken, it is at best a partial resolution to the problem of the beneficial ownership.

Multiple-persons accounts laws try to address these types of problems. Their benefits are many. I summarize only four here.

- A multiple-person accounts law identifies the two assets for which ownership might be claimed: the bank account (asset 1) and the sums on deposit in the bank account (asset 2).
- A multiple-person accounts law prevents an accidental and intentional impairment of either spouses' rights by the simple movement of sums on deposit from one bank account to another.
- A multiple-person accounts law furthers state domestic violence prevention policies.
- A multiple-person accounts law shields financial institutions from liability for honoring the withdrawal request of a bank account owner who is not also the beneficial owner of the sums on deposit being withdrawn.

c. The Uniform Multiple-Persons Accounts Act of 1989

According to the National Conference of Commissioners on Uniform State Laws, twelve U.S. jurisdictions—including Arizona and New Mexico, both discussed below—have adopted the Uniform Multiple-Person Accounts Act (UMPAA 1989 for short). Also adopting the UMPAA 1989, according to the same source, are the U.S. Virgin Islands and Brazil.

The UMPAA (1989) can be adopted within the Uniform Probate Code, as a free-standing Uniform Nonprobate Transfers on Death Act, or piece meal as a supplement to the state's existing legislation.

The UMPAA 1989 is not community property legislation, but it does contain a provision, on the right of depositors who are married to each other. Adopting states can choose to include or omit this language.

The policies UMPAA 1989 address involve three issues that consistently come up in relation to demand deposit (simple bank) accounts:

- Issues related to the beneficial ownership rights to sums on deposit as between depositors.
- Issues related to the existence, validity, and revocability or survivors' benefits.
- Issues related to the protection of the financial institution.

UMPAA 1989 covers demand deposit accounts. The term *demand deposit account* includes bank accounts, savings and loan association accounts, and credit union accounts. Investment accounts are not included within the definition of a demand deposit account.

Additionally, UMPAA 1989 includes a provision applicable to account depositors who are married to each other. Specifically, UMPAA 1989 Art. 2, Sec. 11(b) provides: **"During the lifetime of all parties, an account belongs to the parties in proportion**

to the *net contribution* of each to the sums on deposit, unless there is clear and convincing evidence of a different intent. *As between parties married to each other, in the absence of proof otherwise, the* <u>*net contribution*</u> *of each is presumed to be an equal amount.*" (Italics and underscore added.)

The italicized language suggests a legal presumption, but it does not go on to explain how that presumption can be rebutted. The underscored language above reveals itself as non-community property legislation by how it closes with a provision applicable to "parties who are married to each other."

The UMPAA 1989 Art. 2, Sec. 11 Comment clarifies the rationale for presuming that the person who deposits sums into a joint deposit account remains the beneficial owner of those sums. The Comment says the language of Art. 2, Sec. 11 is based on the idea that because such as depositor does not intend to change the ownership of the sums by the simple act of depositing funds into an account, they lack a donative intent to make an irrevocable gift of the same.

The definition of account under UMPAA 1989 makes clear that a covered account is one that is either in *sole* title or *joint* title.

The traditional phrase "joint account" is too imprecise a label to identify why two or more persons might want their name on the bank account contract. Thus, in the context of marriage, it is useful to recognize that a couple may want to accomplish any number of goals in opening a joint bank account.

They may want to operationalize their genuine belief that they are co-owners of the sums on deposit in the account. If this is the case, then the UMPAA 1989 Art 2, Sec. 11 (b) captures this intent: **"As between parties married to each other, in the absence of proof otherwise, the net contribution of each is presumed to be an equal amount."**

But statute falls short if spouses hold the view that the sums on deposit are not all or partly co-owned. In such a case, the above language does not capture the intent of the parties. Only if the above language is omitted from the adopting statute, does the remaining UMPAA 1989 Art 2, Sec. 11 (b) fragment possibly allow for a rebuttal standard: **"During the lifetime of all parties, an account belongs to the parties in proportion to the net contribution of each to the sums on deposit, *unless there is clear and convincing evidence of a different intent.*"** (Italics added.)

A married couple may name one spouse as a POD beneficiary. If so, then UMPAA 1989 Art 2, Sec.11 (c) provides that **"a beneficiary of an account having a POD designation has no right to sums on deposit during the lifetime of any party."**

A married couple might believe that only one spouse is the true owner of the sums on deposit in the account. Yet, the owning spouse may nevertheless want the other spouse to have access to the account as an agent with authority to withdraw funds either generally or in case of the owning spouse's illness, disability, or death. If so, then then UMPAA 1989 Art 2, Sec.11 (d) provides **"[a]n agent in an account with an agency designation has no beneficial right to sums on deposit."**

Considering the reasons a married couple might open a joint bank account, it is not difficult to understand why a joint bank account set up for one purpose **"may yield unwanted consequences for other purposes."** Uniform Multiple-Person Accounts Act, 8B U.L.A. 3, 5 (2014).

Therefore, to better protect account depositors and financial institutions the UMPAA 1989 proposes the following default rules for all joint bank accounts.

- The ownership of sums on deposit in a joint account is determined by the named depositors' net contributions to the account, which for parties married to each other are presumed to be equal unless established otherwise by clear and convincing evidence.
- Joint account balances transfer on the death of a depositor to the account survivor (or survivors) unless the contract expressly negates survivorship rights.
- A financial institution needs **"definiteness and certainty . . . to be induced to make payments from the account"** making it a key function of the multiple-parties accounts law to allow banks to make payments without also being exposed to liability from **"parties,**

creditors, and successors that arise out of the nature of the funds in the account." Art. 2, Sec. 16, Comment.

- Financial institutions are not responsible for keeping records of the joint depositors' net contributions.
- Net contributions refer to any sums remaining after family expenses have been paid from the account.

These default rules distinguish between the rights of (i) joint depositors who are married to each other versus joint depositors who are not married to each other; (ii) net deposits versus gross deposits; (iii) the financial institution versus the depositors or their creditors; and (iv) accounting for withdrawals made to pay expenses or to buy assets.

These rules do not distinguish between net deposits versus net *character* deposits. Thus, UMPAA 1989 to be adopted by a common law title state or by a community property state.

In the latter type of adoption, the phrase net deposits can be changed to the phrase net *character* deposits. When this happens, the UMPAA 1989, Art 2., Sec. 16 helps identify the correction required to identify net *character* deposits. UMPAA 1989, Art 2., Sec. 16 reads: **"A deposit of community property in an account does not alter the community *character* of the property or community rights in the property, but a right of survivorship between parties married to each other arising**

from the express terms of the account . . . may not be altered by will." (Italics added.)

Without the special presumption for sums on deposit in UMPAA 1989 covered bank account of a married person, the multiple outcomes in a community property state are as follows.

There is typically a line of precedent that holds that sums on deposit in the account of a married person are presumed to be community property. All U.S. community property systems acknowledge as much, especially when it comes to joint accounts, meaning accounts to which both spouses have contractual rights to withdraw sums on deposit.

There can be a line of precedent that the title to the account (sole or joint) determines the character (community or separate) of the sums on deposit in that account.

There can be a line of precedent holding that only the tracing rule (not the account title itself) ultimately determines the character of sums on deposit in any account of a married person.

Adoption of UMPAA 1989, Art 2, Sec. 11 (b) by a community property state—regardless of whether this legislation ultimately gets placed in the state's probate code or elsewhere—constitutes a community property presumption for sums on deposit in a bank account of a married person while the spouses are alive. See UMPAA (1989) Art 2, Sec. 11, Comment.

d. The California Multiple-Party Accounts Law of 1990

The California Multi-Party Accounts Law (CAMPAL 1990 for short) determines ownership between parties, their creditors, and their successors. CAMPAL 1990 was enacted in large part to further the state's domestic violence prevention policies. The idea was to neutralize bad faith attempts by one spouse to impair the other spouse's community property rights in sums on deposit in any bank account titled in one or both spouses' names. It was also enacted to assist with the protection of financial institutions.

CAMPAL 1990 Cal.Prob.Code § 5305(a) sets forth the special community property presumption for sums on deposit in any bank account of a married person. **"[I]f parties to an account are married to each other, whether or not they are so described in the deposit agreement, their net contribution to the accounts is presumed to be and remain their community property."**

This presumption is "special" because it supersedes the general community property presumption as well as the special joint form title community property presumption discussed in Chapter 6 (CFC § 2581). Cal.Prob.Code § 5305(b).

Permissible evidence for rebuttal is set forth in Cal.Prob.Code § 5305(b). But left unclear is whether the evidentiary standard of rebuttal is preponderance of the evidence, which applies to the general community property presumption mentioned in Cal.Prob.Code § 5305(b); or whether the standard is clear and convincing evidence, as set out in Cal.Prob.Code. 5301(a). The spouse who claims that certain sums on deposit are separate property bears the burden of rebuttal. Rebuttal is by one of two allowable methods.

Returning to the issue of permissible rebuttal evidence, one rebuttal method is by tracing. Specifically, the party seeking to rebut the special presumption must identify net sums on deposit by tracing them back to a separate property source. Once such a trace is made, the burden shifts to the community property proponent, who can counter the rebuttal evidence with a written agreement that the sums on deposit are to be community property. See Cal.Prob.Code § 5305(b)(1). See Chapter 6 for more on tracing.

A second permissible rebuttal can be by agreement. Specifically, the party seeking to rebut the special presumption can produce an account specific written agreement between the spouses that expressly provides that the sums on deposit in the identified account are not to be community property. Cal.Prob.Code § 5305(b)(2).

A commingled account is by legal definition a disputed account, California tags the first spouse who commingles a bank account with the duty to keep specialized account records for any future rebuttal effort. See Chapter 6.

A failed rebuttal means that the special community property presumption becomes conclusive as to the sums on deposit in the bank account on the date in question.

Once sums on deposit are characterized, withdrawals on that date can be used to make purchases. The character of any such purchases must be characterized distinctly.

"Net" in this context means any sums remaining after family expenses have been paid from the account. See Chapter 6 for more detail.

Illustration 3.11: During marriage to each other, W and H maintain three bank accounts. Account 1 is a sole account in W's name alone. Account 2 is a sole account in H's name alone. Account 3 is a joint tenancy account in both W's and H's names. Which of the spouses can access Account 1, Account 2, and Account 3?

The answer to who has *access* to the account depends on the bank contract (i.e., the account title).

- *Account 1 is W's sole bank account because it is titled in W's name alone.* W alone has the right of legal access to the account. W alone has the right to obtain private information about the account, and W alone has the right to withdraw sums on deposit from the bank account.

- *Account 2 is H's sole bank account because it is titled in H's name alone.* H alone has the right of legal access to the account. H alone has the right to obtain private information about the account, and H alone has the right to withdraw sums on deposit from the bank account.

- *Account 3 is W's and H's joint account because it is titled in both spouses' names.* Both W and H have the legal right to access the account. Each spouse, even acting alone, has the right to obtain private information about the account. And each spouse, even acting alone, has the right to withdraws sums on deposit from the account.

Illustration 3.12: Same facts as Illustration 3.11, but now the question is who owns the *sums on deposit* in Account 1, Account 2, and Account 3?

The answer to who owns the sums on deposits in the account on a certain date depends on the law of the jurisdiction.

- Under CAMPAL 1990, all sums on deposit in Account 1, W's sole account, are presumed to be community property.
- Under CAMPAL 1990, all sums on deposit in Account 2, H's sole account, are presumed to be community property.
- Under CAMPAL 1990, all sums on deposit in Account 3, W's and H's joint account, are presumed to be community property.

The movement of money from account to account can result in an impairment of rights, including but certainly not limited to:

- Access rights, as when sums on deposit are moved from a joint account to one spouse's sole account.
- Rights of survivorship, as when sums on deposit are moved from a joint tenancy account to a sole account (or a tenancy in common account, or a community property account), or vice versa.
- Rights of devise and descent, as when sums in deposit are moved from a sole account (or a tenancy in common account, or a community property account) to a joint tenancy account.

5. MISCELLANEOUS STATUTORY PROVISIONS THAT CAN AFFECT CHARACTERIZATION

a. The (Now Obsolete) Married Woman's *Separate* Property Presumption

I cover this issue only to underscore the point that a community property system operates on evidentiary presumptions that protect the community. Hence, community property systems no longer rely on separate property presumptions to characterize property even where state constitutions may protect the right of a spouse to own separate property during marriage.

In the context of U.S. community property systems, a married woman's separate property presumption was used in a minority of states up until the mid-1970s, the decade that the legally maintained male management era came to an end as a matter of law. This presumption, typically the only separate property presumption in any given jurisdiction, was rationalized as protection on a titled asset-by-asset basis for the married women who by default was statutorily and generally divested of her legal rights to manage and control community property.

The married women's separate property presumption confirmed as the wife's separate property any titled asset that a husband transferred to the wife in her name alone. The rationale was gift based.

The idea was that since a husband had the legal right to manage and control community property, when a husband transferred property out of the community estate to the wife by a written title in her name alone (*Husband to Wife . . .*), he did so with donative intent to transmute the property to her separate property.

The husband had the burden of rebuttal, which he could meet by presenting proof that he made the transfer to his wife without donative intent.

All U.S. community property states have transitioned from male management to equal or dual management systems. For that reason, the gender specific married woman's separate property presumption is now obsolete.

California and New Mexico once codified the married woman's separate property presumption, but after the transition from male management to equal management and control, that provision was repealed.

In California, the presumption is repealed for all property acquired by a married woman in her name alone on or after January 1, 1975.

In New Mexico, new legislation proposes repealing the married woman's separate property presumption all together. But until that legislation is passed the cutoff date for application of the married woman's presumption is on or after January 1, 1973. Cal.Fam.Code § 803; N.M.Stat.Ann. § 40–3–12(B) (1978).

b. Preserving the Community Property Character of Property in a Revocable Trust

The trust is a product of the common law, not the civil law. Still, use of the trust has been adopted into U.S. community property systems.

California, Idaho, and Wisconsin have specific statutes to preserve the community property character of property held in a revocable trust. The statutes are consistent with estate planning efforts to preserve a stepped-up in basis for the survivor's one-half of community property, as provided by Internal Revenue Code (I.R.C.) § 1014(b)(6).

c. Asset Appreciation versus Rents, Issues, and Profits

The original cost of an asset is called its basis.

Rents are contractual obligations that create for the asset owner a right to periodic payments (i.e., to an income stream). Rents typically derive from real property.

Issues are replicas of the basic asset unit. In an agricultural context, the concept of issues is clear. Issue refers to offspring. In a financial products context, a new issue refers to the process by which a company offers new shares of its stock to investors through an IPO, or a new issue refers to additional shares that increase the total number of shares outstanding, as through a secondary offering.

Profits are defined in multiple ways, but generally the concept of a profit indicates that the owner of an asset has experienced a financial gain from ownership of that asset. One definition (sometimes called net income) is revenue generated from sales of product minus expenses of production and marketing costs. Profits might also be defined as revenue minus costs.

Appreciation is any increase in value over what the original asset cost. (Any decrease in value is called a depreciation.) To realize appreciation, the asset must be sold. Prior to actual severance, a hypothetical appreciation can be calculated by determining what a (hypothetical) willing buyer would pay for the asset.

Appreciation is not the same as rent. Rent is defined as a contract derived asset income stream (rent). An asset may appreciate (or depreciate) yet still produce rents, meaning an income stream. Likewise, stocks and businesses can appreciate or depreciate yet still produce contract derived incomes.

U.S. community property states split in outcome as to separate property rents, issues, and profits.

Most U.S. states (Arizona, California, New Mexico, Nevada, and Washington) follow the so-called American-rule approach, which originated in California. The American rule holds that separate property rents, issues, and profits, because they trace back to a separate property source, are also *separate property during the marriage.*

A minority of U.S. community property states (Idaho, Louisiana, Texas, and Wisconsin) follow the civil-law (or ganancial) rule on separate property rents, issues, and profits. In these states separate property rents, issues, and profits are characterized as *community property during the marriage.* Historically the rationale is usufruct. Modernly, the rational is state constitutionally protected separate property rights. In this minority of states, the parties can reach a contrary agreement as to rents, issues, and profits during marriage, but their agreement must expressly transmute the income stream of the underlying separate property asset from community to separate property *during the marriage.* At the end of marriage, separate property rents, issues, and profits once again become the exclusive property of the separate property owner.

6. STATUTES PROTECTING THIRD PARTIES

Spouses have rights and duties relative to each other. They also have rights and liabilities relative to third parties. For that reason, states enact notice laws that are intended to give third party creditors confidence in transacting with married persons. See Chapter 8 for more on creditors' rights.

Some third-party protection statutes, like the UMPAA 1989, discussed above, and CAMPAL 1990, also discussed above, are designed to protect banks and other financial institutions as well as spouses. Others are designed to permit creditors to transact with one or the other spouse with confidence that the debts and obligations of one spouse will be generally satisfiable against community property.

Despite protection statutes aimed at third parties, transactions between a spouse and a third party do not determine the character of property. Nor do transactions between a spouse and a third party necessarily limit the other spouse's right to manage and control the property that is the subject of the transaction. Instead, state community property laws govern questions about the spouses' rights and duties between themselves, notwithstanding any statutory provisions that may be otherwise intended to protect third parties.

Some third-party protection statutes retain former (rescinded or amended) statutory rights or methods of characterizing assets. The constitutional necessity for retaining such statutes is seldom litigated.

California balances the need to protect a spouse's rights to community real property with the need to encourage third parties to transact with married persons. With respect to real estate transactions, for example, the applicable California statute does this by putting both spouses and third parties on statutory notice that both spouses must join in executing any consequential real estate instrument delivered by a married person to a transferee or encumbrancer. Consequential instruments are defined as those relating to the sale, conveyance, encumbrance, or long-term lease (one year or longer) of the property. See Chapter 8 for more on management and control rights and duties.

When both spouses sign a consequential real estate instrument, a purchaser or encumbrancer of community property who takes in good faith, meaning without knowledge of the marriage relation, generally takes free of the claims of a spouse who did not sign the instrument. If only one spouse signs a consequential real estate document, the burden of proof falls to the third party to show that they lacked notice (actual, constructive or inquiry) of the marital status of the person whose name appears on the document.

Here are a few examples.

In California third parties are protected by constructive (record) notice but held to principles of inquiry notice when it comes to finding out about a prospective mortgagor's or debtor's marital status at the time the consequential real estate instrument is signed. Cal.Fam.Code § 1102.

Other states have different or additional third-party protections when it comes to real estate.

Texas protects a bona fide purchaser who acquires property from a married person without knowledge of the marriage. V.C.T.A. Fam. Code § 5.24(b). Third party protection comes into play only if the property is presumed to be subject to the sole management, control, and disposition of the transacting spouse. This rule comports with the more general Texas rules on community property dual management and control. See Chapter 8.

In Washington, a bona fide purchaser takes real property clear of the community property claim of a spouse whose name does not appear on record title or on a recorded community property claim. See Chapter 3, Washington for more on community property claims.

Thus, at least in the first instance, Washington lends more protection to the bona fide purchaser of Washington real estate titled in one spouse's name alone than it does to the spouse whose name is not on the record title. That said, Washington law also gives the spouse whose name does not appear on title a (short) period to file a community property claim of interest in the real property. A recorded claim of interest challenges the bona fide purchaser's priority position. See Wash.Rev.Code § 26.16.095, discussed in Chapter 3.

7. MISCELLANEOUS STATUTORY PROVISIONS

Before marriage, compiling an inventory of the property that one owns and its value on or near the date of marriage is a practical way to identify (and later prove) a separate property interest in the listed assets.

Some states adopt provisions that authorize a prospective spouse to unilaterally compile and record any such separate property inventory.

California, Idaho, Nevada, and Texas permit a married person to create evidence of the separate character of property by filing and recording an inventory of the property at the time of the marriage.

Nevada provides a way for parties to record a supplemental inventory during the marriage. The Nevada statute delineates one technique for creating an asset-specific separate property inventory and an additional technique for establishing the authenticity of such an inventory.

Louisiana permits **". . . a declaration in an act of acquisition that things are acquired with separate funds . . . ."** LSA-C.C. Art. § 2342. The Louisiana declaration is like an inventory in that it can be created unilaterally by one spouse. It is unlike an inventory in that declarations are made on an asset-by-asset basis, at the time of acquisition.

In the absence of statutory direction, the time to record a separate property inventory is at or reasonably near the date of marriage. If major updates occur, presumably those should also be recorded.

Inventories, in other words, are compiled either before or during marriage as assets are acquired; but they become relevant at the end of a marriage, whether by dissolution or by death, when the community estate is being dissolved. Some states (California is one) encourage, but do not require, parties to inventory all assets, community property and separate property, at dissolution by use of a form provided by the state. See Appendix A, Schedule of Assets and Debts.

A contemporaneously maintained inventory, depending on how carefully it is kept, is in theory persuasive evidence in a dissolution dispute. By contrast, a stale inventory is likely far less persuasive, if it is at all. That said, even a current (recently compiled) contemporaneously maintained inventory will not immunize a separate property proponent from all manner of ambiguities that can arise due to commingling, fungibility, transmutation (changes of character), written agreements, gifts, confusion, contributions to purchase, changes of form, third-party liens and claims, and so on.

8. ALASKA, TENNESSEE, AND PUERTO RICO

Alaska, Florida, South Dakota, and Tennessee do not have default community property systems. However, each state allows a married person what is called a community property option. Because the Alaska and Tennessee options are most developed and different in requirements, I discuss only those two options here.

Puerto Rico and Guam are community property jurisdictions. Puerto Rico differs from the other nine (continental) U.S. community property states in that it allows for liquidation rather than dissolution. I discuss only Puerto Rico here.

a. Alaska

Alaska is a common law equitable distribution state, not a community property state. *Pestrikoff v. Hoff*, 278 P.3d 281 (Alaska 2012). However, Alaska allows married persons to opt into community property ownership as to one, some, or all assets.

The Alaska Community Property Act, found at Alaska Stat.Ann. § 34.77.010 through § 34.77.995 (1998) covers various issues including the classification of property, management and control, transactions between spouses, obligations of spouses, bona fide purchaser protection, community property agreements, life insurance proceeds, and community property agreements and trusts.

To opt into community property requires a community property agreement or trust. The general rule, found at Alaska Stat.Ann. § 34.77.030 (2022) is as follows: **"Except for property that is classified otherwise in this chapter, property of spouses is community property under [Alaska law] only to the extent provided in a community property agreement or a community property trust."**

As to a community property agreement: unless the terms of the community property agreement provide otherwise, management and control is title-based under Alaska Stat.Ann. § 34.77.040 (1998). The big exception here is for sums on deposits in a bank account. In 1996, effective January 1, 1997, Alaska adopted UMPAA 1989 in Alaska Stat.Ann. §§ 13.06.050 and 13.33.201 to 13.33.227.

Formalities for setting up a community property agreement are set out at Alaska Stat.Ann. § 34.77.090 (1998). A community property agreement governs property acquisition while both spouses are domiciled in the state of Alaska. Alaska Stat.Ann. § 34.77.060 (1998).

As to a community property trust, these specifics apply. The terms of the community property trust govern assets transferred to the trust. Formalities for setting up a community property trust are found at Alaska Stat.Ann. § 34.77.100 (2014). A community property trust may be settled by one spouse or both spouses even if neither is domiciled in the state so long as **"... at least one trustee is a 'qualified person ...'"** A qualified person is defined as an individual person who resides in Alaska, an Alaska trust company, or a bank that is organized under Alaska law. Either or both spouses can serve as a qualified trustee so long the fiduciary spouse (or, if both spouses are fiduciaries, at least one spouse) is: **"(1) an individual (A) who ... resides in this state; (B) whose true and permanent home is in this state; (C) who does not have a present intention of moving from this state; and (D)**

who intends to return to this state when away." Alaska Stat.Ann. § 34.77.100(a) (1998).

A community property agreement must be identified as such with a standard notice **"in capital letters"** prominently placed at the head of the agreement. Alaska Stat.Ann. § 34.77.090. A community property trust must be identified in the same way. Alaska Stat.Ann. § 34.77.100(b) (2002).

The purpose of the capitalized notice requirement is to protect third parties who transact with one or both spouses.

b. Tennessee

Tennessee is a common law equitable distribution state. As of 2010, pursuant to Tenn. Code Ann. § 35.17.101–35.17.108 (2010), married persons can opt into a Tennessee community property trust.

There is no requirement that the parties be domiciled in the state. The only requirement is that a qualified trustee manage the trust. A qualified trustee is defined by the above statute as either a Tennessee resident or a company authorized by state law to act as a fiduciary.

Management and control rights must be set forth in the terms of the trust.

c. Puerto Rico

The Puerto Rico community property system derives from articles found in such sources as the Civil Code of Puerto Rico 1902, the Spanish Civil

Code of 1889, and the Civil Code of Louisiana of 1870. Puerto Rico primarily differs from other U.S. community property states in how it uses liquidation rather than dissolution rules.

In Puerto Rico, a conjugal partnership is formed by the act of marriage. The purpose of a conjugal partnership is to acquire property and to meet the spouses' financial obligations during marriage.

At divorce, a conjugal partnership is liquidated as if it were a commercial partnership. P.R. Laws Ann. Title 31, § 381 (1993). It is not dissolved as it is in the other U.S. community property states.

Puerto Rican decisional law underscores the liquidation approach by holding that the determination of property at the end of a marriage cannot be made by the individual spouses. Rather property must be liquidated to pay off the debts, charges, and obligations of the conjugal partnership. Surplus community property shall be divided between the parties if and only if there is property remaining after the liquidation process is over. Often cited foundational cases are *Vivaldi v. Mariani*, 10 D.P.R. 444 (1906), *Succession of Morales v. Kieckoefer*, 17 D.P.R. 304 (1911), and *Orta v. Arzuaga*, 23 D.P.R. 259, 268 (1915).

A federal case that discusses Puerto Rican conjugal partnership law is *Federal Deposit Ins. Corp. v. Martinez Almodovar*, 671 F. Supp. 851 (D. Puerto Rico 1987).

C. INDIVIDUAL STATES

1. ARIZONA

Ariz.Rev.Stat.Ann. § 25–211(A) states the basic community property principle found in the Uniform Marriage and Divorce Act, also know as UMDA 1970 Section 307 Alternative B. The relevant text provides:

> **"All property acquired by either husband or wife during the marriage is the community property of the husband and wife except for property that is:**
>
> **1. Acquired by gift, devise or descent.**
>
> **2. Acquired after service of a petition for dissolution of marriage, legal separation or annulment if the petition results in a decree of dissolution of marriage, legal separation or annulment."**

The above Arizona statute implies an acquisition-based general community property presumption.

Ariz.Rev.Stat.Ann. § 25–318 reads:

> **"In a proceeding for dissolution of marriage, for annulment or for legal separation, or in a proceeding for disposition of property following dissolution of the marriage by a court that previously lacked jurisdiction . . . the court shall also divide the community, joint tenancy and other property held in common equitably, though not necessarily**

> **in kind, without regard to marital misconduct."** (Italics added)

The language explicitly mandates the court to divide joint tenancy and tenancy in common titles as community property is divided in Arizona, which is to say equitably without regard to fault. Equitable division is noted in the above statutory language; so too is Arizona's decision to dissolve property on a no-fault basis. But while the statute is clear on these points, it does not specify two other important issues. They are one, does the statute enable (or not) a special joint title form community property presumption, which would be raised only upon proof of acquisition during marriage? Two, does the statute restrict the evidence that can be presented to prove a separate property interest in a jointly titled asset?

Ariz.Rev.Stat.Ann. § 25–318(A) (2022) turns on a concept of quasi-community property, without using that label.

> **"For the purposes of this section only, property acquired by either spouse outside this state shall be deemed to be community property if the property would have been community property if acquired in this state."**

But the statute has been interpreted in line with *Stephen v. Stephen*, 284 P. 158 (Ariz. 1930), which holds that the character of movable property acquired during marriage is determined by the law of the married person's domicile at the time of acquisition. This could possibly affect ownership of bank accounts and possibly deposits (as not all states have adopted a multiple-party accounts law), cash, businesses, investment accounts, and other potentially high value assets that are classified as movable personal property. A corollary of this rule is that such out-of-state property, if later exchanged for Arizona property, would determine the character of the Arizona property.

Arizona adopted the Uniform Multiple-Persons Accounts Act (UMPAA 1989 for short) in 1994, effective after December 31, 1994. See Ariz.Rev.Stat.Ann. §§ 14–6102, 14–6201 to 14–6227. The section that specifically refers to living parties who are married to each other is Ariz.Rev.Stat.Ann. § 14–6211.

Ariz.Rev.Stat.Ann. § 14–6211 (1995) replicates the suggested UMPAA 1989 language; as such it provides: **"During the lifetime of all parties an account belongs to the parties in proportion to the *net contribution* of each to the sums on deposit unless there is clear and convincing evidence of a different intent. *As between parties married to each other, in the absence of proof otherwise, the net contribution of each is presumed to be an equal amount.*"** (Italics added.)

Ariz.Rev.Stat.Ann. § 25–217 (2024) is an important notice for married persons, and especially for retirees, who move to Arizona.

> **"Marital rights in *property which is acquired in this state* during marriage by persons married without the state who**

move into the state shall be controlled by the laws of this state." (Italics added.)

Together, the above statutes and decisional interpretations suggest that the Arizona law, is highly sensitive to conflict of laws problems stemming from the needs of retirees.

Property onerously acquired in the state during marriage while domiciled in the state is clearly Arizona community property, unless separate property (say funds from a retirement account for example) was used to purchase it.

At dissolution, property in joint title is divided equitably as if it were Arizona community property, as discussed above.

But otherwise, only movable (personal) property acquired while the married person is domiciled in the state is squarely included within the definition of Arizona community property. Movable property acquired elsewhere is characterized by the law of the married person's domicile at the time of its acquisition. Moreover, real estate purchased with funds obtained in another state (funds in an account earned from work conducted while a domicile of another state) might be separate property or community property as governed by the laws of another community property state. So, for example, deferred funds earned in California prior to establishing a retirement residence in Arizona would be California community property earnings.

The implication of these rules for retirees requires analysis of conflict of laws issues as well as of community property laws.

Also, note that characterization and division are separate issues.

Characterization of personal property acquired in another state prior to establishing residence in Ariona, may nevertheless be divided equally or equitably depending on the law of the other jurisdiction. In that case, the outcome that would have prevailed in the parties' previous domicile might be identical to the outcome the parties' reach under Arizona law notwithstanding any holding about the character of the property. Some cases on this point are superseded by statute, but for a general example see e.g. *Rau v. Rau*, 6 Ariz. App. 362, 432 P.2d 910 (1967), citing *Stephens*, supra.

Conflict of laws issues may also extend to management and control rights during marriage. For example, if a married person were to move to Arizona from a common law title state owning a movable asset titled in his or her name alone, that asset would be characterized according to the law of the domicile where it was acquired. If the same married person were to sell that out-of-state asset and use the sale proceeds, to buy Arizona property titled in his or her name alone, the new purchase might also be characterized under the laws of the former domicile. In Arizona each spouse has the exclusive right to manage, control and dispose of his or her separate property; therefore, during marriage, the new purchase would be subject to the sole management and control of the acquiring spouse. For more on management and control, see Chapter 8.

On the community property side of the conflict of laws spectrum, if a married person domiciled in California were to sell California community personal property titled in her or his name alone before moving to Arizona, and then, after reestablishing domicile in Arizona, use the sale proceeds to buy property in Arizona, that property—by application of the tracing rule—seemingly would be controlled by California law, not Arizona law. See *Jones v. Weaver*, 123 F.2d 403 (9th Cir. 1941).

Conflict of laws issues in a dissolution proceeding can be complex. They are raised briefly here only because of Arizona's reputation as a retirement destination.

Retirees who move to Arizona may face additional issues than those discussed above. See Chapter 13 for more on conflict of laws.

At the end of marriage, whether a non-owning spouse is protected or not depends upon how the marriage ends.

In a dissolution, Arizona, being a community property state, does not have an equitable division statute.

If a marriage ends by the death of a spouse, the Revised Arizona Probate Code uses a different statute, Ariz.Rev.Stat.Ann. § 25–211 (2008), to define community property.

At death, Arizona law is potentially far less protective for a retiree who did not earn an income during marriage while domiciled in the state. As a community property state, Arizona does not have a forced share statute. Therefore, in the case of the owning spouse's death, the non-owning surviving spouse's financial future will depend largely on the decedent spouse's estate plan. Rights of survivorship transfer property to the surviving spouse outside of probate. But otherwise, for retirees whose work life was in another state, there may be little or no Arizona community personal property that a surviving spouse can draw on for support.

2. CALIFORNIA

Cal.Fam.Code § 760 states the basic community property principle: **"Except as otherwise provided by statute, all property, real or personal, wherever situated, acquired by a married person during the marriage while domiciled in this state is community property."**

The equality of interest principle is stated at Cal.Fam.Code § 751: community property rights "... **during continuance of the marriage relation are present, existing, and equal ....**" Each spouse acquires a vested one-half undivided interest in a community property asset upon its acquisition.

At dissolution, the spouses can agree by marriage settlement agreement to divide, trade or offset their community property rights as they see fit. If they cannot reach a marital settlement agreement, a factfinder shall dissolve their estate on an asset-by-asset basis in accordance with the equal division rule set out in statutes governing dissolution. In such a case, equal division mandates a 50-50 split for each asset.

California recognizes and names the concept of quasi-community property. For purposes of a dissolution proceeding, quasi-community property is defined by Cal.Fam.Code § 125(a) as property acquired: **"By either spouse while domiciled elsewhere which would have been community property if the spouse who acquired the property had been domiciled in [California] at the time of its acquisition."**

Quasi-community property does not come into existence when one or both spouses establish a domicile in California. To the contrary, any property that one or both spouses own when they establish a new domicile in the state continues to be characterized by the laws of the acquiring spouse's former domicile. It is only when a petition for dissolution is filed in a California superior court that one or both parties are deemed to consent to the characterization of pre-domicile acquisitions in accordance with California community property law. The assets acquired in the pre-domicile jurisdiction are called quasi-community property, but they are divided as if they were community property.

In a probate proceeding Cal.Prob.Code § 66 uses a nearly identical definition of quasi-community property.

Property acquired by a person during a *void* marriage is not within the California community property system; rather, it is individual property, acquired by a single person. However, a *voidable* marriage does acquire community property or quasi-marital property, depending on what the defect in the marriage is, unless the marriage ends by annulment (see statute below).

A person who in good faith believes that their otherwise void or voidable marriage was valid when contracted can obtain a judicial declaration of putative spouse status. A putative spouse has an option to either use the state's quasi-*marital* property system or its general civil laws. A putative spouse, as opposed to a civil claimant, can access rules, rights, and obligations otherwise applicable only to validly married spouses.

Quasi-marital property is defined as **"property acquired during the union that would have been community property or quasi-community property if the union had not been void or voidable, ..."** Cal.Fam.Code § 2251(a)(2).

A general community property presumption is implied from the community property statute—Cal.Fam.Code § 760—by the state evidence code and by a long line of precedent. The general community property presumption is raised by proof that the property in question was acquired by a person during their marriage while domiciled in the state. Once raised, the general community property presumption becomes conclusive as to the asset unless the separate property claimant can rebut the presumption with factual evidence. Rebuttal can be by tracing the asset back to a separate property source or by producing an agreement between the spouses that the asset is not community property. Rebuttal is by the lowest civil standard of proof—preponderance of the evidence. *Marriage of Ettefagh*, 150 Cal.App.4th 1578, 59 Cal.Rptr.3d 419 (Cal.Ct.App. 1st Dist. 2007) states the rationales for the low evidentiary standard as being to equalize the risk of judicial error between the divorcing parties and to effect a no-fault dissolution.

The general community property presumption is applicable after the death of former spouse for a limited period. However, Cal.Fam.Code § 802 exempts from the general community property presumption **". . . any property to which legal or equitable title is held by a person at the time of the person's death if the marriage during which the property was acquired was terminated by dissolution of marriage more than four years before the death."** This provision can be avoided with an estate plan.

For purposes of division of property on dissolution, a special community property presumption for "property acquired by the parties during marriage in joint form" *has been enabled by statute.* Cal. Fam.Code § 2581. The statute is special because it supersedes the general community property presumption. But it is limited in that it applies only in a dissolution proceeding. See Chapter 6 for more on joint form titles. both spouses' names.

For the special joint form title community property presumption, rebuttal is by one of two statutory methods.

Rebuttal option one is a clear statement in the deed or other documentary evidence of title that the asset "**. . . is separate property and not community property . . . .**" Cal. Fam.Code § 2581(a). Either this language is redundant, or it has a potentially more exact meaning that relates to commingling; either way, no case clarifies. Rebuttal option two is a stand-alone written agreement that the titled asset "**. . . . is separate property.**" Cal. Fam.Code § 2581(b). A general agreement (which might suffice to rebut the general community property presumption) will not rebut this special presumption if the asset is not clearly identifiable from the face of the agreement. The special joint form title community property presumption is discussed further in Chapter 6.

A special community property presumption for sums on deposit in any bank account of a married person can be found at Cal.Prob.Code § 5305(a), as part of the state's provisions on nonprobate transfers. This special presumption was adopted in 1990, effective January 1, 1991, and it supersedes both the general community property presumption and the special joint form title community property presumption. The presumption can be raised in a dissolution or in a probate proceeding.

Rebuttal is by one of two statutory methods.

Rebuttal option one appears at Cal.Prob.Code § 5305(b)(1), which provides that a rebuttal is proved if: **"The sums on deposit that are claimed to be separate property can be *traced* from separate property unless it is proved that the married persons made a written agreement that expressed their clear intent that the sums be their community property."** (Italics added). See Chapter 7 for more on the specialized tracing required for rebuttal.

Rebuttal option two appears at Cal.Prob.Code § 5305(b)(2), which provides that a rebuttal is proved if: **"The married persons made a written agreement, separate from the deposit agreement, that expressly provided that the sums on deposit, claimed not to be community property, were not to be community property."**

This special community property presumption for sums on deposit in any bank account of a married person was enacted to further the state's domestic violence prevention policies. For more on the California Multiple-Parties Accounts Law (CAMPAL 1990 for short) see Chapter 7.

Cal.Fam.Code § 780 creates a *special* category of community property for money and property *received in settlement* of a personal injury claim that arose during marriage. Otherwise, the personal injury claim itself is not proprietary (on the theory that an unadjudicated personal injury claim is not transferable on a market) and therefore not subject to characterization even if the claim arose during marriage. Special community property, unlike ordinary community property, is subject to a mandatory assignment rule—found at Cal.Fam.Code § 2603—that favors the injured person. The statute has two nullifying exceptions. One is where **"commingling with other assets of the community estate"** has occurred. Cal.Fam.Code § 2603(b) The other is where **"the interests of justice require another disposition."** Id. For the second exception, no more than one-half of the settlement shall be awarded to the non-injured spouse.

Money and property received as satisfaction for personal injury claims that arose before marriage or after separation are received as separate property of the injured person. Likewise, money and property received as a settlement for personal injury claims against the other spouse are also received by the injured spouse as separate property, no matter when received. See Chapter 5.

The character of an asset determines legal management and control rights. Rights and obligations regarding the management and control of community property come into existence on the date of marriage and continue through dissolution. Cal. Fam. Code § 721, § 1100 (e) and § 1102. See Chapter 8 for more on management and control.

The Judicial Council provides a helpful (but not mandatory) form for inventorying assets at dissolution. The form lists each asset, date acquired, gross fair market value, amount of debt, net fair market value and the petitioner's and respondent's proposal for division of the asset. Separate property claims are noted as well on the form.

3. IDAHO

Idaho Code § 32–906 is the basic statute. It provides, in part that **"[a]ll property acquired after marriage by either husband or wife is community property."** This statute implies, rather than directly states, that property acquired after (meaning during) marriage by both spouses, as with a joint form title, is also community property, a standard discussed further below.

By the same provision Idaho adopts the civil law rule on separate property rents, issues, and profits. **"The income, including the rents, issues and profits, of *all other property*, separate or community,"** is community property, unless it has been specifically transmuted by an agreement between the parties. *All other property* refers to Idaho Code § 32–903 and § 32–904, both codes that define separate property.

Property acquired during marriage in both spouses' names (joint form title) is community property unless the spouses agree otherwise as to the asset. See Chapter 6.

Idaho Code § 32–907 and § 32–908 allow for the filing of a separate property inventory. The statutory provisions are gender specific, but by the holding in *Suter v. Suter*, 546 P.2d 1169 (Idaho 1976), the statute now applies on a gender neutral basis. Cases decided prior to *Williams v. Paxton*, 559 P.2d 1123

(Idaho 1976) are outdated on this issue under current principles of equal protection law.

Idaho law, like California law, preserves the community property character of property held in a revocable trust, per Idaho Code § 32–906A.

4. LOUISIANA

Community property is "... **property acquired during the existence of the legal regime through the effort, skill, or industry of either spouse; property acquired with community things or with community and separate things, unless classified as separate property ...; property donated to the spouses jointly; natural and civil fruits of community property; damages awarded for loss or injury to a thing belonging to the community; and all other property not classified by law as separate property.**" LSA-C.C. Art. 2338.

Louisiana strongly discourages the creation of joint tenancy titles, as discussed in Chapter 6. Property acquired during marriage in joint form title is community property in character.

According to the Civil Code of 1870, the word property is a translation of the civil code concept of patrimony, which breaks property down into *propriete* and *biens*. This definition of patrimony is seldom defined, but when it is, it refers to something like rights and duties inherited from one's ancestors. See e.g. *Dué v. Dué*, 342 So.2d 161, 165 (La.

1977)(characterizing attorney contingency fee contracts as community property).

Other U.S. community property states do not rely on the concept of patrimony, or even use that word. Nevertheless, the concept of patrimony has a long history in Louisiana, but it is unclear how closely courts in the state rely on the concept today. *Propriété* corresponds to homestead rights in land protected by law. Black's Law Dictionary. *Biens* corresponds to things and estate (riches or fortune), two words that are synonymous for purposes of the Louisiana Code. LSA-C.C. 448. The word estate is an important word in common law where it means interest in land. Restatement of Property § 9 (1936). The word estate in the Louisiana Code does not derive from the common law; it derives from the Civil Code of 1824. Athanassios N. Yiannopoulos, *Introduction to the Law of Things: Louisiana and Comparative Law*, 22 Louisiana L. Rev. 756 (1962)(discussing terminology of the Louisiana Code.)

One consequence of relying on the civil law concept of patrimony is that in Louisiana the traditional concept of the marital (or community) regime holds. A marital regime is an entity that holds both assets *and* obligations; and an entity for which both assets *and* obligations are characterized as community or separate property Under LSA-C.C. Art. 2361 obligations **"incurred by a spouse during the existence of a community property regime are presumed to be community obligations."** Obligations that do not benefit the spouses, the family, or the other spouse are not community obligations. LSA-C.C. Art. 2363. In the other U.S. community property states, by comparison, the marriage is not a stand-alone entity. Only the spouses—not the marriage as an entity—assume obligations. That said, community property may nonetheless be responsible for debts incurred by one spouse who, acting alone, incurs the debt. See Chapter 9.

Louisiana adopts a possession-based general community property presumption limited in application to "things." Set out in LSA-C.C. Art. 2340 the presumption states: **"[t]hings in the possession of a spouse during the existence of a regime of community of acquets and gains are presumed to be community, but either spouse may prove that they are separate property."** See also Art. 2342, To elaborate the word *things* has historically been defined to mean all property (as complicated by the concept of patrimony discussed above) acquired during the marriage. *Possession* in the Louisiana community property system has a narrower definition than one might find in general property law: possession, in the context of a marriage in Louisiana, indicates that the spouse holds the property as an owner, not as a caretaker or bailee.

LSA-C.C. Art. 2342, discussed in the previous paragraph, is a gender-neutral update of the declaration rule. Today, either spouse, obviously during marriage, has a right to declare **"in an act of acquisition"** that the asset is **"[a]cquired with separate funds as . . . separate property"** The non-acquiring spouse may concur in the declaration, which results in a double declaration, not a contractual agreement. The **"either spouse may prove"** language is a response to equal protection concerns, as explained by LSA-C.C. Art. 2340 Comment (b). Thus, either one or the other spouse may controvert a declaration with what seems under *Talbot v. Talbot,* 864 So.2d 590, 600 (La. 2003) to be a rebuttal standard for which the court may consider any manner of proof:

> "As a matter of policy and in the interest of fairness, we find that the community presumption contained in article 2340 is rebuttable by either spouse upon a showing by a preponderance of the evidence the separate nature of property brought into the community."

A spouse's intestate heirs and the creditors also have a right to controvert a declaration, regardless of whether the surviving spouse concurred at acquisition. Time limits apply. However, once an asset has been alienated, encumbered, or leased for consideration, a declaration of separate property stands to protect third parties.

Louisiana is in the distinct minority of U.S. community property states on the issue of how best to characterize gifts made *by a third party* to the spouses jointly. *Gifts* may be recast as donations to the community. *Donations* are at LSA-C.C. Art. 1468 and Art. 1469 (which defines the **"Donation Mortis Causa"**. Other states may refer to donations as not gifts, but rather the conferral of a benefit, and often it is difficult to find any definitional language on the distinction. But in Louisiana, thankfully, a bright light gets cast by the LSA-C.C. Art. 1468 definition of inter vivos donations: **"A donation inter vivos is a contract by which a person, called the donor, gratuitously divests himself, at present and irrevocably, of the thing given in favor of another, called the donee, who accepts it."**

There may be an extremely fine line between the common law inter vivos *gift* and the inter vivos *donation*. A *gift* requires proof of declarative (one-sided) donative intent, delivery, and acceptance. *A donation* requires proof of an agreement between the donor and donee that the donor will favor the donee. Chapter 5.

But the basic Louisiana community property statute codifies the rule that *donations* from third parties to the spouses jointly are community property in character. (See the LSA-C.C. Art. 2338 phrase: **"property donated to the spouses jointly; . . ."**).

In other community property states, distinguishing between *gift* and *donation* can be significant, but only if the same distinction holds. A *gift* made by a third party to one spouse alone before or during marriage is the donee-spouse's separate property; and in a clear majority of U.S. community property states even a gift made jointly to both spouses during marriage falls under the definition of separate property unless the donor intended to make a gift to the community and to transfer the gift in joint form title. But a *donation*, as LSA-C.C. Art. 1468 (discussed above) makes explicitly clear, is community property in character upon receipt.

How does the remedies tail wag the gift-versus-donation dog? A gift is the declared intent to give something freely, a gratuitous unenforceable promise made without consideration. A donation, by contrast, is a contract to confer a benefit on another in exchange for a benefit. See LSA-C.C. Art. 1468, discussed above. If the contract is breached, the legal right to sue and any resulting remedy is owned by the community. Since the couple are not a qualified charitable organization, it is unclear how the donation contract is rationalized when a third-party donates to a married couple but suffice it to say that the donation is community in character upon receipt. Untangling this skein is up to the lawyers of Louisiana.

There is an exception to the Louisiana rule on donations, however. Revision Comments from 1979 indicates that if the spouses **"do not live in community,"** i.e., if they have agreed to live in a contractual matrimonial regime, with separation of their property, then **"the donor may not create a community regime for the spouses. In such a case, the property given to them is separate property held in indivision."** Separate property is discussed in Chapter 5.

Louisiana follows the general civil law ganancial separate property income rule. LSA-C.C. Art. 2339 provides in a general statute titled **"Fruits and revenues of separate property . . ."** that the receipts (rents, issues, profits, and other revenues) of separate property obtained during marriage are community property.

The owner may reserve them as separate property by a declaration that is executed and recorded. Recordation presumes acknowledgment (notarization), and both are intended to protect the adversely affected spouse by providing proof, as between the spouses, of the properly recorded declaration as it was made on a set and certain date. The rights of third parties are of secondary concern.

A more specific standard applies to minerals and oil and gas revenues. **"[M]inerals produced from or attributable to a separate asset, and bonuses, delay rentals, royalties, and shut-in payments arising from mineral leases are community property."**

The difference between a general declaration and the specific mineral extraction declaration is this. Generally, separate property fruits are community property during the marriage by usufruct, but then returned to their separate property owner at the end of marriage. Extracted mineral products, on the other hand are exempt from the usufruct rule. LSA-C.C. Art. 2339 bases that exemption on revision comments 1976 of LSA-C.C. Art. 551 which excludes mineral production from the definition of fruits and revenues. The theory behind the exemption is that mineral substances that have been already extracted from the ground are not fruits because their extraction depletes the underlying property, whereas the harvesting of fruits does not.

The community owns (rather than merely enjoys by usufruct) extracted mineral products. Thus, any *income* derived from a mineral lease, community or separate, during marriage is outright community property. The dominant rationale affects management and control rights. There also appears to be an implicit acquisition-based rationale at work in the case law. The justification given is that a mineral lease relates to rights in the underlying real estate, but the extraction of a mineral (oil or gas, for example) requires labor, which belongs to the community during marriage. Therefore, a person can own mineral lease rights prior to marriage, making the lease a separate property asset. But any development of that mineral lease during marriage involves community expenditure or labor thereby bringing the extracted mineral product (and its income) within the principle of community property. The Louisiana rationale contrasts with the Texas rationale on extracted mineral products, discussed below.

Fruits are produced periodically by a thing without a diminution of its substance. Fruits can be natural or civil. Natural fruits are the product of the earth or of animals. Civil fruits are analogous to what are called rents, issues, and profits in other jurisdictions.

Milling v. Collector of Revenue, 57 So.2d 679 (La. 1952), a state tax case, suggests that "bonuses, delay rentals, royalties, and shut-in payments from separate property fall into the community though they are not [explicitly] classified as fruits under Article 551." Here again, the rationale would be that the above assets produce income without diminishing the base property source. In *Milton v. Milton*, 71 So.3d 326 (La.Ct.App. 2011), writ denied 69 So.3d

1150 (La. 2011) the separate property owner of cows petitioned for a reimbursement from the community for income produced during marriage in the form of milk. In denying the separate property owner's reimbursement request, the court characterized the milk as a fruit to which the community was entitled to by right of usufruct during the marriage. See e.g., Yiannopoulos, *Introduction to the Law of Things: Louisiana and Comparative Law*, supra, at 791 (discussing community property and the concept of civil and natural fruits).

Usufruct is a civil law concept defined as **"[a] real right of limited duration on the property of another."** LSA-C.C. Art. 535.

As a personal servitude, usufruct benefits a party in his or her enjoyment. The benefited party is called the "usufructuary;" the burdened party is called the "naked owner." In the marriage context, usufruct creates a *nonreimbursable* right to an income stream created by a separate property asset. This right lasts for the duration of the marriage.

Usufruct is a personal servitude most perhaps analogous in the common law to a profit à prendre (also known as an easement in gross). But Louisiana abandoned the term profit or "profits" (previously found in the English-language version of its Civil Code) early on, calling it an erroneous translation of the French word for "fruits." An extended explanation of the change is provided in LSA-C.C. Art. 551.

Cases sometimes make an analogy between usufruct and beneficial ownership, but any similarity in the context of marriage may be too superficial to make a legal difference. Usufruct gives the community a terminable right to use, but not a right to sue for partition. Whereas beneficial ownership, once confirmed by a court judgment, is outright ownership sufficient to support an action for partition.

Louisiana has the most extensive statutory pattern, outside of the uniform principal and income acts, for defining usufruct. LSA-C.C. Art. 535 and Art. 629 deal extensively with the relationship between the usufructuary and the naked owner as to different categories of property.

As usufructuary, the community has the right to possess and enjoy separate property fruits for the duration of the community regime. The community's usufruct right is free from the interference of the spouse who is the naked owner of the asset. Additionally, absent a contrary testamentary disposition, the law recognizes a right of usufruct in a surviving spouse over the half of the community inherited by the decedent spouse's descendants. See Chapter 12.

5. NEVADA

Nev.Rev.Stat. § 123.220 is the basic statute: **"All property, other than that stated in NRS 123.130** [a section that provides for a written inventory of the separate property of a married person, as discussed below], **acquired after marriage by either**

spouse or both spouses, is community property unless otherwise provided by:

1. An agreement in writing between the spouses.

2. A decree of separate maintenance issued by a court of competent jurisdiction.

3. NRS 123.190 (NRS 123.190 governs appropriated separate property earnings, discussed below.)

4. A decree issued or agreement in writing entered pursuant to NRS 123.259." (NRS 123.259 refers to the division of the community estate in cases where one spouse is institutionalized.)

Nev.Rev.Stat. § 123.190, adopted I 1873 but most recently updated in 2017, says: **"When a spouse has given *written authority* to his or her spouse to appropriate to his or her own use the spouse's earnings, the same, with the issues and profits thereof, is deemed a *gift* from one spouse to the other, and is, with such issues and profits, the latter spouse's separate property."** (Italics added.) This statute is unusual for two reasons. It crosses the line from the earner's exclusive management and control of uncommingled community property earnings (as in Texas) to the donee's outright ownership of the appropriated (gifted) earnings of the donor spouse. And it uses the phrase *written authority*, not written agreement, or written contract, or written declaration, as in other states. See Chapter 5 for more on gifts and Chapter 8 for more on management and control.

Nevada allows for a general community property presumption but, to date, not for a special joint form title community property presumption applicable at dissolution.

The general community property presumption is supplemented by extensive legislation concerning the procedure for and effect of recording a written inventory of the separate property of a married person. The applicable statutes include Nev.Rev.Stat. §§ 123.130 through 123.170, and the following language of Nev.Rev.Stat. § 123.160:

> **". . . the failure to file for record an inventory of [the] . . . separate property [of a married person resident in Nevada] . . . or the omission from the inventory, . . . of any part of such property, . . . is prima facie evidence, as between such married person and purchasers in good faith and for a valuable consideration from the other spouse, that the property of which no inventory has been so filed, or which has been omitted from the inventory, is not the separate property of such person . . . ."**

Nev.Rev.Stat. § 123.140(3) permits supplemental inventories: **"From time to time thereafter, a further and supplemental inventory may be made out, signed, acknowledged, or proved, and recorded in like manner, of all other separate property after acquired by such**

married person, excepting money, and the rents, issues and profits of such person's separate property, included in the original or any subsequent inventory if the same be in money."

6. NEW MEXICO

The code books use the compilation date "(1978)" but be aware that proposed changes were made in 2024.

N.M.Stat.Ann. § 40–3–8(B) (1978) defines community property as **"[p]roperty acquired by either or both spouses during marriage which is not separate property."** The spouses' respective interests in community property are present and vested. Quasi-community property is defined by the same statutory provision.

The general community property presumption is modeled on California law in that the general community property presumption arises from the fact of acquisition during marriage while domiciled in the state. N.M.Stat.Ann. § 40–3–12(A) (1978) provides: **"Property acquired during marriage by either spouses, or both, is presumed to be community property."** The spouse who asserts that the property is all or part separate property in character bears the burden of rebuttal.

In 1984, New Mexico adopted a special joint form title community property presumption. N.M.Stat.Ann. § 40–3–8(B) (1978) called **Classes of Property**. That section refers to separate property, as well. The community property portion of the statute reads in relevant part: **"[C]ommunity property means property acquired by either or both spouses during marriage that is not separate property. Property acquired by a husband and wife by an instrument in writing whether as tenants in common or as joint tenants or otherwise shall be presumed to be held as community property unless such property is separate property within the meaning of (§ 40–3–8) subsection A of this section."** (The 2024 legislative proposal seeks to change "husband and wife" to "during a marriage".) This community property presumption is not limited to a dissolution proceeding, thus supporting the inference that this joint form title community property presumption can be raised in a probate proceeding.

N.M.Stat.Ann. § 40–3–8(A)(5) (1978) provides that the special community property presumption is rebutted for **"property designated as separate property by a written agreement between the spouses, including a deed or other written agreement concerning property held by the spouses as joint tenants or tenants in common in which the property is designated as separate property."**

Rebuttal of the joint form title community property presumption is by proof of one the elements listed in N.M.Stat.Ann. § 40–3–8(A) (1978). Generally, the special joint form title presumption is rebutted with evidence that the jointly titled asset was acquired before marriage, acquired by gift during marriage, or subject to a separate property agreement between the spouses.

Sec. 45–6–211(B) replicates the suggested UMPAA (1989) language; as such it provides: **"During the lifetime of all parties, an account belongs to the parties in proportion to the net contribution of each to the sums on deposit, unless there is clear and convincing evidence of a different intent. *As between parties married to each other, in the absence of proof otherwise, the net contribution of each is presumed to be an equal amount.*"** (Italics added.)

7. TEXAS

The basic community property statute in Texas is V.T.C.A.Fam. Code § 3.002 and § 3.003(a).

This former statute is acquisition-based. It provides that **"[c]ommunity property consists of the property, other than separate property, *acquired* by either spouse during marriage."** (Italics added.) Rebuttal for this *acquisition*-based community property presumption is by the preponderance of the evidence.

The possession-based general community property presumption found at V.T.C.A.Fam. Code § 3.003(a) (West 2006) states: **"Property *possessed* by either spouse during or on dissolution of marriage is presumed to be community property."** (Italics added.) Rebuttal for this *possession*-based community property presumption is by clear and convincing evidence.

Texas originated the homestead concept. Homestead property is a community property title that enjoys exemptions from the reach of creditors. Texas statutory formalities ensure that joint tenancy is intentionally, not accidentally, used. Therefore, there is little need for a special joint form title community property presumption like the one enacted by California. See Chapter 6 for more on joint title forms in Texas.

Texas follows the civil law rule defining separate property rents, issues, and profits as community property during the marriage. But that rule is rationalized by the state constitution, not by reference to usufruct. See Chapter 7.

Moreover, Texas differs from the Louisiana when it comes to extracted mineral products. The Louisiana rationale appears in Section C, Louisiana above.

The Texas rule, by comparison, as stated in *Norris v. Vaughan*, 260 S.W.2d 676, 681 (Tex. 1953), adapts the labor principle, in a possibly diluted form, for gas leases that are acquired before but developed during marriage. For such a lease the labor principle is restricted to proof, offered by the community property proponent (who may be a spouse or an heir in a probate proceeding), that there was "an expenditure of community funds or effort as to impress community character on the gas produced." Absent such proof, the sale proceeds of a separate property mineral lease (i.e., any sale of extracted mineral products) remain separate property. If the lease interest is acquired during marriage—rather than before marriage—with separate property capital, then the profits, mineral products, and sale proceeds are community property outright, subject to a reimbursement right for the lease owner. Norris, supra, is distinguished by *Weed v. Frost Bank*, 565 S.W.3d 397 (Ct.App. 2018).

Arguments have been made to extend *Norris*, supra, to intellectual property. *Alsenz v. Alsenz*, 101 S.W.3d 648 (Tex.App. 2003), a patent case, considered this argument as a matter of first impression. The court noted that the character of the patent was not at issue, only the income received from the patent during marriage. Building on this, the court went on to issue a two-part holding: (i) "a spouse is entitled to an interest during marriage in the revenue stream from intellectual property that was created by the other spouse before marriage" (*Id.* at 654) and (ii) the income stream generated during the marriage from a patent obtained by a spouse prior to marriage is a "revenue" and a "fruit" of separate property; as such, the income stream is community property during the continuance of the marriage. Id. at 654.

There is a practical difference between *Norris* and *Alsenz*. But the cases, read together, illustrate how usufruct rights differ from outright ownership.

Under the rule in *Norris* the oil-and-gas profits, products and sale proceeds are characterized upon the inception of the lease rights (asset #1) and again at the point of mineral or gas extraction from the leased area (asset #2). Thus, if inception of right to a mineral lease is before marriage, then the extracted mineral products of the lease are separate property. This leaves it to the community proponent to show a community expenditure or effort to develop the lease.

But if inception of right to the oil-and-gas lease occurs during marriage, no matter the source of purchase funds, the products of the lease are owned entirely as community property. In the latter case, it is the separate property spouse who must seek a capital reimbursement for any separate property that was used to purchase the lease.

Under the rule in *Alsenz*, the income from a patent issued before marriage is viewed as a secondary income stream generated by the underlying separate property asset (the patent). As such, the inventor controls the patent (asset #1), but the community has a right to the patent royalties during the marriage (income derived from asset #1), even absent proof of a community expenditure or effort to develop the patent. The community's rights end at dissolution, at which time patent royalties once again belong entirely to the inventor. This approach as applied to patents is novel and no doubt subject to change.

Texas has one of the broadest statutory authorizations designed to protect third persons in consequential real estate transactions involving community property. V.T.C.A.Fam. Code § 3.104(b) provides, among other things, that a third person dealing with a married person is entitled to rely on the authority of that married person to deal with the community property. The third party's statutory entitlement can be nullified by the third party's fraud, or by actual or constructive knowledge that the transacting spouse lacked authority to deal with the real estate.

Recording of an inventory of the separate property of a married person is permitted by V.T.C.A.Fam. Code § 3.004, but not required to preserve and prove a separate character claim (as it is in Nevada).

The 1980 amendment to TEX. CONST. ART. XVI, § 15, provides, in part: **"[i]f one spouse makes a gift of property to the other that gift is presumed to include all the income or property which might arise from that gift of property; . . ."**. This clause creates a new presumption in Texas (which, being a civil law rule state as to separate property rents, issues, and profits, would otherwise deem the income from separate property to be community property if received during marriage). The new presumption is that a gift from one spouse to the other of separate property is presumed to include a gift of the future income of that property as well. This provision was likely aimed at federal estate tax questions raised by *Estate of Castleberry v. C.I.R.*, 68 T.C. 682 (1977), which was subsequently reversed by *Wyly's Estate v. C.I.R.*, 610 F.2d 1282 (5th Cir. 1980). Texas law continues to develop on this point. See Chapter 5.

8. WASHINGTON

Washington's basic community property statute is Wash.Rev.Code § 26.16.030 (West 2016), a provision that accomplishes two goals. One, it describes the attributes of community property. And two, it defines the term, mostly by reference to what community property is not.

"Property *not* acquired or owned, as [separate property] is community property." Wash.Rev.Code § 26.16.030

Property prescribed in **RCW 26.16.010** [titled **"Separate property of spouse"**] **and 26.16.020** [titled **"Separate property of domestic partner"**] is **". . . acquired after marriage or after registration of a state registered domestic partnership by either domestic partner or either husband or wife or both, is community property. . . . ."** RCW 26.16.010 and 26.16.020, Washington's separate property provisions are discussed in Chapter 5.

Washington characterizes joint tenancy titles as community property in character absent proof that both spouses *declared* contrary intentions. (To sharpen the use of the word declared, California requires an agreement between the spouses to rebut the special community property presumption for joint form titles, not just double declarations of the spouses.) The state approach calls for what it regards as enhanced joint tenancy creation formalities to steer married persons away from common law concurrent titles and toward community property titles. See Chapter 6.

But even where the parties use a joint tenancy title with the idea of creating separate property interests, there may be litigation over characterization. This is because *during* marriage, a joint tenancy title between married persons defaults to community property upon severance by conveyance. See Chapter 6.

9. WISCONSIN

Wisconsin adopted the Uniform Marital Property Act in Wisconsin, Act 37, 1985, effective January 1, 1986 (WUMPA 1985 for short). The relevant legislation that controls characterization can be found in **The Family. Chapter 766. Property Rights of Married Persons: Marital Property.**

Wis.Stat. § 766.001(2) (2009) states: "**It is the intent of the legislature that marital property is a form of community property.**" The Wisconsin marital property system applies to spouses upon their determination date, which in most cases (given the passage of time from the enactment to today) is the same as the date of marriage or the date of domicile in the state. Wis.Stat. § 766.31(6). For more on determination date, see Chapter 2, Sec. C., Wisconsin.

Wis.Stat. § 766.31(1)–(4) is the basic statute.

Sec. 766.31(1) states the general provision: "**(1) General. All property of spouses . . .**" and not just the property acquired during the marriage "**[i]s marital property except that which is classified otherwise by this chapter and that which is described in sub. (8).**" Sec. 766.31(2) states a marital property presumption. "**(2) Presumption.**

All property" not just property acquired during the marriage, **"[i]s presumed to be marital property."**

Subsections (1) and (2) move Wisconsin as close to a universal marital property system as exists in the U.S. today; while Subsections (8) and (9), discussed below, steer it toward a ganancial system, which is what prevails in all the other U.S. community property jurisdictions.

Wis. Stat. §766.31(3) states the equality of interest principle: **"(3) <u>Spouse's interest in marital property</u>. Each spouse has a present undivided one-half interest in each item of marital property . . . ."** This clause appears to necessitate an item-by-item characterization at dissolution.

Subsection (3) carves out two clear exemptions from the equality of interest principle. Both apply when a marriage ends by death, and both allow for an aggregated value division rather than an asset-by-asset division.

The first exemption is a nonemployee spouse's terminable interest in a deferred employment benefit plan or individual retirement plan (if it is traceable to the rollover of an earlier retirement plan). See Chapter 7.

The second exemption is a decedent-spouse's estate if, by enforceable marital agreement, the spouses opted for an aggregate value division of marital assets (i.e., the division of a hotchpot marital property estate) at the death of one of them, rather than for the item-by-item division envisioned by the statute.

Wis. Stat. §766.31(4) adopts, with articulated exceptions, the rule that all income earned or received from *individual* property during marriage is community property. **"(4) Classification of Income. [i]ncome earned or accrued by a spouse or attributable to property of a spouse during marriage and after the determination date is marital property."**

As discussed below, this subsection amplifies the traditional civil law ganancial rule that the rents, issues, and profits of separate property received during marriage are community property during the continuance of the marriage. But the Wisconsin approach is rule is subject to two additional qualifications, both are listed in the basic statute, and both of which veer Wisconsin away from a universal marital property system toward a ganancial system.

The first qualification is a tracing rule. Sec. 766.31(8) states that property exchanged for or with the proceeds of individual property is individual property. **"Except as provided otherwise in this chapter, the enactment of this chapter does not alter the classification and ownership rights of property acquired before the determination date or the classification and ownership rights *of property acquired after the termination date in exchange for or with the process of property acquired before the determination date.*"** (Italics added.)

The second qualification states a separate property definition. Sec. 766.31(9): **"Except as provided otherwise in this chapter and except to the extent that it would affect the spouses' ownership rights in the property existing before the determination date, *during marriage the interest of a spouse in property owned immediately before the determination date is treated as if it were individual property.*"** (Italics added.) Individual property is defined at and discussed in Chapter 5.

Finally, Wisconsin amplifies the civil law rule on separate property rents, issues, and profits by making the community the owner of those streams of income during the continuance of the marriage. This is different than the Louisiana approach, which gives the community usufruct rights to that same type of income. It is also different from Texas, which subjects a separate property gas lease and any sale proceeds from extracted mineral products obtained during marriage to distinct characterizations.

Wisconsin has not, to date, adopted a special joint form title marital (community property) presumption. Of note, marital title may be held in common law joint tenancy form. See Chapter 6.

Of note is pending 2024 legislation on digital property. See Wis. Stat. § 766.01(e) and (f).

CHAPTER 5
SEPARATE PROPERTY

A. OVERVIEW

Separate property is defined by state statute to include property acquired before marriage; gifts received by a spouse during marriage; and (in some states) the rents, issues, and profits of either.

In most states, title passes when the common law elements for an inter vivos gift are met. States can differ with respect to how a gift to both spouses is characterized. Differences depend primarily on statutory presumptions (as in Louisiana) and on case law regarding the role of donor intent in characterizing the gift.

U.S. community property states split on how to characterize separate property revenues, often referred to as "rents, issues, and profits." See Chapter 4. A few—Idaho, Louisiana, Texas, and Wisconsin—characterize such income as community property during the continuance of the marriage. Most—Arizona, California, Nevada, New Mexico, and Washington—characterize the same as separate property during the marriage.

Community property states split on how to characterize money and property received by a spouse during marriage in settlement of a personal injury claim. Some states characterize all or some personal injury settlements as separate property. Others characterize the same as community property or as special community property. Special community property is owned in undivided shares during the marriage, but assignable to the injured spouse at dissolution.

B. DETAIL

1. PROPERTY ACQUIRED WHILE MARRIED AND DOMICILED IN THE STATE

The word "acquired" has a precise meaning in community property law. It means the date the legal property right or interest comes into existence. Note however that the term differs in usage as discussed below.

In a ganancial system, all property acquired before marriage is separate property. Property acquired during marriage by a person who is married and domiciled in a community property state is presumed community property, as discussed in Chapter 4.

Classic civil law characterizes all gifts as separate property. Property acquired without personal effort is lucratively acquired. Property acquired during marriage through personal labor or work is an onerously acquired. The onerous-lucrative distinction is discussed in Chapters 1 and 4.

Onerous is as broad a term as lucrative, but there can be apparent overlap. Often a business gift is exchanged in lieu of earnings, making it an onerous acquisition. Cases treat accumulations as onerously acquired despite what parties might label the transfer. An onerously acquired "gift" is not a true gift, meaning something transferred for no consideration. It is a business gift, which typically means (depending on the facts) a bargained for exchange. Likewise, the conferral of benefit is not a true gift. The conferral of the benefit is something given with the expectation of reciprocity.

Some analogies are possible to federal income tax cases like *Commissioner v. Duberstein*, 363 U.S. 278 (1960), which treats the business gift as taxable income. Gambling proceeds could be understood as onerous or lucrative depending on the skill involved, but they are more typically characterized by tracing the winnings to their source, lucrative chance.

In *Downer v. Bramet*, 152 Cal.App.3d 837, 199 Cal.Rptr. 830 (Cal.App.Ct. 4th Dist. 1984) an employer labeled as a "gift" a transfer of an interest in a ranch (real estate) to an employee-spouse. Contending that the ranch was separate property, the donee spouse chose not to disclose it to his spouse in their dissolution proceeding. Years later, the ranch was sold. The former wife sued her former husband to establish a community property interest in the ranch sale proceeds. She built her case on these facts: the ranch was given in lieu of pension benefits; the employee spouse had no social relationship with the employer; and the employer had made identical gifts to other employees in lieu of pension benefits. The trial court dismissed the former wife's claim. The court of appeal reversed and remanded.

The importance of *Downer* is that the donor's label (gift), without more, did not necessarily decide the character of the property for purposes of the employee spouse's dissolution proceeding. Instead, the issue on remand was whether the ranch was acquired by the employee-spouse during marriage through onerous means.

2. EARNINGS AND ACCUMULATIONS AFTER A DATE OF SEPARATION

Date of separation is a cornerstone concept in community property law. It is the date, during marriage, that earnings and accumulations become separate property because one or both spouses' decides to proceed with terminating the marriage.

After a date of separation but before the final judgment of dissolution, one or both parties no longer acquire community property in the form of earnings and accumulations. They might have community property savings to draw on. But after a date of separation, community property acquisition ceases.

To prove date of separation, all states accept proof of formal separation. Filing a petition for separation is proof of a date of separation. In states that require formal proof of date of separation, earnings and accumulations continue to be characterized as community property during periods of (informal) physical separation.

Some but not all states also accept proof of physical, or informal, separation.

Physical separation occurs when, for example, one spouse moves out of the marital residence and otherwise communicates their intent to the other spouse to end the marriage. Not all states require that the spouses establish separate residences to prove date of separation.

Informal separation occurs when one spouse communicates to the other that the marriage is over. This method of establishing a date of separation, as noted in the previous paragraph, does not necessarily require that the spouses establish separate physical residences.

In states that allow spouses to establish a date of separation by physical or informal conduct, the transition from characterizing earnings as community property to characterizing them as separate property happens automatically, without the need for court action. Often there is a wide array of facts of life that the parties can draw from to make arguments to prove or disprove a specific date of separation. The issue is not whether there is a date of separation but rather when, as between two competing dates, the date of (informal) separation occurred. One can see the benefit of filing for legal separation as a way to establish a clear date of separation for the parties, their creditors, and any other third parties who may be acting in reliance on what they believe to be an ongoing and intact marriage.

3. INTER VIVOS GIFTS

Property received by gift is ordinarily the separate property of the donee spouse. Louisiana modifies this rule by characterizing as community property **"property donated to the spouses jointly."** LSA-C.C. Art. 2338. So does Wisconsin.

A gift is defined in the common law as a gratuitous transfer made with donative intent. Courts have declined to follow a rigid definition of a gift as being totally without consideration and a sale as being for any consideration.

Wedding gifts to the married couple are often received before marriage. This makes them separate property by timing. It was once possible for a court to hold that wedding gifts were community property by virtue of an oral or implicit transmutation that occurred on the date of marriage. However, today, because most states require written proof of a transmutation, the oral or implied transmutation rationale is no longer sound. Unmarried parties who want their wedding gifts to be characterized as community property can use a premarital agreement. Married parties can use a formal transmutation. See Chapter 2 for more on premarital agreements and Chapter 3 for more on transmutations.

An alternative rationale for characterizing wedding gifts as community property is to focus on the third-party donor's intent in making the gift. In Louisiana, a premarital engagement gift could be construed as property donated to the prospective spouses jointly upon condition of marriage. If so, the engagement gift would (hypothetically) vest in the community upon marriage. LSA-C.C. Art. 2338. *Jones v. Ridgon*, 32 Ariz. 286, 257 P. 639 (1927) indicates that Arizona would go in the same direction as Louisiana; however, the recent case of *Valento v. Valento*, 225 Ariz. 477 240 P.3d 1239 (Ct.App. 2010) signals otherwise. Wisconsin, in the default WUMPA provision, characterizes third party gifts made during marriage to both spouses as marital (community) property unless the third-party donor expresses a contrary intent. Wis.Stat. § 766.31(7)(a).

Texas characterizes gifts (including wedding gifts) as the separate property of the recipients by constitutional provision and by statute. V.T.C.A. Fam.Code § 3.001(a)(2).

California statutory law is silent on the wedding gift issue. However, more generally, Cal.Fam.Code § 770 provides that **"all property acquired by the person after marriage by gift, bequest, devise, or descent"** is separate property.

This suggests that, regardless of the donor's intent, a wedding gift made before or after marriage falls within the definition of separate property. A donor possibly can use a gift transfer deed in joint form to deliver property during marriage to the spouses. In California, for example, property acquired during marriage in any concurrent title will raise the special joint form title community property presumption in a dissolution proceeding. The separate property proponent would then bear the burden of rebuttal. But it is unclear how the rebuttal would be framed, as the argument might have to focus on the meaning of the word "acquired." The California presumption is found at Cal.Fam.Code § 2581 and discussed in Chapter 3 and Chapter 6.

4. PROPERTY ACQUIRED IN EXCHANGE FOR SEPARATE PROPERTY (THE TRACING PRINCIPLE)

Counterintuitively, the largest category of separate property—ignored by statutory schemes (except in Louisiana and Wisconsin), yet completely recognized by judicial decisions, is property received in exchange for separate property. See Chapter 7 for more on tracing.

5. MORE ON SEPARATE PROPERTY RENTS, ISSUES, AND PROFITS RECEIVED DURING MARRIAGE

Asset appreciation is characterized identically to the asset. This is the rule in all community property states, despite a split in authority among the states on how to characterize separate property rents, issues, and profits received during marriage.

The civil law ganancial rule characterize rents, issues, and profits received during marriage as community property. At divorce, any separate property rents, issues, and profits return to the separate property owner.

The American rule characterize the rents, issues and profits of separate property received during marriage as separate property.

Illustration 4.1: A person owns an unencumbered separate property rental unit prior to marriage. The rental unit is separate property. What is the character of the rents received during marriage from this unit?

In a civil law state (Idaho, Louisiana, Texas, and Wisconsin), rents from a separate property rental are community property during the marriage, but they will return to separate property ownership in the event of divorce or death of a spouse. In an American rule state (Arizona, California, Nevada, New Mexico, and Washington), by contrast, rents from a separate property rental received during marriage remain separate property during and after marriage.

States that follow the American rule for rents, issues, and profits explain the break from the civil law ganancial rule depending on their unique histories. Most states reference their state constitutions and precedent, which, because they protect the right to own separate property during marriage, permit tracing. California points to the holding in *George v. Ransom*, 15 Cal. 322, 76 Am.Dec. 490 (Cal. 1860). Louisiana justifies its decision by reference to the civil law concept of usufruct.

As an aside, early on the civil law permitted tracing, but only as to land-for-land exchanges and reinvestments of separate property land sale proceeds in land. See e.g., COMPARATIVE STUDIES IN COMMUNITY PROPERTY LAW 116–117, Jan. P Charmatz and Harriet S. Daggett eds. (1955), citing Law, William Q. de Funiak, PRINCIPLES OF COMMUNITY PROPERTY 2ND 142 (1943) and translations of Spanish commentaries like Gutierrez and Matienzo.

The common law permitted tracing from and to real and personal property.

Illustration 4.2: A spouse owns an unencumbered rental unit as separate property. Assume the spouse sells the rental unit to buy a boat. What is the character of the boat? In all jurisdictions the boat is separate property by the tracing principle. The civil law land-to-land limitation on tracing no longer applies in the U.S. community property states.

Illustration 4.3: A spouse owns an unencumbered rental unit as separate property. The spouse sells the rental unit and deposits the sale proceeds into a joint bank account shared with the other spouse. What is the character of the deposited sale proceeds?

A jurisdictional split may arise on whether the state has adopted UMPAA (1989) or some other legislation that establishes a special community property presumption for sums on deposit in any account of a married person. See Chapter 7 for more on tracing to and from bank accounts.

Illustration 4.4: A spouse owns an unencumbered rental unit as separate property. She uses monthly rents collected from the unit to buy a second rental unit. What is the character of the second rental unit?

A jurisdictional split arises. In most community property states (the American rule jurisdictions), the rents are separate property, and anything purchased with those rents is separate property by the tracing principle. The second rental is thus a separate property asset.

In a minority of community property states (the civil law jurisdictions), the rents are community property during marriage, making any purchase made with those rents, during marriage, community property. This makes the second rental a community property asset.

Any or all of the above outcomes can be altered by a premarital agreement or a valid transmutation.

In the above examples, keep these points in mind.

One, if the owning spouse validly transmutes the rent producing real estate into community property during the marriage, the character of the real estate might change. In some states, transmutation of the underlying property implicitly transmutes that property's rents, issues, and profits. However, in other states, rents, issues, and profits must be expressly identified and transmuted to effect a valid change in their character. See Chapter 3 for more on transmutations.

Two, the mere act of commingling separate property with community property does not automatically transmute the asset. See Chapter 3 for more on the doctrine of confusion and when it applies.

Illustration 4.5: Assume the owning spouse, in Illustration 4.4 above, commingles rent deposits with community property earnings to buy a boat. What is the character of the boat at dissolution?

In in an American rule jurisdiction, the separate property rents retain their character. The boat was purchased with separate and community property. Tracing can be used to identify proportional separate property slash community property shares of ownership.

In a civil law state, rents of separate property that are received during marriage are community property by law, and so are earnings. Therefore, no commingling occurred when rents from the separate property rental were mixed with the separate property owning spouse's community property earnings to buy the boat.

Income streams from separate property are uniformly identified in statutes by the labels "rents, issues, and profits" or "fruits and revenues" (in Louisiana). As discussed above, Idaho, Louisiana, Texas, and Wisconsin, characterize the income of separate property obtained during marriage as community property during the continuance of the marriage. This is the civil law ganancial rule.

An early California case started a contrary trend that gave rise to the now-called American rule. In *George v. Ransom*, supra, the California Supreme Court interpreted a California Constitutional provision (all property owned by the wife prior to marriage shall be her separate property) to include the capital gains of that property. Cal.Fam.Code § 770(a)(3) codifies the holding by providing that "**. . . separate property of a married person includes . . . the rents, issues, and profits" of separate property."** Today, the American rule is embedded in the community property systems of Arizona, California, Nevada, New Mexico, and Washington.

The Texas Supreme Court construed a clause in the Texas Constitution identical to the California Constitutional clause in *Arnold v. Leonard*, 114 Tex. 535, 273 S.W. 799 (1925). The Texas Supreme Court held that the Texas legislature was constitutionally prohibited from characterizing as separate property the rents, issues, and profits accrued during marriage from (the wife's) separate property. Thus, in Texas, by constitutional provision, property owned before marriage includes only the base property, not the capital accumulations of that property.

The American rule split from the civil law rule is only over the character of separate property rents, issues, and profits that are obtained during marriage. There is no disagreement among the community property jurisdictions as to the character of the separate property rents, issues, and profits obtained prior to marriage or after the marriage ends. That income is clearly separate property.

Likewise, there is no disagreement as to the character of rents, issues, and profits obtained from community property obtained during marriage. Each is community property.

Rents and interest payments for the use of property, or money and other items that are renewable, recurrent, and nonconsuming are classified in the category of rents, issues, and profits. Stock or cash dividends are too. See Chapter 4 for more on the civil law definition of fruits, and how that term differs from the concept of rents, issues, and profits.

Profits are capital gains produced by separate property. In Arizona, California, Nevada, New Mexico and Washington, separate property livestock, separate property businesses, separate property taxable investment accounts, and separate property crops can give rise to profits during marriage. See Chapters 4 and Chapter 7 for more on the distinction between income streams and property appreciation.

Depreciating or depleting items produce receipts which are often, but not always, classified in the category of rents, issues, or profits. Among these items are timber, coal, stone, and mineral extraction. Three of the major oil and gas producing states—California, Louisiana, and Texas—are community property states. For more on extracted mineral products, see Chapter 3, Section 3, Louisiana, and Texas.

Complete consumption of the item that produced receipts, such as a legal or equitable life estate or an annuity, poses problems in the states that follow the civil law rule on separate property rents, issues, and profits. If such receipts are labeled the revenue of separate property, a total conversion of separate property into community property could result over time. Conversely, if those receipts are not labeled separate property rents, issues, or profits, then there would be no allocation to the community of the income produced by the assets (which represent holding wealth for a time), which would circumvent the civil law rule. While a proportionate allocation between separate and community is possible, civil law states treat the receipts of such assets as being like a liquidating dividend from a corporation, i.e., as a receipt of capital as opposed to a rent, issue, or profit.

Community property states generally decline to apply many common accounting and economic concepts of income in the interest of keeping the law streamlined. Thus, dividing separate property rents, issues, and profits from property appreciation can raise problems in all jurisdictions. Part of the job of the legislature and the courts is to reach principles that help standardize acceptable accounting methods for those who seek dissolution or probate administration in the state.

As to rents, issues, and profits, in Idaho, Louisiana, Texas, and Wisconsin the dividing line between income (community property) and natural increases (separate property) can be difficult to identify. Except in Arizona, increases in size or bulk do not give rise to separate property; the underlying property simply retains its separate property character. Likewise, increases in market value due to market conditions, including inflation, should not change the character of the property.

Accessions and accretions normally have the same character as the original property

6. MONEY AND PROPERTY RECEIVED FOR PERSONAL INJURY CLAIMS

Personal injury recoveries raise unique issues. As a matter of public policy, a personal injury claim is not itself transferable property. But a personal injury claim can result in a settlement of money and property for the injury.

a. Proper Party to Bring the Personal Injury Action

In the 1970s, male management was replaced with equal management and control. The transition required reconsideration of the necessary party issue.

As for community property, the injured party is the proper party to maintain the personal injury action. When a jurisdiction apportions personal injury recoveries into community and separate elements (some, but not all do), it may be possible that both spouses will be necessary parties to an action.

The spouse to whom separate property belongs is the proper party to maintain an action at law concerning that asset.

b. Spousal Immunity

This ancient common law doctrine forbade certain (or all) types of lawsuits between spouses. The doctrine that barred one spouse from suing another during the marriage was rooted in several systemic concerns expressed in the so-called "unity of husband and wife" rationale. According to that rationale, spouses could not sue each other for reasons such as the public policy of preserving peace and tranquility in the home (regrettably this policy covers up rather than prevents domestic violence); the supposed adequacy of criminal and divorce law; the fear of a flood of social matrimonial disputes in the courts (also a domestic violence cover up); the fear of false testimony, and collusion; and the risk of insurance fraud. These were regarded as legitimate policy justifications upon which to preclude, as a matter of law, one spouse from suing the other spouse for a personal injury during the continuance of the marriage.

Most states have abolished the doctrine of interspousal tort immunity, as has the Restatement. See e.g. *Freehe v. Freehe*, 81 Wash.2d 183, 500 P.2d 771 (1972), *Self v. Self*, 58 Cal.2d 683, 26 Cal.Rptr. 97, 376 P.2d 65 (1962) and *Klein v. Klein*, 58 Cal.2d 692, 26 Cal.Rptr. 102, 376 P.2d 70 (1962). In Wisconsin (and under WUMPA), interspousal immunity is explicitly eliminated in several situations.

(*Freehe*, supra, was overruled by *Brown v. Brown*, 100 Wash.2d 729, 675 P.2d 1207 (1984)(en banc) on different grounds. *Freehe*, supra, characterized a recovery for injuries to a married person by a third-party tortfeasor as community property. *Brown*, supra, characterized the same as separate property except to the extent that the recovery compensated for lost wages which would have been community property, but for the injury.

Immunities do not apply in domestic violence situations. Where one spouse intentionally injures the other, some states provide that money and damages received to settle a personal injury claim against another spouse are the separate property of the injured spouse whether the settlement is received during or after the marriage. In these states, the injured spouse's action for intentional tort can be brought against the other spouse during marriage, or upon separation or divorce. Other states require that an action by one spouse against the other for an intentional tort committed during marriage (or by extension during a period of separation) be brought after divorce, as a subsequent action. Not all states distinguish between intentional and negligent harms when it comes to interspousal torts lawsuits.

Neither do immunities apply in actions by one spouse against another for property and economic torts. To allow spouses to protect their vested property rights in marital property, equitable and partnership related actions between spouses are permitted, often by statute. These can include an action for damages for breach of the spousal fiduciary duty; an action for an accounting of the property; an action to determine the rights and obligations of the spouses; an action for adding a spouse's name to the title of certain marital property or to bank accounts titled solely in the other spouse's name; and claims for impairment of a community property interest (economic torts). See for example Cal.Fam.Code § 1101.

c. The Community Property Defense

Imputed contributory negligence in the context of marriage was sometimes referred to as the community property defense. The community property defense became available when one spouse's personal injuries were caused by a third party and the other spouse's contributory negligence.

The defense worked like this. If one spouse was injured in an accident in which the other spouse was adjudged contributorily negligent, the community property defense barred the community estate from recovering damages. The policy underlying the community property defense was that a negligent spouse should not benefit from his or her own negligence.

Some states, California being one, abrogated the imputed contributory negligence theory as a matter of law, and instead adopted a contribution system.

Under the contribution system, if an injured spouse sues a third party but chooses not to name the other spouse as a defendant, the third party can counter-claim against the unnamed spouse for an adjudication on whether the unnamed spouse was a contributing proximate cause of the plaintiff spouse's injury. If the answer is yes, then the third party can seek a contribution from the contributorily negligent spouse.

In the case of couples who are intentionally or unintentionally not married, different outcomes result.

For nonmarried cohabitants, because they cannot acquire community property, the community property defense is not applicable absent an equitable alteration of the ordinary rules.

For putative marriages, it is possible to be deemed by law to have come into ownership of community property or community property analogies (like, for example, California's concept of quasi-marital property). Such a result could also produce an analogy to the community property defense. Outcomes turn on marriage validity doctrines, which differ from state to state.

Even so, a trend is emerging considering declining marriage rates. In a community property defense jurisdiction, the more lawful the marriage, the more the community property defense applies. The unmarried couple avoids the defense to which a putatively married couple is perhaps subject, and to which a lawfully married couple is certainly subject.

It is possible that these types of litigation-related problems were responsible for any (past) trend toward apportioning personal injury recoveries into their separate and community property elements. In the typical automobile accident case, however, case law in every jurisdiction illustrates how the community property defense could be and was invoked by and for a casualty insurance company to avoid liability, rather than by and for a spouse personally.

d. Reasons for Apportioning Personal Injury Settlements

A personal injury award has different components. Each component is discussed in the next section. Commentators have argued and judges have held that at least some of these components trace to separate property, and thus should be characterized as the separate property of the injured spouse.

Currently, three rationales for such an outcome prevail.

One, the onerous-lucrative rationale recognizes the personal injury cause of action and all recoveries received from third parties as community property, not because they are obtained through labor, but because they are not a gift. One possible limitation of this analysis is the approach taken by Nevada courts that a personal injury remedy is not within the definition of acquisition as set forth in the general community property statute.

Two, the private-slash-personal right rationale considers the personal injury recovery as a settlement of money for damage to a personal right, rather than to a property right. The rationale draws a sharp line between a property claim and a personal injury claim. In California, for example, a property claim can meet the definition of an accumulation, but a personal injury claim cannot because it is personal to its holder. Thus, the personal injury claim is not subject to characterization; whereas money or property received in settlement of a personal injury claim are. The theory is that only the settlement (not the underlying personal injury claim) represents a tradable "accumulation" for purposes of property characterization.

Commentators sometimes counter that a personal injury claim because it can impact earnings, can or should be defined as an accumulation. These commentators focus on how to characterize disability payments made by an employer to an injured worker. Worker's compensation is derived from the employment, which sounds in community, but it is measured by the type of injury, which is said to be personal. Moreover, disability insurance is designed to replace future loss of income, which could be community or separate depending on the parties' marital status at the time the disability arises. From this perspective—the argument goes—depending on the facts of the case, a personal injury claim could be defined as an accumulation in one case but a personal injury claim in another.

Given the conceptual difficulty of breaking down personal injury settlements, including workers compensation, into components, the more accepted view is to name the injured spouse as the community agent for management and control of any personal injury action that arises during the marriage. If the personal injury action is not brought before dissolution, the injured spouse continues as the exclusive manager of the personal injury action once the marriage is over.

If the injured (now-former) spouse decides, after divorce, to pursue the personal injury claim that arose during the prior marriage, any settlement received would be outside of the community property system.

Some U.S. community property states, again California being one, follow precedent that disallows placing a claim that arose during a dissolving marriage into trust with the intention of designing a pro rata division should a settlement be won after the final judgment of dissolution is issued.

The above theories do not acknowledge the argument which defines pain and suffering as a form of labor by the injured party. Nor do they fully address the argument that defines the care of an injured spouse as a form of labor undertaken by the caregiving spouse.

Finally, statutory reimbursements tend to be a systematic way to address the above issues. If the community or the other spouse's separate property estate contribute to care and medical expenses of a spouse who was injured during the marriage, a reimbursement may be due in the event of dissolution.

e. Elements of a Personal Injury Settlement

Most jurisdictions have viewed a recovery for personal injury as containing the following elements (excluding attorney fees):

(i) *Compensation for future earnings:* During the marriage, compensation for future earnings is deemed to be community property. Dissolution could make a portion of the future earnings separate. The courts have not uniformly attended to the risk of how a dissolution would impact the character of the future earnings portion of a settlement. Nor have they uniformly attended to the dissolution risks of allocating a portion to earnings while married and the balance to earnings after divorce.

(ii) *Reimbursement for past medical expenses:* During the marriage, this reimbursement is often given to the community on the rationale that the medical expenses have been paid from community property funds. The better rule appears to require an examination of the character of funds that were used to pay the medical expenses, and to direct the recovery accordingly so as to affect a complete reimbursement. If this latter approach is followed, then any marital estate, whether the community estate or the separate property of the non-injured spouse, can request a reimbursement.

(iii) *Compensation for pain, suffering and disfigurement:* Money received for pain, suffering and disfigurement is generally regarded as the separate property of the injured spouse. Jurisdictions differ on the character of money received for loss of consortium, and for loss of whose consortium.

(iv) *Payments for loss of body parts:* Generally, money (received for lost (meaning severed) body parts) is treated as separate property, especially when the injury is not related to a job. If compensation for a job-related injury is measured by the severity of the injury to the worker, some states hold the award to be community.

(v) *Disability payments:* Compensation for disabilities poses special problems when combined or taken in lieu of retirement benefits. In some cases, a worker may be entitled to either retirement or disability payments, but not both. The rationale focuses on whether an election by an injured spouse to take disability payments impairs the non-injured spouse's right to one-half of community funds in an existing defined benefit (i.e., pension or pension-like) plan.

f. Problems with Apportioning Personal Injury Settlements

One problem with apportioning a personal injury recovery by the nature of the right that has been injured is that there is no certainty that the jury will accurately allocate the total award.

For example, a jury may be aware that a plaintiff's fee for her lawyer will not be paid by direct court award. And knowing this, the jury might increase the amount of the recovery for pain and suffering (a separate property item) to reimburse amounts the community paid to lawyers.

Apportionment problems arise in connection with the expenses and fees paid to personal injury attorneys. If the attorney's fee is deducted from the recovery, should it be allocated to one category or borne proportionately by all categories? If the attorney's fee is deducted proportionately from a recovery in which the jury increased the "pain and suffering" portion in contemplation of the fee, the medical expense reimbursement to the community will not recover one hundred cents on each dollar that the community paid, while the separate property will receive slightly larger payments for pain and suffering. Regardless of the conceptual support for apportioning personal injury money and property received in settlement of a personal injury claim against a third party, a disputed settlement can be deemed separate property, in whole or in part, by statutory default.

In the California community property system, money and property received during a marriage for a personal injury settlement that arose during marriage are entirely community property. But they are a special kind of community property assignable by statute to the injured party in the event of a dissolution, with limited exceptions.

7. LEGAL TRANSITIONS

In each state, historical forms of separate and community property exist. What in a past era was separate property is now community property or vice versa. The reason is that constitutional problems and most statutory changes in the character of property operate prospectively, thus leaving behind a trail of historical forms of community or separate property.

Statutory community property presumptions can be applied retroactively with no constitutional objections. For example, in a line of cases commencing with *Marriage of Buol*, 39 Cal.3d 751, 218 Cal.Rptr. 31, 705 P.2d 354 (1985), which is now superseded by statute, the California Supreme Court held that the retroactive application of Cal.Fam.Code § 2581 (the evidentiary community property presumption that applies in a dissolution proceeding to assets titled in any joint form) neither impairs vested property interests nor violates due process of law. However, anytime a statute adopts a more rigorous standard than before, vested rights are impacted. So, for example, if a written instrument was not required in the past, but a statute is passed to now require a writing, the statute is likely not retroactive out of concern for impacting vested rights. Therefore, a dateline must be drawn to protect those who relied on the prior law. Ultimately this creates a new class of historical community property or separate property that lasts up until the date the statute with the new requirements takes effect. See Chapter 2, Section C, California for examples.

Conflict of laws and legal transitions can also create special categories of separate property within the confines of a state system, as discussed in Chapter 3, Section C, Arizona.

Wisconsin places property acquired prior to its adoption of the community property system in an entirely different category called either "predetermination date" or "unclassified" property. This property is essentially individually owned separate property.

State transitions concerning the character of separate property rents, issues and profits obtained during marriage may create historical, or transitional, forms of community or separate property as well.

The inception of title rule applies in all U.S. community property states, but so may states also have enacted evidentiary community property presumptions. If so, the jurisdictions will split on how to account for post-acquisition commingling, especially in the form of labor and capital contributions. See Chapter 4, Chapter 6, and Chapter 7 for more on community property presumptions and how they apply.

In American rule states, the inception of title rule sets the character of the property on the date of its acquisition, but that character can be changed by commingling.

In civil law rule states, the inception of title rule determines the character of the asset at acquisition, with no changes in character over time. See Chapter 7.

Despite differences, the inception of title rule identifies the date of acquisition. In the community property system, property is characterized at its wellspring, the point where the legal right comes into existence.

But keep in mind that acquisition of property is usually the net effect of a series of acts undertaken over a period. An inventor may have an idea, research existing inventions, work upon and perfect her invention, seek a lawyer and apply for and receive a patent. Clearly the patent is property, and even a formal declaration of a patent right (meaning a formal written title), but is the date of the patent the same as the date that property rights in the invention were acquired? Was the property right acquired before the patent was formally granted?

When property is created, all the various acts and ceremonies necessary to complete a purchase, gift, or conveyance of title are generally deemed to be taken together as of the time of some substantial part. Thus, the point of original acquisition is when the property right *first* comes into existence. Later acts that ratify or confirm the property right are said to "relate back" to the point of original acquisition. The task often is to determine the substantial part that represents the act of "original acquisition" in what may be a series of acts that lead up to the coming into existence of a legal right that is more than an expectation.

In the case of the inventor, it is probable that the time of acquisition will precede the grant of, and even the application for, the patent. For an author, the time of acquisition might very well precede the negotiation of the book contract, or the publication of the book; in most cases it will precede the transfer of royalties from publisher to writer. Somewhere around the time that a working model is made, or a book proposal or manuscript is substantially completed, seems an early but still logical date of original acquisition for this type of property creation.

The marital status of the inventor or author at the time that the substantial part of acquisition occurs will determine the character of the property going forward for purposes of state law. There is a strong argument that an invention for which the substantial act of acquisition takes place during marriage should be characterized as community property. There is also a strong rebuttal that an invention for which the substantial act of acquisition takes place before marriage or after a date of separation should be characterized as separate property.

Examples of property acquired over time are deferred earnings and pension rights for labor exerted, and created products like writings, inventions, and other artistic endeavors.

Celebrity status is characterized by this same analysis.

8. SUMMING UP: ACQUISITION BEFORE MARRIAGE, AFTER A DATE OF SEPARATION, AND THROUGH TO DIVORCE

The existence of a valid marriage is required for the to acquire and own community property. Much of the property parties acquire during a marriage is community property. So too is property they exchange for community property.

However, in U.S. community property systems there is a significant amount of legal support for the ownership of separate property during marriage. Property acquired before marriage is separate property in all states. Property acquired by gift during marriage is separate property in all states. Property exchanged for separate property is separate property in all states.

Most states characterize separate property rents, issues, and profits acquired during marriage as separate property. Only a few community property states characterize the same as community property during the continuance of the marriage.

Earnings and accumulations acquired after a date of separation are separate property in most states.

C. INDIVIDUAL STATES

1. ARIZONA

Ariz.Rev.Stat.Ann. § 25–213 defines separate property by restating the exceptions to community property listed in Arizona's basic community property statute Ariz.Rev.Stat.Ann. § 25–211. Separate property is **"real and personal property"** owned by a spouse **"before marriage and that is acquired by that spouse during the marriage by gift, devise or descent, and the increase, rents, issues and profits of that property . . . ."** Ariz.Rev.Stat.Ann. § 25–213(A).

Separate property is also defined as property acquired after the filing of a petition that results in a decree of dissolution. Here is the relevant language: **"Property acquired after service of a petition for dissolution, legal separation, or annulment is also the separate property of that spouse *if the petition results in a decree of dissolution of***

***marriage, legal separation or annulment.*"** Ariz.Rev.Stat.Ann. § 25–213(B). (Italics added.) This suggests two things. One, Arizona does not allow a date of separation to be established by informal methods. Two, Arizona requires written proof of a date of separation in the form of legal filing that has also resolved in an actual divorce, as established by a final decree of dissolution. This is what it takes to recharacterize what would ordinarily be community property (for example earnings) as separate property.

Until 1970, Arizona case law characterized recoveries for personal injuries as community property. In *Jurek v. Jurek*, 124 Ariz. 596, 606 P.2d 812 (1980)(In Banc), the Arizona Supreme Court followed the lead and logic of commentators and the courts of Nevada and New Mexico by characterizing the compensation for personal injuries caused by a third party as the separate property of the injured spouse, and the compensations for expenses incurred by the community for medical care and treatment and any loss of wages resulting from the personal injury as community property. Otherwise, the apportionment of a personal injury award into its component parts remains the rule in Arizona. *Hatcher v. Hatcher* 188 Ariz. 154, 933 P.2d 1222 (1996).

Windauer v. O'Connor, 107 Ariz. 267, 485 P.2d 1157 (1971)(In Banc), a domestic violence case, held that after divorce a spouse may sue a former spouse to recover damages for an intentional tort that occurred during the former marriage. Note however, that this case predates contemporary domestic violence prevention policies and efforts.

In *Fernandez v. Romo*, 132 Ariz. 447, 646 P.2d 878 (1982)(In Banc) the Arizona Supreme Court abolished the doctrine of spousal immunity in automobile accident cases.

2. CALIFORNIA

California Constitution, Article 1, § 21 ensures that **"[p]roperty owned before marriage or acquired during marriage by gift, will, or inheritance is separate property."**

Cal.Fam.Code § 770 defines as separate property **"[a]ll property owned by the person before marriage; [a]ll property acquired by the person after marriage by gift, bequest, devise, or descent; and [t]he rents, issues, and profits of the property"** described in the statute. Indeed, the so-called "American rule" requiring that separate property income streams be themselves characterized as separate property *during the marriage* has its source in California law, and specifically in *George v. Ransom*, supra.

Cal.Fam.Code § 771 changed on Jan. 1, 2017. It now provides: **"(a) The earnings and accumulations of a spouse and the minor children living with, or in custody of the spouse, after the date of separation of the spouses, are the separate property of the spouse."**

The earnings and accumulations of **"an emancipated minor child"** continue to belong to that child.

Marriage of Davis, 61 Cal.4th 846, 352 P.3d 401 (2015) is abrogated by Cal.Fam. Code § 70 (effective Jan 1, 2017, with minor changes that took effect on Jan 1, 2020.)

> **"(a) 'Date of separation' means the date that a complete and final break in the marital relationship has occurred, as evidenced by both of the following: (1) The spouse has expressed to the other spouse the intent to end the marriage. (2) The conduct of the spouse is consistent with the intent to end the marriage.**
>
> **(b) In determining the date of separation, the court shall take into consideration all relevant evidence.**
>
> **(c) It is the intent of the Legislature in enacting this section to abrogate the decisions in In re Marriage of Davis (2015) 61 Cal. 4th 846 and Marriage of Norviel (2002) 102 Cal. App.4th 1152."**

Personal injury recoveries for a cause of action that accrued during marriage have been community property except between 1957 and 1968, In 1968, California restored the community property character of the personal injury recovery making it a form of special community property. Special because this category of community property is subject to a mandatory assignment rule. The legislature also attempted to eliminate imputed contributory negligence (the community property defense). Cal.Fam.Code §§ 780 and 783.

Currently, Cal.Fam.Code § 780 characterizes money and property received as community property if the cause of action "**. . . arose during the marriage . . . .**". Cal.Fam.Code § 781 (effective Jan. 1, 2020) on the other hand, characterizes as separate property damages money or property received for a cause of action that arose **"after the entry of judgment of dissolution . . . or legal separation . . . [or] while the injured spouse is living separate from the other spouse."** Provisions to reimburse the non-injured spouse's separate property or the community property for any expenses paid **"by reason of the personal injuries"** are set out in that section as well.

In a dissolution proceeding, there is precedent that a personal injury cause of action that arose during the marriage but that was not yet pursued or settled by the end of the marriage, exits the marriage with the injured spouse. *Marriage of Pinto*, 28 Cal.App.3d 86, 104 Cal.Rptr. 371 (1972). Of course, this is a judge made ruling, so the case holding is subject to competing interpretations until the legislature makes a clear statement.

A community property personal injury claim that arises during the marriage results in community property money and property, but as noted above, this category of community property is subject to mandatory division pursuant to Cal.Fam.Code § 2603, which provides that Cal.Fam.Code § 780 personal injury money and settlements shall be assigned to the injured spouse unless economic conditions or the interests of justice require otherwise. The court must assign the settlement to the injured spouse, but the court has discretion to award the noninjured spouse part of the special community property. Discretion is limited by statute. In no case shall the noninjured spouse's share exceed one-half of a personal injury settlement.

Certain purchases made from a personal injury recovery may be assigned to the injured spouse using tracing methods. *Marriage of Devlin*, 138 Cal.App.3d 804, 189 Cal.Rptr. 1 (1982) used the doctrine of tracing to set aside dissolution rules for ordinary community property in favor of assigning to the injured spouse a residence that had been purchased with a personal injury settlement (special community property) during marriage and modified for the injured spouse.

Cal.Fam.Code § 781 characterizes damages arising from a cause of action that one spouse has **"against the other spouse that arose during the marriage"** as the separate property of the injured spouse. Likewise remedies for economic torts based on a breach of fiduciary duty are the separate property of the recovering spouse. Cal.Fam.Code § 1101(g) and (h).

Forfeiture statutes exist throughout the family code to address interpersonal violence in the marital relationship. For example, conviction for the attempted murder of a spouse by the other spouse assigns to the injured spouse **"100 percent of the**

community property interest in the retirement and pension benefits of the injured spouse" in addition to whatever other property the injured spouse is statutorily entitled to, and (by reference to other statutes) attorney fees and court costs. Cal.Fam.Code § 782.5. See a more detailed discussion, see Jo Carrillo, *Financial Intimate Partner Violence: When Assets and Transactions Become Weapons*, 9(4) FAMILY & INTIMATE PARTNER VIOLENCE QUARTERLY 67 (2017).

3. IDAHO

Idaho Code § 32–903 provides that **"All property of either the husband or the wife owned by him or her before marriage, and that acquired afterward either by gift, bequest, devise or descent, or that which either he or she shall acquire with the proceeds of his or her separate property, by way of moneys or other property, shall remain his or her sole and separate property."**

On the issue of separate property revenues received during marriage, Idaho is a civil law state. Idaho Code § 32–906, discussed in Chapter 4, the basic community property statute, characterizes **"[t]he income, including the rents, issues, and profits, of all property, separate or community"** as community property during marriage even if there is no dispute about the separate property character of the underlying asset. For discussion of this section, see *Josephson v. Josephson*, 115 Idaho 1142, 772 P.2d 1236 (Ct. App. 1989), abrogated (on other grounds) by

Bell v. Bell, 122 Idaho 520, 835 P.2d 1331 (1992). Rents, issues, and profits received during may be transmuted from community to separate property during the marriage if **"both spouses, by written agreement specifically so providing, declare that . . . the income, including the rents, issues, and profits, from all or specifically designated separate property be the separate property of the spouse to whom the property belongs."** See Chapter 3 for more on transmutations.

Idaho Code § 32–909 characterizes the earnings and accumulations of **"the wife . . . while she is living separate from her husband [is] the separate property of the wife."** The gender specific language is a remnant of the male-management era. Biased statutory language was held unconstitutional in *Suter v. Suter*, 97 Idaho 461, 546 P.2d 1169 (1976), which also declared earnings after a date of separation to be the community property of the spouses.

Idaho case law initially classified personal injury recoveries as entirely community property. However, *Rogers v. Yellowstone Park Co.*, 97 Idaho 14, 539 P.2d 566 (1974), allowed an Idaho spouse who was married to an employee of the corporate defendant to recover damages for her own pain and suffering as her separate property. The court based its characterization upon the nature of the right violated and the interest damaged (medical expenses paid, future earnings lost, pain and suffering). In the same decision, the Idaho Supreme Court abolished the doctrine of interspousal immunity.

In *Runcorn v. Shearer Lumber Products, Inc.*, 107 Idaho 389, 690 P.2d 324 (1984), a non-injured spouse was permitted to recover for the negligent loss of consortium in a worker's compensation case, reduced by the percentage of negligence attributable to the injured spouse.

4. LOUISIANA

Louisiana defines separate property in a statute that lumps all the topics so far discussed. In LSA-C.C. Art. 2341 as property "**. . . acquired by a spouse prior to the establishment of a community property regime; property acquired by a spouse with separate things or with separate and community things when the value of the community things is inconsequential in comparison with the value of the separate things used; property acquired by a spouse by inheritance or donation to him individually; damages awarded to a spouse in an action for breach of contract against the other spouse or for the loss sustained as a result of fraud or bad faith in the management of community property by the other spouse; damages or other indemnity awarded to a spouse in connection with the management of his separate property; and things acquired by a spouse as a result of a voluntary partition of the community during the existence of a community property regime.**"

"**The natural and civil fruits of the separate property of a spouse, . . .**" are community property during the marriage, unless they are reserved under LSA-C.C. Art. 2339. After the marriage, these separate property natural and civil fruits return to the full ownership of the separate property that produced them.

Under LSA-C.C. Art. 2356 **"The legal regime of community property is terminated by the death or judgment of declaration of death of a spouse, declaration of the nullity of the marriage, judgment of divorce or separation of property, . . ."** or, alternatively if there is a **"[m]atrimonial agreement that terminates the community."** Matrimonial agreements are discussed in Chapter 2. This makes Louisiana a formal separation state, meaning that the date of separation must be established with a written instrument.

In Louisiana, the community estate, and not just the marriage itself, is terminated rather than dissolved. In other states, the marriage is terminated but the community estate is dissolved.

The practical effect of this linguistic distinction is that all property owned after the termination of the marriage (not just earnings and accumulations, as for example in California) is acquired as individually owned property. Thus, after the point deemed by a court to be the irretrievable and irreparable breakdown of the marriage, all property is individual property, meaning property not governed by the community property system. The closest equivalent of individually owned property in the matrimonial regime is separate property. See e.g., *Aufrichtig v.*

Aufrichtig, 796 So.2d 57 (2001) for a review of relevant cases and distinctions between dates of marriage, separation, and termination.

"[P]roperty acquired by a spouse by inheritance or donation to him individually; . . ." is separate property, again, under LSA-C.C. Art. 2341 which is reproduced above.

As discussed above, property jointly donated to both spouses by a third party is community property under LSA-C.C. Art. 2338, but as Revision Comments from 1979 indicate, if the spouses **"do not live in community,"** i.e., if they have agreed upon a contractual matrimonial regime in lieu of the legal one, then **"the donor may not create a community regime for the spouses. In such a case, the property given to them is separate property held in indivision."**

Generally, Louisiana adheres to many distinctions in the law of gifts. Gifts are labeled along a spectrum that ranges from a gratuity to a remunerative conferral of a benefit. For purposes of determining whether a third party's transfer to a donee spouse meets the definition of separate property, therefore, it may be necessary to analyze the factual context in which the transfer was made. Other states include in the definition of separate property only gratuitous transfers that meet the common law elements of a gift.

There is no case law indicating that Louisiana deviates from this approach, however, LSA-C.C. Art. 2343 provides that **"the donation by a spouse to**

the other spouse of his undivided interest in a thing forming part of the community transforms that interest into separate property of the donee. Unless otherwise provided in the act of donation, an equal interest of the donee is also transformed into separate property . . ." as are any of the **"natural and civil fruits of the thing . . ."** Here, "donation" seems to signify a gift. Thus, a gift from one spouse to the other transforms the donor spouse's one-half community property into the donee spouse's separate property. The donee spouse already owns one-half of community property; so, when the donee receives one-half of the donor's community property it is as the donee's separate property. This is how the donee comes into separate ownership of the whole (50% already owned + 50% received as a gift = 100%).

Louisiana has long recognized the distinctive elements of a personal injury action and has also been willing to characterize each part in accordance with the right violated. The recognition was maintained and extended to either spouse in LSA-C.C. Art. 2344, effective January 1, 1980.

As a general rubric, the statutory default holds as discussed above:

"Damages due to personal injuries sustained during the existence of the community by a spouse are separate property."

"Nevertheless, the portion of the damages attributable to expenses incurred by the community as a result of the injury, or in

compensation of the loss of community earnings, is community property. If the community regime is terminated otherwise than by the death of the injured spouse, the portion of the damages attributable to the loss of earnings that would have accrued after termination of the community property regime is the separate property of the injured spouse." This statute is intended to encompass "injuries to the personality of the injured spouse" and "work[er's] compensation benefits." Revision Comments—1979.

5. NEVADA

Nev. Const. Art. 4, § 31 provides, in part: **"All property, both real and personal, of a married person owned or claimed by such person before marriage, and that acquired afterward by gift, devise or descent, shall be the separate property of such person. . . ."**

The state constitutional provision is amplified by Nev.Rev.Stat. § 123.130 (effective July 1, 2017):

"All property of a spouse owned by him or her before marriage, and that was acquired by him or her afterwards by gift, bequest, devise, descent or by an award for personal injury damages, with the rents, issues and profits thereof, is his or her separate property."

Nev.Rev.Stat. § 123.180 provides that while the spouses are **"living separate and apart . . ."** the earnings of **"[a] minor child"** are the separate property of the custodial spouse. Nev.Rev.Stat.

§ 123.180, however, currently omits any reference to the earnings and accumulations of a spouse while living separate and apart from the other spouse. Nev.Rev.Stat. § 123.220, the general community property statute, fills the spouse-spouse gap by providing that all property during the marriage is community property up until **"[a] decree of separate maintenance issued . . . ."** *Forrest v. Forrest*, 99 Nev. 602, 668 P.2d 275 (1983) makes the same point. This rule structure in effect makes Nevada a formal separation state, like Arizona, that requires the separation to resolve in a dissolution. But unlike Arizona, in Nevada, the dissolution must additionally include a decree of separate maintenance.

Nevada has the most extensive legislation concerning the procedure for and effect of recording of a written inventory of the separate property of a married person. The applicable statutes include Nev.Rev.Stat. § 123.140 through Nev.Rev.Stat. § 123.160 (excerpted in Chapter 3 above).

Nevada's courts were among the first to judicially classify any part of a personal injury recovery as separate property. They are also among the first to judicially divide the recovery between separate and community in accordance with the right violated and the damage suffered. By stressing that community property, is acquired onerously the rationale was that personal injury recoveries are not necessarily community. It may take an enormous amount of effort to recover from a personal injury, *but the personal injury claim is not* acquired *onerously*.

So, for example, in *Los Angeles & S.L.R.R. v. Umbaugh*, 61 Nev. 214, 123 P.2d 224 (1942), the court ruled that a monetary recovery for the wrongful death of a child by one spouse does not fall within the meaning of the word "acquired" as used in the general community property statute. By this rationale, during marriage, money and property obtained as a recovery for an injury to one's person is conceptualized as a replacement or exchange for loss rather than as an onerous acquisition.

Nevertheless, the courts and the statutes concede that other aspects of a personal injury recovery like pain and suffering, loss of comfort, and whatever part of the award addresses loss of services and medical expenses are community in character.

In addition to Nev.Rev.Stat. § 123.130 quoted above, Nev.Rev.Stat. § 123.121 provides:

> **"When spouses sue jointly, any damages awarded shall be segregated as follows:**
>
> **1. If the action is for personal injuries, damages assessed for:**
>
> **(a) Personal injuries and pain and suffering, to the injured spouse as his or her separate property.**
>
> **(b) Loss of comfort and society, to the spouse who suffers such loss.**
>
> **(c) Loss of services and hospital and medical expenses, to the spouses as community property.**

2. If the action is for injury to property, damages shall be awarded according to the character of the injured property. Damages to separate property shall be awarded to the spouse owning such property, and damages to community property shall be awarded to the spouses as community property."

6. NEW MEXICO

N.M.Stat.Ann. § 40–3–8(A) (1978) defines separate property in the usual way.

A." 'Separate property' means:

(1) property acquired by either spouse before marriage or after entry of a decree of dissolution or marriage;

(2) property acquired after entry of a decree entered pursuant to Section 40–4–3 NMSA 1978, unless the decree provides otherwise;

(3) property designated as separate property by a judgment or decree of any court having jurisdiction;

(4) property acquired by either spouse by gift, bequest, devise or descent; and

(5) property designated as separate property by a written agreement between the spouses, including a deed or other written agreement concerning property held by the spouses as joint tenants or

tenants in common in which the property is designated as separate property."

N.M.Stat.Ann. § 40–4–3, noted above, is the statute on court sanctioned separation. It reads: **"Whenever the parties to a marriage have permanently separated and no longer live or cohabit together as a married couple, either may institute proceedings in the district court for a division of property, disposition of children or alimony without asking for or obtaining in the proceedings a dissolution of marriage."** Court sanctioned separation is the effectively the same as a legal separation.

Earnings after a date of separation but prior to a court sanctioned (legal) separation or divorce decree remain community property under general principles. New Mexico has no provision for the couple that is estranged (informally separated) but not yet legally separated.

New Mexico has enacted a Family Violence Protection Act (the NMFVPA for short) found at N.M. Stat. Ann. § 40–13–1 through § 40–13–6 (1978). The NMFVPA was passed in 1987. In 2001, amendments allowed for financial remedies and counseling programs. See N.M. Stat. Ann. § 40–13–5 (1978).

Otherwise, the no-fault principle prevails with respect to property matters between spouses. No-fault divorce was recognized as early as 1933—far earlier than in other community property states. Case law prohibits trial courts from considering fault when granting a divorce, dividing property, or awarding alimony. However, *Flores v. Flores*, 84 N.M. 601, 506 P.2d 345 (1973), held that one spouse has the legal right to sue the other spouse for an intentional tort that occurred during a period of separation. Alternatively, an interspousal motion for a protective order can be brought during the divorce process, by way of a motion for debt classification, pursuant to N.M. Stat. Ann. § 40–13–5 (1978), or by way of a tort claim filed after the marriage is terminated, as in Arizona.

N.M. Stat. Ann. § 40–3–8E (1978) follows the American-rule that separate property rents, issues, and profits are also separate property during marriage.

New Mexico has a relatively unenhanced treatment of the character of personal injury recoveries compared to other community property states. In *Soto v. Vandeventer*, 56 N.M. 483, 245 P.2d 826 (1952), where the spouse obtained a tort judgment against a third party, the New Mexico Supreme Court followed Nevada law to characterize the injured spouse's compensation for pain and suffering as separate property, and the compensation for medical expenses, earnings, and loss of service to the community as community property. *Soto*, supra, does not apply, however, unless and until community indebtedness for medical expenses is established: see *Flores*, supra. Subsequent cases extend the *Soto*, supra, rule; see e.g. *Baca v. Baca*, 71 N.M.468, 379 P.2d 765 (1963) (recovery for the wrongful death of a child).

7. TEXAS

Tex. Const. Art. XVI, § 15, as amended in 1948, 1980, 1987, and 1999, defines separate property as **"All property, both real and personal, of a spouse owned or claimed before marriage, and that acquired afterward by gift, devise or descent, shall be the separate property of that spouse; . . ."**

V.T.C.A.Fam.Code § 3.001 further provides:

"A spouse's separate property consists of:

(1) the property owned or claimed by the spouse before marriage;

(2) the property acquired by the spouse during marriage by gift, devise, or descent; and

(3) the recovery for personal injuries sustained by the spouse during marriage, except any recovery for loss of earning capacity during marriage."

To date, Texas follows the civil law ganancial rule of declaring rents, issues, and profits of separate property received during marriage to be community property during marriage. The key to this rule is the *absence* of the phrase "and rents, issues, and profits from separate property" in the constitutional provision that defines separate property. Currently, Texas has no statutory provision that clearly characterizes separate property income streams during marriage. However, case law has consistently interpreted the Texas Constitution to require that separate property rents, issues, and profits obtained during marriage be characterized as community property.

Texas has made various short-lived- and unsuccessful efforts to transition toward the American rule, which recognizes separate property rents, issues, and profits received during marriage as separate property during marriage.

Arnold v. Leonard, 114 Tex. 535, 273 S.W. 799 (1925) held unconstitutional two Texas statutes that attempted to move the state to the American rule. The court held that the Texas constitutional provisions describing the extent of a spouse's separate property rights contain an implied prohibition against the exercise of legislative power to change the specified circumstances in which property is defined as separate property. The rationale holds more generally as well because of reasons discussed in Chapter 1.

Over time, more statutes have been enacted to move Texas toward the American rule majority of U.S. community property states. But these statutes also have been eventually repealed. The result is that Texas continues in the civil law tradition as to rents, issues, and profits derived from separate property during marriage: each is community property.

A proposed constitutional amendment recently in the works did not pass. The amendment would have given courts discretion ("may" instead of "shall") to partition the community property so that once partitioned "the future income from that property" could be characterized as the separate property of a spouse to whom it was assigned.

On a related point, Tex. Const. Art. XVI, § 15 currently permits that spouses may **"agree [in writing] between themselves that the income or property from all or part of the separate property then owned or which thereafter might be acquired by only one of them, shall be the separate property of that spouse."** Moreover, if a spouse makes a gift of separate property to the other spouse, **"that gift is presumed to include all the income or property which might arise from that gift of property."** Thus, a gratuitous transmutation (a true gift) of the underlying separate property will automatically include any future rents, issues, and profits that the property might produce. See Chapter 3 for more on transmutations.

Although V.T.C.A.Fam.Code § 3.001(a)(3), reproduced above, resolves the split character of two elements of a personal injury action, it does not mention reimbursements for proven medical expenses. Case law characterizes lost wages, medical expenses, and other injury related community expenses as community property damages in a divorce action. *Cottone v. Cottone,* 122 S.W.3d 211 (2003), *Wilson v. Wilson*, 132 S.W.3d 533 (2004).

In *Graham v. Franco*, 488 S.W.2d 390 (1972), the Texas Supreme Court upheld the constitutionality of V.T.C.A.Fam.Code § 3.001(a)(3) while declining to define a tort cause of action as transferable property. There, the medical reimbursement element of the recovery was characterized as community in character, but the court also indicated, the pain, suffering and disfigurement elements of the recovery are the separate property of the injured spouse. This view has been followed recently by *Harrell v. Hochderffer*, 345 S.W.3d 652 (2011), where damages for disfigurement, past and future mental anguish, and past and future physical pain and suffering were characterized as separate property of the injured spouse.

In *Whittlesey v. Miller*, 572 S.W.2d 665 (1978), a wife's recovery for loss of consortium was held to result from her independent action, and thus separate in character. Also, such an action was permitted notwithstanding the husband's settlement with the tortfeasor. In *Reed Tool Co. v. Copelin*, 610 S.W.2d 736 (1980), even though the wife's claim against her husband's employer for the negligent loss of consortium was dismissed as derivative under the worker's compensation act, her claim for the *intentional* loss of consortium was allowed. The rationale was that such a recovery would be separate property under V.T.C.A.Fam.Code § 3.001, subject to the wife's exclusive management and control, and thus it was non-derivative.

8. WASHINGTON

Washington's statutes are distinctive in that they do not define separate property so much as they describe incidents of separateness. Wash.Rev.Code has distinct but identical provisions for spouses and domestic partners.

Wash.Rev.Code § 26.16.010 **Separate property of a spouse** provides:

"Property and pecuniary rights owned by a spouse before marriage and that acquired by him or her afterwards by gift, bequest, devise, descent, or inheritance, with the rents, issues and profits thereof, shall not be subject to the debts or contracts of his or her spouse, and he or she may manage, lease, sell, convey, encumber or devise by will such property without his or her spouse joining in such management, alienation or encumbrance, as fully, and to the same extent or in the same manner as though he or she were unmarried." This provision brings Washington into the majority of U.S. community property states that follow the American rule characterizing separate property rents, issues, and profits as themselves separate property even when acquired during marriage.

Wash.Rev.Code § 26.16.020 extends this same language to domestic partners.

Wash.Rev.Code § 26.16.140 provides that if **"spouses or domestic partners"** are **"living separate and apart"** their respective earnings and accumulations are to be characterized as the accumulator's separate property. Washington courts have held that physical separation alone does not establish a date of separation. Rather, "the test is whether by the parties, in conduct have exhibited a decision to renounce the community, with no intention of ever resuming the marital relationship." *Oil Heat Co. of Port Angeles v. Sweeney*, 26

Wash.App. 351, 354, 613 P.2d 169 (1980). A date of separation does not hinge on proof of an intent to divorce; rather it hinges on far more qualitative proof that the parties no longer have "the will to union," a standard discussed in *Estate of Nikiporez*, 19 Wash.App. 231, 574 P.2d 1204, *rev. denied*, 90 Wash.2d 1013 (1978).

In Washington, a chose in action (the right to bring a lawsuit in state or federal court) was historically within the definition of property. *Hawkins v. Front St. Cable Ry. Co.*, 3 Wash. 592, 28 P. 1021 (1892), a case where a husband alone sued a streetcar company for damages suffered by his wife as a result of the streetcar driver's negligence. The defendant streetcar company sought to amend the complaint to include the wife; it argued that husband had suffered no damages and could not recover for the wife's injuries. The trial court refused to include the wife; instead, it instructed the jury that the husband could recover for the wife even if she were not a party to the action. The Supreme Court of Washington discussed the common law as it functions within the Washington community property system before holding that because *all* property acquired during marriage except by gift, bequest, or devise is community property, a chose in action acquired during marriage must fall within the definition of community property. The court supported its argument by reference to the (then) law of California. (Under current California law, a personal injury cause of action property is no longer regarded as transferable property, as discussed above.)

Later cases suggest a reform of the view expressed in *Hawkins*, supra. *Marriage of Brown*, 100 Wash.2d 729, 739, 675 P.2d 1207 (1984) held that because Wash.Rev.Code § 26.16.030 (the basic community property statute) applies only to onerous acquisitions of property during marriage; a personal injury cause of action is not onerous, as discussed above. It is separate property, "except to the extent the recovery compensates the community for lost wages, which would have been community property or injury-related expenses, which the community incurred." Id. at 730.

A statutory change on the issue of interspousal immunity ensued after *Freehe*, supra. This happened when the state transitioned from contributory negligence to comparative negligence and abolished the community property defense by statutes that took effect in 1974. Wash.Rev.Code § 4.22.020 now provides that **"[t]he contributory fault of one spouse or one domestic partner shall not be imputed to the other spouse or other domestic partner . . . to diminish recovery in an action by the other spouse or other domestic partner . . . , or his or her legal representative, to recover damages caused by fault resulting in death or in injury to the person or property, whether separate or community, of the spouse or domestic partner. In an action brought for wrongful death or loss of consortium, the contributory fault of the decedent or injured person shall be imputed to the claimant in that action."**

9. WISCONSIN

To repeat a definition from the general section of this Chapter, in Wisconsin, a married couple's "determination date" is the last date to occur of the following:

- marriage; or
- the establishment of a marital domicile in Wisconsin; or
- January 1, 1986.

Wis.Stat. § 766.31, titled **"Classification of Property of Spouses"** and discussed in Chapter 4 controls. The statute creates three basic property classifications:

- Marital property, which is the equivalent of community property.
- Individual property, which is the equivalent of separate property.
- "Predetermination date property" (also called "unclassified property"), which is all property of spouses is presumed to be marital unless classified otherwise by the spouses or by statute.

"Predetermination date property" is property acquired by one or both spouses prior to their determination date (i.e., prior to the date on which the marital property law first applies to them). This could be prior to marriage, prior to establishing a domiciled in Wisconsin, or (a category of now superseded cases no doubt) prior to Wisconsin's adoption of the Uniform Marital Property Act (UMPA 1983).

Wis.Stat. § 766.31, parallels UMPA 1983 in its basic classification statute, and it adds important specifications:

1. **Trusts:** Wisconsin's statute specifies that a trust distribution of principal or income received during marriage from a trust created by a third person to one spouse is the individual property of that spouse unless the trust provides otherwise. See Wis.Stat. § 766.31(7)(a) above.

2. **Personal injury recoveries:** Wisconsin treats as marital property any amount of personal injury damages attributable to the loss of income during marriage. At the death of the injured spouse any such amounts become the individual property of the surviving spouse. These points are discussed above.

3. **Written consents:** Wisconsin sharply reduced the circumstances under which a "written consent" (a document signed by a person against whose interests it is sought to be enforced) may be used to reclassify marital property into individual property. Such a consent may be used only in relation to life insurance policies; still, a written consent nevertheless remains a valuable planning device for insurance assets. Note however that Wisconsin does authorize marital property agreements, as discussed in Chapter 4.

4. **Unilateral statement for adopting the American rule for individual (separate)**

property rents, issues, and profits: Wisconsin authorizes a legal document analogous to the Louisiana approach of allowing a naked owner to reserve, by written instrument, the right of usufruct to individual (separate) property rents, issues, and profits. The default rule in Wisconsin is that post determination- date rents, issues, and profits from either predetermination date property or individual property are characterized as marital (analogous to community) property by default during marriage.

However, the individual (meaning separate) character of rents, issues, and profits from individual property can be preserved. To do so, an owner must follow statutory formalities for producing a unilateral statement of intent specific to the specific individual (separate) property and the revenues (rents, issues, and profits) that it produces. The statement must be signed, acknowledged before a notary public, and served by delivery or certified mail to the other spouse.

5. **Income from interspousal gifts:** Wis.Stat. § 766.31(10) attempts to avoid adverse death tax results.

With respect to property rights Wis.Stat. § 766.31(8) provides that the basic rule **"does not alter the classification and ownership rights of property acquired before the determination date or ... after the determination date in exchange for or with the proceeds of property acquired before the determination date."** Wis.Stat. § 766.31(9) that property **"is treated as if it were individual property."** This rule focuses in on property acquired during marriage. If that property traces back to separate property, it is separate property. If it traces back to predetermination date property (individual property), it is classified as predetermination date property, meaning individual property.

Wis.Stat. § 766.31(7) defines individual, me (analogous to separate, property) as:

> **"Property acquired by a spouse during marriage and after the determination date is individual property if acquired by any of the following means:**
>
> **(a) By gift during lifetime or by a disposition at death by a 3rd person to that spouse and not to both spouses. A distribution of principal or income from a trust created by a 3rd person to one spouse is the individual property of that spouse unless the trust provides otherwise.**
>
> **(b) Except as provided in s.766.625(2)(b)1., in exchange for or with the proceeds of other individual property of the spouse.**
>
> **(c) From appreciation of the spouse's individual property except to the extent that the appreciation is classified as marital property under s. 766.63.**

(d) By a decree or marital property agreement or reclassification agreement under sub (10) designating it as the individual property of the spouse.

(e) As a recovery for damage to property under s. 766.70, except as specifically provided otherwise in a decree or marital property agreement.

(f) As a recovery for personal injury except for the amount of that recovery attributable to expenses paid or otherwise satisfied from marital property and except for the amount attributable to loss of income during marriage. . . ."

(g) By classification under s. 766.625(2), designating an account and the digital property in an account, including the content of electronic communications, as defined in s. 711.036(6), as the individual property of the holding spouse.

To reiterate the rule of the subsections in more accessible language.

A gift made by a third party to one spouse alone is individual property of the donee spouse. *In re Czerneski*, 330 B.R. 240 (Bkrtcy. E.D. Wis. 2005).

Subsection (a) also sidesteps the multiple-party accounts problems that can arise when trust distributions are deposited into a bank account by the trustee or by the trust beneficiary. Rather than use the multiple-party bank account rules, Subsection (a) focuses on the distributions. Unless the trust document provides otherwise, those distributions are classified as individual property. Despite this change of focus from the place deposited to the distribution, it continues to be easy to commingle trust distributions with marital property. Anytime it is easy to commingle property, it is just as easy to reach the point of confusion, a point at which automatic transmutation occurs. It is unclear whether confusion would shift to the analysis toward the multiple-party accounts laws.

Subsection (b) classifies as individual property anything that is exchanged for or purchased with sales proceeds from individual property. Whether property can be traced back to individual property is a question of fact. The finding of which will be upheld unless it is clearly erroneous. The issue here is one of identity. Was the claimed property exchanged for or purchased with individual property? Tracing method is a question of law.

Subsection (f) characterizes money and property received in settlement of a personal injury claim as individual property with exceptions for loss of income, as discussed below.

Subjection (g) is new legislation on digital property, a topic on which Wisconsin leads the way.

At a spouse's death **"[t]o the extent that marital property includes damages for loss of future**

income arising from a personal injury claim of a surviving spouse, the surviving spouse is entitled to receive as individual property that portion of the award that represents an income substitute after the death of the other spouse." Wis.Stat. § 766.31(7m).

As noted above, Wisconsin follows the civil law rule that separate property rents, issues, and profits obtained during marriage are marital property. But, at least with respect to interspousal gifts, if one spouse makes a gift of the revenue producing property it is accepted as individual (separate) property; so too is the revenue of that individual (separate) property characterized as individual (separate) property. **"If a spouse gives property to the other spouse and intends at the time the gift is made that the property be the individual property of the donee spouse, the income from the property is the individual property of the donee spouse unless a contrary intent of the donor spouse regarding the classification of income is established."** Wis.Stat. § 766.31(10).

D. QUESTION AND ANSWER

(1) Before her marriage to H, W is an employee of ABC Corp., and W owns 100 shares of ABC Corp. stock.

(2) During marriage, W receives 100 additional shares of ABC Corp. in a 2-for-1 split.

(3) The next year, W receives 10 additional ABC Corp. shares as a 5% stock dividend.

(4) Additionally, the value of ABC Corp. rose due to two factors: the intrinsic value of the business and inflation.

(5) ABC Corp. declared cash dividends of $5,000 each in years 3, 4 and 5 of W's and H's marriage. In these same years, there were no stock splits or dividends.

(6) W earned a salary for professional services in the amount of $100,000 for each of years 1 through 5.

(7) W earned pension benefits in the form of investments in a general account managed by ABC Corp., for each of years 1 through 5.

(8) During marriage, W is injured by a negligent driver. She settles her personal injury claim against that driver for $10,000.

Characterize each of the eight elements above as community (CP) or separate property (SP).

Assume:

General community property principles apply.

There are no marital agreements nor (where permitted) unilateral declarations between W and H as to the character of the above elements.

W and H are still married.

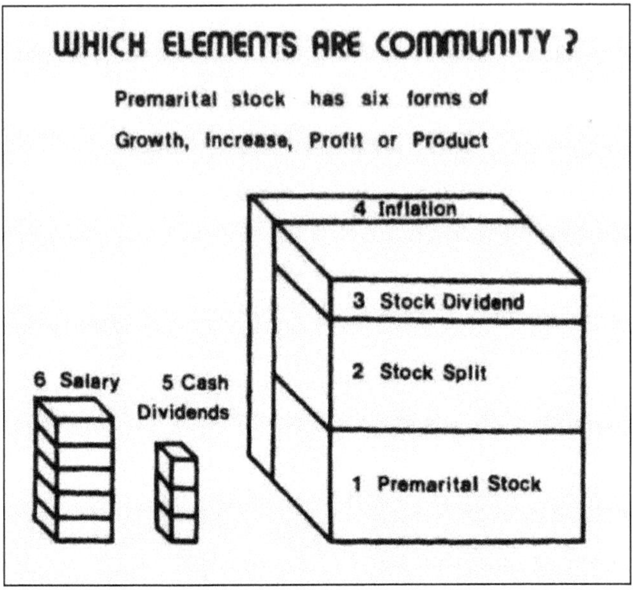

1. SP: The 100 shares of stock W owned before marriage are W's separate property.

2. SP: The 2-for-1 stock split is a "mere" change in form. Although the additional 100 shares are received during marriage, the additional 100 shares trace back to the original 100 shares of stock, which are separate property in character. Thus, the additional 100 shares of ABC Corp. stock are W's separate property.

3. SP: The stock dividends here took the form of additional shares of the company. Sometimes stock dividends look more like an income item (especially when cash dividends alternate with it), but stock

dividends tend to be classified as a change in form rather than as rents, issues, or profits. Thus, the additional 10 shares that make up the 5% stock dividend trace back to W's separate property, making those 10 shares separate property.

4. SP: The increase due to inflation is not a change in form. The principle is that an unrealized change in value does not alter the character of the property. The value of the shares fluctuates from market day to market day, but any fluctuation does not change the separate property character of the underlying shares. Thus, W continues to own 210 shares of ABC Corp. stock as her separate property no matter its value (up or down) on a particular market day.

5. CHARACTERIZATION DEPENDS ON THE JURISDICTION: Cash dividends, once distributed, fall within the definition of rents, issues, and profits. Here, the income producing asset is W's separate property. In the American rule majority (Arizona, California, Nevada, New Mexico, and Washington), the cash dividends distributed by the ABC Corp. during marriage are the separate property income of W's 210 separate property shares of ABC Corp. stock as such the dividends are characterized as W's separate property. In the minority civil law states (Idaho, Louisiana, Texas and Wisconsin) the cash dividends, although derived from W's separate property ABC stock holdings, are characterized as community property during the marriage.

6. CP: In all the community property states, income earned from any onerous source (salary,

wages, tips, barter) is community property if acquired during the marriage while domiciled in the state.

7. COMMINGLED: In all community property states, deferred earnings, including pension rights, are community property if earned during marriage. Here, because W was employed by ABC Corp. before and during marriage, her pension benefits are commingled and subject to apportionment. Apportionment will likely follow the time rule: W's separate property share of ABC Corp. pension benefits can be calculated by dividing the number of years W was employed by ABC before marriage by the total number of years she was employed by ABC Corp. The community property share of W's pension benefits will be calculated by dividing the number of years W was employed by ABC during marriage by the total number of years W was employed by ABC Corp. See Chapter 7.

8. CHARACTERIZATION DEPENDS ON THE JURISDICTION: In some states, W's personal injury settlement is her separate property. In other states, because the cause of action arose during the marriage and was obtained during the marriage, the personal injury settlement is community property. Among the former group of states, any part of the recovery that compensates for loss of income may be characterized as community property, depending on state law. Among the latter group of states, some may deem W's personal injury recovery a special type of community property mandatorily assignable to the injured spouse in the event of dissolution.

CHAPTER 6

JOINT TENANCY MEETS COMMUNITY PROPERTY

A. OVERVIEW

Common law concurrent title forms—specifically the *joint tenancy with the right of survivorship* title and the *tenancy in common* title—are not part of the community property system. Their origin is the English common law system. Even so, married persons in most U.S. community property states are not precluded from using either of these two title forms.

In a community property system, common law joint form titles are most often allowed to work as designed.

But when a marriage ends by dissolution, not death, legal confusion has and sometimes still does arise.

But before we discuss problems, here is an inventory of concurrent title forms—also called joint form titles—and their origin.

1. TYPES OF JOINT FORM TITLES

Concurrent titles and their origin:

Tenancy in common [TIC]	Common law origin
Joint tenancy with the right of survivorship [JTWROS]	Common law origin
Tenancy by the entirety [TBE]	Common law origin
Community property [CP]	Civil law origin
Community property with the right of survivorship [CPWROS]	A contemporary hybrid title first enacted in California
Homestead right [HR]	Texas community property origin

a. Tenancy in Common

Tenancy in common (TIC for short) is the default concurrent title for real estate.

A TIC is designed so that two or more persons—referred to herein as "joint tenants" or "tenants"—can own property while continuing to retain individual rights of devise and descent to the titled asset. An added feature of the TIC is that parties can own the property in unequal shares. With a TIC title, if one tenant dies, his or her proportional share of the TIC titled asset passes through a probate process, whether by devise or by intestate succession (if the decedent does not have a valid will).

Illustration 6.1: H and W acquire title to Blackacre during marriage in fee simple absolute as tenants in common (TIC). H devises Blackacre to C. Assume H dies before W. Upon H's death, H's one-half interest in Blackacre passes through H's estate to C. The result is that C and W own Blackacre as tenants in common.

b. Joint Tenancy with the Right of Survivorship

Joint tenancy with the right of survivorship (JTWROS for short) is the opt-in common law concurrent title for real estate.

A JTWROS is designed so that two or more people can own property together under an agreement that each will waive his or her testamentary rights to the titled property in exchange for a guaranteed right of survivorship. One requirement of the JTWROS title is that parties hold equal shares.

The joint tenants' agreement is recited in the deed itself with whatever language state law requires. At common law four unities were required to create the JTWROS title: unity of (1) time, (2) title, (3) interest, and (4) possession. Some states, like California, still require the four unities to be met, but they also relax the unity of time in cases where a person who already has title to the property conveys it *to themself and the other person* (or persons) as JTWROS (for example, *O to O and A as joint tenants with the right of survivorship*).

Assume that two persons acquire property during marriage in JTWROS. The title is designed so that when the first joint tenant dies, his or her interest in the asset automatically (without the need for court action) vanishes, and the surviving tenant automatically (again, without the need for court action) steps into ownership of the whole property outside of a probate process and free of the claims of the decedent's estate or heirs.

Illustration 6.2: H and W acquire Blackacre during marriage in fee simple absolute as JTWROS. Assume H dies before W. H devises his share in the property to C. At H's death, H's interest vanishes, and W automatically becomes the sole owner of Blackacre by right of survivorship. As to Blackacre, H's estate and heirs, including H's beneficiary C, have no claim against W for ownership of the property.

c. Tenancy by the Entirety

Tenancy by the entirety (TBE for short) refers to a common law marital title. The TBE is designed as a unitary title, meaning that it is not a concurrent title with two owners, but rather a single title owned by the marital entity. The TBE can only be created in roughly half of the 41 common law title states, and then only by those married couples who expressly opt to use it.

To create a TBE, five unities are required: (1) title, (2) time, (3) interest, (4) possession, and (5) marriage.

A TBE cannot be created in any of the community property jurisdictions and, to be fair, it is not needed in them. The TBE is a sort-of opt-in version of the automatically acquired community property title. However, once a TBE is validly created in a state that allows its use, it can be recognized as valid in the community property state where the parties seek dissolution, depending on countervailing state policies that protect creditors' rights.

The Texas homestead, discussed below, has been more accurately likened to a TBE because it (too) requires five unities, and the parties must opt into the use of the homestead option. The Texas homestead is not a common law interest so much as it is a distinct interest created by the Texas Constitution to allow married couples to shield their concurrently held family home from the reach of a decedent spouse's creditors.

d. Community Property

Community property is the community property system default title. The use of the *community property* title (CP title for short) is restricted to married persons (and, in some community property states, to registered domestic partners) who are domiciled in the state when the titled asset is acquired. With the traditional CP title, both spouses own the asset during their lifetimes; at the death of one spouse, his or her one-half interest passes by devise or intestate succession.

Illustration 6.3: H and W are married and domiciled in a community property state. They acquire Blackacre (wherever situated) taking a CP title. H devises his CP title interest in Blackacre to a third party, D. Assume H dies before W. Upon H's death, H's one-half CP interest in Blackacre passes to D through a probate process. The consequence is that D and W own Blackacre as tenants in common (since W and D are not married). (Spousal and family protections may delay D's rights to seek partition of the property.)

The CP title form, as to any state, can only be acquired by persons who are married to each. other.

e. Community Property with the Right of Survivorship

Community property with the right of survivorship title (CPWROS for short) is restricted to those community property states that permit its creation by statute, and (within those states) to married couples and (in some states) registered domestic partners. See for example Cal.Civ.Code § 682.1.

The CPWROS is a hybrid title form insofar as it applies the right of survivorship to the CP title. CPWROS allows spouses to waive testamentary rights with respect to the titled asset in exchange for a right of survivorship. At death, the property is characterized as community property, but the decedent spouse's interest vanishes, leaving the surviving spouse to automatically step into ownership of the whole.

Illustration 6.4: H and W are married and domiciled in a community property state. They acquire title to Blackacre in fee simple absolute using a CPWROS title. Assume H dies before W. At H's death, H's interest vanishes at his death, and W automatically becomes the sole owner of Blackacre by right of survivorship. W takes outside of the probate process, free of the claims of H's estate and heirs.

f. Homestead Rights

A *homestead right* allows a spouse to exempt certain property from forced sale for the payment of the other spouse's debts, typically those debts not related to a purchase money mortgage, taxes, and some contractors' liens.

Texas, Idaho, and Nevada create a homestead, either by constitution or by statute, between the spouses from community property (or possibly even from the separate property). Idaho and Nevada do so by statute. Wisconsin, by statute, authorizes something like the Texas homestead right. Wisconsin calls its family protection "survivorship marital property."

Texas, by state constitutional provision, gives the surviving spouse the right to establish a homestead in community or (even) in separate property. The homestead right is a vested property right, not just a personal exemption to keep property out of the reach of creditors, but it is often referred to as an "exemption." Its duration can be for the lifetime of the surviving spouse.

Tex. Const. Art XVI, § 16 states the parameters of the homestead right. Interpretive Commentary explains the purpose of the homestead right as being to preserve the integrity of the family as the basic unit of society; to provide the family with a home notwithstanding certain debts; and to allow "pioneers a sense of freedom and independence." *Id.*

The first Texas homestead exemption was passed with no debate in 1839. But the creditors' lobby quickly took notice and annulled the exemption in February 1840. By December 1840, the exemption was reenacted. When Texas was annexed by the U.S., the constitutional convention enshrined the homestead in the state's Constitution of 1845, Art. VII, § 22 (42 votes in favor; 14 votes against) to protect it from the vagaries of state politics.

Other states, like California, do not enshrine a homestead right in the state constitution. Instead, married couples can choose to opt into one of the two available survivorship title forms (the JTWROS or the CPRWOS) if they want a titled asset to pass automatically upon the death of a spouse to the surviving spouse. Today California is a lien theory state, so the surviving spouse must assume any purchase money loans and taxes owed upon the death of the decedent spouse. The right of survivorship allows property to pass outside of probate. The legal consequence of a nonprobate transfer is that the surviving spouse is protected from the decedent spouse's probate creditors.

All community property states employ probate code family protections that could be labeled homestead rights; however, most state protections are enacted by statute, not enshrined in the state constitution (as in Texas).

2. COMMON LAW CONCURRENT TITLES IN A COMMUNITY PROPERTY SYSTEM

Joint titles are the point at which the common law system routinely gets overlaid onto the community property system.

It is not uncommon for married persons to hold property using common law concurrent titles (the TIC and the JTWROS, assuming JTWROS title creation is permitted in the jurisdiction), or some combination thereof. In fact, in vertically developed urban areas, like San Francisco, one building may be held in various forms of joint titles and sole titles, as supplemented by contracts.

Still, as discussed above, TIC and JTWROS have their historical origin in the English common law system, meaning that they are outside of any community property system, traditional or modern. Technically, common law concurrent titles are characterized as concurrently owned separate property. The CP title form, by contrast, has its historical origin in the continental European community property system. The CP or CPWROS titles are also concurrently owned, but they are characterized as community property in the event of dissolution and death.

States have attempted to close the conceptual gap between the common law concurrent and the community property title forms in at least four ways.

The first strategy a state might use is to enable the use of CPWROS in the hope that more married couples will use it.

The second is to steer married property owners away from using the JTRWOS title by raising the bar for opting into it. Here the idea is to direct married property owners either to a CP or a CPWROS title or its equivalent such as the homestead right.

The third is to treat joint titles (and especially the JTWROS) as community property in character for all purposes unless the separate property proponent can produce evidence that the married title holders had a contrary intent.

The fourth is to enable a special community property presumption that characterizes common law joint titles as community property for purposes of a dissolution proceeding. The presumption, because it is an evidentiary assist for the community, is rebuttable by the separate property proponent.

Most appreciating or costly assets like realty, stock certificates, vehicles, and boats have documents of title. Spouses commonly hold assets in joint title, whether by deed, registration, or even the will of a third-party testator.

Document recitals that meet state JTWROS requirements for creation are prima facie evidence of this agreement between the beneficial title holders: the parties will own the property concurrently until the death of the first title holder, at which point the property will pass to the survivor outside of probate.

Why is this a nonprobate transfer? Because at death, the deceased title holder's interest disappears, and the surviving title holder automatically steps into ownership of the whole, as noted above.

Automatic here means without the need for a court judgment. To be sure, after the death of the first tenant, the title must ultimately be changed to reflect the change in ownership. But this can be done privately. A court process is not needed to change the title. Neither is it needed to confirm the title change.

This is the parties' agreement if the marriage ends by death. But—and this is a big but—what happens if the marriage ends by divorce?

JTWROS recitals do not necessarily reflect the spouses' intentions or expectations as to the character of the titled asset if the marriage ends by dissolution.

Consider these scenarios.

- The spouses take a JTWROS title to avoid probate if one of them dies. But they are uninformed or misinformed as to how the title might function if the marriage ends by divorce.
- The spouses take a JTWROS title to avoid probate if one of them dies. But they have conflicting unspoken intentions about what the character of the property should be if the marriage ends by divorce.
- The spouses take a JTWROS title only because they believe the property is owned by one spouse, and they want the other spouse to be able (or required) to act as an agent.

The joint bank account, while not a true JTWROS can create similar and additional problems. See Chapter 7 for details on bank accounts.

Here are some bank account basics.

- A bank account is different than an investment account.
- A bank account is an asset, the ownership of which is determined by the title to the account.
- The sums on deposit in the account are an asset, the ownership of which is determined by deposits.
- Community property sums flow to and through bank accounts. Separate property sums may too. Therefore, sums on deposit in a simple depository bank account are easily commingled during marriage by the act of depositing money.
- Assets that are purchased with sums on deposit withdrawn from a bank account may, depending on the case, take on the character of the purchase funds.
- A safe-deposit box signature card, in some cases, may raise questions about the community or separate character of any item in the box, and especially of untitled items like rings and heirlooms. This happens, for example, when a joint rental agreement declares that the box *and its contents* are held in "joint tenancy." Contemporary law tends to

subject the box and each of its contents to distinct legal analysis; but a common error is to assume that ownership of the box determines ownership of its contents.

B. DETAIL

1. PREVALENCE OF THE COMMON LAW JOINT TENANCY TITLE FORM

With an expensive trust, parties can avoid the cost, delay, publicity, and inconvenience of probate administration with respect to the assets held in the trust. For relatively little expense, a JTWROS title can serve the same purpose of avoiding probate, but only as to the titled asset. For that reason, a JTWROS title is considered a useful asset-specific estate planning tool.

In the typical situation, the family home is the married couple's single most valuable asset. Often that asset has been purchased with a purchase money loan that is being repaid during marriage with community property earnings. Because of the importance of the asset to the family, the couple may be given to understand that they should take title to the asset in both of their names, "in case one of them dies." Their express intentions are that if the marriage should end by the death of a spouse, the titled asset will fall outside of the decedent spouse's probate estate.

Normally the legal and tax ramifications of the choice between the JTWROS and CP title forms are not apparent to the parties at the time of the transaction, a time when they are married and (obviously) still alive. The ramifications (only) become clear later in time when the marriage ends.

But if the marriage ends by dissolution the issue will be whether the JTWROS asset is community property or concurrently owned separate property. One would assume that the value of the asset would be split equally between the spouses, but if the asset is community property that will depend on state law. Take a state like Arizona: if the asset is deemed community in character, equitable (not equal) division is the rule. If it is deemed a concurrently owned separate property JTWROS, equal division is the rule by design of the title. Additionally, a JTWROS could raise management and control issues, as well as, in some states, questions about the court's jurisdiction to partition the asset.

If the marriage ends by death, the concurrent title will function as designed as designed. Common law titles will be characterized as separate property. CP titles will be characterized as community property. The parties' intentions will be furthered, but there may be additional benefits/consequences like those discussed below.

2. JOINT TENANCY COMPARED WITH COMMUNITY PROPERTY

JTWROS, TIC, CP and CPWROS may be regarded as distinct in a community property state for one purpose or another.

Some states, like California, give married couples who want a joint title the option to choose between JTWROS, TIC, CP title, or CPWROS for purposes of disposition at death. Other states, like Washington, use doctrinal crossover methods by which the severed JTWROS of two married persons defaults to CP title rather than to TIC (as would be the case in a common law jurisdiction).

Arizona, California, Idaho, Nevada, and Washington permit the CPWROS title form or its equivalent if the spouses expressly opt into it. Wisconsin, with its concept of survivorship marital property, is the exception to the opt-in rule. Texas uses the homestead right to exempt property from the reach of the decedent spouse's conveyees and general creditors.

Only the use of CPWROS or Wisconsin survivorship marital property make clear that the spouses acquired the asset with the intention (i) that it be characterized as community at dissolution or death and (ii) that the survivor be guaranteed ownership of the whole by right of survivorship. And only the Texas homestead makes clear that, while survivorship is feature of the homestead, its real purpose is to protect the homestead from the decedent spouse's creditors.

Moreover, on its face, a JTWROS recital in a deed may be interpreted to indicate that the spouses opted *for* the JTWROS form and *against* the (traditional) CP title form. But the face of a deed and the parties' intentions as to why they decided to use one deed form instead of another may be remembered quite differently in the event of a dissolution. For that reason, some states (Idaho) place very little trust in using deed recitation language as the basis for a default rule.

At dissolution, a community property state can express and recognize a strong public policy interest in furthering equity between the spouses. If so, the state can enact a special presumption or other type of rule that treats common law joint titles—the JTWROS and the TIC—as community in character *for purposes of the dissolution proceeding only*.

At the death of a spouse a JTWROS recital better captures the parties' expectations, namely that the survivor would take automatic ownership outside of probate. (The non-hybrid traditional CP title transfers by probate, not by right of survivorship.) Therefore, the historical tendency has been to interpret JTWROS recitals as separate property in character. This leaves it to the community property proponent to prove that notwithstanding the separate character of the JTWROS deed, the parties transmuted the asset from separate to community property. Transmutation formalities apply, meaning that any alleged rebuttal agreement would have to comply with the state transmutation rules, as discussed in Chapter 3.

But if the surviving spouse steps into ownership of the whole at the other spouse's death, what else would motivate a surviving spouse to argue that a JTWROS should be community property in character?

One answer is income tax valuation.

When a marriage ends by the death of a spouse, the surviving spouse may eventually sell the titled asset. The Internal Revenue Service rules for calculating the basis of an asset in the decedent's gross estate work out so that a JTWROS asset produces more income tax liability for the surviving spouse than does a CP titled asset. See the Illustrations below.

Among the contexts in which there is a heightened risk of litigation over the characterization of joint form titles are the following:

a. Dissolution Proceedings

If state law allows a court to award the separate property of one party to the other; or if state law provides that the division of community property upon divorce shall be "equal" (50–50); or if fault has been eliminated as a basis for the apportionment or division of spouses' property, then the character of concurrently held property may have little practical relevance.

However, in states where the court does not have jurisdiction over separate property in a dissolution proceeding, character questions may become more pressing.

b. Severance

A JTWROS can be severed (terminated) by one spouse acting alone. Severing the JTWROS cancels the right of survivorship, but it does not necessarily end the concurrent ownership between the spouses unless the severance is by conveyance to a third party.

If one spouse severs a JTWROS title by conveying his or her interest to him or herself (through a straw person or directly if permitted by state law), then the two spouses continue as concurrent owners, but without the right of survivorship. The severance means that the title form defaults to TIC, in most states. Or, as in Washington, to CP title. See Section C, Washington, Wash.Rev.Code § 64.28.040.

Severance is, therefore, a consequential transaction between the spouses for how it restores each spouse's rights of devise and descent as to the titled asset.

c. Probate Law Interaction

A salient difference between the four concurrent title forms becomes clear when a marriage ends by the death of one of the spouses.

Assets titled as JTWROS and CPWROS are owned by the surviving spouse without being subject to probate administration. For these titles, the right of survivorship ensures as much.

Assets titled in TIC or CP title are subject to the whole of probate administration unless a probate code statute provides the surviving spouse with an exception or exemption.

Probate assets are subject to the claims of the decedent spouse's creditors, beneficiaries, and nonspousal heirs.

d. Tax Consequences of a Sale After Death

Another salient distinction between the types of joint form titles pertains to how the character of property owned by the first spouse to die can affect the income tax liability of the surviving spouse who sells the property.

Generally, the gain from the sale of property is computed by subtracting the seller's basis from the amount realized in the sale. I.R.C. § 1001. When property is acquired by a surviving spouse (the income taxpayer) from a decedent spouse, the income taxpayer's adjusted basis in the property is **"the fair market value of the property at the date of the decedent's death."** l. I.R.C. §§ 1014(a) and 1014(b)(6).

For the income taxpayer, if his or her spouse holds JTWROS titles at death, those properties are subject to inclusion in the decedent's gross estate. The taxpayer "acquires" that property from the decedent only to the extent that the JTWROS property is included in the decedent's gross estate. As set forth in I.R.C. § 2040, the taxpayer's basis is equal to what the decedent claimed on the estate tax return.

I.R.C. § 2040 labels a joint tenancy title where the decedent and the spouse are the only joint tenants, as a qualified joint interest. It further specifies that the value included in the gross estate for that property **"is one-half the value of the qualified joint interest."** Id. This means that the taxpayer is entitled to one-half of the fair market value of the qualified joint interest (the JTWROS) property as an adjusted basis in the property.

Illustration 6.5: During marriage B and C purchased a house for $100,000 and they took title as JTWROS (Time 1). When B died the fair market value of the house was $500,000 (Time 2). Assume that at B's death, the house is characterized as concurrently owned separate property. Since the JTWROS is one in which B and spouse C were the only joint tenants, it meets the definition of a qualified joint interest under the I.R.C. 2040 (Time 3). In consequence of Time 1, Time 2, and Time 3, one-half of the house falls into the decedent's gross estate and gets a step-up in basis to $250,000 for B's federal estate tax purposes. C is subsequently deemed to have acquired B's one-half interest by a transfer from B's estate. (Time 4). Assume C, in the same tax year, sells the house for $500,000 (Time 5).

How much of a gain would the surviving spouse realize at the sale of the house for purposes of income tax liability?

The answer is $250,000.

To answer this question, (i) characterize the house, (ii) determine the step-up in basis, and (iii) calculate the income taxpayer's gain when the house is sold.

- The house was purchased during marriage but titled in JTWROS (Time 1).

- At B's death the JTWROS title required that the house be characterized as concurrently owned separate property (Time 2).
- The taxpayer acquired an interest in the house valued at $250,000 from the decedent's estate (Time 3).
- The taxpayer's basis is valued by reference to the sale price ($500,000) minus the one-half interest (valued at $250,000) that the taxpayer already owned as a joint tenant during the decedent's life (Time 4).
- The seller's gain from the sale of property is computed by subtracting the taxpayer's basis ($250,000) from the amount realized in the sale ($500,000). Using this I.R.C. formula, the taxpayer's gain is $250,000 of taxable income from the sale, in the year the house was sold for $500,000. (Time 5).

What if the house had been held in CP or CPWROS title at the death of the first spouse to die? Or, what if the jurisdiction is one that treats JTWROS as community property? Would the surviving spouse have realized the same gain at the sale of the house for purposes of income tax liability?

Illustration 6.6: During marriage B and C purchased a house for $100,000; they took title in CP (Time 1). When B died the fair market value of the house was $500,000 (Time 2). Assume that the house is characterized as community property. The decedent's interest in the house, because it is community in character, is not included in the decedent's gross estate for federal estate tax purposes (Time 3). The rationale is that I.R.C. § 2056 contemplates that the house will be taxed when the surviving spouse dies.

How much of a gain does the surviving spouse realize from the sale of the house in CP title for purposes of income tax liability?

The answer is $0.

- The house was purchased during marriage and titled in CP (Time 1).
- At B's death the CP title meant the house was characterized as a community property (Time 2).
- The taxpayer acquired no value from the decedent since the community property house was not included in the decedent's gross estate (Time 3).
- The taxpayer's basis is $500,000, the value of the house at B's death (Time 4).
- The taxpayer's gain from the sale of property is computed by subtracting the taxpayer's basis ($500,000) from the amount realized in the sale ($500,000). This leaves C with no gain (or a gain valued of $0) from the sale, in the year of the sale.

Key differences between the JTWROS and the CP titles:

- A JTWROS title is includable in the gross estate of the decedent, the CP title is not. I.R.C. § 2040.
- Because the JTWROS was only between the spouses, one-half of the value of the house is included in the decedent's gross estate by federal statute. The surviving spouse acquires that one-half value from the decedent as a transfer. I.R.C. § 2040.
- A CP title is not includable in the decedent's gross estate and thus is not used to calculate the value of a transfer from the decedent to the surviving spouse. I.R.C. § 2040.
- The marital deduction was passed to address tax differences between JTWROS and CP.

Spouses who want the right of survivorship feature of the JTWROS with the federal estate and income tax savings feature of the CP title, can use a CPWROS, if allowed in the community property state where they are domiciled.

The above illustrations are intended to make a simple point: in the event of one spouse's death, different title forms may have unintended federal (and state) income tax consequences for the surviving spouse who later sells the property.

To address such consequences, at least one state—New Mexico—extends its statutory joint title form community property presumption to probate proceedings. Other states heighten JTWROS creation requirements to steer married persons toward using CP title. But in most states, the title of property at the death of a spouse determines its character, with JTWROS and TIC characterized as the decedent spouse's separate property absent evidence to the contrary.

3. CREATING THE JOINT TENANCY

JTWROS is an opt-in title form for real estate. For that reason, the intention to create a JTWROS must be evident if not expressly stated in the conveyance (deed or will) by which the title is taken.

What kind of language indicates an express statement that property be held as JTWROS?

a. "Joint"

The word "joint" in a title document, without more, is insufficient to create a JTWROS.

The legal rationale is that the word "joint" is too general a word to capture the parties' agreement to waive constitutionally protected rights of devise and succession as to the titled asset. Occasionally, courts will accept the word "joint" when used by a non-lawyer, but some supportive evidence that the parties' intended to create a JTWROS (or at least no contradictory evidence) also may be required.

b. "Joint Tenancy"

Seemingly, the clearest minimum language needed to declare a JTWROS is the term "joint tenancy." California, for example, requires that a "joint tenancy" be expressly declared as such in the deed or the will that creates it; but California law does not also require that the election "with a right of survivorship" be explicitly spelled out in the title document. Cal.Civ.Code § 683.

c. "Joint Tenancy with the Right of Survivorship"

Texas requires that the right of survivorship (which is the main incident of the JTWROS) be spelled out as such in the deed or the will that creates it. Other formalities also apply.

d. Deed Declarations and Extrinsic Evidence to Hold the Property as Separate Property

In some states, deed declarations (recitals) of "joint tenancy" or "joint tenancy with the right of survivorship" are enough to create the JTWROS title.

But in other jurisdictions, a JTWROS cannot be created merely by declaration in a deed. Additional extrinsic formalities must be met, as in Texas and Washington. The legal rationale for such an outcome is that a title document is not reliable enough to indicate whether the spouses reached a specific agreement as to the character of the titled asset.

4. THE SPECIAL JOINT FORM TITLE COMMUNITY PROPERTY PRESUMPTION

Prior to the mid-1980s, courts in community property states analyzed on a case-by-case basis the parties' intentions and expectations in choosing one joint form title form over another. Judicial results were inconsistent which made the precedents themselves inconsistent.

The problem (very simply stated) took this form: The couple used community property funds to purchase property that they then titled in JTWROS. Under general common law principles, the title form presumptively controlled its character; and thus, rebuttal rested with the joint tenant—in this case the community property proponent—to show that the actual title was of a different character (community) notwithstanding the JTWROS title form. The *historical* rationale for placing the burden on the community property proponent was that community property purchase funds had been transmuted into separate property via the JTWROS deed. Another historical rationale was that the deed was a first agreement between the spouses to characterize the property as separate. That "first agreement" could be altered, but only by a subsequent (second) agreement between the spouses that their intent was that the titled asset would be community property in character if the marriage were to end by dissolution.

An agreement is defined as a bilateral communication between the spouses. An unexpressed belief ("I thought the house was 'ours' "), a unilaterally stated belief ("I often said that the house was 'ours' "), or a misunderstanding ("I thought that JTWROS was the same as community property") were and still are insufficient to prove that the parties replaced the first agreement (declared in the deed itself) with a subsequent contradictory agreement.

In the pre-1980 era of easy transmutation, an oral or implied second agreement was sufficient to rebut the JTWROS title document. Today a writing is required to prove the existence of the agreement.

Today, easy transmutation is no longer the trend: Transmutations must be in writing. Some states require an express declaration by the adversely affected spouse. Plus, transmutations are scrutinized for voluntariness and the absence of unconscionability, as discussed in Chapter 3.

Nearly every community property jurisdiction has adopted an approach that works to characterize property acquired under *any* joint form title as community *for purposes of a dissolution proceeding*. (Among the U.S. community property states that permit joint tenancy titles, Nevada has been the only holdout.) The rebuttal burden shifts to the separate property proponent to show a subsequent inconsistent agreement that the parties intended to characterize the property as separate in whole or part.

In terms of what constitutes a writing, some states allow the second (rebuttal) agreement to be established either by a clear statement in the title document or by an extrinsic agreement. Other states allow a broader range of evidence like circumstantial evidence or tracing to prove the rebuttal standard. Either way, the policy goal is to further the state's interest in equitable *and* consistent dissolution outcomes.

California explicitly asserts that its special joint form title community property presumption serves a compelling state interest. Cal.Fam.Code § 2581 further provides that an asset acquired during marriage in *any* joint title form (JTWROS, TIC, CP, or CPWROS) with funds of *either* character (community or separate) is presumptively community *in a dissolution proceeding*. Rebuttal rests with the separate property claimant. The range of rebuttal evidence is set forth (and thus limited) by statute. Additionally, rebuttal evidence is subject to other statutory tests to guard against unconscionability and coercion.

Illustration 6.7: During marriage, H and W buy a house in California. They take title to the house as JTWROS. No other agreements are made between H and W as to the house. When H and W *file for dissolution*, what is the character of the house? Here, the house is presumptively community property by application of a special community property presumption set out in Cal.Fam.Code § 2581. This special presumption supersedes the general community property presumption.

Illustration 6.8: Same facts as in Illustration 6.7 except that at purchase H and W also sign a written agreement (extrinsic to the deed) stating that H intends to keep a fifty-percent separate property interest in the house to reflect the percentage of H's separate property contribution to purchase. In a dissolution proceeding, the community property presumption is raised by the joint form deed (the "first agreement"). H, as the separate property proponent, has the burden to rebut the presumption by a preponderance of the evidence. H can do so by producing the subsequent contradictory agreement (the "second agreement"). Assuming the second agreement is enforceable, it will control the characterization of the house for purposes of the dissolution.

Depending on the state, a separate property contributor who cannot rebut the presumption may be permitted to request a reimbursement either as a matter of court discretion or as a statutory right. In some states, California again being the example just discussed in Illustration 6.7 and Illustration 6.8, reimbursement is by statutory right, but it is without interest, payable upon partition, and limited by depreciation. (Not all community property states allow a statutory reimbursement in these circumstances.)

Illustration 6.9: During marriage, H and W buy a house in California for $100,000. They use $50,000 of community property and $50,000 of W's provable separate property funds to buy the house. H and W take title as JTWROS. They reach no other agreements about the character of the house. When H and W petition for dissolution, they sell the house for $500,000. By application of the statutory joint form title community property presumption the house is *entirely* (100%) community property at dissolution due to the absence of rebuttal evidence. But W is statutorily entitled to a reimbursement of $50,000, without interest. At the sale of the house, the reimbursement to W must be paid off the top:

$500,000 – $50,000 = $450,000. The remaining $450,000 is entirely community property, to be split equally between H and W ($225,000 each). Also, any appreciation is community property with each spouse entitled to a 50% share.

Distinguishing between basis and appreciation is discussed further in Chapter 7.

Illustration 6.10: During marriage, H and W buy a house in California for $100,000. They use $50,000 of community property and $50,000 of W's provable separate property. They take title as joint tenants. At that time, W and H also sign a written agreement that W will keep a 50% separate property ownership interest in the house in the event of dissolution. When H and W dissolve their marriage, they sell the house for $500,000. The house is presumptively community property by application of the statutory community property presumption. But now W can rebut the presumption by producing the second agreement, which establishes that the house is concurrently owned by the community property estate (50%) and by W's separate property estate (50%). Note that the second rebuttal agreement controls pro rata shares of ownership. Moreover, because the terms of the rebuttal agreement mirror the actual net character contributions to purchase, no transmutation has occurred. The house is owned one-half by the community (with each spouse owning a 50% interest of that one-half) and one-half by W's separate property estate.

Chapter 7 covers these issues further.

5. NOMINAL TITLE, "FOR CONVENIENCE"

Why would a married couple specify "joint tenancy" if they did not intend to transmute their community property into separate property? Popular explanations include

- Statements that the form of title was "nominal," i.e., in name only. (The adhesion character of financial institution forms and practices makes such explanations reasonable.)
- Belief that the joint tenancy account was only intended as an agency account on which the names of both parties were listed "for convenience only."

These arguments have a reasonable ring and are often accepted by courts. The trier of fact has the last word in making such determinations. The trier is called upon to exercise its discretion based upon the often-self-serving oral testimony of the parties (or one of them) that they intended exactly the opposite of what they previously signed a formal document saying they intended.

The "convenience" explanation is often used with nonspousal joint tenancies to indicate that the original depositor of the funds in a joint bank account did not intend to create a form of concurrent ownership, but only intended to create an agency so that the second person could withdraw the sums on deposit in the account for the benefit of the first person.

6. JOINT BANK ACCOUNTS

In many jurisdictions, special statutory rules exist for deposits of money in financial institutions, as discussed in Chapter 4. Although the term "bank account" is used in this book, each jurisdiction has several different kinds of financial holding devices ("accounts," "shares," "certificates of deposit," "money market certificates," and so on) and institutions (savings banks, credit unions, brokerage firms, whether brick-and-mortar or on-line). Precision is required in practice to determine which type of device, in which type of institution, is dealt with by a particular statute.

For married persons, a "joint" bank account is created when the parties open an account in both of their names. A joint bank account can also be created when one spouse "adds" the other's name to a pre-existing account. Financial institutions generally have detailed provisions on preprinted cards or on-line forms that the parties must complete to open or modify a bank account. Generally, these forms are very specific in their "agreement" that the account is to be JTWROS and, more to the point, that either signatory has the contractual right to withdraw sums on deposit in the account in full and on demand during his or her life or upon death (as determined by a beneficial designation or a disposition).

Despite the bank signature card contract verbiage, bank accounts do not fall within traditional definitions of JTWROS. This is because of the statutory abrogation of the requirement of the four unities of time, title, interest, and possession. That is, in the context of a joint bank account, the parties (here we are assuming spouses) have full access to the joint bank account during their lives; this means that the bank can (without liability for misdelivery of funds) honor a request by either party, acting alone, to withdraw all the sums on deposit from the account. Depending on the net character of the sums on deposit in the account, an excess withdrawal is conceptually contrary to the usual JTWROS rule that a joint tenant can, at severance, affect only his or her proportionate share of the total.

In the context of marriage, even joint bank accounts predictably give rise to tracing issues because many acquisitions can be traced to or through a bank account. If the account is *un*commingled, then an asset purchased from the account takes on the character of sums on deposit that were used to make the purchase.

But what if a spouse claims that the account is commingled with community property and separate property sums on deposit?

If we assume that community property sums on deposit in a joint bank account are sufficient to make the purchase on the date in question, then even if separate property sums on deposit are (i) provable on the date of the purchase and (ii) sufficient to make the purchase, that purchase should be characterized as presumptively community in character, with rebuttal determined by state law.

Chapter 7 covers the characterization of accounts, sums on deposit in an account, and purchases made from commingled accounts.

7. JOINT SAFE-DEPOSIT BOXES

Safe-deposit box agreements sometimes declare that all contents of the safe deposit box shall be joint tenancy between the co-tenants of the box. Such a declaration, if intended, can be binding upon the parties in the absence of a statute providing otherwise (such as exists in California or Nevada).

If one spouse predeceases the other, the legal issue becomes whether the joint tenancy rental agreement is sufficiently clear, specific, or fair enough to transmute the character of each community property asset or title stored in the box. In most states, even case law holds that the title to a safe-deposit box does not determine the title to the assets and the titles stored in the box. However, when it comes to untitled assets, control and possession can raise significant questions about who owns the asset.

Even in the era of easy transmutation, reconciling a conflict between a safe-deposit signature card and a document in the safe-deposit box was uncertain, especially if the document was registered in the name of one or both spouses in a form of ownership other than joint tenancy, e.g., community property. The issue for courts in those cases was whether the safe-deposit signature card should prevail over the express registration of the particular asset.

In the era of formal transmutation, each asset, in theory, should be characterized independently. In other words, the simple act of placing an asset in a safe deposit box, without more, should not transmute the asset; nor should it create an exception to an asset-by-asset characterization rule. The best practice is to hold that a safe-deposit box signature card is not a title-changing transmutation with respect to the assets that are stored in the safe-deposit box unless there is proof of a valid transmutation as to any asset in question.

If a deed or stock certificate is registered in one name but located within a safe-deposit box whose safe-deposit signature card declares that all contents of the box shall be joint tenancy, then the battle of paperwork probably should be resolved in favor of the express statement of title that is relatively more specific, i.e., the stock certificates rather than the safe-deposit box agreement.

Another method of resolving conflicting paper titles is to give effect to the later-in-time document. Formal transmutation rules diminish legal uncertainty in these cases.

8. SUMMING UP: JOINT FORM TITLES AT DISSOLUTION AND DEATH

There are four concurrent title forms. They are the TIC, the JTWROS, the CP title and the CPWROS. The problem that JTWROS and TIC can cause in a community property system stems from the fact that those titles have their origin in the English common law, which makes them technically separate property in character.

For purposes of a dissolution proceeding, most community property states presume or else treat property acquired during marriage in any joint title form as community in character. These rules serve the policy of making (and keeping) the law consistent so that parties and their advisors can better plan how to use a particular joint form title for a particular purpose (dissolution or death, probate avoidance or tax liability, and so forth).

C. INDIVIDUAL STATES

1. ARIZONA

Under general law, the TIC is the default concurrent title for real estate, but parties can create a JTWROS by **"express words** [that] **vest the estate in the survivor on the death of a grantee or devisee."** Ariz.Rev.Stat.Ann. § 33–431(A) and (B).

Ariz.Rev.Stat.Ann. § 33–431(C) permits, in any deed recorded from or after December 31, 1994, the creation of **"[c]ommunity property with right of survivorship."** Spouses must opt into this title form with **"express words** [that] **vest the estate in the surviving spouse on the death of one of the spouses."**

Key to understanding joint tenancy title is the inception of title rule. In Arizona, although the "marital rights" of married persons who move to

Arizona are governed by Arizona law (see Ariz.Rev.Stat.Ann. § 25–217 discussed in Chapter 3), their "property rights" may ultimately be governed by another state's law. True, Arizona law employs a quasi-community property principle, but case law routinely applies the inception of title rule along with the tracing principle to analyze whether property acquired while domiciled in another state falls within the Arizona community property principle.

As a touch point, property acquired during marriage while domiciled in Arizona with Arizona community property labor or earnings is clearly Arizona community property. But property acquired otherwise may give rise to a characterization dispute.

For Arizona community property, partition of the joint titles of parties who file a petition for dissolution in Arizona is equitable without regard to fault as set forth in Ariz.Rev.Stat.Ann. § 25–318(A): **"In a proceeding for dissolution of the marriage, or for legal separation . . .** [the court] **shall assign each spouse's sole and separate property to such spouse. It shall also divide the *community*, joint tenancy and other property held in common equitably, though not necessarily in kind, without regard to marital misconduct."** (Italics added.)

Implied in this language is the possibility, in the context of dissolution, that there exist joint tenancy titles that are separate in character (*separate* joint tenancy and other property held in common equitably) and those that are community in character (*community* joint tenancy and other property held in common equitably), depending on state law. These legal differences may be of consequence in the context of a dissolution proceeding for at least three reasons.

One, the difference between a community joint tenancy title versus a separate property joint tenancy title is the difference between judicial discretion versus property right. Ariz.Rev.Stat.Ann. 25–318(A), above, mandates a judge to **"equitably"** divide *community property* joint tenancy titles. Equitable division does not necessarily mean 50-50. The common law rules, by comparison, require that a *separate property* joint tenancy title meet and maintain four unities (time, title, interest, and possession). Unity of interest means that the parties own equal shares of the property—this turns out to be simple arithmetic in the case of married joint tenants, since, by right, each spouse would own one-half of the whole.

Two, the difference between Arizona community property joint titles, more generally, and the joint titles of other community property states in the context of litigation comes down to rebuttal. Arizona follows the inception of title rule, which looks to when the original property right came into existence, not to the date the joint title was executed. If there is a discrepancy between the two dates, the inception of title rule encourages parties to produce evidence of intent as to character with respect to the earlier date.

In a dissolution proceeding, rebutting a joint title characterized as community property in Arizona (in a divorce proceeding) could require an analysis of the following elements. Timing (when was the property in joint title acquired?); domicile (where did the parties live when the property was acquired?); source of funds (what is the character of the funds that contributed to the purchase of the property in the first place?)

Marriage of Flower, 223 Ariz. 531, 225 P.3d 588 (Ct. App. 2010) held that a court may consider statutory and non-statutory factors in assessing the equities of a particular case under Ariz.Rev.Stat.Ann. § 25–318. An analysis of joint title starts with the inception of title rule (what was the parties' intent as to character when the property was acquired?). From there it allows a judge to consider all other past, present, and implicitly future factors. Relevant are factors casting light on whether the parties intended the property to be community or all or part separate in the context of a dissolution proceeding. Once these determinations are made, equitable division can ensue.

If title was taken in joint title in a different community property state, standards for rebuttal might be difficult to meet. In Arizona, for example, rebuttal turns on proof of the parties' intent, but no particular type of rebuttal evidence is required. In California, by contrast, joint form titles are presumed to be community property unless the parties can produce a clear statement in the deed or an extrinsic written agreement of a definite intent of one or both spouses to keep a separate property interest in the titled property.

Of course, if the parties are indifferent to how the joint tenancy is ultimately characterized, then these legal differences are irrelevant to the outcome. But if the parties are in dispute, or if equitable turns out to be a far distant cry from equal, what appears to be a hair-line distinction between treating a joint title as community or separate can be material.

Three, community property not disposed of by a divorce decree is held thereafter by the parties as tenants in common. Here again, proportional ownership may become a post-dissolution issue to litigate. If one party made no significant financial contribution to the property, then the other party would have a basis upon which to argue that the noncontributor's share should be minimal.

In a dissolution proceeding, to sum up, joint titles might be divided equitably (for Arizona community property), equally (for common law joint tenancy), or according to proportional contributions to acquisition (for common law tenancy in common titles). Considering the above variations, and notwithstanding the habits of law practice, the Arizona statute is not as predictive as one might hope, especially given that Arizona has historically been a place where people choose to retire after a lifetime of working in another jurisdiction.

In the context of a marriage terminated by death, *Baldwin's Estate*, 50 Ariz. 265, 274–275, 71 P.2d 791, 795 (1937) affirms that community property is the preferred joint title form between Arizona spouses, but then recognizes that spouses domiciled in the state have a right to hold property as joint tenants with right of survivorship. A court is permitted to rebut a community property joint tenancy "only where it clearly appears that both spouses have agreed that the property should be taken [as joint tenants and not as community property]." Proof of a rebuttal is predicated on a showing that the disadvantaged spouse knew that the deed provided for a right of survivorship. Without evidence of specific knowledge concerning how the right of survivorship works, however, the mere insertion in the deed of right of survivorship language would not only defeat the community property law but also defeat the rights of the decedent's heirs.

2. CALIFORNIA

California permits the creation of community property with the right of survivorship when such is **"expressly declared in the transfer document . . ."** and **"[s]igned or initialed by the grantees."** Cal.Civ.Code § 682.1. California is a common law state, therefore, the four unities (time, title, interest, possession) are required to create a joint tenancy. But California has also modernized its law to allow unilateral creation (*O to O and A as joint tenants with the right of survivorship*), an update to the law that relaxes the unity of time.

A different but similar civil code section covers what language is required to "expressly declare" the intent to create a joint tenancy. Cal.Civ.Code § 683. Use of the words **"joint tenancy"** suffice to demonstrate an intent to take property concurrently by right of survivorship. (*O conveys to B and C as joint tenants*).

Generally, a joint tenant has the right of unilateral severance. *Riddle v. Harmon*, 102 Cal.App.3d 524, 162 Cal.Rptr. 530 (1980) veered from the common law to permit unilateral severance of a joint tenancy (*O conveys to O*). But *Riddle* was decided before the passage of Cal.Fam.Code § 2581, the special community property presumption for joint form titles obtained during marriage, and before new legislation on the obligations of spouses in a transaction between them.

In *Riddle*, supra, the parties were married and yet the court did not discuss the impact of marriage on severance. The severance of a joint tenancy is a consequential transaction because it involves rights of devise and descent; for that reason, joinder (both spouses signature on the severing document) would be required under Cal.Fam.Code § 1100(a) and Cal.Fam.Code § 1102. Spousal partnership duties set forth in Cal.Fam.Code § 721 are yet another basis for distinguishing *Riddle*, supra, in a contemporary case involving a unilateral severance of a joint tenancy title held by married persons.

A general statute attempts to counteract *Riddle*, supra, to protect the interest of third parties. Cal. Civ. Code § 683.2 requires that a deed affecting severance to a third party be recorded. Penalties apply as set forth in Cal.Civ.Code § 683.2(b), which acknowledges that a joint tenancy may be unilaterally severed, but also sets forth recording requirements to ensure that the severance is effective as to **"[t]he rights of a purchaser or encumbrancer for value in good faith and**

without knowledge of the written agreement." Subdivisions (a) and (b) waive joinder for purposes of severance. Nevertheless, where the parties named in the title are married to each other, the more specific joinder requirement in Cal.Fam.Code § 1102 supersedes Cal.Civ. Code § 683.2.

As explained above, an asset acquired during marriage in any joint form title is presumed to be community property *for purposes of a dissolution or legal separation*. California adopted a community property joint form title presumption in 1984. Cal.Fam.Code § 2580 and § 2581 state the policy and provide: ***"For the purpose of division of property on dissolution of marriage or legal separation of the parties*, property acquired by the parties during marriage in joint form, including property held in tenancy in common, joint tenancy, or tenancy by the entirety, or as community property, is presumed to be community property."** (Italics added.) Rebuttal is by a clear statement in the title document, or by an (extrinsic written) agreement between the spouses that the titled asset is not to be community property in whole or part for purposes of a dissolution proceeding.

When the court concludes that a joint form title is entirely community in character, Cal.Fam.Code § 2640 applies to give a separate property contributor a statutory right of reimbursement, without interest. **"Contributions to the acquisition of property"** are defined under Cal.Fam.Code § 2640(a) as **"downpayments, payments for improvements,**

and payments that reduce the principal of a loan used to finance the purchase or improvement of the property but do not include payments of interest on the loan or payments made for maintenance, insurance, or taxation for the property." Reimbursements are made without interest or adjustment for changes in monetary value and, under § 2640(b), **"may not exceed the net value of the property at the time of the division."**

Retroactive application of the Cal.Fam.Code § 2581 joint form community property presumption has been held to be constitutional. *Marriage of Buol*, 39 Cal.3d 751, 759, 218 Cal.Rptr. 31, 705 P.2d 354 (1985)(in bank). The rationale is that the use of an evidentiary presumption does not disturb vested property rights. Chapter 13 discusses California retroactivity.

Reimbursement under Cal.Fam.Code § 2640, on the other hand, is non-retroactive and applies only from January 1, 1984 forward. *Marriage of Heikes*, 10 Cal.4th 1211, 44 Cal.Rptr.2d 155, 899 P.2d 1349 (1995). By this case, a separate property contribution to the purchase of an entirely (100%) community property asset made before January 1, 1984, is a presumptive gift to the community under *Marriage of Lucas*, 27 Cal.3d 808, 166 Cal.Rptr. 853, 614 P.2d 285 (1980). But this case was superseded by Cal. Fam. Code § 2640 on this issue giving rise to a so-called anti-*Lucas* approach. Thus, that same contribution to purchase, if made *on or after January 1, 1984*, is a presumptive no-interest loan to the community, subject to the statutory reimbursement discussed above.

At the death of a spouse, the joint form titles function as designed. Any issues with creation or severance are covered by decisional law and whether the jointly titled property is JTWROS or TIC, or CP or CPWROS. Rebuttal of character is permitted.

Unique limitations on safe-deposit boxes are imposed by statute. Cal.Civ.Code § 683.1 states that safe-deposit box rental agreements shall not create a joint tenancy in the contents of the box, and **"[a]ny such contract or other arrangement purporting so to do shall be to such extent void and of no effect."**

Cal.Civ.Code § 682.1, which as discussed above permits the parties to declare a CPWROS, provides that CPWROS should be treated as JTWROS for purposes of passing property at death without the necessity of probate. Severance of a CPWROS can be accomplished unilateral severance, however, so long as the act of severance comports with spousal partnership fiduciary duties.

3. IDAHO

In Idaho, a joint form deed is community property, unless there is clear and convincing evidence that the spouses intended to hold the property as joint tenants. Recitations in the deed itself (like for example a declaration of rights of survivorship) are not sufficient to meet the rebuttal standard. Therefore, in Idaho, the CP title remains the default title in Idaho for married persons even if the property is titled in a joint form with a common law origin.

CPWROS is available to married persons who opt to use it. CPWROS can be created by grant, by transfer, or by devise to a husband and wife. See Idaho Code § 15–6–401. Divorce or annulment terminates a CPWROS per Idaho Code § 15–6–402.

For more on protection from the reach of a decedent spouse's creditors, see Chapter 9.

4. LOUISIANA

In Louisiana, a joint form deed is characterized as community property. Louisiana has avoided much of the litigation concerning common law titles by disallowing the creation of the joint tenancy title form. *Winsberg v. Winsberg*, 56 So.2d 730 (La. 1952).

5. NEVADA

Nev.Rev.Stat. § 111.064(2) recognizes both traditional community property and CPWROS: **"A right of survivorship does not arise when an estate in community property is created in a married couple, as such, unless the instrument creating the estate expressly declares that the married couple take the property as community property with a right of survivorship. This right of survivorship is extinguished whenever either spouse, during the marriage, transfers the spouse's interest in the community property."**

The distinction between community property and joint tenancy is highlighted by Nev.Rev.Stat. § 123.030: **"A married couple may hold real or personal property as joint tenants, tenants in common, or as community property."**

Spouses must affirmatively opt into joint tenancy, however. The existence or non-existence of a joint tenancy must affirmatively appear in the deed per Nev.Rev.Stat. § 111.065(1), which has the effect of transmuting community property into joint tenancy **"[w]hen expressly declared in the transfer to be joint tenancy . . ."** Therefore, the act of opting into a joint tenancy deed transmutes any community property (such as purchase funds) into separate property thus shifting the burden to the community property proponent to prove otherwise. The same rule holds for personal property.

Additionally, Nev.Rev.Stat. § 111.065(2) provides: **"A joint tenancy . . . may be created by a written transfer, agreement, or instrument."** The word **"may"** was held to be mandatory (meaning the equivalent of a shall) in *McKissick v. McKissick*, 93 Nev. 139, 560 P.2d 1366 (1977).

Nevada recognizes a homestead (defined in Nev.Rev.Stat. § 115.010). When the homestead is declared upon community property it is deemed to be held as community property with right of survivorship, Nev.Rev.Stat. § 115.060.

6. NEW MEXICO

New Mexico has a fairly long list of proposed legislation at the time this Nutshell goes to press; many of the proposals are language updates. Key among the proposals is to change "husband and wife" to "the parties to a marriage." On the topic of joint titles, for example, the newly proposed N.M.Stat.Ann. § 40–3–2 (1978) states: **"*The parties to a marriage* may hold property as joint tenants, tenants in common or as community property."**

A joint form title community property presumption appears in N.M.Stat.Ann. § 40–3–8(B) (1978). That presumption applies to **"[p]roperty acquired by either or both spouses during marriage that is not separate property."** The presumption appears in the next sentence of the statute: **"Property acquired during a marriage by an instrument in writing whether as tenants in common or as joint tenants . . . shall be presumed to be held as community property unless such property is separate property within the meaning of Subsection A of this section."** Chapter 5 for a discussion of Subsection A.

The New Mexico statutory presumption applies to acquisitions during marriage, but the presumption is not on its face limited to a dissolution proceeding (as it is in California).

The application of the *presumption* itself is retroactive (as it is in California). See *Swink v.*

Sunwest Bank, 955 F.2d 31 (10th Cir. 1992) and *Swink v. Fingado*, 115 N.M. 275, 850 P.2d 978 (1993).

Additionally, N.M.Stat.Ann. § 47–1–16 (1978) does away with heightened proof requirements for the purposes of *establishing* a joint tenancy: **"An instrument conveying or transferring title to real or personal property to two or more persons as joint tenants, to two or more persons and to the survivors of them and the heirs and assigns of the survivor, or to two or more persons with right of survivorship, shall be prima facie evidence that such property is held in a joint tenancy and shall be conclusive as to purchasers or encumbrancers for value. In any litigation involving the issue of such tenancy a preponderance of the evidence shall be sufficient to establish the same."** Note, the preponderance of the evidence standard used for rebuttal because the presumption effectively relates back to the date of the spouses acquired the asset. For a transmutation case, a higher standard of proof (discussed below) for rebuttal applies.

Rebuttal of the special joint form community presumption is by proof of any one of the following, as delineated in N.M.Stat.Ann. § 40–3–8(A) (1978), amended in 1990,

- Timing (acquisition before marriage). N.M.Stat.Ann. § 40–3–8 (A)(1).
- Gift (acquisition during marriage. N.M.Stat.Ann. § 40–3–8 (A)(4).

- Agreement (the parties executed a second agreement that the asset titled in joint form was all or part separate property). N.M.Stat.Ann. § 40–3–8 (A)(5). Here, the second agreement must at least be specific enough to identify the property as separate in character.

- Tracing (acquisition during marriage, but with separate property funds). Here, the separate property proponent must show by a preponderance of the evidence that acquisition funds were separate property. See *Chavez v. Chavez*, 56 N.M. 393, 244 P.2d 781 (1952).

Acquisitions and transmutations are treated as different classes of property. An acquisition is not necessarily a transaction between the spouses. See Chapter 3 for more on transmutations.

Because it is relevant to the rebuttal standard, it makes sense to discuss here that as between the spouses, a transmutation must "be established by clear, strong and convincing proof, which is a higher standard than the preponderance of evidence" standard allowed for acquisitions. *Trimble's Estate*, 57 N.M. 51, 253 P.2d 805 (1953). The *Trimble*, supra, is meant to "subject transactions between spouses to common law rules controlling actions of persons occupying confidential relations with each other." *Fletcher's Estate v. Jackson*, 94 N.M. 572, 579, 613 P.2d 714 (Ct. App. 1980). See Chapter 3 for more on the *Trimble* Rule.

N.M.Stat.Ann. § 45–2–804 (1978), amended in 2011 and effective January 1, 2012, governs revocations of probate and nonprobate transfers by divorce.

7. TEXAS

Holding title in JTWROS does not appear to be as commonly used in Texas as in other community property states (except Louisiana, which does not permit joint tenancies). Perhaps this is because Texas is the birthplace of the "homestead" concept, discussed in Section A.1 above.

Texas Const. Art. XVI, § 52 enshrines and describes the homestead right: **"On the death of the husband or wife, or both, the homestead shall descend and vest in like manner as other real property of the deceased, and shall be governed by the same laws of descent and distribution, but it shall not be partitioned among the heirs of the deceased during the lifetime of the surviving husband or wife, or so long as the survivor may elect to use or occupy the same as a homestead, or so long as the guardian of the minor children of the deceased may be permitted, under the order of the proper court having the jurisdiction, to use and occupy the same."**

Considering the homestead option, as far as testamentary rights go, there is little need for married persons to opt for a JTWROS title. The reason is that the Texas homestead is akin to a durable community property with the right of survivorship (CPWROS) title. Durable means that the title survives the death of the first spouse through to the death of the second surviving spouse who is using or occupying the property. Practitioner commentary leans in agreement of this point of view.

Indeed, Texas has an inconsistent decisional history of forbidding (or not) the creation of a JTWROS from property that is community in character. *Ricks v. Smith*, 159 Tex. 280, 318 S.W.2d 439 (1958), allowed the strategy; but *Ricks* was overruled by *Hilley v. Hilley*, 161 Tex. 569, 342 S.W.2d 565 (1961), which held that the JTWROS argued for could not be created from community property because the acquisition during marriage was not by gift, but by exchange of community property.

The Texas Legislature amended the predecessor of V.T.C.A.Prob.Code § 46 by adding a final sentence specifically allowing "any husband and his wife . . ., by written agreement, [to] create a joint estate out of their community property, with rights of survivorship." But the Texas Supreme Court declared this quoted portion of the probate code unconstitutional in *Williams v. McKnight*, 402 S.W.2d 505 (1966), citing *Hilley*. The Texas Legislature subsequently deleted the overruled sentence from the Probate Code, which has itself been repealed and replaced with an Estates Code, effective January 1, 2014. See Chapter 11.

Nevertheless, if the married persons insist on placing community property into a JTWROS, Texas permits the use of a valid JTWROS so long as the married persons follow a process, known (at least in California) as the Texas two-step.

The Texas two-step turns on the rule that property purchased by Texas spouses with separate (as opposed to community) funds may be held as JTWROS, with the undivided one-half interest characterized as concurrently held separate property. Thus, the two-stepping spouses must first partition the community property into separate property (step 1), and then execute written survivorship agreements for the separate properties (step 2). *Holmes v. Beatty*, 290 S.W.3d 852, 52 Tex.S.Ct.J.967 (2009). Together, the title (which ideally explicitly uses the statutorily mandated "right of survivorship" language) and the written survivorship agreements (which also make the right of survivorship explicit) serve as predictably solid proof of the spouses' intent to hold the property as JTWROS.

V.T.C.A.Prob.Code § 46, repealed 2009, effective Jan. 1, 2014, by the Texas Estates Code, is captioned **"Joint Tenancies."** The probate version of the Texas two-step permits parties to create a joint tenancy by a deed *plus* a written agreement **"[t]hat the interest of any joint owner who dies shall survive to the surviving joint owner or owners, ..."** A deed standing alone will not create a joint tenancy since **". . . no such agreement shall be inferred from the mere fact that the property is held in joint ownership."** This section does not apply to spouses regarding **"their community property . . ."**.

Through a series of amendments in 1948, 1980, 1987, and 1999, Tex. Const. Art. XVI, § 15 came to permit spouses to engage in more liberal transmutations, as discussed in Chapter 3. These amendments *appear* to give rise to the right to create a joint tenancy with the right of survivorship directly from community property. Evidence for this is in the following language: **"spouses may agree in writing that all or part of their community property becomes the property of the surviving spouse on the death of a spouse."** It is unclear how this liberalization interacts with the two-step process described above.

8. WASHINGTON

As between nonmarried persons, Wash.Rev.Code § 64.28.010 sets out the requirements for creating a JTWROS: "**Joint tenancy shall be created only by written instrument, which instrument shall expressly declare the interest created to be a joint tenancy. . .**"

Wash.Rev.Code § 64.28.020. Subsection (1) makes the TIC the default joint title and allows for JTWROS: **"Every interest created in favor of two or more persons in their own right is an interest in common, unless acquired by them in partnership, for partnership purposes, or unless declared in its creation to be a joint tenancy, as provided in RCW 64.28.010, or unless acquired by executors or trustees. . . ."**

However, Subsection (2) states that interests in common in the names of spouses or registered domestic partners are **"presumed to be community property."** In other words, even when Washington spouses set out to use the JTWROS deed form, the character of the asset defaults to community property.

Wash.Rev.Code § 26.16.120 additionally allows spouses to enter into a community property agreement to dispose of community property by survivorship. **"Community property agreements"** are contractual, not testamentary, under the rationale of *Norris v. Norris*, 25 Wash.App. 290, 605 P.2d 1296 (1980). Any property subject to such an agreement is presumptively community property, unless established otherwise. Under the same code section, community property agreements, by statute, must meet a high standard of formality. Enforceability is determined **"by the execution of an instrument in writing under their hands and seals, and to be witnessed, acknowledged and certified in the same manner as deeds to real estate are required to be ...."** The Washington approach took effect on January 1, 1985. Wash.Rev.Code § 64.28.040(3).

For married persons and domestic partners, Washington courts have extended the common law requirements for the creation of a joint tenancy with the right of survivorship. The four unities are required, but so too is clear and convincing evidence of the written intent of both spouses to convert a community property title into one with the right of survivorship. A community property agreement ensures that the specific property will pass by survivorship; it does not transmute that property into separate property.

A question sometimes raised about the Washington community property agreement approach is whether the emphasis upon the formality of the agreement (written, sealed, signed, witnessed, acknowledged, and certified) by which survivorship is affixed to community property may impose too high a standard for the layperson.

One answer to the hyper-formality argument is that similar formalities for deeds (and the requirements for wills) have long served a ritual and an evidentiary function. Formalities impress upon parties the legal importance of the document being executed: this serves the ritual function. Formally executed documents provide clear and convincing evidence of the parties' specific intent as to the asset: this serves the evidentiary function.

Another answer is that it appears under the law that a JTWROS title between married persons is presumptively community property both for purposes of dissolution and death. Arguably, the newly adopted approach simplifies, rather than complicates, the interface between the common law titles and the state community property system. The idea is that a simplified approach better protects the marital estate.

In Washington, joint titles between spouses are presumed to be community in character. By executing a community property agreement, the parties can opt for a right of survivorship as to any particular asset. The property covered by the community property agreement remains community in character, but it passes by survivorship. Thus, what the parties are agreeing to is analogous to CPWROS.

Wash.Rev.Code § 64.28.040(1) states: **"(1) Joint tenancy interests held in the names of both spouses or both domestic partners, whether or not in conjunction with others, are presumed to be their community property, the same as other property held in the name of both spouses or both domestic partners. Any such interest passes to the survivor of the spouse or survivor of the domestic partner as provided for property held in joint tenancy, but in all other respects the interest is treated as community property."**

Wash.Rev.Code § 64.28.040(2) speaks to severance: **"Either person in a marriage or either person in a state registered domestic partnership, or both, may sever a joint tenancy. When a joint tenancy is severed, the property, or proceeds of the property, shall be presumed to be their community property, whether it is held in the name of either spouse, or both, or in the name of either domestic partner, or both."**

Sometimes the question of which concurrent title the spouses' intended to use comes up even when a third party, rather than the spouses themselves, prepared or issued the disputed title.

For example, in *Estate of Olson*, 87 Wash.2d 855, 557 P.2d 302 (1976), the court held that a separate property JTWROS is not established by one spouse's unilateral act of drafting and later executing a promissory note and real estate mortgage that referred to the property as joint tenancy with the right of survivorship. The court held that in the absence of an express written declaration by the marital community (i.e., a mutual declaration by each of the spouses) that the interest created was to be a joint tenancy (that is a common law title form), the property remained community property (albeit with the Wash.Rev.Code 64.28.040(1) mandated right of survivorship). See also, *Rogers Walla Walla, Inc. v. Ballard*, 16 Wash.App.81, 553 P.2d 1372 (Ct.App. 1976), *review denied* 88 Wash.2d 1004 (1977) and *Graves v. Beutler*, 112 Wash.App. 1018 (2002). (*Graves* is not reported in P.3.)

Lambert v. Peoples National Bank of Washington, 89 Wash.2d 646, 574 P.2d 738 (1978)(en banc), decided in the male management era, involved a purchase of mutual fund certificates over a long period of time (1950 to 1972) by a wife who was acting as de facto manager. At issue were the mutual fund certificates that she purchased with community property sums withdrawn from a bank account. Most of those certificates had been issued by the financial institution in a joint tenancy with the right of survivorship form; but some of them had been issued in tenancy in common. In an action between the husband's estate and the wife's conservator, the Washington Supreme Court upheld the characterization of the certificates as community property on the rationale that both spouses had not mutually declared consent to the change (from community property to JTWROS) as is required by Washington law. Dispositive were the following: the wife alone managed the community finances, the husband had limited English proficiency, and the parties were uninformed as to the function of the different concurrent titles.

Written evidence of both spouses' intentions as to title form is often difficult to locate. Banks retain signature cards, and vehicle registration records are centrally located. But brokerage account records may be incomplete or prospective only. Additionally, the background papers for a promissory note (as opposed to the deed of trust or mortgage) may also be difficult to locate. Promissory notes are not necessarily recorded in the public title record. Real estate mortgages and deeds of trust, on the other hand, are routinely filed, by the encumbrancer, in the public record in the county where the real estate is located.

Of historical interest is that the JTWROS has had a difficult struggle for existence in Washington. Wash.Rev.Code § 64.28.010(1), above, which permits JTWROS for persons who are not married to each other, dates back to a 1960 initiative. *Holohan v. Melville*, 41 Wash.2d 380, 249 P.2d 777 (1952)(en banc) is obsolete because of subsequent changes in the law, but it contains a useful history of joint tenancies in Washington.

9. WISCONSIN

A joint tenancy deed executed on or after January 1, 1986, is characterized as survivorship marital property. A similar deed executed before January 1, 1986, remains joint tenancy.

Otherwise, Wisconsin blasts through the common law title interface with community property problem. Wis.Stat. § 766.60(4) by authorizing the holding of marital property in survivorship form:

"(4)(a)Spouses may hold property in any other form permitted by law, including but not limited to a concurrent form or a form that provides survivorship ownership. [T]o the extent the incidents of the tenancy in common or joint tenancy conflict with or differ from the incidents of [marital] **property classification . . . , the incidents of the . . . joint tenancy, including the incident of survivorship, control."**

But Wis.Stat. § 766.60(5) authorizes a special form of marital property called **"survivorship marital property"**:

"(5)(a)If the words "survivorship marital property" are used. . . , the marital property so held is survivorship marital property. On the death of a spouse, the ownership rights of that spouse in the property vest solely in the surviving spouse by nontestamentary disposition at death. . . ."

The Legislative Council notes that the most significant differences between joint tenancy and survivorship marital property are, one, the income tax treatment of basis at the death of a spouse and, two, the right of a joint tenant to unilaterally opt out of (destroy) the right of survivorship.

Income tax basis at the death of the spouse differs depending on the character (individual or marital) of the property in question is discussed in Section B, above.

The ability to destroy the right of survivorship in survivorship marital property depends upon both the form in which the property is held and on whether the entire ownership interest or only a portion of it is transferred.

Wis.Stat. § 766.605 contains a rule covering the Wisconsin homestead, which is a primary residence (owned or rented) surrounded by a limited amount of acreage, depending on whether the property is urban or rural (up to one acre if the homestead is not part of a farm and up to 120 acres if it is part of a farm). According to the statute **"A homestead acquired after the determination date which, when acquired, is held exclusively between spouses with no 3rd party is survivorship marital property if no intent to the contrary is expressed on the instrument of transfer . . . ."** Under this statute, unless a contrary intent is shown, a deed of realty to a husband and wife (and no other person) as grantees creates survivorship marital property if the realty is in fact a homestead. If the deeded realty is not a homestead, the spouses have full testamentary rights as to the property since the property is marital property without a right of survivorship.

A homestead is given additional protections than the double step up in basis under federal income tax law for the surviving spouse, discussed in Section B above. State law also protects eligible homestead property from the reach of many of the decedent spouse's creditors.

Wis.Stat. § 766.60(4)(b)1.(a) states that if **"a document of title, instrument of transfer or bill of sale"** after the determination date expresses an intention to establish a joint tenancy or a tenancy in common, the property is, respectively survivorship marital property or marital property.

Similarly, Wis.Stat. § 766.60(4)(b)2 states:

"A joint tenancy or tenancy in common exclusively between spouses which is given to the spouses by a 3rd party after the determination date is survivorship marital property or marital property, respectively, unless the donor provides otherwise." This important provision clarifies situations were a third-party donor makes a gift to the spouses, of an asset titled in both their names, during their marriage. The Wisconsin rule is inclusive in its coverage and sensible in its outcome.

CHAPTER 7
CHARACTERIZATION PROBLEMS

A. OVERVIEW

This Chapter focuses on the mechanics of characterization for purposes of a marital dissolution.

1. GENERAL APPROACHES

a. Overriding Contracts, Transmutations, and Special Community Property Presumptions

Before applying the material in this chapter, determine whether the parties have overriding contract or proof of transmutation. Enforceable contracts and transmutations will control the outcome.

b. Community Property Presumption

Identify the community property presumption at play under state law *and* how to rebut that specific presumption.

c. Some General Rules of Apportionment

Decide if two or more marital estates have contributed to the purchase or increase in value of the relevant asset.

A marital estate can be community property, the separate property of one spouse, or the separate property of the other spouse.

A contribution may be funds to purchase or an improvement that increases the value of the property. Other contributions might be labeled as the conferral of a benefit by one estate upon another. A conferral of a benefit might be understood as something less than a contribution to purchase but something more than a true gift. See Chapter 5 for more on doctrinal differences between gifts, conferred benefits, and contributions to purchase.

Commingled assets must go through an accounting.

Accounting is a remedy. Accounting methods are determined by law.

Profit-sharing may be allowed or not depending on state law. Otherwise, a court may order a reimbursement to a marital estate that conferred a benefit on another marital estate.

After deciding that there is no overriding premarital agreement, transmutation, or applicable superseding community property presumption, consider these general points.

- The inception of title rule provides that the character of an asset is set or determined at the time the asset is acquired.
- An asset is acquired on the date that legal rights to it come into existence.
- An asset can be acquired by purchase or by other legal methods.

- When an asset is acquired by purchase, the source of purchase funds may and likely will factor into the characterization process.

d. Apportionment for Specific Categories of Assets

Loan proceeds acquired by a person during marriage while domiciled in the state are generally characterized as community property. If acquired prior to marriage, the loan proceeds are accounted for as separate property even if the loan principal is repaid during marriage.

Many loan agreements give the lender control over dispersal of proceeds for purchase and over management decisions in case of borrower default. How the loan proceeds are distributed, along with the terms of the loan contract, can set or determine (depending on state law) the character of the asset at purchase.

Loan proceeds can be distributed in at least one of two ways.

One way to release loan proceeds is to transfer them directly to a third-party seller on behalf of the spouses. Under this model, the lender does not transfer control of the loan proceeds to the borrowers. Additionally, the lender retains control of asset in the event of default.

If the borrowers do not come into possession of the loan proceeds, then the character of the loan is decided by when the loan proceeds are transferred to the seller. If the loan proceeds are transferred during marriage, the loan is presumptively community in character. For this fact pattern, most states allow rebuttal by the lender's intent test. The lender's intent test is clearly met if a lender relied *solely* on the separate property of the obligor spouse in originating the loan.

The lender's intent rebuttal makes sense if one considers that the lender is asserting control over the loan proceeds in relation to the borrower. Thus, if the lender has identified the borrower as the spouse with sufficient separate property to guarantee the loan, and if the lender has secured the loan solely with that spouse's separate property assets, then the loan proceeds are themselves separate property.

A few states allow rebuttal by the community purpose method of characterizing loan proceeds. Under this test, a loan is community property if it was obtained for a community purpose, but separate property if it was obtained for a non-community purpose. Drawing the line between community and non-community purpose can require much in the way of the court's time and energy.

A second way to release loan proceeds is to transfer them directly to the borrowers' bank account by direct deposit. A direct deposit constitutes relinquishment of possession and control of the loan proceeds to the borrower by the lender.

Here again the loan proceeds are presumptively community property if acquired during marriage, this is so no matter how the bank account is titled. Rebuttal is allowed, but rebuttal will require tracing the loan proceeds *to and through* the bank account into which the lender deposited them. Whether rebuttal requires simple or specialized records depends on state law. In this scenario, where the lender releases the funds directly the spouses, it is possible for a borrower to acquire loan proceeds, or the right to loan proceeds (as with a line of credit), prior to marriage, only to have those proceeds be properly characterized as community property during the marriage.

Secured credit acquisitions made before marriage in all states, come to the marriage as separate property by application of the inception of title rule.

A secured credit acquisition is the purchase of an asset with a loan that is distributed to the seller of the asset by the lender on behalf of the borrower who later marries. The lender in this scenario does not relinquish control of the loan proceeds to the borrower. Rather, the lender transfers the loan proceeds directly to the seller as part of the sales transaction. Additionally, the loan is secured by the asset itself signaling that the lender retains control over the management of the asset in case of default.

The following rules apply to cases where all three facts are established.

Fact 1: *prior to the marriage of the borrower*, the lender advanced loan proceeds directly to a third-party seller on behalf of a single borrower, and the lender secured the loan with the asset purchased.

Fact 2: *during marriage*, the community helped repay the separate property loan principal.

Fact 3: *an accounting is requested at sale or end of marriage* to help determine what proportion of the asset became community property, if any, and what proportion remains separate property, if any.

The California leads the way in the apportionment approach. It does this by recognizing what the courts have labeled a vested "pro tanto interest" in the community that arises as of the date of its first contribution to purchase. The character of the purchase is initially *set* as separate property by the inception of title rule. But over time, if the community's contribution to purchase grows, the community's unwritten pro tanto interest gives rise to a pro rata ownership interest in the asset. Thus, an asset that started out as entirely separate property at its purchase, becomes commingled over time, which is to say co-owned between the separate property purchaser and the community property. Since partners share profits, and because the community has established a pro rata share of ownership in the property, the community is entitled, by right, to its pro rata share of any calculated or hypothetical appreciation.

In contrast to the California approach is the Texas approach.

Texas leads the way with the *reimbursement* approach. By this approach, the character of the purchase is *determined* as separate property at its purchase. Any benefits conferred by a different estate are reimbursed by the benefited estate. The goal is to prevent unjust enrichment of the benefited estate. Whether a reimbursement is due is for the court to determine. Appreciation is not shared because no matter the judge's decision, the inception of title rule applies so that the property's character, as *determined* on the date of its acquisition, holds steady to and through the marriage.

Separate property businesses: A separate property business is defined in one of two ways. It can be a business started or acquired before marriage. Or it can be a business started or acquired during marriage with provable separate property funds. Community labor added to the separate property business can give the community a claim, but to what? At dissolution or sale of the business, the accounting problem becomes how to compensate the community for its contribution, large or small, to the growth of separate property business. Where the community does not contribute to business growth, it may be entitled to a reimbursement for uncompensated community property labor contributions.

In all community property states, the inception of title rule determines the character of the business upon dissolution or death. In other words, no matter the court's decision about how to address the community's claim against the separate property business, the business remains separate property in and after the dissolution.

Pension benefits (deferred compensation) and other deferred employment benefits are apportioned using a time rule—so called because time employed is how interests in and out of marriage are determined. The time rule divides the time of participation in the employment benefit during marriage (the numerator) by the total time of participation in the employment benefit (the denominator).

Life insurance: Term life insurance policies take on the character of the funds that paid the last premium payment. The last premium payment is the payment that was made before the evitable contingency in the contract—here the death of the insured spouse—occurred.

So, for example, if in the month of X's death, X, who leaves a surviving spouse Y, paid a term life insurance with community property, then the life insurance proceeds are entirely community property in character. Assume X named only a non-spousal POD beneficiary Z on the life insurance contract. Z would be entitled, by the POD term in the life insurance contract, to 50% of the insurance proceeds as against X's spouse Y. Y, although not named as POD, is nevertheless entitled to Y's community property share of 50%.

If X had paid for the last contract term with 20% separate property and 80% community property, then Z would be entitled to 60% (20% of the separate property proceeds + 40% of the community property proceeds = 60% total) of the insurance proceeds as against Y, who would be entitled to 40%, (80% ÷ 2 = 40% total), or one-half of the community property share of the proceeds.

If X paid the last contract term entirely with separate property, then Z would be entitled to 100%

of the insurance proceeds as against Y, who would take 0%.

Whole life insurance savings components, or savings components of term policies (if any) are apportioned between the character of funds that contributed to the savings component.

These basic principles and steps listed above are a starting point for specific types of assets.

Additional complications may arise in each jurisdiction, and in each case, depending on the circumstances.

2. COMMINGLING BASICS

Commingling is very easy to do.

States have made strides toward simplifying bank deposit problems. Still, bank deposits can be commingled, as when different character deposits are made to the account. Purchases can be commingled, as when different character funds contribute to the purchase.

Business profits can become commingled as when community property labor helps make the business profitable.

Deferred compensation plans and pension benefits can be commingled as when earnings are acquired while single versus while married (pensions), or while married versus after a date of separation (pensions), or by different character deposits (in the case of defined contribution plans like 401(k)s, IRAs and so forth), or by acquisition of preferred rights from an employer (stock options).

When commingling occurs, different outcomes are possible depending on how the asset is treated under state law.

a. The Inception of Title Rule

The keystone to a ganancial community property system is the inception of title rule.

That rule provides that the character of an asset is *set*, or in some states *determined*, on the date of its acquisition. The date of acquisition is when legal rights to the asset come into existence.

If the asset is purchased before marriage, that asset comes to the marriage as the owner's separate property.

If the asset is purchased while married and domiciled in the state, that asset comes into the marriage as community property.

If, over time, a different character of property contributes to the acquisition of an asset, depending on state law, that asset can become commingled unless the contribution is de minimis. There may be state law that distinguishes between a contribution to purchase and the conferral of a benefit.

Illustration 7.1: Prior to marriage H buys a house with a down payment of $500,000 and a $500,000 purchase money loan secured by the house. Title is in H's name alone. Assume that on the date of marriage, H no longer has a mortgage, and all security interests on the house have been released. On the date of H's marriage to W, the house is characterized as entirely (100%) H's separate property.

Illustration 7.2: Same facts as Illustration 7.1 except that on the date of marriage, H has paid off all but $200 of the $500,000 mortgage loan. Assume further that during the marriage H pays off the remaining principal portion of the loan with $200 of community property earnings. In all jurisdictions the house is likely characterized as entirely H's separate property in accordance with the definition of separate property (the house is owned by H prior to marriage and thus it comes to the marriage as H's separate property). Most states would treat the $200 payment as the conferral of a benefit rather than as a true contribution to purchase, thereby allowing W to make a reimbursement claim for $100, which is her one-half of the $200.

What is the difference between a contribution to purchase versus the conferral of a benefit in this case?

If the $200 is treated as a contribution to purchase, it can be overlooked as de minimis compared to the original purchase price of the asset. This rationale includes a total of two steps: step one, naming as implausible the conclusion that a payment of $200 to a $1,000,000 purchase is evidence of an acquisition to purchase; and step two, naming the far more plausible idea that such a "contribution" is not evidence of a contribution at all because it is de minimis relative to the purchase price of the house.

If the $200 is treated as a conferral of benefit, the issue will be whether it unjustly enriches the benefited estate to not reimburse W's one-half of $200.

If a court finds (implausibly) that W has a 0.0002% pro rata interest, the house will need to have a market appreciation of $500,000 for W to walk away with the same $100 payment from H that she can get by asking for a simple reimbursement. Therefore, unless there is appreciation of more than $500,000, reimbursement is the efficient way to go.

b. The Concept of Pro Tanto Ownership

Pro tanto, pro rata, fractional, and commingled are similar term often interchanged by lawyers and judges who write opinions and orders. Despite their apparent interchangeability in legal parlance, each term can have a slightly different meaning in a formal sense.

Pro tanto	Latin for so much or to a certain extent. Can be used in law to describe a partial release of a debt or obligation.
Pro rata	Latin for in proportion. In English, a percentage share or a proportional share of the whole.
Commingle	To combine funds or properties that are co-owned into a common fund or property.

Fraction	To separate out something larger into smaller component parts.
Apportion	To divide and allocate.

In a state like California which not just follows but created the so-called American rule, a separate property credit acquisition brought to the marriage and titled in the purchasing spouse's name alone is separate property at its inception. This is by application of the inception of title rule. However, during marriage, if the separate property loan is repaid with community property earnings, then case law recognizes the vesting of a *pro tanto* interest in favor of the community. The interest is vested, which simply means that at the point the pro tanto interest is recognized, the house is newly regarded as a *commingled,* asset, one co-owned between the separate property owner and the community.

Illustration 7.3: Assume a house is purchased with a loan before marriage and state law allows for vesting of a pro tanto interest. Title is in the purchasing spouse's name alone. On the date of the first community contribution to purchase, a pro tanto interest in the community vests. If mortgage payments are made throughout the marriage, at dissolution, all community mortgage principal payments will count as community contributions to purchase. The sum of these community mortgage principal payments is then divided by the purchase price of the house to determine the community's pro rata (fractional) share of ownership. If the house has appreciated in value, the community is entitled, as a matter of property right, to its pro rata share of asset appreciation too. Transaction costs are borne by the parties in their respective pro rata shares, with community property costs split in half.

Proportional ownership works well for some types of assets (for example, securities) but less well, if at all, for other types of assets (for example, property acquired by adverse possession). Louisiana has been the state least willing to recognize proportionate ownership in accordance with a contribution to acquisition approach.

It is as likely that, for whatever reason, the community might prefer a reimbursement. But this option makes most sense when an asset has depreciated in value from purchase to accounting.

Illustration 7.4: During marriage H buys a car for $10,000. He takes title in his name alone. H uses $2,500 of provable separate property funds (SPH) plus $7,500 in community property (CP) cash to pay the remainder of the purchase price. The car title shows that it was acquired during marriage while H was domiciled in the state, therefore, the car is *presumptively* 100% community property despite the sole title in H's name. However, H has the option to rebut the general community property presumption by proving that he made a separate property contribution to the purchase of the car. If H's rebuttal attempt succeeds, he can prove that his separate property has a pro rata (percentage) share of 25% ($2,500 SPH ÷ $10,000 car purchase price = 25%). In this case, the car, would be regarded as commingled, meaning owned 25% as H's separate property and 75% as community property.

An alternate outcome could be that H concedes that the car is entirely community property but seeks a $2,500 reimbursement to cover his provable separate property contribution to purchase.

Illustration 7.5: Same facts as 7.4 except that the car has depreciated in value. He sells it for $3,000. Rather than seek co-ownership, H can opt for a reimbursement of his $2,500 purchase contribution. H's reimbursement has priority, so it gets paid first. The community share of $500 is split by the spouses, but only after reimbursements are paid.

If the car had been sold for $1,000 instead of $3,000. H would still get a reimbursement, but only in the amount of $1,000.

c. Ownership versus Reimbursement

In a general sense, what is the difference between ownership and reimbursement in the context of marriage?

Ownership presumes a spouse who has a legal right to the thing in question and rights of management and control as well.

Reimbursement presumes a spouse who is in the status of a lender in relation to the community. Because of this status, the spouse who seeks a reimbursement is entitled to return of whatever funds were extended to help purchase the asset.

Most U.S. states follow the so-called American rule approach. Take for example, a house purchased prior to marriage with a loan but paid for during marriage with earnings. In those states, the inception of title rule *sets* the character of the asset, but with the first contribution to purchase, the pro tanto obligation comes into existence. The pro tanto obligation results in a vested pro rata share that, once established (proven), the court is mandated to recognize. Recognition by the court essentially divests the separate property owner's title in the amount of the community's pro rata share.

Currently, the American rule requires a two-step accounting before title can be cleared for sale. Step one identifies contributions to purchase of different characters. Step two calculates pro rata (fractional) shares of asset ownership.

In contrast to the American rule approach, some states follow the traditional civil law approach. In civil law states, the inception of title rule *determines* the character of the asset from purchase through to sale or dissolution. Any benefits conferred by the community on a separate property owner are *reimbursed* to prevent unjust enrichment of the benefited estate. The court's authority is broad on the issue of preventing unjust enrichment. But unlike in American rule states, where a court recognizes that the house is co-owned, in civil law states the tool for preventing unjust enrichment is singular: the judge has the authority to impose an equitable lien on the benefited property in favor of the estate that conferred the benefit. See Section 4 below.

Under both rules, the community that contributes to a separate property purchase becomes a lien holder. But in American rule states, the lien protects an ownership right whereas in civil law states the lien protects a reimbursement right.

Illustration 7.6: X and Y, a couple domiciled in a community property state, decide to marry. Assume that soon *before* the date of the marriage X buys a house for $100,000 using a down payment of $25,000 and a $75,000 purchase money loan secured by the house (Time 1). X takes title in X's name alone; no changes in title are made during the marriage. X does not refinance the loan at any time during this problem. Assume further that *during* marriage earnings pay X's mortgage principal (Time 2) and that X subsequently files for dissolution of marriage (Time 3).

In an American rule state, the inception of title rule for X's house is *set* on the date of purchase, but it can change with a contribution to purchase made with a different character of funds. At dissolution, when the character contributions are accounted for, the law will apportion the house pro rata between X and the community of X and Y.

In a state that follows the civil law, such as Texas, the inception of title rule *determines* the character of the house as entirely separate property, with no change in character possible going forward. When the community confers a benefit on X's separate property, the community may become eligible for a reimbursement depending on whether it meets statutory elements. To enforce the reimbursement judgment a court has authority to order an equitable lien on X's house.

Keep in mind that not all contributions to purchase lead to commingling. In the above examples, title was in one spouse's name alone. But notice what occurs when X, as separate property owner, explicitly decides to make the community a co-owner of the asset.

Illustration 7.7: Same facts as Illustration 7.6 except that *during* marriage the purchasing spouse X whose name is on title signs a joint form deed, as grantor, in a state that allows the unilateral creation of concurrent titles. The joint form deed reads "*X to X and Y as joint tenants with the right of survivorship.*" No other agreements are made between the spouses about the character of the house at the time that the deed is delivered. Assume the community confers a benefit on X by paying down the purchase money mortgage principal. At dissolution, if the state has a special community property presumption for assets in joint form title, the house is presumed to be entirely (100%) community property for purposes of the dissolution proceeding. In this case the house will not have a separate property ownership component, but this is the result of positive action taken by X the original separate property owner. X changed the deed form from sole to joint form without also obtaining a second agreement rejecting the community property outcome.

d. Transmutations by Operation of Law

It is easy to commingle an asset. Too much commingling can lead to confusion.

The aptly named doctrine of confusion applies when community and separate property components can no longer be identified.

The doctrine of confusion allows a court to find a transmutation by operation of law when component character parts of an asset are no longer identifiable by an accounting or by reference to records. In such a case, the entire asset becomes conclusively community property in character.

The rationale of the doctrine of confusion is gift-based. Donative intent is found when the separate property contributor allows their separate property contribution to become unidentifiable relative to commingled community property. Delivery of the gift occurs at the point of confusion.

Illustration 7.8: Same facts as Illustration 7.6 above for a house purchased *before* marriage, except that *during* marriage the purchasing spouse refinances the house multiple times and keeps no clear financial records. Assume that when the parties file for dissolution, the purchaser's separate property contribution to the house cannot be identified, even by the low preponderance of the evidence standard.

Here, the doctrine of confusion is raised to protect the community. The elements of the argument are based on the common law of gifts. The element of donative intent is established by facts showing the separate property owner decided not to keep records. The delivery element is established by facts showing that the separate property share could no longer be identified relative to the community property share. Acceptance of the gift by the community is presumed absent facts showing otherwise.

3. TRACING BASICS: FOLLOWING THE MONEY TRAIL

Because commingling is common, records kept by the parties may and likely are required to trace assets back to purchase or funds back to acquisition dates. Tracing is an investigative technique commonly referred to as following the money trail. Tracing is also an equitable remedy that originated with the common law of trusts.

Tracing can be relatively basic or specialized depending on the facts of the case and law of the jurisdiction. In this context, tracing refers to the process of using investigative techniques to identify character component percentages of an asset by (most commonly) a preponderance of the evidence standard.

Parol evidence is acceptable in some cases to establish the character of money (or even sums on deposit).

Accounting with basic records, which run the gamut from rudimentary to elaborate, are more reliable than parol evidence if the records are kept contemporaneously relative to the purchase. Records prepared for litigation are suspect because they increase the risk of perjury.

Accounting with specialized bank account records is, in some cases and in some jurisdictions, necessary to successfully rebut an applicable community property presumption as to sums on deposit in a bank account. Here again, contemporaneous record keeping is preferred if not required.

In the community property sphere, specialized bank records can be used to answer three issues. The first is what is the character of sums on deposit on a particular date. The second is what is the character of sums that were withdrawn from the account on a certain date. The third is what were those withdrawn funds used to purchase.

In the marriage context, specialized records are something of a musical three-part invention. Part one is identifying separate property deposits and withdrawals. Part two is identifying community property deposits and withdrawals. Part three is applying the family expense presumption so that family expenses are deducted first from community property sums on deposit. These three tasks, applied together, identify net *character* deposits and withdrawals *on a given calendar date.*

Specialized records are not required to add a burden to spouses' lives. Rather, they serve a systemic function.

A state can require specialized records to require factual and temporal clarity. Clearer information means that the evidentiary standard of proof can remain at the lowest preponderance of the evidence. Here, the strategic trend seems to be toward favoring more detailed and accurate contemporaneously kept records over general records to shore up community property presumption rebuttal efforts.

Some states do not require specialized records, but they consequently adopt the higher clear and convincing standard of proof. In some ways, the same outcome is ensured. The party with the clearest records will have a more convincing story. So even here, the strategic trend will be toward favoring more detailed and accurate contemporaneously kept records over general records.

Contemporaneous accounting requires the keeping of consistent records over time to reflect when character-specific deposits and withdrawals are made.

Accounting with start-date/end-date values (aka total recapitulation accounting), establishes values at significant points in time (as opposed to contemporaneously on a day-to-day or periodic basis). Start dates and end dates are most commonly milestone dates.

Rationales for tracing are three.

The first rationale is constitutional. Some state constitutions protect the right to own separate property during marriage. Tracing is the investigative work that helps protect that right.

The second rationale is informational. Tracing is the investigative work that underlies rules such as the inception of title rule, and that helps identify contributions to purchase and conferrals of benefit.

The third rationale is remedial. A pro rata ownership share comes into existence as an unwritten title. American rule states recognize that the pro rata ownership share is a vested interest that gets formally secured by the asset during the dissolution process.

Likewise, a statutory right of reimbursement is an unrecorded debt. All states recognize the reimbursement as a loan that gets formally secured by the asset during the dissolution process. The tool for securing the ownership share or the loan is the equitable lien.

4. OWNERSHIP VERSUS REIMBURSEMENT FOR UNCOMMON ACQUISITIONS

The American rule approach for credit acquisitions is temporally dynamic, but it may be historically static. The goal of the American rule—which has been adopted widely across the U.S.—is to vest the community contributor with its proportional share of ownership; of course, to do so requires divesting the beneficial title holder of that same share of ownership. As for community property states, California, Nevada, and New Mexico follow the American rule approach.

The civil law rule approach for credit acquisitions is temporally static with the goal of protecting separate property owners from a court order that divests them of the community (or marital) pro rata share. Of the community property states, Arizona, Idaho, Louisiana, Texas, and Washington follow the civil law rule approach. Under this approach, a reimbursement may be due based on proof of the value of the benefit conferred on the separate property owner by the community.

To be sure, even in a civil law state, a community can purchase a pro rata share. But the rule is that gratuitous transfers from one marital estate to another are, by default, understood to be conferral of benefits, not contributions to purchase.

Under both approaches these time points are dispositive.

Time 1 is the date of the inception of title.

Time 2 is the date of the first contribution to purchase *or* conferral of benefit by an estate of a different character.

Time 3 is the date of a sale or dissolution, which is itself a partition process. At this time, the value of each contribution or conferred benefit is added up

Illustration 7.9: A spouse buys a house *before* marriage (Time 1). Title is in the purchaser's name alone. The house is paid for during marriage with community property earnings (Time 2). In all jurisdictions, the inception of title rule (Time 1) decides the original character of the house as the purchasing spouse's separate property.

(Time 2) On the date of the first separate property loan principal repayment made with community property, states split on the issue of whether the community acquires a qualified vested ownership or alternatively a reimbursement right.

(Time 3) The community is either awarded its pro rata ownership share, as in American rule states. Or else it acquires a right to ask for a reimbursement of any benefit it conferred, as in civil law states, where the reimbursement is awarded to prevent unjust enrichment of the benefited estate.

Many, but not all, credit acquisition cases involve mortgaged real estate secured by the purchased asset. Mortgage funded acquisitions are time-based in the sense that the asset is purchased from a seller but paid for over time. Therefore, if a house is paid for in cash, a different form of accounting may be required.

Here are additional time-based acquisition problems in this area. In each of these examples Time 1 is prior to marriage. Time 2 is during marriage. Time 3 follows Time 2. Different results are reached in different states, and sometimes within the same state, depending on the method of acquisition.

LARGE PURCHASE MADE WITH A REAL ESTATE CONTRACT: H, a single person, enters a contract to purchase (in Louisiana, "bond for deed" for) Blackacre (Time 1). H pays the consideration from his earnings during marriage (Time 2). After full payment is made, H receives title to the real estate (Time 3).

MORTGAGE FORECLOSURE: W, a single person, sells Blackacre and takes back a mortgage from her buyer (Time 1). H's buyer defaults (Time 2).

W, as creditor, takes a deed in lieu of foreclosure during marriage (Time 3).

LAND PATENT: H, a single person, enters land under a federal land grant (Time 1); a patent is issued during H's marriage to W (Time 2). Years later, H files for dissolution (Time 3).

ADVERSE POSSESSION WITHOUT COLOR OF TITLE, EXAMPLE 1: W enters adverse possession (or prescription) without color of title while single and begins her claim against a negligent owner of land (Time 1). During marriage, the limitation period runs thus vesting W with title by adverse possession title (Time 2). W seeks dissolution (Time 3).

ADVERSE POSSESSION WITH COLOR OF TITLE, EXAMPLE 2: W enters adverse possession (or prescription) without color of title while single and begins her claim (Time 1). During marriage, the limitation period runs thus vesting W with title by adverse possession title (Time 2). W obtains a quiet title action in her favor (Time 3).W seeks dissolution (Time 4).

ADVERSE POSSESSION WITH COLOR OF TITLE, EXAMPLE 3: W enters adverse possession without color of title while single and begins her claim (Time 1). During marriage, the limitation period runs thus vesting W with title by adverse possession title (Time 2). W does not bring a quiet title action before she files for dissolution (Time 3).

CONTINGENT FEE: W, an attorney, enters a contingent fee contract while single (Time 1). W renders legal services to her client and obtains a verdict and judgment in her client's favor (Time 2). The verdict is upheld on appeal, W's judgment is executed, and funds are finally made available for payment after the final judgment in W's dissolution proceeding (Time 3).

PERSONAL INJURY CLAIM: W, a single person, pursues a malpractice claim against a doctor for a duty established at Time 1, and breached at Time 2. W does not discover the injury until during her marriage to H, at Time 3.

EMPLOYMENT BENEFITS (PENSION): W, a single person, is employed by ABC Corp. and W's pension rights vest (Time 1). W's pension rights increase in incremental percentages during her marriage; and eventually, W's pension rights mature subject to conditions that will not be completely removed until W retires (Time 2). While still employed, W files for dissolution (Time 3).

At what time in the above examples is the asset acquired for purposes of the community property principle. When is the inception of title? Time 1? Time 2? Time 3? Time 4, in some cases?

The inception of title theory usually characterizes property at the point in time when an actionable property right is established, whether it be contingent or vested. A term life insurance contract on a living person, the forfeitable pension rights of an employee, the not yet perfected claim of an adverse possessor are each mere expectancies that may become contingent and eventually vested rights. An expectancy is not a property right or interest, and hence it is not subject to division at dissolution or death. By comparison, a contingent property right, even though it may not soon become possessory, can be the basis for a legal claim.

Thus, in the adverse possession examples above, notice that the claimant's legal right to the property does not come into existence until the statute of limitations bars the negligent owner from bringing a suit to regain the property. If the adverse possessor quiets title and obtains a court judgment in their favor, the date of acquisition will relate back to the original entry. Thus, the date of title acquisition may be far earlier than the date of the court judgment that perfects the title.

The foregoing issues are presented here in connection with a time span that extends from before, through and after marriage. Similar problems can arise when a period starts while married persons change domiciles from one jurisdiction to the another.

Occasionally, a court will use all-or-nothing approaches than an apportionment approach. The court might do this by declaring that an asset that is the product of both community and separate contributions is entirely community property (or entirely separate property) rather than a proportion of each character. The likelihood of this approach varies according to the jurisdiction, the type of asset in question, and the form the community contributions (cash, loan proceeds, labor).

B. DETAIL

1. TRACING TO AND THROUGH COMMINGLED BANK ACCOUNTS

A bank account is commingled if it holds both community property and separate property funds. Multiple party accounts laws refer to what might generally be called "funds" or "money," as "sums on deposit" in the bank account. Bank accounts are referred to as depository or depositary (with a "a") accounts.

If the Uniform-Persons Accounts Act (UMPAA 1989) or, as under the California Uniform-Parties Accounts Law (CAMPAL 1990), all sums on deposit in any depository (bank) account of a married person are presumptively community property absent admissible rebuttal evidence. See Chapter 4 for more on statutory multiple-persons and multiple-parties accounts laws.

a. Techniques and Options

A commingled bank account is a disputed account as a matter of law. This is because commingling a bank account exposes the community property funds to the risk of impairment.

Spouses are in a confidential relationship with each other. The legal significance of such a relationship is that each spouse has a general duty not to take any unfair advantage of the other spouse in a transaction between them. See Chapter 8 for more on duties between spouses.

Sums on deposit are most commonly community property in character.

Rebuttal as to separate property deposits is possible with character specific bank records.

Specialized records are account specific records that are contemporaneously kept.

Contemporaneously kept records means that the records being offered for rebuttal are prepared at or around the time deposits and withdrawals are transacted; contemporaneously kept records reduce the risk of perjury in a later proceeding.

Net character deposits show sums on deposit in the account after family expenses are paid.

The family expense presumption subtracts family expenses from community property sums on deposit first, and then from separate property sums on deposit if community funds are exhausted.

Depending on state law, separate property funds used to pay family expenses (expenditures for consumable goods) may be regarded as a gift to the community absent evidence of a written reimbursement agreement between the spouses.

b. Common Law Equitable Claims

The Restatement (First) of Restitution (1937) proposes that a claimant who traces assets through a commingled fund into a product of the fund be limited—even as against a conscious wrongdoer—to a share of the product **"in such proportion as his money bore to the whole amount of the fund."**

Restatement (First) of Restitution § 210(2). This same provision gives an equitable claim against the property for *reimbursement* to the owner of money which is wrongfully mingled by another and subsequently used to acquire property. The Restatement section also allows the alternative remedy of a *constructive trust* if **"the wrongdoer knew that he was acting wrongfully."**

The Restatement (Third) of Restitution and Unjust Enrichment (2011) §§ 58 and 59 is an updated version consistent with the rules presented in the Restatement (First) of Restitution (1937). The Restatement 2011 suggests **"permitting the claimant (as against a wrongdoer) to claim the entire advantage of beneficial withdrawals that can be attributed to the claimant's funds."** Restatement (Third) of Restitution & Unjust Enrichment § 59 (2011).

It is still too soon to tell whether the Restatement (Third) will be accepted by courts as useful in community property disputes. That said, there is at least one important difference between the First and Third Restatements of Restitution and Unjust Enrichment. It has to do with the difference between remedy for reimbursement—the equitable lien—versus the remedy for restitution—the constructive trust.

If there is a limit on which claim can be used, here is the breakdown:

- *Equitable lien* imposed on the commingled bank account: the Restatement (First) of

Restitution (1937), provides in § 211 that the lien attaches to the money remaining in the account and upon the proceeds of the part of the account that was withdrawn. See also Sec. 212.

- *Restitution*: here the idea is to restore the claimant to lost property, opportunity costs, or to a previous situation.

As a practical matter the difference between an equitable lien and restitution lies in what can be recovered. This difference becomes material when an asset appreciates over time. In such a case, the *creditor* of a debt secured by an equitable lien upon the property does not benefit if the property increases in value, whereas an *owner* of an interest in the appreciating item (by constructive trust) does benefit.

The Restatement (Third) of Restitution and Unjust Enrichment §§ 54 through 61 describe how tracing establishes the link between the transaction that gives rise to the claim and the property in question. Practically speaking, tracing is the investigative tool that gives the innocent party the information necessary to make the choice between a constructive trust (i.e., to own a fractional share in the claimed property) or an equitable lien (i.e., to have, as a creditor, a secured position in the asset for the dollar amount owed by the wrongdoer).

The question of whether to prefer an asset or an asset-based remedy versus an equitable lien may arise for any number of reasons, economic and noneconomic. The psychological difference may be strong between owning a percentage of an asset (via a constructive trust) versus being entitled as a creditor to a reimbursement that is secured by an equitable lien on the asset.

c. Conversion Damages

The Restatement (Third) of Restitution and Unjust Enrichment (2011) additionally provides that a party who gains a benefit in breach of a fiduciary duty is liable for damage. This is a general principle, but it clearly applies in the dissolution context.

In the case of commingled funds, the managing spouse is a spouse who is in a confidential relationship with the non-managing spouse by the fact of the marriage. That spouse can be liable for conversion, a common law cause of action.

The conversion cause of action accrues at the point of commingling (which is when the account becomes disputed) or, in states permitting the extension of a statute of limitations, by the discovery rule (which is the point in time when the harm is discovered). A cause of action in conversion can also arise when a spouse is unjustly enriched by the impairment caused to the other spouse's community property interest in the subject property.

The Restatement imposes liability for conversion at the point of commingling, regardless of the commingling converter's intention or state of mind. The reason is the commingling converter obtains advantages that come from *sidestepping disclosure, negotiation, contracting, and payment*. A breach of fiduciary duty claim addresses these issues. The converter's degree of fault does and should become relevant, not in dividing property (as all community property states have adopted no-fault dissolution), but in assessing damages.

2. SEPARATE PROPERTY BUSINESSES

As set forth above, a separate property business is defined as a business started before marriage or during marriage with provable separate property funds

In the case of a separate property business, total recapitulation accounting is most often used. This requires proof of the value of the business at the start and at the end of marriage.

Marriage does not automatically transmute separate property into community property in the U.S. Therefore, absent a transmutation, the premarital business comes to the marriage as separate property. A separate property business also can be started or bought during marriage with provable separate property capital. Therefore, the value of the business on the date of marriage or on the date of start-up is necessary to establish the baseline separate property value of the business (*Element 1*).

The fair market value of the business at the time of dissolution or death of its owner identifies the business's increased value over time, if any (*Element 2*).

The relationship between Element 1 and Element 2 above is that the business starts as a separate property business, and the inception of title rule determines its character for purposes of dissolution. A mere change in value of the separate property business does not change its character.

Element 3 is a hypothetical look at what the start-up capital would have returned had it been invested in reasonably safe securities. This number represents separate property rents, issues, and profits that are also characterized as separate property.

Element 4 is the level of community property labor on a scale from minimum to substantial.

The relationship between Element 3 and Element 4 is that while separate property rents, issues and profits belong to the separate property, excess profits are characterized as the community property, but only if the community helped grow the business.

Labor includes management efforts. Normally all cash earnings partly or completely withdrawn (or overdrawn) in the form of salary are treated as a business expense, not as a contribution to the profitability of the business.

Ideally, a business will generate enough value to equal the total of capital contributions, returns on capital, and excess profits. Ideally, useful financial records will be available to identify the relative contributions of management versus capital. It is only because the ideal situation seldom if ever exists those adjustments of the type described in this chapter are necessary.

Considering the less-than-ideal situations that abound at dissolution, disputes can arise over where to draw the line between reasonable profits—which are characterized as the separate property owner of the business—or excess profits—which are characterized as community property depending on the facts of the case.

a. The American Law Approach versus the Civil Law Approach

In American law states rents, issues and profits of separate property received during marriage are separate property. In these states, the method is to subtract separate property profits from total profits. What remains is excess profits. Excess profits, if any, are characterized as community property.

In civil law states, by contrast, Element 3—profits—is characterized as community property during the marriage by usufruct. At dissolution profits once again belong to the separate property business owner.

All states allow the separate property owner's business records to be admitted into evidence. However, the amount, timing, and nomenclature of distribution from the business is within the control of the managing spouse. Therefore, business records as to what constituted salary and what dividends were reinvested may not be objective (or in some cases even kept). Additionally, because the records are kept for purposes other than dissolution (like tax purposes or liquidity reports), they often are not accurate on the type of data required to apportion business profits at dissolution.

Many states direct courts to use the doctrine to further a policy of doing substantial justice between the parties.

b. More on the American Law Approach: *Pereira* Apportionment versus *Van Camp* Reimbursement

When community property management, in the form of labor, helps generate business profits, the issue of how to apportion total profits can be handled in one of two ways.

Alternative 1—known as the *Pereira* approach—provides that business profits (not the business itself) can be apportioned between the separate and community property.

Alternative 2—known as the *Van Camp* approach—provides that profits belong entirely to the separate property, but the community is due a net reimbursement for the benefit it conferred on the business in the form of labor.

c. *Pereira v. Pereira*: The Apportionment Approach

In *Pereira v. Pereira*, 156 Cal. 1, 103 P. 488 (1909) the California Supreme Court used a total recapitulation accounting method to apportion the *profits* of a separate property saloon business. The community's interest, created by adding a quantum of labor into the business, was discussed as a right to *excess profits*. The value for excess profits was measured by the difference in value between the fair market value of the business at divorce minus the sum of the following: original separate property capital at marriage plus a fair rate of return on that original capital. The fair rate of return is calculated at simple interest to account for family expenses.

This holding became known as the *Pereira* method.

The *Pereira* holding can be expressed as a formula.

$$\mathbf{FMV@_{divorce} - (FMV@_{marriage} + FRR) = Excess\ Profits}$$

Where:

- **"FMV@divorce"** is the value of the separate property business at the end of the marriage.
- **"FMV@marriage"** is the value of the separate property business on the date of marriage (or the value of the startup separate property capital during marriage).
- **"FRR"** is the hypothetical fair rate of return on the original separate property capital calculated at simple interest.
- **"Excess profits"** are what remains after the separate property is compensated for the use of its capital during the relevant time period. This is the community property component of the profits.

Losses are normally not shared by the community under *Pereira*. Rather, the community takes its excess profits as a creditor of the separate property business. Since the community is not a co-owner of the business it does not suffer losses.

The scope of covered businesses is broad. Brick-and-mortar businesses (bakeries, retail stores, and so forth) are obviously covered under this rule, but so too are any other profit-making arrangements. Taxable investment accounts brought to the marriage or started during the marriage with provable separate property funds have been treated as separate property businesses. Law and other professional firms, consultancy firms, rental property, and any other enterprise undertaken for profit are as well. Even arrangements of family trusts that name the separate property business owner as beneficiary have been consolidated into a fictional entity that gets treated as a separate property business for purposes of apportioning business profits of a separate property business in a dissolution.

d. *Van Camp v. Van Camp*: The Reimbursement Approach

Van Camp v. Van Camp, 53 Cal.App. 17, 199 P. 885 (1921) held that separate property rents, issues and profits retain their original character where growth of the underlying business is due to a factor other than community property labor. Under this formula, the community is entitled to a reimbursement for its net labor contribution to the business. Net labor means any uncompensated labor that was put into the business minus any family expenses paid from the business.

The *Van Camp* holding can be expressed as a formula:

FMV@divorce − (CP labor − Family expenses) = SP

Where:

- **"FMV@divorce"** is the fair market value of the separate property business at divorce.
- **"CP labor"** is the value of community property labor contributions to the business over the time in question.
- **"Family expenses"** are family expenses paid from the business over the time in question.

For purposes of calculating the value of uncompensated community property labor, benchmark salary figures can be used if actual records are not available. Family expenses are then subtracted from community property labor costs but only if those family expenses were actually paid from the contested business.

e. Excess Profits or Reimbursement?

In jurisdictions that follow the American rule, the court has discretion to select the formula—*Pereira* or *Van Camp*—that furthers substantial justice between the parties.

An award of excess profits is generally favored as a policy matter because it compensates the community property independently of any salary or wage that may have been paid to one or both spouse(s) from the business during marriage.

In California, *Pereira* is also favored as a doctrinal matter by application of the labor quantum standard of *minimum-plus labor*, as set forth in *Beam v. Bank of America,* 6 Cal.3d 12, 98 Cal.Rptr. 137, 490 P.2d 257 (1971), discussed below in Section C, California. In other states (Wisconsin) *substantial labor* is the labor quantum standard.

An award of excess profits may be preferable even if the community was compensated during marriage for its labor. The reason is that labor and profits are distinct components of the business. Labor is a business expense. Profits are a return on business capital. Thus, even when the community is compensated by the business for its labor, depending on the amount of labor that went into the growth of the business, the community can still be entitled to an award of excess profits as a way to achieve substantial justice between the parties.

A reimbursement is indicated when a lower quantum of community labor, as determined by state law, goes into the business. If too little community labor goes into the business, or if that labor is not tied to profitability, then a net reimbursement may be more appropriate than an award of excess profits.

There is greater variation within each jurisdiction than there is between jurisdictions in the methods used to apportion profits of a separate property business. The decided cases have almost always dealt with a successful business. If a business has no profits, then there is little reason to set out on accounting for what does not exist.

f. Type of Business Organization

The rules of this section apply to unincorporated sole proprietorships and partnerships as well as to corporations. The existence of a close (i.e., entirely or predominately owned by a married person) corporation seems to increase the problems and lead to apportionment questions. This is because in a closely held corporation, the business owner normally has substantial control in deciding whether to reinvest or distribute profits, decide salary, restrict the sale of stock, and so forth.

The separate entity for tax purposes causes greater formality in the arrangement and in the quality of business records than does an untitled business. A salary is more likely to be paid if it obtains more income advantages than a dividend; but, on the other hand, corporate earnings may be retained.

Accountants may compute the fair market value of the business by including an intangible asset known as "good will" to account for the profitability of the business. If good will is included in a computation at dissolution, it may create a speculative paper profit. Moreover, after the business is apportioned, the owner of the separate property business must pay the community, as creditor, as noted above. In such a case, the obligation may subject the business to added debt which may negatively impact from the business owner's ability to meet other obligations of importance from the business, such as spousal support or child support payments.

Often it makes more sense to distinguish between the close corporation on the one hand and a publicly traded corporation on the other hand (even though both are "corporations") than it does to distinguish between corporations and unincorporated businesses. Idaho has case law making just such a distinction.

Complex problems in all states have arisen when, at divorce, an owner of a closely held family corporation transfers shares of stock to his or her other family members as part of a strategy to avoid repaying the ex-spouse creditor.

The divorce court occasionally disregards the corporate entity in its discretion, especially if it seems to have been used to conceal assets or to obtain unfair advantage in the dissolution proceedings for the shareholder spouse.

g. Contrasts to Community Property Doctrines

There are several areas where different rules seem to apply to the separate property businesses.

In some states community property law is altered by an express modification of the Uniform Partnership Act 1914 (UPA for short) or the Revised Uniform Partnership Act of 1997 (RUPA for short) so that a partnership interest is not community property.

Credit acquisitions by a business, especially a corporation, may be subject to the business accounting rules as opposed to the rules concerning the purchase of assets with borrowed funds, a topic discussed next.

3. CREDIT ACQUISITIONS

a. General Principles

When an expensive asset (like a house) is purchased with borrowed funds, title to the real estate is taken subject to the mortgage lien or a deed of trust. In cases where contributions to the principal payments on the purchase loan are of different characters, jurisdictions split on whether or how to apportion the purchase, depending on whether the purchase is made before or during marriage. Arizona, Idaho, Washington, Louisiana, and Texas follow the civil law inception of the title rule where the character is determined at the point of purchase. California, New Mexico, Nevada, and Wisconsin follow the so-called American pro tanto approach where the character is set at the point of purchase but can change over time.

b. Character of Loan Proceeds (Borrowed Funds)

In all jurisdictions loan proceeds obtained during marriage are presumed to be community property. So too is credit and creditworthiness. How the separate property proponent rebuts this presumption as to borrowed funds that flow into the marriage depends on how the funds have been dispersed.

If the funds are dispersed directly to the borrower through a bank account, the rules on sums on deposit in any bank account of a married person come into play.

If the funds are dispersed directly from the lender to the seller of an asset on behalf of the married borrowers, then the funds are community property in character subject to one of two rebuttal tests. One is the lender's intent test, the other is the community purpose test See Sec. A. above).

Assessing the character of borrowed funds is useful to either establishing an ownership share or to determining whether a reimbursement is due.

California uses the lender's intent test which can be stated as follows: loan proceeds obtained during marriage, if advanced by the lender to the seller on behalf of the spouse(s), are presumptively community property unless the lender intended to rely *solely* on separate property in extending the loan. *Marriage of Grinius*, 166 Cal.App.3d 1179, 212 Cal.Rptr. 803 (1985), clarifying *Gudelj v. Gudelj*, 41 Cal.2d 202, 259 P.2d 656 (1953), which failed to cite precedent.

In this situation, Washington alternatively uses the community purpose test which can be stated as follows: credit obtained during marriage is either community or separate property depending on whether the funds served a community purpose.

Note that during marriage the identity of the spouses who sign the promissory note is not determinative of the character of the funds obtained. Nevertheless, a spouse's signature is important because it represents a personal contractual obligation incurred by that spouse toward the lender. As such, a spouse can expose their separate property to liability for the loan by their signature. See Chapter 9 for more on creditors rights.

c. Loans Obtained Prior to Marriage

The pro tanto approach originated in California law with *Vieux v. Vieux*, 80 Cal.App. 222, 251 P. 640 (1926). That early twentieth century case articulates the principle that by helping to repay a separate property purchase loan on separate property real estate, the community obtains a vested pro tanto interest by operation of law. The interest results in a vested pro rata ownership share that grows with every loan principal payment. The title to the real estate in this case was taken in one spouse's name only, but the in the dissolution the court recognize that the house had become commingled, thus giving both spouses an ownership interest. The husband owned the separate property interest and one-half of the community property interest; the wife owned one-half of the community property interest.

Marriage of Moore, 28 Cal.3d 366, 169 Cal.Rptr. 662, 618 P.2d 208 (1980) sets forth the basic accounting methodology for quantifying the community property pro rata interest. Because that interest is an ownership share, it entitles the community its share of *total* appreciation, if any. Total appreciation is that increase in asset value that occurs between purchase and dissolution.

Marriage of Marsden, 130 Cal.App.3d 426, 181 Cal.Rptr. 910 (1982) uses the *Moore* formula for quantifying proportional interests, but applies the community share of ownership only to *marital* appreciation. This case is used when premarital appreciation can be proved. Premarital appreciation is that increase in asset value that occurs from purchase to marriage. Marital appreciation is that increase in asset value that occurs from the date of marriage to the date of dissolution (or the death of a spouse).

The *Moore,* supra, and the so-called *Moore/ Marsden* approaches hold that the historic purchase price (the contract price) of the asset is the denominator for purposes of calculating character pro rata shares. Other states use a different price point as the denominator. New Mexico, for example, uses of the value of the asset on the date of marriage.

See Section C, California for more on both approaches.

d. A General Approach

The character of a credit acquisition purchased with different character funds is determined in the following order.

All the following steps assume that title to the asset in question is in one spouse's name alone.

Step 1: Rule out an enforceable agreement or valid transmutation. Either will prevail, regardless of other factors, including the form of title.

Step 2: Apply the inception of title rule to either determine *or to* set *the character of the asset*. If the asset securing the loan was acquired *before* marriage, its inception of title is separate property. In such a case, the burden of making a case for a pro rata ownership interest falls on the community. Alternatively, if the asset was acquired *during* marriage, the inception of title rule characterizes the property as community, leaving the burden of rebutal to the separate property claimant.

Check the form of paper title—the deed to the property. The form of the title does not necessarily control ownership of the asset in a community property jurisdiction. What the form of title determines is which community property presumption applies (the general presumption or the specific joint form title presumption) and more to the point, what evidence is needed to rebut that specific presumption.

Step 3: Apply the inception of title rule to the loan proceeds. If the loan proceeds are obtained *prior* to marriage, the loan is separate property. If the loan proceeds are obtained *during* marriage, they are presumptively community property. The separate property proponent carries the burden of rebuttal, most likely by the lender's intent test.

Step 4: What character are capital contributions, such as the down payment and loan principal repayments? Down payments and loan principal repayments are contributions to purchase in some states and conferrals of a benefit in others. Interest, taxes, insurance, and maintenance expenditures are accounted for as family expenses.

For property purchased with a separate property loan *before* marriage, check to see if loan repayments have been made *during* marriage with community property funds. These loan repayments will count as either a contribution to purchase or as the conferral of a benefit by the community on the spouse whose name is on title.

For property purchased with a community property loan *during* marriage, check for separate property funds that went into the purchase. Again, depending on the state, these moneys will either be counted as contributions to purchase or as a conferral of a benefit.

Step 5: What is state public policy? There are two main theories that determine the character of property that was acquired on credit.

American rule states use this rationale to support apportionment by pro rata shares. The narrative underlying this theory is that there was a point at which the parties implicitly agreed that the community's contribution to the purchase of the property would be in exchange for a pro rata share of ownership.

Civil law states use a different rationale for supporting a reimbursement. Here the idea is to prevent unjust enrichment of the benefited estate, meaning the estate (community or separate) that purchased the property in the first place.

4. DEFERRED COMPENSATION

a. Types of Deferred Compensation

In accordance with the basic rules discussed in Chapters 4 and 5, deferred compensation earned during marriage is presumptively community property.

Defined *benefit* plans correspond to the increasingly rare traditional pension benefit. A defined benefit plan falls into the definition of earnings, even if those earnings are not distributed until a later date. The pensioner is an annuitant, not an investor or a depositor. Moreover, defined benefit plans are generally coordinated with Social Security benefits.

Stock options, profit sharing plans, traditional pension distributions are also examples of defined benefit plans, because all are based on the employment relationship, not on the actual contributions made by the employee or the employer to an identifiable investment fund whose performance is reported to the employee by means of regular statements.

Defined *contribution* plans correspond to retirement savings accounts to which the employee contributes for purposes of investment. The employer may, but need not, match the employee's contribution to an account in the employee's name. Here the value of a defined contribution plan depends upon the amount of actual employee contributions to the plan made over time, and the rate of return obtained on invested contributions. The term defined contribution plan is broad enough to include many different vehicles such as tax deferred and tax protected accounts. Examples include a 401(k) or 403(b) account, an Individual Retirement Account (IRA), or a Roth IRA, all of which at the time of this publication are still in permitted by federal law.

Some employment benefits, like medical and dental plans, do not create divisible assets. Rather, they are in the nature of expense-reducers.

Other benefits, like bonuses and employer-guaranteed loans are routine enough that they do not raise special community property problems. What matters for these assets is timing: only benefits earned during marriage while domiciled in the state are characterized as community property.

The remaining benefits raise issues of characterization that must comply with the Internal Revenue Code and, depending on the case, with other potentially complex sections of federal laws like the Employee Retirement, Income Security Act of 1974 (ERISA for short), the Retirement Equity Act of 1984 (REACT for short), or even specific statutes related to civil service employees, military employees—the Uniformed Services former Spouses' Protection Act of 1984 (FUSFSPA for short)—public employees, or health insurance transfers—the Consolidated Omnibus Budget Reconciliation Act of 1985 (COBRA for short). These federal laws are outside the scope of this Nutshell.

b. Severance, Death, Disability, and Retirement Benefits

As a form of deferred compensation, historically (at least) employers sometimes provide one or more benefits designed to alleviate financial problems caused by retirement, disability, or death of an employee. Each benefit can raise problems and issues in community property dissolutions.

Unconditional severance pay is typically regarded as a form of deferred compensation for services previously rendered. As such, severance pay is subject to community property rules by timing, the question being whether the pay was earned for a period during marriage while domiciled in the state.

Stock options may or may not be compensation for past, present, or future services. But to the degree they are an alternative to a salary structure offered for tax purposes, they fall within the definition of work compensation and as such are subject to community property rules, if earned during marriage while domiciled in the state. Timing issues related to the granting and exercising of stock options can raise apportionment questions.

So, for example if an employer compensates an employee in pay and in shares of stock, both forms of compensation constitute earnings. But if an employer compensates an employee in pay, with stock options that promise purchase of stock at a set price in the future, more complicated apportionment issues can arise. See Section C California.

Life insurance problems include unresolved contingencies and dramatic value change between the underlying contract and the contract proceeds.

Whole life insurance policies are valuable prior to payout and, as such, are subject to community property rules, including apportionment, if entirely or partially acquired during marriage while domiciled in the state.

Term life insurance policies insure a person at death with renewability roughly based on an assessment of the insured's risk factors for an untimely death. Employers sometimes provide group term life insurance programs. The renewability of group term life insurance policies is not dependent on the insured's actual risk factors; it is dependent on other factors like the employee's continued employment and the employer's ongoing economic decision to continue offering its employees the group plan. Term life insurance, group term life insurance and term health insurance contract policies each represent a liability that loses its (potential) pay out value once the contract term expires, at which point the policy become worthless unless it is renewed.

A term life insurance *contract* is characterized for purposes of identifying its character by the last premium rule. That said, the contract itself is typically not an asset subject to division at dissolution—it has no cash value. The contract simply goes with the party who is willing to make the next premium payment or, if the contract is part of a group life insurance plan offered by an employer, it goes with the employed party at the end of marriage.

Life insurance *proceeds*, however, are funds distributed on the death of the insured. The last premium rule decides the character of these funds. If the last premium was paid by funds of different characters, then the proceeds will be apportioned by character contributions, with proportional character shares decided by reference to the last contract payment that was made before the insured's death. Gifts of life insurance proceeds are discussed in Chapter 5.

Federal law preempts distribution matters related to Veteran's insurance. Likewise to Federal Employee's Group Life Insurance (FEGLI), a group term life insurance program offered to most federal employees.

Wissner v. Wissner, 338 U.S. 655, 70 S.Ct. 398, 94 L.Ed.2d 424 (1950) held that a community property claim contrary to the insured's express designation is precluded by federal statute. The pre-emption ruling was based on language in FEGLI that the insured **"shall have the right to designate"** and change the beneficiary at all times and that payments of proceeds **"shall be exempt from the claims of creditors, and shall not be liable to attachment, levy or seizure by or under any legal or equitable process whatever, either before or after receipt by the beneficiary."** Exemption from the claims of creditors would mean dispositions in a dissolution action that reimburse the community.

Disability insurance plans have an evitable contingency (injury), as opposed to the inevitable contingency of life insurance (death). Until the evitable contingency has occurred, the right to disability insurance is a mere expectancy. When the contingency occurs, the inception of title rule looks to the marital status of the recipient to determine the character of the payments. Because disability payments are often designed to replace salary and are further contingent upon the survival of the intended recipient, the question is whether each payment's character should be determined separately. If each payment is not so characterized, the risk is that a spouse may divorce the disabled employee and take one-half of all disability benefits, leaving the injured spouse without means of support. The difficulty of characterizing recoveries for personal injuries is analyzed in Chapter 5; many of the same principles apply to disability payments.

As to the employee spouse who is entitled to either disability pay or retirement pay but not both, courts have generally held that the employee option cannot defeat the spouse's right to one-half of the community property retirement benefits. Under such a holding, the disability receipts are characterized as community property to the extent that retirement pay would have been so characterized.

Chapter 11 of Title 38 U.S.C.A. 301 et seq. covers disability during the line of military duty and pre-existing injuries or diseases aggravated after the separation of military service. The Federal Uniformed Services Former Spouses Protection Act (with its lisping acronym FUSFSPA 1984) does not authorize direct payments of retired disability pay to a former spouse. Disability payments are also protected by the Veterans Benefit Act, 10 U.S.C.A. 1408(a)(4)(B). See below and Chapter 12. For more on military retirement discretionary pay see Chapter 13.

Pension rights may be in the form of a (future) pension right in a retirement fund or (for an already retired worker) it may be in the form of a (current) dollar amount payable for the life of the retired employee. As such pension rights are an annuity. Both disability and retirement payments are usually contingent upon the survival of the annuitant unless the annuitant has contracted with the employer to extend a diminished retirement payment in exchange for extending payments for the life of a surviving spouse or registered domestic partner. Either way, whether we are discussing a future or a current payment right, pension rights are deferred compensation subject to community property rules.

With respect to pension benefits, the difficulty arises because retirement income annuities are earned by a prolonged period of employment that may overlap married and unmarried periods, or periods of domicile in both community and non-community property states during the employee's life. When either is the case, it calls for an allocation to or apportionment between the separate and community components.

Difficulties arise in valuing and dividing the pension asset upon divorce. Is a retirement pension one asset or a series of payments?

A minority of states may apportion the pension as a savings account. This method apportions by actual money contributions, sometimes augmented by an interest factor for the period that the funds have been held by the retirement fund.

The clear trend, however, is to use the *time rule.*

The time rule holds that the community property share of the pension can be apportioned by a ratio of time earned while married divided by the total time employed.

Here is the formula:

$$\frac{\textit{Time married}}{\textit{Total time employed}} = \textit{CP \% of the pension}$$

$$\frac{\textit{Time unmarried}}{\textit{Total time employed}} = \textit{SP \% of the pension}$$

The time rule makes a rough cut because the task of apportioning a pension benefit otherwise can be too complex for courts to handle efficiently thus increasing the expense of dissolution for the parties.

California gives a court full authority to "**make whatever orders are necessary or appropriate to ensure that each party receives the party's full community property share in any retirement plan, whether public or private, including all survivor and death benefits.**" Cal.Fam.Code § 2610. Louisiana has held that the court should apportion based on the money contributed by each estate. Wisconsin describes the marital property element by statute.

See below for more on ERISA, Qualified Domestic Relations Orders (QDROs), or court orders that direct a retirement plan to pay a portion of a participant's benefits to another person, an alternate payee, who may be a former or current spouse or a child), and state *nunc pro tunc* judgments, meaning court judgments that retroactively correct earlier rulings.

c. Division upon Divorce of Retirement and Disability Benefits

Since both retirement and disability provisions are dependent upon the outcome of so many contingencies, courts have had difficulty in dividing the community property while providing for pre-vesting and post-vesting contingencies (further employment, election to retire, not dying etc.), some of which include options within the control of the employee. California has set the theme that normally the wage-earner is given the retirement plan especially where there are balancing assets which can be given to the nonwage-earner as an offset.

Federal law has two attitudes toward retirement plans.

As to *private* retirement plans, The Employee Retirement Income Security Act of 1974 (ERISA), 29 U.S.C. §§ 1001 to 1381 demands that they not act like government plans. With private plans the variation in state law turns on vesting of rights in the employee, leaving the issue of apportionment one for the dissolution.

As to pensions *from* the *government*, discussed next, the employee has no vested right until the prescribed term of service has been rendered; the emphasis is upon the absence of enforceable rights of the employee.

ERISA regulates, at the federal level, retirement funds sponsored by a private employer in which the employee (participant) spouse is eligible for benefits or able to make contributions to the plan over time. The intention of the federal government to preempt the field by ERISA is shown in 29 U.S.C. § 1144, which declares that ERISA's provisions **"shall supersede any and all State laws insofar as they may now or hereafter relate to any employee benefit plan. . . ."** In *Egelhoff v. Egelhoff*, 532 U.S. 141 (2001), the U.S. Supreme Court wrote an extensive explanation of the factors involved in determining whether ERISA preempts state law.

Under 29 U.S.C.A. 1056(d)(3)(A), only a valid **"qualified domestic relations order,"** or QDRO, can provide an exception to the anti-assignment clause of ERISA, and to the express federal preemption provision of that statute. Thus, only by a valid QDRO, can a state court address *and create enforceable community property interests* in a federally regulated pension.

d. Government Retirement Plans

There is a dividing line between governmental and private retirement plans. The statutory schemes by which public employees are granted retirement benefits have adopted an imperious attitude if one considers that a recipient has no right to the retirement or other benefits until their prescribed term of service has been rendered, as defined by federal rules. Benefits are given as a matter of governmental largess.

None of the states follows the old Spanish distinction by which bonus payments to married soldiers who received other compensation were treated as gifts and therefore separate property. The statutory language and approach of governmental employee retirement plans did, however, emphasize the non-vested nature of the retirement allowance; this emphasis led the courts in California and Texas to adopt a short-lived doctrine that retirement funds subject to certain contingencies were not vested and therefore could not be community property. Both jurisdictions have reversed the holding, but the dichotomy between governmental and private pension plans remains.

Military retirement pay is an example.

Prior to the June 25, 1981 operational date stated in FUSFSPA, 10 U.S.C.A. § 1408, which removed the federal pre-emption found to exist in *McCarty v. McCarty*, 453 U.S. 210, 101 S.Ct. 2728, 69 L.Ed.2d 589 (1981), federal military disposable retirement pay could not be characterized as community property. To do so would impermissibly vest the non-military member spouse with the benefit.

However, the enactment of the FUSFSPA, 10 U.S.C.A. § 1408 reverses the result in *McCarty*, supra, as to disposable retired pay.

FUSFSPA § 1408(c) states the general rule: **"Subject to the limitations of this section, a court may treat disposable retired pay payable to a member for pay periods beginning after June 25, 1981 either as property solely of the member or as property of the member and his spouse in accordance with the law of the jurisdiction of such court."**

By this language, federal law recognizes that a court ordered outcome, such as **"a division of community property (including a division of community property)"** that states payment of amounts **". . . expressed in dollars or as a percentage of retired disposable pay . . ."** may be different depending on whether the state is a community property jurisdiction or not. FUSFSPA § 1408(a)(2)(b)(iii) and (3).

Retired disposable pay means the total monthly retired pay a member is entitled to less overpayments, forfeitures, disability elections, and annuity elections for a spouse or former spouse. FUSFSPA § 1408(a)(4)(A).

Mansell v. Mansell, 490 U.S. 581, 594–595, 109 S.Ct. 2023, 104 L.Ed.2d 675 (1989) interpreted FUSFSPA § 1408(a)(4)(A)(iii) to mean that a state cannot treat as divisible community property "the waived portion" of the veteran's retirement pay that becomes "nontaxable disability benefits." *Mansell*, supra, involved a disability waiver that *preceded* the divorce.

Howell v. Howell, 581 U.S. 214, 137 S.Ct. 1400, 197 L.Ed.2d 781 (2017) raised the same issue in a case where the spouse with the military retirement benefit opted to reclassify disposable retirement pay as disability pay after divorce. In *Howell*, supra, the veteran spouse was an active member of the Air Force when he divorced. The Arizona divorce court characterized the veteran's military retirement as community property; it then awarded the nonveteran spouse a one-half interest in the veteran's pension whenever the veteran retired in the future. One year later the veteran retired. At the time between divorce and retirement, both the veteran and his former spouse received a fifty-fifty share of the husband's (future) monthly retirement pay. Thirteen years after the divorce, the husband was adjudged 20% disabled due to a military service injury. At that time, he opted to waive $250 of his retirement pay to receive nontaxable disability benefits. As to the veteran, his retired disposable pay was reclassified as disability benefits, so he received the $250 back in the form of disability pay. But wife lost the $250 waived share from her retirement pay. Wife sued.

The Arizona courts ordered the former husband to reimburse the former wife for the amount that her monthly payments were reduced by his disability waiver. *In re Marriage of Howell*, 238 Ariz. 407, 408, 361 P.3d 936, 937 (2015), citing *Mansell*, supra. The former husband petitioned for certiorari to the U.S. Supreme Court.

Ultimately, the U.S. Supreme Court took the case and held that the state court judgment ordering the veteran to reimburse his former spouse for the difference in pre- and post-disability waiver outcomes was without regard to the veteran's disability. Therefore, it (impermissibly) vested the former nonveteran spouse in the veteran spouse's nontaxable disability benefits. In creating a disability pay exemption for the FUSFSPA § 1408(c) community property provision, the court recognized that federal pre-emption could work a hardship on divorcing parties, and restated the pre-1981 rationale, as stated in *McCarty*, supra, but as applied to disability pay only.

> "The basic reasons *McCarty* gave for believing that Congress intended to exempt military retirement pay from the state community property laws apply *a fortiori* to disability pay. See 453 U.S. at 232–235, 101 S.Ct. 2728 (describing the federal interests in attracting and retaining military personnel.) And those reasons apply with equal force to a veteran's post-divorce waiver to receive disability benefits to which he or she has become entitled." *Howell*, supra, at 1406.

The outcome in *Howell*, supra, is consistent with the late-twentieth century trend among community property states to assign money and property for bodily injury (an analog to disability benefits) to the injured spouse upon dissolution.

The application of the federal supremacy clause (U.S. Const. Art. 6, Cl. 2) to community property is discussed in Chapter 13.

Federal statutes by which retirement benefits are awarded may provide that the benefits are for the employee only (non-transferable personal interest) and thus cannot be assigned or reached by process or by attachment (spendthrift provision).

The federal Social Security program has the most widespread retirement coverage of any retirement plan. There is no definitive statement that such benefits are the separate property of the recipient, but it is probable that the Supreme Court of the U.S. would characterize all benefits received under the Social Security program as separate property of the recipient.

Federal law is also inconsistent when it comes to recognizing community property rights in federal governmental benefits and private annuity plans. On one hand, Social Security (retirement) benefits are separate property of the recipient employee despite state community property laws. On the other hand, the Retirement Equity Act (REACT) amendment to ERISA creates a "super community property" interest for the surviving spouse in death benefits. Under REACT, a QDRO may assign pension rights to a former spouse, even if the participant spouse opts to continue working past the (maturity) date at which he or she is eligible to retire with such rights. The REACT right of a surviving spouse applies in community property states to community property and to non-community property interests.

C. INDIVIDUAL STATES

1. ARIZONA

Bank accounts and sums on deposit. Commingled sums on deposit are presumptively community property unless the separate property deposits can be "explicitly traced;" rebuttal rests with the separate property proponent by "clear and satisfactory evidence." *Cooper v. Cooper*, 130 Ariz. 257, 260, 635 P.2d 850, 853 (1981)(in banc). Insubstantial amounts will not transmute the character of the account. *Battiste v. Battiste*, 135 Ariz. 470, 662 P.2d 145 (1983). No presumption of a gift arises when identifiable separate property funds—meaning deposits that are in fact traceable to a separate property source—are deposited in the spouses' joint checking account. *Bowart v. Bowart*, 128 Ariz. 331, 625 P.2d 920 (Ct. App. 1980).

All these cases pre-date the multiple-parties accounts law movement.

Separate property businesses. Separate property business profits—as distinguished from the underlying separate property business—fall under the Ariz.Rev.Stat.Ann. § 25–213(A), which defines the rents, issues, and profits of separate property as separate property. All other property obtained during marriage that is not acquired by gift, devise or descent is community property under the general statute, Ariz.Rev.Stat.Ann. § 25–211.

And yet, in the separate property business context, rents, issues, and profits of the business are "earnings," even though they derive from separate property. *Rueschenberg v. Rueschenberg*, 219 Ariz. 249, 196 P.3d 852 (2008) recognized the inconsistency between Arizona's adherence to the American rule on rents, issues, and profits and its treatment of the same as "earnings" in the separate property business context. The case reconciled the inconsistency in favor of the general community property statute Ariz.Rev.Stat.Ann. § 25–211.

A line of cases starting with *Evans v. Evans*, 79 Ariz. 284, 288 P.2d 775 (1955) allows the separate property proponent to rebut the community property presumption. Proof required is that "earnings" obtained during marriage from rents, issues and profits were derived mainly from the inherent nature of separate property. Specifically, this means that rents, issues, and profits were derived from separate property capital and capital investment, not from community labor. If such proof is made, "earnings" are redefined as "rents, issues, and profits" under the separate property statutory provision of Ariz.Rev.Stat.Ann. § 25–213(A).

In *Cockrill v. Cockrill*, 124 Ariz. 50, 601 P.2d 1334 (1979) the Arizona Supreme Court reversed its prior all-or-nothing rule in favor of apportioning separate property profits depending on their source (underlying property or community labor). The stated policy goal was to achieve substantial justice between the parties. There, the issue of apportionment was remanded back to the trial court only to bounce back again to the court of appeal in

Cockrill v. Cockrill, 139 Ariz. 72, 676 P.2d 1130 (1983).

Credit acquisitions. Arizona applies the inception of title rule to separate property acquired prior to marriage. Ariz.Rev.Stat.Ann. § 25–213. Separate property retains its character even if community property mortgage principal payments are made, unless the spouses agree otherwise, or the asset is transmuted by operation of law. Community property that is transmuted by a disclaimer deed signed by the adversely affected spouse is separate property as well. *Femiano v. Maust*, 248 Ariz. 613, 463 P.3d 237 (Ct. App. 2020).

In the above instances, the community property can acquire an "equitable lien" against the separate property under the rule in *Drahos v. Rens*, 149 Ariz. 248, 717 P.2d 927 (Ct.App. 1985). In this case, the husband purchased a $21,000 residence one day prior to marriage, using a $7,000 downpayment and a $14,000 loan. At dissolution, the house was valued at $80,000. The trial court, applying the inception of title rule, characterized the house as separate property and awarded the community an "equitable lien" on the residence. The residence remained separate in character. On appeal, the court affirmed the separate property characterization of the house but remanded the case to the trial court for recalculation of the lien. The case was strongly criticized on equitable grounds for characterizing the house as separate property when it was purchased the day before the parties married. Offsetting any injustice was that the court's accounting method included an equity (appreciation) value in the lien amount.

Ariz.Rev.Stat.Ann. § 25–318, discussed in Chapter 9, allows a court to vindicate the community's capital contribution through an "equitable lien." See *Lawson v. Ridgeway*, 72 Ariz. 253, 261–62, 233 P.2d 459, 467–68 (1951). Cases have taken several divergent paths from that beginning, and courts are not restricted by prior holdings because of the equitable nature of the lien.

That said, the general idea, sometimes called "the *Drahos* formula", seems to be that the lien should be calculated by the "amount spent formula" or by the "value-at-dissolution formula." *Barnett v. Jedynak*, 219 Ariz. 550, 55, 200 P.3d 1047, 1052 (Ct.App. Div. 1 2009). *Valento v. Valento*, 225 Ariz. 477, 482, 240 P.3d 1239, 1244 (Ct.App. Div. 1 2010) applied *Barnett* to articulate a hybrid reimbursement approach, seemingly based on *Marsden* (a California case discussed in Section C, California below).

The Value at Dissolution Formula:

- *When property appreciates during the marriage:* The prescribed value-at-dissolution of the community's interest in appreciated separate property (the so-called community equitable lien) reimburses the community for its contribution to the loan principle plus its proportional share of asset appreciation:

$$C + \left(\frac{C}{B} \times A\right) = \textit{value of CP lien}$$

Where:

- A represents the appreciation in value of the property during the marriage,
- B equals the purchase price
- C equals the community contributions to loan principal repayments. Notice how a reimbursement for C (the C before the plus sign) is *added* to the community's proportional share of asset appreciation (the C divided by B ratio that appears after the plus sign). This is part of the formula, and it assists with clarity.
- *When property depreciates and equity is positive:* The community is reimbursed for its loan principal payments plus its proportional share of asset appreciation.
- *When the property depreciates, and equity is negative:* The community lien can be valued by this proposed formula:

$$C - \left(\frac{C}{B} \times D\right) = \textit{value of CP lien}$$

Where D equals the depreciation in value of the property during the marriage, B is the fair market value on the date of marriage, and C is the community contributions to loan principal or market value. Here again C is reimbursed for its contributions to the loan principal payment minus its proportional share of asset depreciation.

Note that a depreciation, while a loss in market value, is usually recorded in the form of a tax deduction and therefore it should be a positive number for purposes of the above formula.

According to *Valento*, supra, the above formula is "a restatement of *Barnett*, supra, in a declining market." Id. 482, 1244. Here, community contributions enhance the separate property owner's equity position by decreasing the principal balance of the loan. This is true even if the property owner eventually owes more on the mortgage than the property is worth on the market. Id. 483, 1245.

Capital improvements are reimbursed under the value-at-dissolution formula. The community is entitled to share in the enhanced value of the property due to the expenditure of community funds. Not reimbursed are noncapital improvements, taxes, interest, and maintenance.

The intent of the lender test is not used in Arizona. Credit obtained during marriage is community property. Yet some Arizona cases have ignored the credit portion of the acquisition in determining the character of the property by tracing only to the down payment.

Work related benefits. Inception of title was given support in a dictum in *Rothman v. Rumbeck*, 54 Ariz. 443, 96 P.2d 755 (1939), which indicated that that rule would be applied to life insurance. The inception of title rule was cited with approval more recently in *Everson v. Everson*, 24 Ariz.App. 239, 537 P.2d 624 (Ct.App. 1975) and *Bell-Kilbourn v. Bell-*

Kilbourn, 216 Ariz. 521, 169 P.3d 111 (Ct. App. 2007). But * * * abrogated * * *

Retirement benefits are apportioned on a time basis.

In compliance with *Howell*, supra, protecting disabled military veterans is the plain language of Ariz.Rev.Stat.Ann. § 25–318.01. Added in 2010 and updated effective July 24, 2014, the statute mandates that **"[I]n making a disposition of property [at dissolution] a court shall not do any of the following:**

1. **"Consider any federal disability benefits awarded to a veteran for service- connected disabilities pursuant to 10 U.S. Code Sec. 1413 or 39 U.S. Code Ch. 11."**

2. **Indemnify the veteran's spouse for any prejudgment or postjudgment waiver or reduction in military or retainer pay related to receipt of disability benefits.**

3. **Award any other income or property of the veteran to the veteran's spouse or former spouse for any prejudgment or postjudgment waiver or reduction in military or retainer pay related to receipt of the disability benefits."**

2. CALIFORNIA

Bank accounts and sums on deposit. As noted above, California has adopted and enhanced uniform laws on multiple parties' bank accounts. Enhancements started in the case law, but eventually California enacted the California Multiple Parties Accounts Law (CAMPAL 1990 for short), is part of its Probate Code. See Chapter 3 for more on CAMPAL 1990.

As a brief review of Chapter 4, an account title determines access to the account. Ownership to sums on deposit are analyzed as a distinct issue.

The CAMPAL 1990 applies only to bank accounts, and it includes a special community property presumption for sums on deposit in any bank account of a married person. This special community property presumption supersedes both the general community property presumption and the special joint form title presumption. The result is that sums on deposit in any demand deposit account of a married person are presumptively community property in character. The separate property claimant has the burden of rebuttal. That burden can be met by tracing, using specialized records, or by producing an agreement, specific to the account, that all or some sums on deposit in the account are not community property. The preponderance of the evidence standard applies.

CAMPAL legislation follows the holding in *See v. See*, 64 Cal.2d 778, 51 Cal.Rptr. 888, 415 P.2d 776 (1966). Especially relevant are the rules developed in relation to purchases made from a commingled account. In *See*, supra, a case that is consistent with CAMPAL 1990, the California Supreme Court ruled that an *intentional purchase*, during marriage, from a disputed account (meaning an account that was commingled or undisclosed) titled in one spouse's name alone is presumptively community property. Rebuttal *as to the intentional purchase* rests with the separate property proponent. Assuming the intentional purchase is titled in one spouse's name alone (in *See*, supra, assets were titled in the account holder's name alone) the general community property presumption applies to that asset. Rebuttal requires proof that separate property funds made or assisted with the purchase. If the funds were withdrawn from a bank account, then proof that the funds were separate property in character requires specialized account records. For ease of understanding, these records can be called *See*-compliant records.

What are *See*-compliant records?

First, they are records contemporaneously kept for a specific bank account. Contemporaneous records reduce the risk of perjury. Records prepared for litigation increase the risk of perjury.

Second, they are records that show character specific deposits and withdrawals. Clear records allow parties to go to a specific date to identify the character of sums on deposit in an account on that date. Unclear records simply show that there are sums on deposit in the account on certain dates, but they do not specify the character of those sums.

Third, for the sake of clarity, the records should show that the record keeper applied the family expense presumption, which requires that family expenses first be deducted from community property deposits. On dates where the community property sums on deposit were not sufficient to cover a family expense, then the expense is deducted from the separate property sums on deposit in the account.

Fourth, if steps one through three above are met, then on the date that funds are withdrawn to make a purchase, the records show whether community property sums in the account were (or were not) exhausted. If there were community property sums on deposit in the account, then the inference is that the purchase was made with community property sums. If the parties believe otherwise, they can declare as much in a separate written document. But if community property sums on deposit were exhausted on the date of the purchase, then the inference is that the purchase was made with separate property sums.

Tracing methods set forth in *See*, supra, are also consistent with CAMPAL 1990.

Practitioners occasionally report that they rely on forensic records to prove an ownership interest in an asset purchased with sums withdrawn from a bank account. But there is a meaningful difference between creating records for purposes of a dissolution proceeding versus preparing already existing records for the same purpose. On the eve of dissolution, one might reasonably employ an accountant to review already existing *See*-compliant records; this kind of review should not raise the same specter of perjury that creating new records for dissolution purposes does.

In fact, creating records in anticipation of litigation is counter to the parameters set forth in *See*, supra, and in CAMPAL 1990 for at least two reasons. One, the duty to keep specialized records arises on the date that the account is first commingled; that date may precede dissolution by years or even decades. Two, the first spouse who commingles the account has the legal duty to keep records. Thus, it is the parameters of this legal duty that presupposes not just keeping records for the sake of clarity, but also keeping records to comply with a duty that arose from commingling the account. Remember, every commingled account is a disputed account on the issue of ownership of sums on deposit. It is disputed because the act of commingling is an act of conversion.

Forensic records can take many forms; but they are questionable and even inadmissible for several reasons other than that they go against the letter of the law. It is a significant breach of law and policy for a court to permit the use of an accounting method that turns a community property interest, which is vested, into an interest that is effectively contingent upon dissolution. Two, because the duty to keep records arises on a date during marriage when the commingling occurred, it may be reversible error to permit a spouse who breached their duty to introduce records prepared for litigation. Three, forensic records, unless they start from the date of any initial commingling and move forward to the date of dissolution, may violate the inception of title rule, as well as misapply the family expense presumption. Four, records created in anticipation of dissolution increase the risk of perjury.

Tracing money withdrawn from an account is allowed only as to intentional purchases that are untitled or titled in one spouse's name alone. Any assets purchased in joint title form continue to be governed by Cal.Fam.Code § 2581. See Chapter 4.

The *Hicks-Mix-Murphy* line of cases allows for the prospective use of *See*-compliant records. This line of cases allows a separate property proponent to plan separate property purchases, during marriage, by using contemporaneous *See*-compliant financial records to show that on or near the date of a purchase (i) both the community property and the separate property sums on deposit were sufficient to make the purchase; (ii) the separate property owner signed a written declaration of intent to use separate property funds to make the purchase; (iii) the purchase was, in fact, subtracted from separate sums on deposit available on or near the date of purchase; and (iv) the separate property purchaser disclosed the purchase as separate in character to the other spouse, optimally before the purchase was made. The written declaration of intent must be extrinsic to the account records. In *Marriage of Mix*, 14 Cal.3d 604, 122 Cal.Rptr. 79, 536 P.2d 479 (1975) the court affirmed the non-discretionary rule that *See*-compliant records must be prepared contemporaneously, not in anticipation of litigation; *Estate of Murphy*, 15 Cal.3d

907, 126 Cal.Rptr. 820, 544 P.2d 959 (1976) applies these rules in the probate context.

Cal.Fam.Code § 721(b) states that spouses are in a confidential relationship, and as such have a general duty not to take any unfair advantage of the other. A breach of this general duty can occur where a separate property proponent gains **"any unfair advantage over the other in a transaction between them . . ."** This statute also includes specific duties based on the Revised Uniform Partnership Act. See Chapter 8.

Separate property businesses. Courts have considerable discretion to do substantial justice between the parties in accounting for the community's interest, if any, in a separate property business. Keep in mind that court holdings are expressed arithmetically, but arithmetic expression does not change the fact that the cases are applying law.

Under *Pereira v. Pereira*, 156 Cal. 1, 103 P. 488 (1909) if community property contributes more than a minimum amount of labor (the minimum-plus standard for short) to a separate property business, then the community is entitled, as a creditor of the business, to excess profits.

Here is the *Pereira* holding expressed as a formula:

FMV@ disso – (FMV @ marriage[1] + FRR) = excess profits

---

1 Assumes a separate property business brought to the marriage.

Pereira is discussed in Section B above.

Beam v. Bank of America, 6 Cal.3d 12, 98 Cal.Rptr. 137, 490 P.2d 257 (1971) held that a non-tax deferred investment account brought to the marriage falls within the definition of a covered separate property business. *Beam*, supra, sets the level of labor that gives rise to a community interest as "more than minimal," hence the "minimum-plus" standard mentioned in the previous paragraph.

Under *Van Camp*, a minimum quantum of community labor, entitles the community to a reimbursement for its net labor contribution to the business.

Here is the *Van Camp* holding expressed as a formula:

FMV@ disso – (CP labor – Family expenses) = SP

Van Camp is discussed in Section B above.

Marriage of Imperato, 45 Cal.3d 432, 119 Cal.Rptr. 590 (1975) allowed for "reverse *Pereira*" apportionment for a community property business that appreciates in value during a period between a date of separation and a dissolution proceeding, but its holding was called into question in 2022.

Marriage of Koester, 73 Cal.App.4th 1032, 87 Cal.Rptr.2d 76 (1999), held that the incorporation during marriage of a business that was brought to the marriage is a change in form, not an acquisition during marriage under Cal.Fam.Code § 2581.

Credit acquisitions. California recognizes the existence of a vested pro tanto interest for community property contributions to the purchase of separate property.

The following law applies only when the asset (usually a house) is titled in one name alone. In a dissolution proceeding, joint form titles are presumed community property; rebuttal is by agreement, not tracing as discussed in Chapter 3.

In determining the pro tanto interest, community contributions to purchase come into play when a credit acquisition is made before marriage, then paid down (or off) during marriage. Refinancing can complicate the original picture.

A short note on the difference between a pro tanto and an equitable interest is useful here. The pro tanto interest comes into existence when a borrower pays off a loan. When the community pays mortgage principal for the original borrower, that borrower obtains a vested pro tanto interest relative to the lender. As between the original borrower and the community, this translates into a pro rata vested share of ownership. Ownership signals that the asset is commingled, and since only owners have a right to appreciation; ownership also signals that the appreciation is owned in pro rata shares. An equitable interest does not come into existence except through judicial action, usually at the end of the marriage. An equitable lien signals that the asset remains solely owned by the spouse whose name is on the title deed, but the community has a secured interest as to any reimbursement amount the court deems just.

Vieux v. Vieux, 80 Cal.App. 222, 251 P. 640 (1926) articulated a twofold rationale in support of the pro tanto approach. The first rationale was the implied contract rationale: community property contributions to purchase of a separate property asset are proof that the parties impliedly agreed that the community would get a proportional share of ownership in exchange for helping the debtor spouse pay off the mortgage loan. The second rationale was to prevent unjust enrichment of the separate property title holder.

Marriage of Aufmuth, 89 Cal.App.3d 446, 152 Cal.Rptr. 668 (1979), and *Marriage of Moore*, 28 Cal.3d 336, 168 Cal.Rptr. 662, 618 P.2d 208 (1980) affirmed the rationales presented in *Vieux*. Moreover, each rationale went on to become the basis for establishing a contributing estate's pro tanto share (and thus their pro rata ownership share for purposes of dissolution) relative to the historic contract price of the disputed credit acquisition.

Aufmuth, supra, overruled in part, still stands for the proposition that loan proceeds obtained during marriage constitute a community property contribution to purchase.

Moore, supra, stands for the proposition that loan proceeds obtained before marriage are a separate property contribution from which community loan principal repayments are subtracted. (Interest, taxes, and insurance payments are not contributions to purchase; they are categorized as family expenses.) Contributions to purchase are ultimately reimbursed, but the ratio derived from dividing community property contributions by the historical purchase price of the asset results in a percentage share of ownership of the asset. That percentage is the community's pro rata ownership share of the total appreciation.

Marriage of Marsden, 130 Cal.App.3d 426, 181 Cal.Rptr. 910 (1982) allows for the apportionment of credibly proven marital appreciation. *Marsden*, supra, also confirms that, as a matter of law, the denominator in the *Moore*, supra, formula shall be the contract price (called the "historic purchase price" in *Marsden*, supra), not the fair market value of the house at marriage.

In a *Moore-Marsden* analysis, each estate's proportional share of ownership is calculated by use of *Moore*, supra. But that pro rata share is then multiplied by *marital* appreciation (or depreciation), meaning the change that occurs from the date of marriage to the date of dissolution. The *premarital* appreciation/depreciation, and premarital loan principal repayments are characterized as separate property acquired before marriage.

Marriage of Sherman, 133 Cal.App.4th 795, 35 Cal.Rptr. 137 (2005) clarified that the fair market value of a residence for purposes of apportioning the property is as of the date of trial, not the date of separation. *Sherman*, supra, also disallowed rental value of the separate property residence to be factored in as a credit for the separate property estate.

As stated above, loan proceeds obtained *prior* to marriage are separate property under the general rules set forth in Chapter 5. Loan proceeds obtained *during* marriage are presumptively community property under the general rules set forth in Chapter 4. *Aufmuth*, supra, holds that loan proceeds are a positive contribution to purchase; and if acquired during marriage they constitute a community property asset—in other words, loan proceeds acquired during marriage, even though a debt, factor into the accounting as a plus, not as a negative. If the separate property claimant wishes to rebut a community property presumption as to loan proceeds, the lender's intent test is the appropriate method for doing so if the purchase funds were transferred directly from the lender to the seller, as discussed in Chapter 4.

Marriage of Grinius, 166 Cal.App.3d 1179, 212 Cal.Rptr. 803 (1985) controls as a practical, if not a legal, matter. In *Grinius*, supra, the court went to the trouble to "restate the applicable standard: loan proceeds acquired during marriage are presumptively community property; unless the lender intended to rely *solely* on a spouse's separate property and did in fact do so." Id.

The *Moore*, supra, formula applies when there is no or little asset appreciation prior to marriage. Practically, this can occur when the separate property owner buys the property close to, but still before, the date of the marriage.

Marsden, supra, applies when the separate property owner can credibly prove that the house appreciated in value between the date of purchase and the date of marriage.

Here are the elements of analysis for *Moore*, supra: (i) the downpayment; (ii) the loan proceeds; (iii) the loan principal repayments; and (iv) the historic purchase price.

Each contributing estate's percentage of ownership is determined by adding up that estate's contribution to purchase and dividing it by the historic purchase price. (Interest, taxes and insurance payments are not included because they are family expenses, as discussed above.)

Here is the *Moore*, supra, holding expressed as a two-step formula:

Step one: determine pro rata shares of ownership.

$$\frac{SP\ dpmt + (SP\ loan - CP\ contribution)}{HPP} = SP\%$$

$$\frac{CP\ contribution}{HPP} = CP\%$$

Step two: Multiply pro rata shares by appreciation (or depreciation) to apportion the asset appreciation.

$$SP\% \times App\ (or\ Dep) = SP\ share\ of\ the\ App/Dep$$

$$CP\% \times App\ (or\ Dep) = CP\ share\ of\ the\ App/Dep$$

If premarital appreciation has been established by the separate property claimant, apportion only marital appreciation (or depreciation).

Marital appreciation equals the fair market value at dissolution minus the fair market value at marriage, a value that must be established by credible evidence such as a professional appraisal conducted on or near the date of marriage.

If there is no provable premarital appreciation, apportion total appreciation (or depreciation).

Total appreciation equals the fair market value at dissolution minus the fair market value at purchase.

If a separate property proponent cannot establish an ownership interest (for example where there is an unrebutted joint form title presumption or where the separate property proponent fails to rebut the general presumption), the asset is entirely community property. In that case, the separate property contributor is nonetheless entitled to a statutory reimbursement, without interest and subject to value limitations.

Cal.Fam.Code § 2640, the general reimbursement provision, creates a right of reimbursement that applies only when the asset in question is entirely (100%) community property: **"[I]n the division of the community estate . . . unless a party has made a written waiver of the right to reimbursement or has signed a writing that has the effect of a waiver."** Absent such a waiver, **"the [separate property contributor] shall be reimbursed for the party's contributions to the**

acquisition of [entirely community] property. . . ." Tracing determines the amount of the reimbursement, which **"shall be without interest or adjustment for change in monetary values and may not exceed the net value of the property at the time of the division."**

Retroactive application of § 2640 was held to be unconstitutional; the addition of a writing requirement being the reason. *Marriage of Heikes*, 10 Cal.4th 1211, 44 Cal.Rptr.2d 155, 899 P.2d 1349 (1995).

Marriage of Walrath, 17 Cal.4th 907, 72 Cal.Rptr.2d 856, 952 P.2d 1124 (1998) held that the § 2640 right to reimbursement carries over in the event that the original property is refinanced and the (refinanced) loan proceeds are used to a secure a community asset. If the finance record becomes too complicated to decipher, the doctrine of confusion applies, and the asset can be deemed entirely (100%) community property.

For purposes of a separate property reimbursement, Cal.Fam.Code § 2640 defines **"[c]ontributions to the acquisition of property,"** as including **"downpayments, payments for improvements, and payments that reduce the principal of a loan used to finance the purchase or improvement of the property. . . ."** By the same statute, contributions to purchase **"do not include payments of interest on the loan or payments made for maintenance, insurance, or taxation of the property."**

The legislature modified the rule of *Marriage of Lucas*, 27 Cal.3d 808, 166 Cal.Rptr. 853, 614 P.2d 285 (1980) for purposes of dissolution. Current Cal.Fam.Code § 2640 includes capital improvements within the express meaning of contribution to purchase and provides that they shall be reimbursed.

Are contributions to the improvement of property within this definition? Generally, ordinary improvements fall under the rubric of family expenses, as such they are not reimbursable absent a contract providing otherwise. Also not reimbursable are non-capital contributions such as insurance, taxes, interest, and ordinary maintenance, as noted above. This distinction appears in the case law as well.

Work related benefits. Business goodwill falls within the community property system. Celebrity identity does too, as it is a property right, recognized and protected from commercial use without prior consent, by Cal.Civ.Code § 3344. No cases so hold, but presumably a celebrity identity, developed via labor during marriage while domiciled in the state is divisible at dissolution. Elite professional status (talent) has been treated as distinct from celebrity identity, and thus as an asset that falls outside of the community property system; here the courts regard talent, (independently of any income stream it produces) as too personal to its holder to be treated as divisible property. *Marriage of McTiernan & Dubrow*, 133 Cal.App.4th 1090, 35 Cal.Rptr.3d 287 (2005). The rules are just beginning to be articulated.

Cal.Fam.Code § 2641 is a specific reimbursement statute for community contributions to one spouse's education or training. The rule favors threshold marriage dissolutions, meaning cases where the parties are married for a short time, invest in an education for one spouse, but otherwise own no or little divisible property. The reimbursement belongs to the community (not solely to the non-student spouse); and it is limited to community property contributions to the direct expenses of an income enhancing education or training. *Direct* expenses are reimbursable: tuition, books, fees, supplies, school related travel, and so forth. Payments that reduce the principal portion of an educational loan count as a reimbursable direct expense. Educational loans are mandatorily assigned to the student spouse at dissolution absent an agreement between the spouses otherwise. Indirect educational expenses (e.g., rent, utilities, cable, etc.) are not reimbursable under this statute, but they may form the discretionary basis for a spousal support award to the nonstudent spouse under Cal.Fam.Code § 4320(b).

California uses the apportionment rule to characterize any savings component (cash surrender value) of an ordinary (sometimes referred to as a whole) life insurance policy; both the chose in action and the savings component are divisible on dissolution. See the *Blethen v. Pacific Mutual Life Ins. Co. of Cal.*, 198 Cal. 91, 243 P. 431 (1926) line of cases.

Term life insurance represents a contractual liability that expires at the termination of the specific contract term unless and until the insured dies. Only at the death of the insured, are proceeds paid out. For this reason, term life insurance without a savings component has no cash surrender value. It protects against the death of the insured, but as a person gets older or ill the product becomes more difficult to obtain. Rather than risk a loss, the language of insurance puts blames the individual for "becoming uninsurable" thus making renewal rights, if any, an issue at dissolution.

Disagreement exists at the court of appeal level as to how to characterize a term life insurance policy. In the interests of facilitating dissolution, *Estate of Logan*, 191 Cal.App.3d 319, 236 Cal.Rptr. 368 (1987) follows *Marriage of Lorenz*, 146 Cal.App.3d 464, 194 Cal.Rptr. 237 (1983) and rejects *Marriage of Gonzalez*, 168 Cal.App.3d 1021, 214 Cal.Rptr. 634 (1985). *Logan*, supra, held that a term life insurance policy is not a community asset subject to division on divorce. The rationale is that the term life insurance contract is worthless once the contract term expires.

Even if not divisible, the term life insurance is characterizable by the last premium rule. In the context of spousal managerial rights and duties, naming a beneficiary is an act that disposes of property after death. Thus, each spouse can only dispose of one-half of the proceeds of a community life insurance policy.

Marriage of Spengler, 5 Cal.App.4th 288, 6 Cal.Rptr.2d 764 (1992) involved renewal rights on a group term life insurance policy offered by an employer. *Spengler* agreed with *Logan* that the term life insurance policy is not itself a divisible asset at divorce, but *Spengler* disagreed with the *Logan* dictum that a renewal right could be community property "if the insured becomes uninsurable during the marriage." Id. Thus *Spengler* held that the employment-related policy, despite the husband's terminal illness and uninsurability, was a mere expectancy dependent upon the employer's continuance of the group insurance plan for all its employees. As a mere expectancy, the life insurance renewal right was not property, and therefore it was not subject to community property laws. By the same rationale, any community property interest in term health insurance ends on dissolution. *Marriage of Havins*, 43 Cal.App.4th 414, 50 Cal.Rptr.2d 763 (1996).

Severance pay is normally understood as deferred compensation. Severance pay was discussed in *Marriage of Horn*, 181 Cal.App.3d 540, 226 Cal.Rptr. 666 (1986), *Marriage of Skadden*, 19 Cal.3d 679, 139 Cal.Rptr. 615, 566 P.2d 249 (1977). A turbulent line of precedent can be found in *Marriage of Gram*, 25 Cal.App.4th 859, 30 Cal.Rptr.2d 792 (1994), which was disapproved of by *Marriage of Lehman*, 18 Cal.4th 169, 74 Cal.Rptr.2d 825, 955 P.2d 451 (1998), which was not extended by *Marriage of Steinberger*, 91 Cal.4th 1449, 111 Cal.Rptr.2d 521 (2001).

Stock options were discussed in *Marriage of Hug*, 154 Cal.App.3d 780, 201 Cal.Rptr. 676 (1984). There the court held that the options were subject to community property rules, and that, given complications raised by issues of timing, their allocation is subject to court discretion.

Disability benefits were discussed in *Marriage of Rossin*, 172 Cal.App.4th 725, 91 Cal.Rptr.3d 427 (2009), a case of first impression. There, the court characterized disability benefits as separate property on a two-part showing. One, the disabled spouse had acquired the disability rights (by contract) prior to marriage and thus entirely with separate property funds. Two, the insured's intention was to replace income in the event of injury, not to supplement retirement.

In *Regents of the University of California v. Benford*, 128 Cal.App.4th 867, 27 Cal.Rptr.3d 441 (4th Dist. 2005), a non-employee spouse who predeceased the participant spouse was precluded from devising her community property interest in the university retirement plans. To get around this ruling, the participant spouse would have had to elect a lump sum (rather than an annuity) upon retirement.

Marriage of Stephenson, 162 Cal.App.3d 1057, 209 Cal.Rptr. 383 (1984) discusses the method for apportioning a defined benefit plan. *Marriage of Bergman*, 168 Cal.App.3d 742, 214 Cal.Rptr. 661 (1985) discusses the method for apportioning a defined contribution plan.

For the interplay between ERISA and California law, see *Kennedy v. Plan Adm'r for Dupont Sav. & Inv. Plan*, 555 U.S. 285, 129 S.Ct. 865, 172 L.Ed.2d 662 (2009). For a discussion and explication of ERISA and the necessity of creating a valid QDRO for purposes of Cal.Fam.Code § 2346, which authorizes a court to enter a judgment *nunc pro tunc* in any dissolution proceeding that seeks to reserve jurisdiction over decedent's ERISA pension, see *Marriage of Padgett*, 172 Cal.App.4th 830, 91 Cal.Rptr.3d 475 (2009).

Generally, California continues to apportion retirement benefits most often by use of the time rule. The ultimate decision of what denominator to use, however, (time, points, contributions) is left to the discretion of the court, but the denominator should make sense in the context of the pension plan. If the employer uses points, the court also should probably use points. See for example *Marriage of Poppe*, 97 Cal.App.3d 1, 158 Cal.Rptr. 500 (1979). Calculations can be laborious, expensive, and subject to intense scrutiny, as illustrated by *Marriage of Green*, 56 Cal.4th 1130, 158 Cal.Rptr.3d 247, 302 P.3d 562 (2013).

3. IDAHO

Accounts and sums on deposit in an account. *Gapsch v. Gapsch*, 76 Idaho 44, 277 P.2d 278 (1954) is an often cited case on commingling of separate and community property. For a purchase from commingled sums on deposit, Idaho does not require specialized records to rebut the general presumption.

Separate property businesses. Idaho follows in civil law on separate property rents, issues, and profits. Thus, in Idaho, separate property rents, issues and profits are community property during the continuance of the marriage. Additionally, *Gapsch*, supra, is often cited for the principle that the natural enhancement of separate property remains part of the underlying separate property. (Natural enhancement presumably refers to asset appreciation, not asset income streams.) Despite this legal scaffolding, it may still be necessary to seek an accounting at dissolution or death. What gets accounted for are profits that can be traced back to separate property elements versus profits that can be traced back to community property elements.

Idaho Code § 32–906 was amended to read **"[t]he income, including rents, issues and profits, of all property, separate or community, is community property. . . ."**

In *Speer v. Quinlan*, 96 Idaho 119, 525 P.2d 314 (1974) and in *Simplot v. Simplot*, 96 Idaho 239, 526 P.2d 844 (1974) the Idaho Supreme Court held that retained corporate stock dividends are not income or rents or profits as that term is used in Idaho Code § 32–906. The rationale is that until corporate stock dividends are distributed, they remain the property of the corporation. *Swope v. Swope*, 112 Idaho 974, 739 P.2d 273 (1987) declined to extend *Simplot*, insofar as it held that the earnings of a partnership, whether retained or distributed, are income under Idaho Code § 32–906. The rationale relied on in *Swope*, supra, is that a partner has a vested interest in partnership earnings, whether retained or distributed.

Speer, supra, also held that retained corporate earnings do not constitute commingling, even when the separate property business owner has substantial influence in the decision to reinvest the corporate stock dividends in the company. The *Speer* court was unwilling to allocate the closely held corporation, even though the separate property proponent was the majority shareholder who made the decision to reinvest the stock dividends. The divorce court had discretionary power to divide the community property in a just manner to protect the community's rights with an equitable lien, but it could not stop the business owner from transferring shares to his family. Thus, the wife was granted an equitable lien on a percentage of the withheld corporate stock retained by her former spouse's separate property business, but that ruling led to substantial post-divorce litigation over who, among the separate property business owner's family members, owned the disputed shares of stock.

Idaho uses a benchmark salary test to determine the amount of the business attributable to the community estate as compensation for its labor. *Speer*, supra, stated that the trial court should adequately compensate the community for its labor at the standard rate it would take to "secure a non-owner employee to perform the same services which were rendered by the community." Id. 135, 330. Once the compensation rate is determined, any rents, issues and profits obtained during marriage are apportioned between labor (the community's reimbursement) and natural increase (the underlying business).

Credit acquisitions have received disparate treatment in Idaho, but generally Idaho follows the inception of the title rule. An early bankruptcy case, *Wilkerson v. Aven*, 26 Idaho 559, 144 P. 1105 (1914), seemed to allow the separate property character of the down payment to determine the character of the property overall. The actual source of payments was used on a condition subsequent basis in *Cargill v. Hancock*, 92 Idaho 460, 444 P.2d 421 (1968). The civil law inception of title approach was followed in *Estate of Freeburn*, 97 Idaho 845, 555 P.2d 385 (1976), a case recently cited by *Credit Bureau of Eastern Idaho, Inc. v. Lecheminant*, 149 Idaho 467, 235 P.3d 1188 (2010).

Work related benefits. Idaho has moved toward the last premium rule for community property term life insurance proceeds. *The Travelers Insurance Company v. Johnson*, 97 Idaho 336, 544 P.2d 294 (1975). This case was followed in *Thompson and Thompson*, 2011 WL 2694245 (U.S. Bankruptcy Court, D. Idaho (2011).

Whole life insurance policies with a savings component continue to be governed by the inception of title rule.

In *Banner Life Insurance v. The Mark Wallace Dixson Irrevocable Trust*, 147 Idaho 117, 206 P.3d 481 (2009), the court announced a move toward Washington's "risk payment theory" for characterizing proceeds. The court articulated the risk payment rule as follows: A life insurance policy acquired during marriage is presumed community property unless the last premium was paid for with separate property.

Pensions are apportioned on a time basis between periods when the employee was or was not married and domiciled in Idaho. *Ramsey v. Ramsey*, 96 Idaho 672, 535 P.2d 53 (1975). *Ramsey* was overruled by *Rice v. Rice*, 103 Idaho 85, 645 P.2d 319 (1982) insofar as it conflicted with *McCarty*, supra, (discussed above and in Chapter 12).

Congress effectively overruled *McCarty*, supra, in 1982 with the FUSFSPA, 10 U.S.C.A. § 1408 (1982), which permits the states to apply **"the law of the jurisdiction of such court"** to treat certain **"disposable retired or retainer pay"** as **"property of the member and his spouse."**

Rice, supra, in turn, was subsequently overruled by *Griggs v. Griggs*, 107 Idaho 123, 686 P.2d 68 (1984), a case in which the Idaho Supreme Court exercised its plenary justification power under Art. § 5 and § 9 of the Idaho Constitution to reinstate the holding in *Ramsey*, supra, allowing apportionment on a time basis for military retirement pay.

In the case of divorce, Idaho Code § 32–712 provides that the existence and extent of retirement benefits, including **"social security, civil service, military and railroad benefits"** is a factor which bears upon a **"just"** assignment of community property. **"Just"** division need not be an equal division under the discussion in *Griggs*, supra. Thus, consideration of such benefits under Idaho Code § 32–712(7) need not run counter to the reasoning of *Hisquierdo v. Hisquierdo*, 439 U.S. 572, 586, 99 S.Ct. 802, 810, 811, 59 L.Ed.2d 1 (1979), which held that to allow an offsetting award to the non-employee spouse would defeat the purpose of barring the anticipation of covered government pensions and benefits.

While Idaho Code § 32–712 provides that **"the community property must be assigned by the court . . . ,"** it also gives the court discretion to give **"due consideration"** to federally protected retirement benefits in making a **"just"** assignment.

4. LOUISIANA

Accounts and sums on deposit. Louisiana historically required greater clarity of intent to preserve the separate character of property acquired by exchange during marriage. LSA-C.C. Art. 2342 carries on this tradition by requiring a declaration of separate property on an asset-by-asset basis, at the time of acquisition. The use of a declaration presumably applies to accounts and to deposited sums. A separate property declaration can be controverted by a community property proponent who traces the asset back to a community source. LSA-C.C. Art. 2342, as discussed in Chapters 3 and 4.

LSA-C.C. Art. 2343 and Art. 2343.1 cover commingling issues. Under the first provision, a spouse may **"transform a community property interest into separate property;"** when this occurs by an act of donation, **"an equal interest of the donee is also transformed into separate property . . . [to] form part of the donee's separate property."** Under the second provision, separate property can be transferred to the community, and it retains its character if there is no

"stipulation that it shall be part of the community." Note however that in *Graffeo v. Graffeo*, 576 So.2d 596 (La.App. 1991), a change in the title of a bank account was sufficient stipulation of an intent to transmute the account from separate to community.

Separate property businesses. LSA-C.C. Art. 2368 allows a statutory scheme by which a separate property business retains its separate character even during marriage. If the business increases in value because of **"uncompensated common labor or industry of the spouses,"** then **"the other spouse is entitled to be reimbursed from the spouse whose property has increased in value one-half of the increase attributed to the common labor."** The business owner can rebut the reimbursement with evidence that some or all the growth was the result of non-labor factors. *Bordelon v. Bordelon*, 942 So.2d 708 (La.App. 2006).

Credit acquisitions. The inception of the title rule had a variation in Louisiana that looked to the time of vesting, rather than purchase. In a bond for deed for the purchase of an immovable (called a contract for deed or a real estate contract in other jurisdictions), the inception of title arises when the contract for the sale of realty is made, but the time of vesting in the purchaser does not occur until the deed is delivered, often years many years after execution, when all contract obligations have been fulfilled by the purchaser.

The use of community property funds to pay a separate property obligation is covered by LSA-C.C.

Art. 2364. The use of separate property funds to pay a community property obligation is covered by LSA-C.C. Art. 2365. Purchase money mortgage cases are reported under both provisions.

Contributions to purchase (mortgage principal payments), use, improvement or other benefits are covered by LSA-C.C. Art. 2366 (community to separate) and LSA-C.C. Art. 2367 (separate to community).

Generally, if property of one character has been used to satisfy a purchase money mortgage obligation of another character, under the inception of title rule, the character of the property does not change, but a reimbursement may be due to the contributing estate to avoid unjust enrichment. The same is true for contributions to acquisitions more generally, as this is the civil law approach. See also *Betz v. Riviere*, 29 So.2d 465 (La. 1947). However, an inconsistent line of cases takes the American rule approach, starting with a now rather historical case, *Curtis v. Curtis*, 388 So.2d 816 (La.App. 1980), an equal management era case that recognizes proportional ownership on the theory that reimbursement is not adequate to keep up with inflation.

Work related benefits. LSA-C.C. Art. 2369 provides that **"[A] spouse owes an accounting to the other spouse for community property under his control at the termination of the community property regime."** This obligation is not predicated upon a showing of fraud, as it is under LSA-C.C. Art. 2354, discussed in Chapter 7. The accounting is due as matter of course, but it applies going forward only to property under one former spouse's control at the termination of the community. Retirement benefits, insurance contracts, corporate stock, former community enterprises, usufruct, and the like would be covered under the provision.

Louisiana has applied the inception of the title rule to life insurance policies and proceeds. *Succession of Verneuille*, 45 So. 520 (La. 1908). At the termination of the community, a reimbursement is due for a community life insurance policy with a cash surrender value that gets allocated to one spouse. Reimbursement is not the amount of one-half of the premiums paid, but rather one-half of the cash surrender value of the policy at the time of partition and award, if any. *Westcott v. Westcott*, 11 So.3d 45 (La.App. 4 Cir. 2009). There is no right of reimbursement for term life insurance without a cash surrender value. *Connell v. Connell*, 331 So.2d 4 (La. 1976).

In *Sims v. Sims*, 358 So.2d 919 (La. 1978), the Louisiana Supreme Court apportioned retirement benefits between the contributing estates on the basis of contribution, not time. See LSA-C.C. Art. 2336. The effect of the ruling was to except private retirement plans and benefits from the inception of title rule. At the termination of the community, each spouse is entitled to a pro rata share of the retirement assets based on a ratio of character contribution divided by total value of plan.

In the public retirement fund area, Louisiana tracks the federal approach of deciding that some retirement funds do not belong to the community of acquets and gains. *Kennedy v. Kennedy*, 391 So.2d 1193 (La.App. 1980) involved the Firefighter's Pension and Relief Fund, *Scott v. Scott*, 179 So.2d 656 (La.App. 1965) involved the State Teacher's Retirement System, and *Brouillette v. Brouillette*, 51 So.3d 898 (La.App. 2010) involved Combat Related Special Compensation Benefits. Relief from the harshness of this rule for the nonemployee spouse is given in the form of a right of reimbursement to the community for any contributions that were made to the separate property retirement system.

5. NEVADA

Accounts and sums on deposit. Purchases made during marriage from a commingled account are presumptively community property absent clear and convincing evidence otherwise. *Malmquist v. Malmquist*, 106 Nev. 231, 238, 792 P.2d 372, 376 (1990) recites the presumably pre-CAMPAL 1990 California approach on this topic.

Separate property businesses. The rents, issues and profits of separate property obtained during marriage are also separate property, following the American rule approach. Historically, Nevada followed the all-or-nothing approach to rents, issues, and profits of a separate property business. But *Johnson v. Johnson*, 89 Nev. 244, 510 P.2d 625 (1973) disallowed the all-or-nothing approach and instead adopted the California approach as stated in *Beam v. Bank of America*, supra, which confirms that *Pereira*, supra, and *Van Camp*, supra, provide rival accounting methods. Today, the preferred accounting method in Nevada is *Pereira*, supra. But the court has discretion to use the method that will achieve substantial justice between the parties.

A relatively recent Nevada application of *Van Camp*, supra, is *Devries v. Gallio*, 128 Nev.Adv.Op. 63, 290 P.3d 260, 263 (2012). There, the wife owned a separate property cattle ranch during the 12-year marriage. The husband introduced evidence of the growth in the value of the wife's business, but "minimal evidence of what labor, if any" the community had contributed. Id. After extensive tracing of the cattle company growth, the trial court applied *Van Camp*, supra, because the increase in value of the wife's business "appeared to come solely from the sale and acquisition of cattle and equipment . . . purchased with [the wife's] separate property or the rents thereof." *Id.*

Credit acquisitions. Nevada courts have recognized that the community is entitled to a pro rata ownership share for contributions to the purchase of separate property. *Robison v. Robison,* 100 Nev. 668, 670, 691 P.2d 451, 454 (1984).

As to apportionment, *Malmquist v. Malmquist*, 106 Nev. 231, 238, 792 P.2d 372, 376 (1990) announced that Nevada would follow a slightly modified version of California law, and specifically of *Aufmuth/Moore* apportionment, as discussed in Section C, California above.

Work related benefits. Deferred compensation in the form of pension benefits is apportioned by time.

Term life insurance is not divisible upon divorce. Term life insurance proceeds are characterized by the last premium rule.

The savings component of a whole life insurance, if any, is apportioned based on character contributions.

6. NEW MEXICO

Accounts and sums on deposit. Purchases from commingled bank accounts are community property unless the separate property proponent can trace the asset back to separate property funds. New Mexico does not appear to have tracing rules specific to commingled bank accounts, thus suggesting that courts allow the total recapitulation method of accounting. Copies of checks, records of deposits, bank account statements, purchase receipts, and possibly even the separate property claimant's testimony may be used to rebut the community property presumption.

Separate property businesses. *Laughlin v. Laughlin*, 49 N.M. 20 (1944) involved a separate property agricultural enterprise made profitable by community property labor. New Mexico's Supreme Court rejected the approach in *Estate of Pepper*, 158 Cal. 619, 112 P. 62 (1910), the start of yet a different line of California cases that involve separate property agricultural enterprises. Instead, the court opted for *Pereira*, supra, accounting. The New Mexico Supreme Court specifically cited the *Pereira*, supra, excess profits versus *Van Camp*, supra reimbursement approach with approval since in New Mexico (as in California) rents, issues, and profits of separate property are also separate property. *Laughlin*, supra, held that even in the case of a separate property agricultural enterprise, the separate property is entitled to the rental value of the land (either in cash or in the proceeds of crops sold from it), while the community property is entitled to the balance of income produced from the land by the labor, skill, or management of the parties.

Credit acquisitions. For credit acquisitions, *Dorbin v. Dorbin*, 105 N.M. 263, 731 P.2d 959 (1986) holds that New Mexico has long apportioned interests where property is purchased with separate *and* community property; pro rata shares are based on capital contributions to purchase. Where an asset is acquired with a separate property downpayment and a separate property loan *and* where community property principal payments are made to the separate property loan, the estates' shares are the ratio of their respective contributions to purchase divided by the value of the asset upon marriage.

Dorbin, supra, cited *Chance v. Kitchell*, 99 N.M. 443, 659 P.2d 895 (N.M. 1983) to affirm the use of a modified California *Moore/Marsden* formula. In New Mexico percentages are determined by dividing contributions by the value of the property on the date of marriage, not by the historic purchase price (i.e., the contract price) as in California. The policy in apportioning interests is to seek substantial justice between the parties.

Neither New Mexico case law nor statutes authorize a reimbursement for payment of interest, taxes and insurance.

Work related benefits. New Mexico applied the inception of title rule for determining the character of "war risk" life insurance proceeds, *White's Estate*, 43 N.M. 202, 89 P.2d 36 (1939). *Phillips v. Wellborn*, 89 N.M. 340, 552 P.2d 471 (1976) moved toward the last premium rule. But otherwise, pension benefits are characterized by marital status when earned, and thus can be adjudged commingled. *LeClert v. LeClert*, 80 N.M. 235, 453 P.2d 755 (1969).

7. TEXAS

Accounts and sums on deposit. Texas cases recognize a community property presumption when separate and community property are commingled so that they cannot be separately traced. In addition, V.T.C.A.Fam.Code § 3.102(b) provides a presumption concerning management, control and disposition of commingled community property, as discussed in Chapter 7.

For funds in a bank account to be characterized as separate property, the burden is on the separate property proponent to prove by clear and convincing evidence. *Vardilos v. Vardilos*, 219 S.W.3d 920 (2007), *Pearson v. Fillingim*, 332 S.W.3d 361 (2011). The separate property claimant's testimony, without corroborating evidence, is not sufficient. *Sprague v. Sprague*, 363 S.W.3d 788 (2012).

Separate property businesses. Texas follows the civil law rule on separate property rents issues and profits. This means that income earned by separate property funds is community property during the marriage, as discussed in Chapters 4, 5, and 7.

Credit acquisitions. Loan proceeds (borrowed money) obtained during marriage are presumed to be community property unless the creditor agreed to look "only" (the standard in California is "solely") to the separate property of the contracting party for satisfaction of the credit extended. *Goodloe v. Williams*, 302 S.W.2d 235 (Civ.App.1957). Unpublished opinions continue this rule. V.T.C.A.Fam.Code § 3.402(a)(4)(C) codifies this lender's intent test in its definition of an "economic contribution," as discussed in the next paragraph.

V.T.C.A.Fam.Code § 3.401 et. seq. allows for claims for economic contribution and reimbursement to avoid what V.T.C.A.Fam.Code § 3.402, effective September 1, 2023, specifically calls unjust enrichment. The claim for reimbursement **"exists when one or both spouses use property of one marital estate to confer on the property of another marital estate a benefit which, if not repaid, would result in unjust enrichment to the benefited estate."**

The claimant must prove that a benefit was conferred by a marital estate **"on the property of another marital estate,"** the value of the benefit conferred, and the unjust enrichment that will occur if the conferring estate is not reimbursed. V.T.C.A. Fam.Code § 3.402 (a).

Marital estate means the community property or the separate property of either spouse. V.T.C.A. Fam. § 3.401(4).

A benefit conferred can fall under one of three categories: the payment of debt, liability or expense; an improvement that increases the value of the real estate; or labor that goes beyond normal maintenance. § 3.402(c). Sub-chapter E includes an "equity and good conscience" standard: a reimbursement is due for a benefit conferred that in equity and good conscience should have been borne by the benefited estate in the first place.

Consistent with the civil law inception of title rule, an economic contribution claim does not affect the character of the asset. V.T.C.A.Fam.Code § 3.404(a), explicitly states, in subsection (b), that **"the claim for reimbursement ... does not create an ownership interest in property, but does create a claim against the property of the benefited estate by the conferring estate. The claim matures on dissolution of the marriage or the death of either spouse."** In *Langston v. Langston*, 82 S.W.3d 686, on subsequent appeal 183 S.W.3d 479 (Ct.App. 2002), a trial court was held to have abused its discretion when it awarded an ownership interest to a contributing estate. Abuse of discretion, because the mandated statutory remedy is not a transfer of ownership, but rather a reimbursement secured by an equitable lien in favor of the conferring estate. V.T.C.A.Fam.Code § 3.406.

Offsets are allowed. The party seeking the offset has the burden of proof. 3.402(h).

A statutory right to waive, release, assign or partition a claim for **"economic contribution"** by a premarital or marital property agreement is found at V.T.C.A.Fam.Code § 3.410.

Finally, and of interest as compared to articulated statutory frameworks, V.T.C.A Fam.Code § 3.411 states that **"the remedies provided by this subchapter are** not **exclusive and are in addition to any other remedy provided by law."**

Work related benefits. Generally, the definitions of community and separate property, along with the conceptual guide of the inception of title rule help characterize assets like non-ERISA governed insurance policies. *Marriage of Skarda*, 345 S.W.3d 665 (2011). Whether property is separate, or community is determined by its character at inception, and this general rule seems to apply to life insurance policies.

If an insurance contract is community property at the time of the insured spouse's death, then the surviving spouse is entitled to one-half the proceeds as his or her share of the community estate; this is so even if the deceased spouse designates a nonspousal POD beneficiary. *Amason v. Franklin Life Ins. Co.*, 428 F.2d 1144, 1146–47 (5th Cir. 1970).

At dissolution, when the life insurance policy has a cash value, the inception of the right rule holds that the ownership of the community property life insurance policy remains co-owned by the (now) ex-spouses as tenants in common absent a valid property settlement concerning the term life insurance policy or a divorce court division of the policy. Each tenant in common gets a one-half share of the insurance proceeds in the event of the death of the insured. Alternatively, where the policy itself does not have a cash value after divorce—as with a term life insurance policy—then the unmatured policy—because it has no property value—is not subject to division, as was explained in *Grost v. Grost*, 561 S.W.2d 223 (1977).

A term life insurance policy that is separate in character that gets reissued during the marriage becomes community property by the last premium rule. *Newberry v. Newberry*, 351 S.W.3d 552 (2011); and *Person v. Fillingim*, 332 S.W.3d 361 (2011).

8. WASHINGTON

Accounts and sums on deposit. All property acquired after marriage is presumptively community property in character, even property in TIC or JTWROS title form. Wash.Rev.Code § 64.28.020 states that an interest in favor of two (or more) persons is an interest in common, and that a joint tenancy can be created in the state. But that code section—for which there is newly proposed legislation—also provides that interests in common in the names of persons who are married to each other (or RDPs) are **"presumed to be their community property."** Thus, a bank account in the name of two married persons is presumptively community in character, as are sums on deposit acquired during marriage. The spouses can opt, by community property agreement, for a right of survivorship; but a community property agreement does not change the character of the account from community to separate. What the community property agreement does is, one, impress upon the parties that they are agreeing to dispose of community property by survivorship and, two, provide clear and convincing written evidence of each spouse's intent. See Chapter 6.

In 1885 Washington abrogated the doctrine of survivorship as an incident of joint tenancies. Later, exceptions were made for demand deposit accounts of various sorts. Commentary explained that what Washington abolished was the technical appending of the right of survivorship to the joint tenancy once the four unities had been met (as in the common law). Washington did not bar the use of a JTWROS, so long as there was written evidence of the parties' intent to dispose of the property by survivorship.

For married persons, the right to agree to a right of survivorship is secured by Wash.Rev.Code § 64.28.030, again if there is written evidence of intent. See Chapters 4 and 6. Moreover, the above statute expressly states that, as to bank deposits and community property agreements, the law **"shall not restrict the creation of a joint tenancy in a bank deposit . . . , nor restrict the power of both spouses or both domestic partners to make [community property] agreements . . . ."**

Moreover, if the spouses use a community property agreement to dispose of sums on deposit by right of survivorship, the account and the sums remain community in character. The account is community property because it is included in a community property agreement; the sums on deposit are community property because they are acquired during marriage absent proof to the contrary and held within a community property account.

Separate property businesses. In allocating the profits of a separate property business to which community labor has been added, the courts in Washington have looked at the respective importance of labor or capital in the business and have considered the sufficiency of amounts withdrawn from the business as salary. The Washington approach—called the segregation approach—is intended to give the separate property owner the authority to self-apportion the business. The rationale is that the court should not second-guess the separate property business owner on management issues and on the more particular issue of how business records are or should be kept during the marriage.

Credit acquisitions. In determining the character of property acquired on credit, Washington follows the general community property presumption. Several local peculiarities and inconsistencies have developed and appear to be in play.

For example, consistent with other community property states, Washington's general approach is to treat borrowed funds and promissory notes obtained during marriage as community property. But rebuttal is not by the lender's intent test. Rather rebuttal is by proof of one of the following: (i) the spouses had an agreement to treat the funds as separate property, (ii) the loan was secured by separate property, or (iii) most generally, the funds were not intended to be or in fact were not used for a community purpose.

The character of an asset purchased with acquired borrowed funds depends on the character of the downpayment *and* on the character of the purchase loan. In *Merkel v. Merkel*, 39 Wash.2d 102, 234 P.2d 857 (1951), one spouse acquired two parcels of land, one before marriage and one during marriage by inheritance; each parcel was subject to a mortgage secured by its respective parcel. The court ruled that both parcels were separate property, both mortgages were separate property obligations, and that the use of community property funds to repay the separate property obligation gave rise to a right of reimbursement in the community. See also, *Marriage of Johnson*, 28 Wash.App. 574, 576, 625 P.2d 720 (1981).

Barlow v. Barlow, 107 Wash.App. 1050, 2001 WL 933382 (2001) adds to *Merkel* and *Johnson*. In *Barlow*, supra, the wife took out an equity line of credit on her separate property during marriage for the purpose of constructing a community property house on a different parcel. The trial court characterized the loan as a community obligation (not a separate one) because it was for a community purpose ("the couple's dream house"). On appeal, this characterization was held to be within the trial court's discretionary power. If the money was borrowed for community purpose, the court ruled, the borrowed funds were community in character. For more on characterizing contract obligations, see Chapter 9.

Washington has granted an equitable lien when separate and community property are commingled by an improvement made by one character of property to the other. The value of the lien is the value of the improvements. Likewise when the separate property of one spouse is used to improve the separate property of the other spouse, as in *Estate of Trierweiler,* 5 Wash.App. 17, 486 P.2d 314 (1971). Washington also indicates that the measure of the lien is the amount expended rather than the amount by which the value of the improved property is enhanced.

Work related benefits. A life insurance policy is analyzed as property, not as a mere expectancy. Therefore, historically, whole and term life insurance policies (and their proceeds) were apportioned using a ratio of character contributions to premiums, *Coffey's Estate*, 195 Wash. 379, 81 P.2d 283 (1938). Of note, however, is that the last premium rule emerged in Washington for term life insurance policies in a dissent in *Small v. Bartyzel*, 27 Wash.2d 176, 185, 177 P.2d 291, 397 (1947).

The risk-payment theory was adopted in *Aetna Life Ins. Co. v. Wadsworth*, 102 Wash.2d 652, 689 P.2d 46 (1984). There, the court held that a married insured has the testamentary right to dispose of one-half of the proceeds of a community property life insurance policy. *Aetna Life Ins. Co.*, supra overruled *Small,* supra.

The time rule was applied to a pension in *Marriage of Jacobs*, 20 Wash.App. 272, 579 P.2d 1023 (1978). See also *Farver v. Department of Retirement Systems of State of Washington*, 97 Wash.2d 344, 644 P.2d 1149 (1982). The percentage of benefits earned during the marriage is subject to division under Wash.Rev.Code § 26.16.030, which is the general community property statute. Percentages earned outside of marriage are separate property under Wash.Rev.Code § 26.10.10 or 26.10.20. See also *Arnold v. Department of Retirement Systems*, 128 Wash.2d 765, 912 P.2d 463 (1996).

9. WISCONSIN

Commingled property generally. Wis.Stat. § 766.63 states the general rules for commingled property and improvements and businesses:

(1) Except as provided otherwise . . . mixing marital property with property having any other classification reclassifies the other property to marital property unless the component of the mixed property which is not marital property can be traced.

(2) Application by one spouse of substantial labor, effort, inventiveness, physical or intellectual skill, creativity or managerial activity to either spouse's property other than marital property creates marital property attributable to that

application if both of the following apply:

(a) Reasonable compensation is not received for the application.

(b) Substantial appreciation of the property results from the application.

Notice that subsection (1) above raises more than a presumption in favor of the marital community. It reclassifies the entirety of the commingled property unless the individual (separate property) component can be traced.

Subsection (2) above uses a substantial labor standard to determine which of any covered property is transmuted by default into marital property. Transmutation by law occurs if the marital partnership is not reasonably compensated for its labor contribution *and* if the property in question has substantially appreciated because of the marital labor contribution. This standard appears to meld the excess profits (*Pereira,* supra) and reimbursement (*Van Camp,* supra) approaches in recognition that the marital partnership's substantial investment in an appreciated enterprise is a reasonable basis upon which the marital partnership can claim a superior property interest in the enterprise relative to the individual owner.

Work related benefits. Life insurance policies and proceeds are extensively treated in Wis.Stat. § 766.61. The general idea is that the ownership interest and proceeds of a life insurance issued after a determination date are marital property regardless of the classification of property used to pay the premiums.

Deferred employment benefits are extensively covered in Wis.Stat. § 766.62. Generally, **"a deferred employment benefit attributable to employment of a spouse occurring after the determination date is marital property."** Various mixed property scenarios and multipliers are detailed in the statute.

PART 3

MANAGEMENT AND CONTROL

CHAPTER 8

MANAGEMENT AND CONTROL

A. OVERVIEW

Property ownership comes with management and control rights.

Management and control rights include but certainly are not limited to, the right to use, consume, destroy, abandon, sell, convey, donate, encumber, mortgage, lease, expend, assign, create a security interest in, dispose of, place into trust, initiate or defend a legal action over, and otherwise exercise control or decision-making power over an asset and its component parts.

The trend in community property states is to extend equal management and control rights to either spouse, each of whom can act alone, but this is not universal among the estates. Thus, management and control rights depend on the asset and on the jurisdiction.

During marriage, management rights and liabilities extend to community property, including any commingled with separate property. At the end of a marriage, retroactive analyses related to liabilities can involve management and control rights.

B. DETAIL

1. MANAGEMENT AND CONTROL: A CATALOGUE OF OPTIONS

Most U.S. community property states have adopted equal management and control legislation for community personal property. That legislation typical refers to equal rights with this word: "either." Either spouse means each spouse, even acting alone, has the same (equal) absolute power of disposition, over the community personal property.

Rules for real property may differ on key points.

The equal management and control language affords a dazzlingly broad grant of control to either spouse. The apparent freedom of the absolute power of disposition standard should not be taken literally. The standard is modified by recognition (often statutory) that the spouses are in a confidential relationship that gives rise to a fiduciary duty that comes into existence, as a matter of law, on the date of marriage.

Every state has gradations of control, depending on the asset.

- *Sole* control, meaning exclusive control by default, for entirely separate property.
- *Equal* control for community personal property.
- *Joint* control for community real property.
- *Dual* control, as in the Texas system.

- *Primary* control, used in some states for community property businesses.
- *Exclusive* control, meaning sole control obtained by court order over a specific community property asset for a limited time.

States differ on general matters. Brief examples follow to illustrate the point.

Arizona is unique by how it allows one spouse to make a gift of identified community property earnings to the other spouse. Upon delivery, the gifted earnings become the separate property of the donee spouse.

In Louisiana, significant amounts of management and control are given to the spouse who registers movables (personal property) in his or her name alone.

Texas is unique for its dual management system. In Texas, spouses have sole management, by statutory default, over community property that each would have owned individually had the marriage not existed. If one spouse's solely managed property becomes commingled with the other spouse's solely managed community property, dual management becomes the default rule for any commingled *community* property in the lot.

With respect to a community property business, California, Louisiana, Nevada, Washington, and Wisconsin recognize the right of one spouse to exercise "primary control" over that business. Primary control is not the same as exclusive control.

Primary control means the manager of a business has somewhere between sole (the top point of a spectrum of control) and equal (the middle point of a spectrum of control) over day-to-day aspects of the business management. The main limitation on primary control is this: if the managing spouse decides to transfer substantially all the business assets to a third party, he or she is statutorily required to obtain the consent of the non-managing spouse. Consent is not necessarily the same as joint control. Here it is important as a reporting and documentation function.

Exclusive control can happen in extraordinary circumstances like if one spouse moves for a protective order to obtain exclusive control over one or more community property assets to protect it from dissipation by the other spouse. Or exclusive control can happen in the most mundane circumstances, like for example when a spouse has a separate property asset that was never commingled with community property.

How do we think of management and control rules at a meta level? One way is to balance the rights of spouses as between each other. Another is to balance the rights of spouses in relation to third parties. A third way is to understand the balance of rights between spouses (who get systemic protections by the very fact of their valid marriage) in relation to the public fisc, which might be called on to pay the bill when systemic protections for a vulnerable spouse do not work for whatever reason.

Statutes and cases normally distinguish between real and personal community property.

a. Community Personal Property

Personal property is defined as all property not real property. A wide range of assets fall into the category of personal property. Money, stock, bonds, pension rights, employment contracts, sums on deposit, furniture, clothing, cars, and companion animals are examples of personal property.

Community personal property is typically governed by the equal management and control rule. Either spouse acting alone has absolute power of disposition, other than testamentary, over community personal property. Some transactions, however, undertaken by one spouse require, by statute, the consent of the nonacting spouse. Actions that require the consent of the nonacting spouse generally involve gifts—true gifts—from one spouse to a third party, or low value transfers of property of a personal nature such as clothing and furnishings of the family.

Specific statutory provisions allow the spouses to agree to a different scheme of management and control in Idaho, Texas, and Wisconsin. In Louisiana, a spouse may expressly renounce the right to concur in actions which would otherwise require both spouses to join in a transaction.

The consent of a spouse may be obtained in advance by a power of attorney in accordance with statutory provisions in California, Idaho, Nevada, and Texas. Generally, an action requiring consent can be ratified after the fact, expressly or by acquiescence, and during life or after death (by means of an estate plan that validates the acting spouse's transaction).

In California, one spouse may bring a motion to dispense with the consent requirement, on a transaction-by-transaction basis. This can happen when the other spouse arbitrarily refuses to give consent, or is physically or mentally incapacitated, or has been absent from the family for a prolonged period. Cal.Fam.Code § 1101(e). Wisconsin has a similar provision that permits a court to appoint a conservator or guardian to exercise a disabled spouse's right to manage and control marital property. Wis.Stat. § 766.51(7).

When both spouses do not act, the statutory remedy is to give the nonacting spouse a cause of action either in conversion (against the spouse who initiated the transaction) or in replevin (against the transferee).

b. Community Real Property

Real property is broadly defined as land and structures affixed. Items of personal property become part of the realty if they are affixed.

Community real property transactions, if they are consequential, require the joint action ("joinder") of both spouses. Practically speaking, joinder means that both spouses must sign any document that affects community property rights in the asset.

Arizona and Washington require joinder for the purchase of community property real estate. The absence of joinder exposes the transaction to a claim for avoidance, brought either by the other spouse or a third party.

c. Separate Property

The rule is exclusive management and control when it comes to entirely (100%) separate property.

d. Commingled Property

Once separate property is commingled with community property, the equal management and control principle may and likely will attach to the entirety of the commingled property. See e.g. *Marriage of Walker*, 138 Cal.App.4th 1408, 42 Cal.Rptr.3d 325 (2006).

The result is that managers of commingled community *personal* property have equal management and control rights over the whole. Shares are pro rata, but the marital estate with the lesser pro rata share has the same management and control rights as the marital estate with the greater share does.

For community *real* property, in a state where both spouses must join in (sign) consequential real estate documents, joiner has a title clearing function as the community property right can be unwritten. A consequential real estate document is one that effects a legal change.

e. Partnership Fiduciary Duties

In the American community property system, the marriage itself is not an entity like a partnership or a corporation. We say marriage is a partnership, but we mean that metaphorically. If anything, spouses engaging in identifiable transactions are joint venturers and as such equity may require that the court recognize their duties to each other for purposes of carrying out that joint venture. When the venture goes sour, many states permit a court to create a remedy—often a resulting or a constructive trust—to protect the spouse who was adversely affected by the transaction. Wisconsin does so by statute, as does California

California, by statute, explicitly specifies that spouses are in a fiduciary duty akin to that of nonmarital business partners. Cal.Fam.Code § 721. The duty requires good faith and loyalty in a general sense across the transactions of married life. Good faith is often defined in case law as honesty in fact. Loyalty is linked to financial disclosure.

Special rules can apply in a transaction between the spouses.

In terms of statutory protections, first and foremost, neither should take any unfair advantage of the other in the transaction itself, as marriage is a confidential relationship. Cal Fam. Code § 721. This standard is not an arithmetical standard. (In a transaction between themselves, one spouse might come out arithmetically ahead.) Rather this is a relationship standard: neither shall abuse the trust of the other in the relationship as to the transaction.

If a breach of the fiduciary duty impairs the non-managing spouse's past, present or future community property interest in the (mis)managed property, Cal.Fam.Code § 1101 provides a series of (apparently) independent claims by which the impaired spouse can sue the alleged impairing spouse for breach of fiduciary duty. Remedies include court ordered accountings, title changes, consent waivers, and damages (with court costs and attorney's fees).

Protection of third parties is furnished by several provisions without much uniformity among the states. California, Idaho, Washington, and Wisconsin include express provisions that validate certain pre-existing documents. Washington protects mechanics and materialmen liens. New Mexico has express provisions for management based upon the form of documentary title to personal property. Nevada and Wisconsin have a specific provision concerning payments from employee benefit plans.

2. THE PARTNERSHIP FIDUCIARY STANDARD

Under the obsolete male management model, a fiduciary standard of varying stringency was generally imposed upon the husband in his role as the legal manager of the community property estate. Real property transactions more typically required joint action between the spouses (a wife's signature on a consequential real estate document), but personal property transactions did not.

The joinder requirement protected the husband's relationship with the third party. When it came to community personal property, the husband, acting alone as a managing agent of the community, had exclusive control over all personal property transactions involving money, encumbrances, securities, bonds, businesses, tort causes of action, tort settlements, bank accounts, retirement accounts, monetized home equity, and so forth. Depending on the jurisdiction, the husband was held to fiduciary standards that could range from good faith on the lax end to (far less commonly) the fiduciary duties of a professional trustee on the strict end.

The range of standards continues today. But it is applied in gender neutral form to the legal manager (either spouse) who transacts with community personal property as the de facto managing spouse for that transaction.

Generally, standards become an issue upon proof of any unfair dealing by a spouse in a transaction with another. Specifically, that factual proof gives rise to a presumption of undue influence to protect the spouse who would be impaired by the transaction if it were given legal effect. Unless the presumption is rebutted (with evidence of voluntariness, usually), the de facto managing spouse is exposed to legal liability on several grounds. Those grounds may be breach of good faith; failure to keep records; failure to make records accessible to the other spouse for inspection and copying; failure to disclose financial information; impairing a nonacting spouse's past, present or future community property interest; obtaining an advantage over the other spouse by fraud, duress, undue influence, oppression; or any other issue of concern to the judge. All of these are example grounds for challenging a de facto manager's conduct as unfair dealing.

On the other extreme of the fiduciary standard, some cases have gone so far as to suggest that a spouse is a "trustee" in relation to the community. But what kind of trustee?

A professional trustee has multiple statutory duties—like the duty to make the trust property productive (or else suffer surcharge against one's own property); the duty to follow certain investing strategies like modern portfolio theory (which allows a trustee to invest in equities) or the legal list (which limits the trustee to investments in bonds or well-secured first mortgages); the duty to account on a periodic basis (or suffer removal from the trustee position).[1] During the marriage, a spouse may not (and likely will not) meet the exacting and formal standard of a professional trustee as to the transaction in question, much less as to all assets of the marriage.

A joint venturer—a general business partner—by contrast, owes partnership fiduciary duties to partners, but the business partner's duties are

---

1 Langbein, *The Uniform Prudent Investor Act and the Future of Trust Investing*, 81 Iowa L. Rev. 641, 643 (1996).

measured by a far less exacting standard than are the professional trustee's duties. Plus, in terms of breach of fiduciary duty claims the general business partner's liability is limited by the business judgment rule in a way that the professional trustee's liability is not. The business judgment rule tends to recognize only claims that arise from acts of gross negligence.

Between the doctrinal extremes of what constitutes a "fiduciary" duty are several possible alternatives. Most have had or still have adherents in some community property states.

The duty not to commit fraud is clearly a part of the de facto managing spouse's obligation in every state. By contrast, loss due to the actions of a negligent or incompetent spouse are (still) considered risks of the marriage in most jurisdictions.

Success of an employed spouse in his or her career is not required by the law. Although what bars a claim in today's world for breach of an employment contract due to non- or substandard performance by the employee spouse? If the contract is entered into during marriage, it belongs to the community, and any impairment of a present or future community property contract right theoretically should be actionable.

A manager is permitted to be inept, inefficient, or clumsy, so long as he or she is honestly so; but here again, the inept de facto manager may be liable if ineptness is adjudged the direct cause of an impairment to the other spouse's past, present or future community property interest. Cal.Fam.Code § 1101.

Transaction facts are required to make any case.

Arguments that the entire marriage impaired one spouse at the expense of the other spouse are too broad to be persuasive in the way required here.

Still, one could rephrase into the language of today a century of case law in each of the U.S. community property jurisdictions. Appellate cases and statutory transitions are proof that at the end of a marriage, given the nature of the dissolution process, each spouse may, should, and could be called upon to account for his or her stewardship of the community property.

So, what inhibits accounting issues from being raised more routinely?

3. TIME FRAMES

Statutes that govern management and control of community property are most likely to come into play at the termination of the marriage by dissolution. Perhaps this is because spouses manage their finances, as a practical matter, without the aid of the law. It is only when marital discord or dissolution arise that the law becomes a tool to challenge past acts of management and control

As a case-management matter, time frames for analysis can include several periods. There is the period before the marriage. The period during the marriage. There is the time after a date of separation.

There is the time during the dissolution proceeding. There is the time after the final judgment of dissolution is signed, especially if the parties continue to hold property together. Of course, children raise different issues not covered in this Nutshell, given its focus on property matters.

As a doctrinal matter, explanatory materials that collect cases of a certain historical era (pre-mid-1970s) are normally decided on the now-obsolete male-management principle (the idea that the husband was the legal manager of the community property by virtue of his gender alone). These mid-1970s explanatory sources were decided before the sea change that equal management and control brought to community property law. Hence, they should not control, and if they do, they must be assessed for implicit gender bias on management and control issues. Implicit bias because pre-mid-1970s the male spouse (the husband) had the legal right of management and control on the theory (however unfounded in any particular marriage) that men were more financially able than women.

Liability for debts is often linked to management and control. See Chapter 8.

4. GIFTS

Gifts and low value transfers have historically been contentious areas because they can involve a spouse who is wrongfully attempting to dissipate the community property in anticipation of a dissolution.

Spanish law gave the husband the right to make gifts of community property to third persons as part of management and control of community personal property. The legal limit to this power was that the husband could not defraud his wife. Most community property states followed the Spanish law, even when they incorporated the common law to determine if a gift had in fact been made.

Today, U.S. community property states that give spouses statutory equal management and control rights (and all do) also clearly note when the consent of the nonacting spouse is required. Consent, therefore, is a corollary right that belongs to the nonacting spouse in certain types of transfers. Consent gives the nonacting spouse the right to challenge an acting spouse's decisions, as to eligible transactions, on a transaction-by-transaction basis. With transactions for which consent was required but not obtained, the transaction between the acting spouse and the third party is subject to challenge by a claim for replevin or conversion. Replevin is a suit brought against the current possessor of the item to seek its return. Conversion is a suit brought against the transferor spouse (among others) for damages.

Additionally, the trend has been and still is to offer some default protection to third parties in transactions with a married person. Transactions that involve gifts or even market value transfers of family furniture and clothing can be negotiated and conducted by one spouse. But here again, statutes tend to give the nonacting spouse the right to consent. Where consent is missing, the nonacting spouse has the right to challenge the transaction by suing either the third party (replevin) or the other spouse (conversion).

Some states, California is an example, extend the non-acting spouse consent requirement from gifts to low-value transactions and even to market value transactions.

a. Gifts of Community Property Made by One Spouse to the Other Spouse

As to community personal property, a *gift* is a gratuitous transfer. Under the common law, dispositive elements for proving a gift are donative intent, delivery, and acceptance.

A *low value transfer* depending on the facts can be a gift, the conferral of a benefit, or a sale. An example might be a case where one spouse sells the $20,000 family piano for $10 to a friend.

A *sale* involves a market transfer, typically of highly personal items such as clothing or family furniture. When these items are sold, no matter the price, the nonacting spouse's consent is required.

Gifts of community property, real or personal, from one spouse to the other spouse pose few problems so long as transmutation formalities are met where applicable. It may be that the state exempts tangible gifts of a personal nature, made under certain conditions, from transmutation formalities.

Transmutations are discussed in Chapter 3.

b. Gifts or Low Value Transfers of Community Personal Property Made by One Spouse to a Third Party

A nonmutual gift is a gratuitous (free) transfer made by one spouse to a third person without the nonacting spouse's consent. The transfer will meet the common law elements of a gift and pass title to the third party upon delivery of the item. But can it be challenged by the nonacting spouse?

Generally, the answer is yes on the ground that the nonacting spouse owns an undivided one-half interest in the community property and has an equal right of management and control over the asset. The nonacting spouse therefore has a legal right, stemming from ownership of the asset, to seek replevin or conversion damages.

Two other general ideas are useful to bear in mind at this point. The law does not bother with trifles. But neither should it tolerate fraud. The area the between trifle and fraud is gray.

Small customary gratuities remain fully within the general management power of a spouse and, as such, they do not require the other spouse's consent even though they may be gifts made without the consent of the nonacting spouse. Louisiana has codified and extended this rule. In Louisiana **"concurrence of the spouses"** is required by statute, except that **"a spouse acting alone may make a usual or customary gift of a value commensurate with the economic position of the spouses at the time of the donation."** LSA-C.C. Art. 2349.

In California, either spouse has full management powers to make a nonmutual gift of community personal property. But because written consent is required, if a spouse makes a nonmutual gift of community personal property to a third party, the absence of consent gives the nonacting spouse a cause of action to avoid the transfer. The result is that the gift giver and the third-party gift recipient (who may want nothing more to do with the spouses) are both exposed to legal action if the nonacting spouse opts to bring a claim to recover the property or its value.

Nevada and Washington require the "express or implied consent" of the non-acting spouse for nonmutual gifts.

Wisconsin requires that both spouses act together to create gifts that exceed a specific dollar amount per donee in a calendar year. If the gift exceeds that annual dollar amount, it may still be valid if it is reasonable in relation to the economic position of the spouses.

Value limitations, like the one that appears in Wisconsin law, appear throughout the community property statutory law. Their purpose is to protect creditors. They protect creditors by dissuading one spouse from attempting to shield assets by transferring them, gratuitously, to third parties and away from the creditor seeking satisfaction. Avoiding creditors is a form of fraud, and thus it makes the gift a fraudulent transfer subject to avoidance under statutes like the Uniform Fraudulent Transfer Act.

That said, there are ways around getting immediate or pre-transfer consent. California has adhered to inconsistent rules on gifts requiring the consent of both spouses. A gift made to a third party—and keep in mind that a third party can be an adult child—is essentially voidable at the option of the living non-consenting spouse. But what if the non-consenting spouse dies before such action can be taken? Can the survivors interpret their testamentary documents for evidence of authorization through a general power of attorney or a trust or estate plan that is consistent with the making of the gift. The answer in *Spreckels v. Spreckels*, 172 Cal. 775, 158 P. 537 (1916) was yes. Posthumous consent to a gift can satisfy the transfer.

The area the between trifle and fraud might be gray, but it exists; and it is the aggrieved spouse who draws the line in any given case. A gift made to a third party with the fraudulent purpose of injuring the nonacting spouse by impairing their property interest is a harm with legal remedies. Likewise, a gift made by undue influence, mistake, or misrepresentation is a harm with legal remedies.

Relevant to the analysis of whether a gift is more trifle than fraud are the following factors. What is the relationship of the donee to the donor? What is the value of the gift as compared to the community estate? What motivated the gift? These are all potential factors that courts have considered in determining whether one spouse's gift to a third party is in fraud of the other spouse's community property rights.

Illustration 8.1: Without the other spouse's knowledge, a spouse gives an adult sibling $3,000 of community property cash. The net worth of the community estate is $500,000.

In most states, the argument for avoiding the gift is that it was nonmutual. Nonmutual means that the nonacting spouse did not consent to the gift before it was made or ratify it after. The lack of consent gives the non-consenting spouse a cause of action for avoidance. And for that reason, the donee's title is voidable through the applicable limitations period. Once the nonacting spouse is barred from bringing their claim, the gift recipient acquires good and merchantable title.

The fact that the gift is small relative to the total value of the community estate may be relevant to an impairment claim, but it is less relevant to the avoidance claim. It is the nonacting spouse who decides if the gift is a trifle or a fraud; they make their decision known by invoking the legal system (or not). California uses this approach.

Louisiana and Wisconsin, by contrast, consider the value of the gift relative to the total community property estate value. Here the gift is $3,000 and the total community property net worth of $500,000, the court would have discretion to dismiss the nonacting spouse's claim as a trifle.

Illustration 8.2: Same facts as 8.1 above except that the net worth of the community estate is $5,000.

The argument in favor of avoiding the cash gift still depends on state law.

The California analysis remains the same, but its ragged economic limits are revealed. Is it practical for *this* nonacting spouse, whose community has a total net worth of $5,000, to devote funds to avoiding the gift? If not, then the gift, while deemed more a trifle than a fraud, is in fact a potentially catastrophic impairment of this community's estate, one that the law can remedy, but one that the nonacting spouse, whose interest in the community property estate, might not be able to pursue absent a statute that provides for attorney's fees in just this kind of case.

The analysis in the other states changes. Here the $3,000 gift made from the $5,000 marital estate is nonmutual—the first ground for avoiding it. And the gift is a substantial percentage of the total net worth of the community property estate—the second ground for avoiding it. Not only is the nonacting spouse's interest impaired (the nonmutual gift) but the couple's creditors are put at risk by the gift giving spouse's act, which can be characterized as a liquidation of the community property estate. If the gift is made for a greater family purpose some courts might deem it valid. But if the gift is a large part of the total community estate, equity-based arguments in favor of avoiding the gift likely outweigh creditor-protection arguments in favor of confirming it.

Illustration 8.3: Same facts as 8.2 above except that the $3,000 cash gift is made to a nonspousal sexual partner.

The argument for avoiding the cash gift is now threefold. One, the gift of community personal property was nonmutual. Two, the gift of $3,000 is a substantial sum relative to the $5,000 net worth of the community. Three, the intimate nature of the donor spouse's relationship to the third-party donee could increase the likelihood that the donor spouse—who is the acting spouse—may make more gifts over time to this recipient—the acting spouse's nonmarried intimate party—without the consent of the nonacting spouse. Without spousal consent, this transfer has the appearance of an undisclosed (secretive) gift. Clearly if one secret gift impairs the nonacting spouse's present and future community property interest and puts creditors' rights at risk, then a whole series of secretive gifts will only exacerbate the problem. Once the creditors' rights argument is raised, the fact that the nonconsenting spouse did not take legal action likely will fall flat.

The point is simple: when creditors' rights are implicated, a new party enters the fray alongside the aggrieved spouse—the creditor. If one spouse is liquidating the community estate by gratuitous secret transfers to a nonmarried intimate partner, then the law on fraudulent transfers is very likely to be implicated.

c. Portion of the Gift That Is Set Aside

If the donor spouse makes a gift to a third person without the consent as in California, Nevada, Washington, or more than the permissible standard as in Wisconsin, or in fraud of the non-consenting spouse's rights (as in other states), what remedies are available if the non-consenting spouse sues the third party?

Is the purported gift void ab initio or voidable?

How much of the gift should be set aside? One half? All in excess of the standard? All or a fraction based on the value of the gift at the time of its delivery?

In an equal management jurisdiction, because either spouse has the power to manage and control community personal property, any gift made by one spouse, acting alone, to a third party is voidable, not void. In other words, delivery of the gift transfers title, but that title is subject to the claims of the non-consenting spouse who has a period of limitations to avoid the gift or recover its value as of the time of transfer, as discussed above.

A claim for avoidance (replevin or conversion) can be initiated by the non-consenting spouse against the third-party donee or against the donor spouse (or his or her estate). In some states, the non-consenting spouse can also sue the donor spouse to recover impairment damages to the claimant's interest either in the community property or in the entire community property estate (as in California). A court might place the property into constructive trust for the benefit of the non-consenting spouse or creditors. See for example Chapter 9, Section C, Wisconsin.

In short, the law balances three issues.

One, it defines the equal management rule to include gifts that are made to a third party by one spouse acting alone. But two, it protects the third-party donee by making title to the gift voidable (not void) upon delivery. And three, it protects the non-consenting spouse by providing a basis, often statutory, upon which he or she can challenge the transfer during the limitations period.

Keep in mind that if the transfer meets the common law elements of a gift, then title passes. What the state family law statute does, then, is not invalidate the gift itself but rather demote the title just enough to protect the recipient of the gift. The recipient receives not good title but voidable title. And because the gift is valid, as between the donor spouse and the third-party donee, the gift is valid upon delivery. And because the nonacting spouse who properly seeks legal recourse has rights, that spouse can recover 100% or 50% depending on when the action is brought.

If the action is brought during the marriage, the spouse acts as an agent for the community and thus recovers 100%.

If the challenge is brought in a dissolution proceeding, the spouse acts in their individual capacity and thus recovers 50%.

If the non-consenting spouse insists on retrieving *the property itself*, he or she must sue the third-party donee or (if the property was subsequently transferred) the current possessor of the property.

If the non-consenting spouse sues for the *value* of the gift, the amount that can be declared void and brought back into the community estate might vary as follows.

- If the marriage is still in existence, the non-consenting spouse can seek to recapture the entire value of the gift (100%) on behalf of the community estate.

- If the community has been terminated (whether by agreement, physical separation (in some states), court action, or death), the non-consenting spouse has the right to recapture one-half of the value (50%) of the gift.

- Another remedy which is possible at the termination of the community is to award to the non-consenting spouse, from the community property remaining on hand, one-half the value of the gift. With this technique, if enough community property remains on hand, the non-consenting spouse need not sue the gift recipient to recover value.

A one hundred percent (100%) recovery, when the marriage is intact, prevents a de facto managing spouse (the donor spouse in this context) from giving progressive halves of the community estate away by successive unconsented to gifts of community property. In Wisconsin, the non-consenting spouse may recover the property or a compensatory judgment equal to the amount by which the gift exceeded the permissible standard. When the marriage is still in existence, recovered property is characterized as community property.

A fifty percent (50%) recovery, when a marriage is ending, allows the other one-half of the property to remain with the third-party donee on one of two standard theories. The first is that from the perspective of the end of the marriage, the transfer is tantamount to dissolution. Hence, the donor has the right to make a gift of 50% of the community property now being dissolved. The second is that under the common law of gifts the donor's title (one-half of the gifted community property) irrevocably transferred to the donee upon delivery; here, the law is understood to protect the community during the marriage. The donor is not protected as an individual and indeed should be estopped from challenging the validity of a gift intentionally made and delivered

d. Gifts Made by One Spouse to a Nonspousal POD Beneficiary in a Term Life Insurance Policy

One of the most frequently litigated issues, especially at the end of a marriage by death, concerns gifts of community property in the form of the proceeds of a term life insurance policy.

Disputes arise because of this clash: On one hand, purchasing a term life insurance contract is a *nontestamentary* act involving community personal property; as such, it is an act governed by equal management and control rules. But on the other hand, designating a pay-on-death (POD) beneficiary is a *testamentary* act; as such, it is outside the scope of equal management and control rules.

This raises questions. With respect to term life insurance, what exactly is the gift and when exactly is it made? Is it made at the time that each premium is paid? Is it made when the policy matures, which is to say when the insured party dies and the insurance company disposes of the proceeds to the POD beneficiary?

If the policy has not yet matured (i.e., if the insured policy owner is alive) a "gift" might be construed as having been made to a third party with each premium payment that was made while the third-party POD was named a beneficiary on the life insurance contract. In such a case the "gift" is really a series of multiple gifts that, together, are properly defined as the sum of cash used to pay the policy premium(s). If the premiums constitute a significant value of the total community property estate, the question of consent gets raised. Did the insured get the non-insured spouse's consent to name a nonspousal POD on the life insurance contract?

If the policy has matured (i.e., the insured is deceased) the "gift" occurs when the POD beneficiary receives the life insurance proceeds, meaning the contract pay out. Where relevant, the proceeds (usually a much larger gift than the gift of premiums) are measured against the net community estate remaining after the payment of debts.

In jurisdictions that distinguish between testamentary and nontestamentary acts in the management and control of community personal property, the character of the policy is important. If the policy is a separate property asset, then the decedent had sole management and control, which then gave the decedent the right to name a nonspousal POD beneficiary for the entirety (100%) of the proceeds. But if the policy is community property in character, then even though the insured had equal management and control, that control did not extend to matters testamentary. In this context, the phrase matters testamentary does not mean that the proceeds will, do or can fall into the deceased's probate estate. Rather, it means more generally that the insured, prior to death, decided to dispose of only their 50% of the policy proceeds upon death.

How much the named POD beneficiary takes depends on state law.

In a state where the naming of a POD beneficiary falls within the category of a transfer that will occur after the death of the insured. Thus, it is a nonprobate disposition. As such, a decedent spouse had the right to make (only) a gift of his or her 50% of the community property proceeds, which leaves the surviving spouse with his or her 50%.

Additionally, the revocability or irrevocability of the POD beneficiary designation is a key touchstone for determining what the gift is and when it was made.

Normally the beneficiary designation is revocable up until the policy matures. There can be a gift of the premium payments as well as a gift of the contract proceeds. But the contract proceeds can only be delivered upon the death of the insured.

An irrevocable beneficiary designation, by contrast, effects an immediate gift not just of all subsequent premium payments, (the gift of cash to pay the premium) but also of the policy proceeds Some uncertainty exists concerning the retention of other rights which can indirectly change the beneficiary, such as the right to surrender the insurance policy, the right to borrow against the policy or the right to allow coverage to expire by the nonpayment of premiums. Generally, however, such rights are disregarded, or considered to be in the nature of conditions subsequent upon an otherwise-completed gift of the life insurance premiums.

Insurance company practices and protective statutes reduce the probability that the insurer will be called upon to pay the proceeds twice. Many companies request or even require that the spouse of the insured policy owner indicate, in writing, his or her consent to any nonspousal POD. By consenting to the other spouse's POD, the consenting spouse relinquishes any community property interest he or she might have to the proceeds upon the insured's death.

Additionally, most states have enacted statutes that permit insurance companies to pay out policy proceeds in accordance with the POD beneficiary designation unless the surviving spouse asserts his or her claim in a timely manner. This practice permits insurance companies to make fast pay outs. If the spouse does assert a claim contrary to the beneficiary designation, the company usually pays the money into court and interpleads the claimants. Interpleader protects the insurance company from paying twice, but it does not determine legal right to the proceeds. Absent interpleader, the spouse asserts his or her claim first against the insurance company; but if the insurer has already paid the proceeds, the spouse is left to assert a claim against the contract POD beneficiary.

The source of the above rules is the management and control limitation upon gifts made by a managing spouse to third parties. It is possible that a reciprocal arrangement between nonspousal business partners to name each other as life insurance beneficiaries would be supported by consideration. If so, that arrangement would be treated as a bargained for exchange—a contract—not an avoidable gift.

C. INDIVIDUAL STATES

1. ARIZONA

Arizona follows a managerial system based on an equal management and control statute that covers both community personal and community real property.

The management and control statute applies to community property generally. It is found at Ariz.Rev.Stat.Ann. § 25–214:

> **"A. Each spouse has the sole management, control and disposition rights of each spouse's separate property.**
>
> **B. The spouses have equal management, control and disposition rights over their community property and have equal power to bind the community.**
>
> **C. Either spouse separately may acquire, manage, control or dispose of community**

property, or bind the community, except that joinder of both spouses is required in any of the following cases:

> **1. Any transaction for the acquisition, disposition or encumbrance of an interest in real property other than an unpatented mining claim or a lease of less than one year.**
>
> **2. Any transaction of guaranty, indemnity or suretyship."**

Since 1913, one spouse (historically the wife) was recognized as having a right of action against the other spouse (historically the husband) for conversion of separate property. *Eshom v. Eshom*, 18 Ariz. 170 (1916).

Additionally, the court has discretion to consider actual damages. Ariz.Rev.Stat.Ann. § 25–318(c) provides that the equitable division process **"does not prevent the court from considering all actual damages and judgments from conduct that results in criminal conviction of either spouse in which the other spouse or child was the victim, excessive or abnormal expenditures, destruction, concealment or fraudulent disposition of community, joint tenancy and other property held in common."** The divorce implications of this topic are discussed further in Chapter 9.

2. CALIFORNIA

California adopts a managerial system based on equal management and control. The system is straightforward, yet it turns on four distinctions. One, the distinction between community *personal* property and community real property: only community personal property is governed by the equal management and control rule. Two, the distinction between community property *business enterprises* and other property: enterprises are personally property governed by a primary management and control rule. Three, community *real property*, whether held for personal use or business use is governed by a joint management and control rule. Four *specifically selected community property assets, by court order,* can be brought under the exclusive control of one spouse for a limited period.

Equal management and control for community personal property. As to community personal property, **"[e]ither spouse has the management and control of the community personal property . . . with like absolute power of disposition, other than testamentary, as the spouse has of the separate estate of the spouse."** Cal.Fam.Code § 1100. The clear limitation on this rule, with respect to community personal property, is that gifts, low value transfers, and transfers of furniture, and clothing may not be made **"without the written consent"** (or ratification) of the non-acting spouse. Cal.Fam.Code § 1100(b) and (c). The statute does not explicitly require prior consent, which is why lifetime or posthumous ratification (after the fact consent) is permitted.

Primary management and control for a community property business. A community property business, which is community personal property, is exempt from the equal management and control rule. Instead, a community property business is governed by a superseding **"primary"** (not sole) management and control provision. See Cal.Fam.Code § 1100(d). The manager of a community property business **"may act alone in all transactions,"** except that the managing spouse must give **"prior written notice to the other spouse of any sale, lease, exchange, encumbrance, or other disposition of all or substantially all of the personal property used in the operation of the business . . . , whether or not title to that property is held in the name of only one spouse."** Id.

Joint management and control for community real property. As to community real property, Cal.Fam.Code § 1102 (effective Jan. 1, 2020) provides that **"either spouse has the management and control of the community property,"** . . . but both spouses must execute **"an instrument by which that community real property or an interest therein is leased for a longer period than one year, or is sold, conveyed, or encumbered."** The joinder requirement contemplates consent prior to the transaction.

The real estate specific rule was adopted in early statehood. It does not apply in transactions between spouses. Rather it protects bona fide good faith lessees, purchasers and encumbrancers who take **"without knowledge of the marriage relation."** Cal.Fam.Code § 1102(c).

A nonjoining spouse gets limited protection from this rule in the sense that a nonjoining spouse can petition a court to avoid the consequential real estate document (instrument) that fails to meet the joinder requirement. Joinder requires both spouses' signature for community property; so, a failure to meet the joinder requirement simply means that both spouses did not sign the document. The caveat here is that the absence of joinder, if challenged, at most cancels the document that lacks the claimant's signature. It does not cancel any underlying debt that was created by the instrument. Nor does it cancel the entire transaction. *Lezine v. Security Pacific Financial Services, Inc.*, 14 Cal.4th 56, 58 Cal.Rptr.2d 76, 925 P.2d 1002 (1996).

Subject to the limitations of the lender's intent test, borrowed funds obtained during marriage are presumed to be community personal property, as discussed in Chapters 4, and 7. This is so even if the loan proceeds are monetized home equity fraudulently obtained by one spouse acting without the knowledge or consent of the other spouse.

Exclusive control by court order. During a dissolution and during a marriage, it is possible for a spouse to petition for exclusive control of a specific asset to prevent its impairment or dissipation by the other spouse.

Additionally, the California Family Code has specific provisions that can (by an injured spouse's option) or do (automatically) provide a legal basis for divesting an abusive spouse of community property or for otherwise affecting his or her rights of management and control. Some statutes apply in a dissolution proceeding. See for example Cal.Fam.Code § 2045. Other remedies are trigged by the wrongdoer spouse's conviction of an enumerated crime against the other spouse See for example Cal.Fam.Code § 4324 and § 4324.5. Other statutes apply categorically to enumerated assets or titles. See for example Cal.Fam.Code § 1101.

California has adopted the Domestic Violence Prevention Act (the DVPA for short) within its Family Code. See Cal.Fam.Code §§ 6200 et seq. DVPA provisions cover domestic relations broadly. Hence the DVPA is potentially broad enough to reach acts of financial violence, whether the parties are married or not.

Preventing undue influence. As to all community personal property, Cal.Fam.Code § 1100(e), a self-updating provision, incorporates the most recently amended version of Cal.Fam.Code § 721(b) in cases involving the management and control of community personal property.

Spouses, by the fact of marriage are in a confidential relationship with each other as a matter of law. While spouses have the right to transact freely, Cal.Fam.Code § 721(b) (effective Jan 1., 2020) provides that ***"in transactions between themselves,* spouses are subject to the general**

rules governing fiduciary relationships that control the actions of persons occupying confidential relations with each other." (Italics added.)

The fiduciary relationship is a partnership duty, not a trust duty. But keep in mind that the marriage itself is not a juridical entity. The spouses are generally held to be in a confidential relationship as a matter of law, and in transactions between themselves they are as joint venturers. As such, when the spouses transact between themselves, *for purposes of that transaction*, each is equated to a nonmarital business partner or a joint venturer (more laxly) not to a professional trustee.

So, for example the spouses have no general duty to keep records. But if records are kept, the recordkeeping spouse, relative to the other spouse, is required to provide access to those records for purposes of inspection and copying, and to provide disclosure of financial information.

Additionally, if one spouse asks the other questions about the transaction, honesty is required in the answer.

And, if the acting spouse obtains a profit, that profit must held in trust for the community. Here, a trust—as to the profits only—comes into existence as a remedial requirement as set forth in Revised Uniform Partnership Act of 1997 (RUPA).

Cal.Fam.Code § 721(b) incorporates RUPA by reference.

Cal.Fam.Code § 1101 sets forth elements of proof and remedies for any breach of fiduciary duty impairment claim.

Generally, Cal.Fam.Code § 1101(a) gives a spouse **"a claim against the other spouse for *any breach* of the fiduciary duty that *results in impairment* to the claimant spouse's present undivided one-half interest in the community estate, including, but not limited to, a single transaction or a pattern or series of transactions, which transaction or transactions *have caused or will cause* a detrimental impact to the claimant spouse's undivided one-half interest in the community estate."**

It is important to notice that the causation element covers past and present actions (*has caused or will cause*). To date, no court has clarified what constitutes proof of a future impairment.

Same with the impairment claimed. An impairment need not be to a transacted asset, nor is it limited to a transacted asset. Rather, an impairment is broadly conceived as a transaction that does or can impair the (whole of the) community property estate.

Recovery percentages, court costs, and attorney fees are set out in Cal.Fam.Code § 1101(g)—50% plus attorney fees and court costs for impairments due to what might be considered ordinary negligence—and (h)—100% and court costs for impairments resulting from fraud, oppression, or malice as defined in the state penal code.

More generally under Cal.Fam.Code § 1101, a claimant spouse can sue: for an accounting; to add a name to **"community property held in the name of the other spouse alone"** with some business exceptions; and to **"dispense with the requirement of the other spouse's consent"** if the "proposed transaction is in the best interest of the community" and **"consent has been arbitrarily refused or cannot be obtained due to physical incapacity, mental incapacity, or prolonged absence of the nonconsenting spouse."** Limitation periods are set forth in the statute.

For term life insurance policies, the character of the last premium paid determines the character of insurance proceeds for that period, as discussed in Chapter 7.

An act, undertaken while alive that determines the disposition of property upon death is excluded from the reach of Cal.Fam. Code § 1100(a). Naming a POD beneficiary is not the management and control of community personal property so much as it is a testamentary disposition. Either spouse, acting alone, has equal management and control rights to make a gift of his or her one-half of a community property life insurance proceeds by naming a nonspousal POD beneficiary. But neither spouse has the power to dispose of the their spouse's one half of the policy proceeds by that same act. Thus, a community property life insurance policy that names a nonspousal (third party) POD beneficiary, without the express consent of the uninsured spouse, is subject to the claims of the uninsured spouse.

If the claim is brought during the life of the insured spouse, it will be cast as an unconsented to (nonmutual) gift of 50% of the term policy premiums. The sum of premiums that paid for the policy while the nonspousal POD was named divided by one-half equals the value of the nonmutual gift made.

If the claim is brought after the death of the insured spouse, the claim of the surviving spouse is for 50% of the proceeds. This is like the risk-payment theory outcome developed by Washington. See Chapter 7 for more on term life insurance.

3. IDAHO

Idaho Code § 32–912 adopts a managerial system based on equal management and control.

"Either the husband or the wife shall have the right to manage and control the community property, and either may bind the community property by contract, except that neither the husband nor wife may sell, convey or encumber the community real estate unless the other joins in executing the sale agreement, deed or other instrument of conveyance by which the real estate is sold, conveyed or encumbered, and any community obligation incurred by either the husband or the wife without the consent in writing of the other shall not obligate the separate property of the spouse who did not so consent; provided, however,

that the husband or wife may by express power of attorney give to the other the complete power to sell, convey or encumber community property, either real or personal. All deeds, conveyances, bills of sale, or evidences of debt heretofore made in conformity herewith are hereby validated."

Idaho Code § 32–906 characterizes the income of all property, separate or community, as community. This brings the separate property rents, issues, and profits received during marriage under the state equal management and control rule. However, if separate property rents, issues, and profits obtained during marriage are transmuted into separate property, the property becomes subject to the management of **"the spouse owning the property."**

Under Idaho Code § 32–916: **"The property rights of husband and wife are governed by this chapter, unless there is a marriage settlement agreement entered into during marriage containing stipulations contrary thereto."**

4. LOUISIANA

Louisiana follows a managerial model that is based on equal management and control and is consistent with the state's civil law tradition.

Ownership in Louisiana is allodial (freehold), though, of course, all land titles originate with the U.S. federal government. Allodial ownership confers present, direct, and exclusive ownership over the thing owned, without bifurcation into legal and equitable interests. Instead, usufruct rights are recognized. Usufruct is discussed in Chapter 5 and Chapter 7.

Louisiana statutes distinguish between "immovables" (land) and "movables" (not land), and between property rights and contract rights.

LSA-C.C. Art. 2346 provides: **"Each spouse acting alone may manage, control, or dispose of community property unless otherwise provided by law."** Concurrence—which sounds much like the joinder requirement of other jurisdictions—of the spouses is required for specified transactions.

When **"concurrence is required by law,"** LSA-C.C. Art. 2353 provides that **"the alienation, encumbrance, or lease of community property by a spouse is relatively null unless the other spouse has renounced the right to concur."** This rule applies to community property businesses (and other enterprises) as well. It is unclear what the word "relatively" refers to; it might be akin to the common law concept of voidable title.

The concurrence of both spouses is statutorily required for **". . . the alienation, encumbrance, or lease of community immovables, standing, cut, or fallen timber, furniture or furnishings while located in the family home, all or substantially all of the assets of a community enterprise, and movables issued or registered as provided by law in the names of the spouses jointly."** LSA-

C.C. Art. 2347(a). Also, by this provision, concurrence is required for **"the harvest of community timber."** LSA-C.C. Art. 2347(b). The organizing principle of this and the next statute is "the community enterprise" not the category of property or the transaction type as in other states.

LSA-C.C. Art. 2348 provides: **"A spouse may expressly renounce the right to concur in the alienation, encumbrance, or lease of a community immovable or some or all of the community immovables, or community immovables which may be acquired in the future, or all or substantially all of a community enterprise. He also may renounce the right to participate in the management of a community enterprise. The renunciation may be irrevocable for a stated term not to exceed three years."**

LSA-C.C. Art. 2349 controls donations—gifts in some other states—made by one spouse to a third party. This statute provides that a spouse acting alone **"may make a usual or customary gift of a value commensurate with the economic position of the spouses at the time of the donation."** The provision, in effect, gives spouses the right to exercise exclusive control over the donated property. As discussed in the main body of this chapter, a gift is a transfer that meets the common law elements of donative intent, delivery, and acceptance. A donation, by comparison, is the contractual conferral of a benefit. This statute seems arguably to treat "gift" as synonymous with "donation."

LSA-C.C. Art. 2350 covers a community property business. It provides: **"[t]he spouse who is the sole manager of a community enterprise has the exclusive right to alienate, encumber, or lease its movables unless the movables are issued in the name of the other spouse or the concurrence of the other spouse is required by law. A community enterprise is a business that is not a juridical person."** (Amended in 2017.) This general provision, as legislative comments make clear, governs when the specific rule on concurrence, found at LSA-C.C. Art. 2353, is deemed inapplicable by application of this general rule. The short answer is that this general rule can be invoked "in favor of commerce" when deemed necessary.

Louisiana includes exclusive control provisions for the following:

- LSA-C.C. Art. 2351: **"A spouse has the exclusive right to manage, alienate, encumber, or lease movables issued or registered in his name as provided by law."**
- LSA-C.C. Art. 2352: **"A spouse who is a partner has the exclusive right to manage, alienate, encumber, or lease the partnership interest."**

When community property is impaired by fraud or bad faith, a cause of action accrues on behalf of the adversely affected spouse. LSA-C.C. Art. 2354 creates liability **"for any loss or damage caused by fraud or bad faith in the management of the community property."** Case law recognizes, within this provision, a duty to disclose. For example, one spouse's pattern of failure to disclose financial information was found by a jury to be fraud in *Theriot v. Theriot*, 622 So.2d 257 (La.App. 1993), writ denied.

5. NEVADA

Nevada follows a managerial system based on equal management and control.

Equal management of community property is governed by Nev.Rev.Stat. § 123.230, which is based on California law. Notice that the statute requires joinder (both spouses must sign) for consequential real estate transactions; and it allows primary control for community property businesses.

> **"A spouse may, by written power of attorney, give to the other the complete power to sell, convey or encumber any property held as community property or either spouse, acting alone, may manage and control community property, whether the community property was acquired before, on or after July 1, 1975, with the same power of disposition as the acting spouse has over his or her separate property, except that:**
>
> **1. Neither spouse may devise or bequeath more than one-half of the community property.**

2. Neither spouse may make a gift of community property without the express or implied consent of the other.

3. Neither spouse may sell, convey or encumber the community real property unless both join in the execution of the deed or other instrument by which the real property is sold, conveyed or encumbered, and the deed or other instrument must be acknowledged by both.

4. Neither spouse may purchase or contract to purchase community real property unless both join in the transaction of purchase or in the execution of the contract to purchase.

5. Neither spouse may create a security interest, other than a purchase money security interest as defined in NRS 104.9103, in, or sell, community household goods, furnishings or appliances unless both join in executing the security agreement or contract of sale, if any.

6. Neither spouse may acquire, purchase, sell, convey or encumber the assets, including real property and goodwill, of a business where both spouses participate in its management without the consent of the other. If only one spouse participates in management, he or she may, in the ordinary course of business, acquire, purchase, sell, convey or

encumber the assets, including real property and goodwill, of the business without the consent of the nonparticipating spouse."

Notwithstanding the above basic management and control provisions, it appears that an employed spouse has heightened control, relative to that spouse's employer, over employee benefits. Practically speaking this is the case across the board in all community property states, at least during the continuance of the marriage. But Nev.Rev.Stat. § 123.240 elevates the concept to a statutory rule in the sense that the employer is statutorily shielded from liability: **". . . whenever payment or refund is made to an employee, former employee, or his or her beneficiary or estate pursuant to a written retirement, death or other employee benefit plan or savings plan, such payment or refund shall fully discharge the employer and any trustee or insurance company making such payment or refund from all adverse claims thereto . . ."** unless notice is given to the employer of the surviving spouse's claim prior to the payout.

Nev.Rev.Stat. § 123.250 gives each spouse the power of testamentary disposition over his or her interest in the community property, with or without the other spouse's consent. The numerical limit on this power appears to be one-half.

6. NEW MEXICO

New Mexico follows a managerial system based on equal management and control.

N.M.Stat.Ann. § 40–3–14 (1978) provides that **"either spouse alone has full power to manage, control, dispose of and encumber the entire community personal property."**

Subsections (B) and (C) of that same code section create title and agreement-based exceptions where sole or joint management become the rule:

> **"B. Where only one spouse is:**
>
> > **(1) named in a document evidencing ownership of community personal property; or**
> >
> > **(2) named or designated in a written agreement between that spouse and a third party as having sole authority to manage, control, dispose of or encumber the community personal property which is described in or which is the subject of the agreement, whether the agreement was executed prior to or after July 1, 1973; only the spouse so named may manage, control, dispose of or encumber the community personal property described in such a document evidencing ownership or in such a written agreement.**

C. Where both spouses are:

(1) named in a document evidencing ownership of community personal property; or

(2) named or designated in a written agreement with a third party as having joint authority to dispose of or encumber the community personal property which is described in or the subject of the agreement, whether the agreement was executed prior to or after July 1, 1973; both spouses must join to dispose of or encumber such community personal property where the names of the spouses are joined by the word "and." Where the names of the spouses are joined by the word "or," or by the words "and/or," either spouse alone may dispose of or encumber such community personal property."

As for community real property, joinder is required.

Except for purchase-money mortgages, **"the spouses must join in all transfers, conveyances or mortgages or contracts to transfer, convey or mortgage any interest in community real property and separate real property owned by the spouses as cotenants in joint tenancy or**

tenancy in common." Additionally, the spouses must join in **"all leases of community real property or separate real property owned by the spouses as cotenants in joint tenancy or tenancy in common if the initial term of the lease, together with any option or extension contained in the lease or provided for contemporaneously, exceeds five years or if the lease is for an indefinite term."** N.M.Stat.Ann. § 40–3–13 (1978).

7. TEXAS

Texas uses a dual management system that gives each spouse sole management and control over separate property and over community property (including personal income) that would have been separate had the person not been married.

Once one spouse's community property is commingled with the other spouse's community property, however, the rule becomes one of joint management and control for the commingled property.

The statutory provisions for management, control and disposition of separate and community property and the protection of third parties are as follows:

V.T.C.A.Fam.Code § 3.101 gives each spouse **"the sole management, control, and disposition of that spouse's separate property."**

V.T.C.A.Fam.Code § 3.102 provides that **"during marriage each spouse has the sole management, control, and disposition of the**

community property that the spouse would have owned if single." This power extends to **"personal earnings; revenue from separate property; recoveries for personal injuries; and the increase and mutations of, and the revenue from, all property subject to the spouse's sole management, control, and disposition."**

Under V.T.C.A.Fam.Code § 3.102(b) **"If community property subject to the sole management, control, and disposition of one spouse is mixed or combined with community property subject to the sole management, control, and disposition of the other spouse, then the mixed or combined community property is subject to the joint management, control, and disposition of the spouses, unless the spouses provide otherwise by power of attorney in writing or other agreement.**

Except as provided in Subsection (a), community property is subject to the joint management, control, and disposition of the spouses, unless the spouses provide otherwise by power of attorney in writing or other agreement."

V.T.C.A.Fam.Code § 3.104:

"(a) During marriage, property is presumed to be subject to the sole management, control, and disposition of a spouse if it is held in that spouse's name, as shown by muniment, contract, deposit of funds, or other

evidence of ownership, or if it is in that spouse's possession and is not subject to such evidence of ownership.

(b) A third person dealing with a spouse is entitled to rely (as against the other spouse or anyone claiming from that spouse) on that spouse's authority to deal with the property if:

(1) The property is presumed to be subject to the sole management, control, and disposition of the spouse; and

(2) the person dealing with the spouse:

(A) is not a party to a fraud on the other spouse or another person; and

(B) does not have actual or constructive notice of the spouse's lack of authority."

When joint management and control applies, gifts made by one spouse to a third party can be avoided by the other spouse. Once challenged, the person who attempts to uphold the gift has the burden to prove that the gift was reasonable under the circumstances in which it was made. Texas retains the civil law fraud test for the setting aside of a gift by the manager of the community, but it extends the test to cover the concept of constructive fraud.

Texas upholds many community property life insurance beneficiary designations when the beneficiary is a relative or former relative whom the insured had a legal duty to support. The existence of the duty negates fraud upon the spouse so long as the community funds expended for the insurance are not unreasonably out of proportion to the community assets remaining.

8. WASHINGTON

The statutory provisions for management and control in Washington are found at Wash.Rev.Code § 26.16.030, reproduced below. Joint management and control rules govern consequential real estate transactions. Primary management and control rules govern where one spouse alone manages a community property business. Otherwise, Washington is a managerial system based on equal management and control.

Unlike in California, where the various management and control rules appear throughout the family code, here the rules are collected in RCW 26.16.030, with exceptions marked out for RCW 26.16.010, RCW 26.16.020, and RCW 62A.9–107, all hyperlinked in the next paragraph.

> **"Property not acquired or owned, as prescribed in RCW 26.16.010 and 26.16.020, acquired after marriage or after registration of a state registered domestic partnership by either domestic partner or either husband or wife or both, is community property. Either spouse or**

either domestic partner, acting alone, may manage and control community property, with a like power of disposition as the acting spouse or domestic partner has over his or her separate property, except:

(1) Neither person shall devise or bequeath by will more than one-half of the community property.

(2) Neither person shall give community property without the express or implied consent of the other.

(3) Neither person shall sell, convey, or encumber the community real property without the other spouse or other domestic partner joining in the execution of the deed or other instrument by which the real estate is sold, conveyed, or encumbered, and such deed or other instrument must be acknowledged by both spouses or both domestic partners.

(4) Neither person shall purchase or contract to purchase community real property without the other spouse or other domestic partner joining in the transaction of purchase or in the execution of the contract to purchase.

(5) Neither person shall create a security interest other than a purchase money security interest as defined in RCW 62A.9–107 in, or sell, community

household goods, furnishings, or appliances, or a community mobile home unless the other spouse or other domestic partner joins in executing the security agreement or bill of sale, if any.

(6) Neither person shall acquire, purchase, sell, convey, or encumber the assets, including real estate, or the good will of a business where both spouses or both domestic partners participate in its management without the consent of the other: PROVIDED, That where only one spouse or one domestic partner participates in such management the participating spouse or participating domestic partner may, in the ordinary course of such business, acquire, purchase, sell, convey or encumber the assets, including real estate, or the good will of the business without the consent of the nonparticipating spouse or nonparticipating domestic partner."

A spouse or domestic partner may protect his or her marital rights to property that is titled in the other spouse's name alone. The spouse does this by filing and recording a written instrument that identifies his or her interest in the property. The instrument provides record notice to third parties. When a spouse fails or decides not to protect marital rights in the above manner, the result is that **"full**

legal and equitable title" passes to **"any actual bona fide purchaser"** who had no knowledge of the marriage and could not have obtained knowledge of the marriage. Wash.Rev.Code § 26.16.100.

9. WISCONSIN

Spouses are held to the standard of good faith with respect to marital property. Wis.Stat. § 766.15 provides:

(1) "Each spouse shall act in good faith with respect to the other spouse in matters involving marital property or other property of the other spouse. This obligation may not be varied by a marital property agreement.

(2) Management and control by a spouse of that spouse's property that is not marital property in a manner that limits, diminishes or fails to produce income from that property does not violate sub. (1)."

A spouse has a claim against the other spouse for breach of the duty of good faith resulting in damage to the claimant spouse's property. A statute of limitations gives the claimant spouse 6-years, from the time actual knowledge of the breach of the duty of good faith is acquired, to file a complaint. Wis.Stat. § 766.70(1) sets out this and other remedies. Wis.Stat. 766.70(dm) includes **"an interest in digital property"** but does not elaborate on the scope of the statute.

The management and control statute, Wis.Stat. § 766.51, reads as follows:

"(1) A spouse acting alone may manage and control:

(a) That spouse's property that is not marital property.

(am) Except as provided in subs. (2) and (3), marital property held in that spouse's name alone or not held in the name of either spouse.

(b) Marital property held in the names of both spouses in the alternative, including marital property held in a form designating the holder by the words '(name of one spouse) or (name of other spouse).'[2]

(d) A policy of insurance if that spouse is designated as the owner on the records of the policy issuer.

(e) Any right of an employee under a deferred employment benefit plan that accrues as a result of that spouse's employment.

(f) A claim for relief vested in that spouse by other law."

---

2 The statute omits any reference to (c), suggesting a clerical error.

By the same statute at § 766.51(1m)(a), "**. . . for the purpose of obtaining an extension of credit for an obligation [incurred by a spouse in the interest of the marriage or the family], a spouse acting alone may manage and control all of the marital property.**"

Also, under Wis.Stat. § 766.51(b), note that:

- Joinder (both spouses must sign) is required for marital property held in the names of both spouses—this is not a special community property rule so much as it is a fact of holding title in two names: and
- Either spouse's right to act alone in managing and controlling marital property does not extend to enumerated business interests.

Wis.Stat. § 766.51(1m)(b)(4) provides that: "**the right to manage and control marital property permits gifts of that property.**"

Related to this provision, Wis.Stat. § 766.53 sets out relevant value limitations, as follows.

"**A spouse acting alone may give to a 3rd person marital property that the spouse has the right to manage and control only if the value of the marital property given to the 3rd person does not aggregate more than either $1,000 in a calendar year, or a larger amount if, when made, the gift is reasonable in amount considering the economic position of the spouses. Any other gift of marital property to a 3rd person is subject to** [the recovery remedy during marriage set out at [§ 766.70(6)] **unless both spouses act together in making the gift. Under this section and for the purposes of** [§ 766.70(6)'s recovery remedy during the marriage], **in the case of a gift of marital property by a spouse to a 3rd person in which the donor spouse has retained an interest, the gift shall be valued at the full value of the entire transfer of marital property, regardless of any retained interest or interest donated to the other spouse. For purposes of this section only, a gift of a life insurance policy by a spouse to a 3rd person shall be valued at the amount payable under the policy if the insured died at the time the gift was made."**

The remedies available to a non-consenting spouse for gifts of marital property made by the other spouse to a third person are set out in Wis.Stat. § 766.70(6) to (8).

CHAPTER 9
LIABILITIES

A. OVERVIEW

Most community property states in the U.S. are ganancial systems. In these states, the marriage is not a legal entity with its own power to incur liability. Instead, each is an agent for the community with actual, implicit, and apparent power to incur liabilities. Community property assets belong in undivided shares to the spouses. Hence, those assets are not beyond the reach of either spouses' personal creditors. The ganancial model looks to gross assets when determining general creditors' rights, but then marshals those assets by character.

A civil law approach exists in which the marriage is a legal entity. It incurs its own liability independent of the marital partners. At dissolution, assets and liabilities are characterized. The community entity model deducts community liabilities from gross community assets in a sort of partnership entity liquidation process.

MANAGERIAL MODEL VERSUS COMMUNITY ENTITY MODEL

ASSETS: Both managerial and community entity models characterize assets as CP or SP.

LIABILITIES (MANAGERIAL MODEL): gross assets, marshaled by character, pay general liabilities.

VERSUS

LIABILITIES (COMMUNITY ENTITY MODEL): CP liabilities are repaid from gross CP assets. SP liabilities repaid from gross SP assets

The term liability is generic. Louisiana uses the term "obligation." The term liability is used without regard to the date upon which the obligation was incurred; the way in which it was created; or the time schedule for payments due.

Liabilities break down into three broad categories: contract, tort, and other.

A contract liability is an obligation that one spouse or both spouses incur by exchange and agreement with a third party or with each other. Typically, a contract liability is memorialized by signing a written document that can be enforced as a contract in a court of law.

A tort liability is a legal obligation that arises on the part of the tortfeasor when the tort occurs.

Other liabilities are legal obligations as well arising from orders like court judgments, support orders, or child support orders. A tax debt falls into this category as well.

In a managerial state, marshaling is the process whereby the creditor determines which character of property—community or property—is reachable first, and which character of property—community or separate—is temporarily exempt. Property is exempt from paying an obligation if it is not subject to levy by the sheriff.

In a case where a community property asset is the first to be levied, the separate property falls into the category of temporarily exempt property. For the community, the levied asset is entirely reachable by the creditor of either spouse because community property is owned in undivided shares.

Some states limit a judgment creditor to reaching the debtor-spouse's undivided one-half of any levied community property. But even in these states, the creditor's repayment can and often does result in an unfortunate outcome. That is that the non-debtor spouse comes to own the property in an undivided one-half share with the creditor. This outcome can lead to a next round of litigation or negotiation, now between the creditor and the non-debtor spouse, over partition of the asset.

Alternatively, in a case where the creditor is initially limited to reaching separate property, community property falls into the category of temporarily exempt property. As such it remains beyond the debtor-spouse's creditor's reach during the levy process. If there are no available separate property assets or if separate property assets become insufficient to repay the debt, then the creditor may benefit from going back to court to marshal the next-in-line community property asset(s).

Marshaling is an issue when the creditor is entitled to reach both community and separate property assets. The answer to how to exercise the option of community or separate property depends on at least two factors. What character of property is reachable first (community or separate?) by statute?

And are any assets, because of their character, temporarily exempt from the reach of the creditor in the first round of the levy process?

State law varies widely in terms of how much protection it extends to a debtor who is married and their spouse.

B. DETAIL

Among the areas of divergence in various states are the following, in order of importance.

1. WHEN WAS THE LIABILITY INCURRED?

A liability can be incurred before, during, or after marriage.

2. WHAT TYPE OF LIABILITY IS AT ISSUE?

A liability can be incurred by contract, tort, or by legal judgment or process? As discussed above support orders and tax debts are examples of general obligations.

3. WHO INCURRED THE TYPE OF LIABILITY AT ISSUE?

How did the liability come into existence and for what reason?

As noted above, there are three possible characters of property that a creditor can or may seek to reach: community property; one spouse's separate property; or the other spouse's separate property.

a. A Contract Liability

A contract debt arises when a contract is signed. A contract debt can be incurred during marriage by one spouse acting alone. It can also be incurred by both spouses acting together. If one spouse incurs the debt, he or she may do so by personal liability and as the manager of the community estate; or that spouse may become liable by statutory obligation.

Even if the contract is signed only by one spouse acting alone, the judgment creditor can typically reach the community property before reaching the separate property of the married person who signed the contract. A signature makes a spouse personally liable on the contract.

General management and control statutes make both spouses personally liable on the contract.

A court judgment will name the liable party.

b. A Tort Liability

A tort liability arises when the tort occurs. One spouse alone may be the tortfeasor. Or both spouses may be tortfeasors. States differ on the reason why a tort judgment creditor should be permitted to reach community property for the wrongful actions of one spouse. One theory is that the tort occurred during the marriage. The other theory is that the tort arose from conduct that benefitted the community. What connects these rationales is the idea that a tort, occurring during marriage, can arise out of conduct that initially benefits the community but then veer off into conduct that has no community purpose whatsoever. See e.g., *deElche v. Jacobsen*, 95 Wash.2d 237, 622 P.2d 835 (1980) (*en banc*) (Horowitz J., dissenting), discussed below in Section C, Washington. In such a case, the community property may be exempt from the reach of the tort creditor. Or, as in most states for a case like this, community assets are marshaled into second place, after the judgment debtor's separate property.

A few U.S. community property states hold that one-half of the community assets may be deemed exempt for purposes of satisfying a separate tort judgment. If so, the judgment creditor can reach the tortfeasor spouse's separate property first, and the tortfeasor's one-half interest in the community property second, but the tortfeasor cannot reach the non-tortfeasor spouse's one-half of the community property. New Mexico achieves this result by statute. Washington achieves it by case law in certain circumstances. How to split the property becomes the next issue, as community property is owned in undivided shares.

c. Other Obligations

Other obligations typically arise by court judgment. State law determines what property the sheriff can and cannot levy against. *Non-exempt* property can be levied. It is reachable by a creditor. *Exempt* property cannot be levied. It is shielded from a creditor's reach, if not temporarily (due to marshaling), then permanently for a reason set forth in state law.

To sum up, on the statutory side of things, the community property rules for dealing with liabilities do not enjoy the same degree of consensus that the rules for characterizing assets do. There are many similarities among the states, there are also material differences.

4. LIABILITY OF COMMUNITY PROPERTY

If a spouse has the legal authority to control the community personal property, then that spouse acts as an agent of the community. This, of course, makes the community property subject to the reach of creditors.

a. Liability for Contracts Signed During Marriage

The safest ground in this area of quicksand is the sure liability of the community property for contracts signed during marriage.

Community debts are satisfied against community property by signature, type of claim, time, managerial authority, and purpose.

Voluntary liens. No state protects debtors from their voluntarily signed liens. For that reason, when it comes to community real property, most community property states require that both spouses sign any document consequential to that asset. Known as *joinder* laws, these statutes simply require both spouses to sign any consequential document. If a consequential real estate document is signed only by one spouse, the spouse who did not sign may have a remedy—even if a very limited and time sensitive one—against the signing spouse or the third-party who seeks to enforce the document in question. See Chapter 8 for more on spousal management of real property.

Contracts expenses: Unsecured contract debts incurred during the marriage are presumed to be family expenses. Rebuttal is with evidence that the expenses were not for the benefit of the community.

Here, the idea is that the spouses have a legal duty to support each other and their children by the present marriage in the manner to which the family has become accustomed. *Necessaries of life* refers to contract debts for the family's standard of living. *Common necessaries* refer to contract debts for basic living expenses like rent, food, and clothing. Both categories of expenses clearly fall within any family expense presumption because they benefit the community.

Debts for common necessaries and necessaries of life qualify contract creditors to execute a judgment in this marshaling order: non-exempt community property assets; the separate property assets of the spouse who signed the contract; and the separate property assets of the spouse who did not sign the contract. Signing the contract puts the spouse into privity of contract with the creditor.

Expenses that *exceed* the community's ordinary standard of living give the community a defense against the creditor that extended non-covered goods or services. So do expenses that are *contrary* to the community purpose. Here, the idea is that the creditor should seek satisfaction from the spouse who incurred the non-covered expense.

If a liability incurred during the marriage is adjudged to not benefit of the community, some states allow the judgment creditor to levy on the debtor's separate property first and on the debtor's one-half of the community property second, as mentioned above. Other states marshal the assets so that the judgment creditor must levy on the debtor's separate property first, before seeking permission to levy on the entirety of the community property.

The community purpose doctrine is not necessarily an explicit part of the statutory creditors' rights scheme in managerial states like California, Idaho, New Mexico, Texas, and Wisconsin; plus, it is out of favor with courts in Washington. Nevertheless, if a judgment creditor's rationale for being able to seize property is that either spouse acting alone can serve as an agent for the community, then legal questions of express, implied, and apparent authority are sometimes litigated, just as they would be in a nonmarital partnership.

b. Liability for Contracts Signed After a Date of Separation

Obligations incurred after a date of separation can fall within the general duty of support, and they are often contractual.

After a date of separation, both spouses have the right to manage and control accumulated community property, if any exists.

If one spouse is more productively employed than the other, the spouse in need of support may incur contractual debt for *common necessaries*, a term defined as basic living expenses, as discussed above.

The contracting spouse has authority to use banked community property. But if that source of funds is exhausted or nonexistent, then then the contracting spouse is liable in first position. But, if the contracting spouse's separate property funds are exhausted, then the creditor can satisfy a default against the other spouse's separate property.

c. Liability for Contracts Signed Before a Date of Marriage

Historically, civil law concepts exempted community property (or at least one-half of it) from liability for premarital obligations; the rationale was that the debts, if they pre-exist the marriage, are not contracted on behalf of the community. The exemption proved extremely inconvenient for creditors since all income (whether earned or, under the traditional civil law rule, generated by an existing separate property asset) is characterized as community property during marriage. If the married couple had only income from work, the rules of the community property system effectively barred the creditor from satisfying the premarital obligation.

Today, there is a tendency to subject community property to premarital liabilities.

One reason is practical: people increasingly use credit cards to pay for family expenses. Credit card debt is revolving debt. As such it is re-contracted each month.

Another reason is analytical: the obligations that a spouse brings to the marriage certainly impact, and probably negatively, the community if the spouse intends to use earnings, obtained during marriage while domiciled in the state, to satisfy the debt.

The third is an equity consideration: What kind of law, for the price of a marriage license, would allow a debtor to frustrate the claims of their premarital creditors with a so-called "two-dollar bankruptcy" (the pre-inflation price of a marriage license)? Such a law would increase the risk of fraud against prospective spouses as well as against creditors.

Despite these reasons, subjecting the entire community to liability for a premarital obligation was not favored in the civil law. Historically, a distinction was based upon whether the debtor was the manager of the community. At other times, the decision to hold the community liable for premarital debts turned on whether the debtor was the producer of the community income. Both distinctions tended to subject the community to liability only when the earning spouse was also the debtor.

Today, under the managerial model, either spouse, acting alone has the legal authority to manage and control community personal property. By virtue of the legal right to manage and control, spouses (and creditors) can expect that the premarital creditors of either spouse may or probably will be able to reach all community property assets to satisfy an unsecured debt in default. Marshaling rules may apply. But these rules will only temporarily exempt the community property so that the creditor can first reach the debtor's separate property.

That said, there are statutes and methods that allow a spouse, to exempt a portion of the community property to protect it from the reach of their spouse's premarital creditors.

Additionally, the range of rules below illustrates the extent to which U.S. community property states can and have diverged from their civil law origin as well as from each other.

- Arizona holds community property liable for the premarital separate debts or other liabilities of a spouse, but only to the extent of the value of that spouse's *contribution to* (not interest in) the community property. Ariz.Rev.Stat.Ann. § 25–215.
- California allows a spouse to fully exempt (shield) his or her (actual) community property *earnings* from **"a debt incurred by the person's spouse before marriage."** Cal.Fam.Code § 911. To qualify as a debt incurred before marriage, the debt must be a nonrevolving debt. Moreover, the protected earnings must be fully removed from the

debtor spouse's reach to qualify for the exemption.

- Early Idaho precedent permitted a premarital creditor of the husband, but not a premarital creditor of the wife, to reach community assets. The gender specificity of the precedent is an obsolete holdover from the male management era discussed above.

- Louisiana permits a premarital creditor to reach the community property but provides for reimbursement between the spouses upon termination of the marital regime.

- Nevada provides that one spouse's share of the community property is not liable for the debts of the other spouse if contracted before marriage. The statute, by its own terms, only exempts nonrevolving debt.

- New Mexico lists separate debts by statute. It then allows separate debts (including premarital obligations of either spouse) to be collected from the debtor spouse's one-half *interest in* (not contribution to, as described in Arizona above) the community property. Marshaling rules require that the creditor prove they tried to reach the debtor spouse's separate property before attempting to seize that spouse's one-half interest in any listed community property. This reverses a prior rule that sought to exempt the entirety of community property from the reach of separate debt creditors.

- Texas, a dual management state, allows the satisfaction of all premarital debts from commingled community property that is under dual control. It subjects property under the sole management and control of one of the spouses only to the premarital debts of that spouse, and not to the premarital debts of the other spouse.

- Washington shields the non-debtor spouse's separate property from the reach of premarital creditors, but then earmarks the debtor spouse's community property earnings and accumulations as subject to levy.

- Wisconsin provides that an obligation incurred by a spouse before or during marriage that is attributable to an obligation arising before marriage (contract), or to an act or omission occurring before marriage (tort), may be satisfied only from property of the spouse that is not also marital property (including the unique Wisconsin "unclassified" or "all other" property). Such debts can also be satisfied from that part of marital property that would have been individual property of that spouse but for the marriage. The category of property that would have been individual property but for the marriage most obviously refers to separate property income streams. See Chapter 5, Section 3, Wisconsin.

d. Liability for Tort Liability Adjudged Against One Spouse

Money and property to be paid for a tort claim are obligations that arise from a court judgment or a case settlement.

Tort obligations: The tort creditor is in an entirely different position than the contract creditor.

For negligent torts, the issue might be phrased in terms of the reasonableness of insuring against the risk.

For intentional torts, a different set of issues asks whether the tortfeasor was acting as an agent of the community when the tort occurred. Such issues secondarily implicate the community purpose doctrine: if the conduct from which the tort arose benefitted the community, then the judgment debtor should be permitted to reach non-exempt community property.

In the civil law system, the separate property of one spouse was not liable for the "delict" (roughly defined as the tort or crime) of the other spouse. Similarly, only the community property managed and controlled by the wrongdoing spouse was subject to liability, and then only if the delict was committed while the manager was engaged in an activity that benefitted the community.

Today, some trends for tort liability are as follows:

- The community is liable in Arizona and Louisiana for a tort committed by the person who is a manager of the property if the activity that gave rise to the tort was being performed for or resulted in a benefit to the community or the other spouse.

- California, New Mexico, and Washington follow a marshaling approach by which the community property can be reached even for a tort that did not benefit the community. In such a case, by statute, the separate property estate of the tortfeasor is primarily liable, but all or at least one-half of the community estate, depending on the jurisdiction, remains secondarily liable. If all the community property is reached by the creditor, the community obtains a right of reimbursement against the tortfeasor spouse.

- Texas subjects the community to liability by statute.

- Wisconsin provides that an obligation incurred by a spouse for a tort during marriage may be satisfied from property of that spouse which is not marital property ("all other property" in the words of the statute) and from that spouse's interest in marital property.

e. Liability for Other Obligations

Most jurisdictions assume that spousal support for a previous spouse and support payments to the children of a prior or different relationship are nonrevolving premarital judgment debts.

This makes a spousal or child support order from a prior marriage or relationship satisfiable first from the judgment debtor's separate property.

In some states—California is an example—if the debtor's separate property is nonexistent or insufficient to satisfy the support obligation, then the community property of the debtor's subsequent marriage is liable. The reason for allowing a child support order from a prior marriage to be defined as an obligation of the current marriage is that state has a compelling interest in seeing that support judgments are enforced. The rules are intended to protect parties who rely on the execution of support judgments. Moreover, they support the collection of support judgments, which are reputed to be among the most difficult to collect.

If a judgment debtor's community property from a current marriage must be used to satisfy a support order from a prior marriage or relationship, some states provide the current community with a right of reimbursement against the judgment debtor. The reimbursement may or may not be with interest. It is payable (either voluntarily or as a lien) from the judgment debtor's existing or after-acquired separate property.

Louisiana has arrived at the opposite conclusion. In Louisiana, the obligation arises not because of the termination of the first marriage, but because of the passage of time during the second marriage. By this rationale, a support order from a first marriage comes to be categorized as a community obligation of the second marriage. It is unclear whether the current community is entitled to a credit should the marriage end. The logic of the Louisiana approach, it seems, may be more difficult to explain to the second spouse than the logic of the California approach.

f. Liability of One-Half of the Community

If a debt cannot be collected from *both* halves of the community property, may the creditor collect against one-half of the community?

The problem is theoretical because on one hand, if analytic stress is placed on the concept of *ownership*, the community is owned concurrently by the two spouses in undivided shares. This means that one-half of the community is the property of the debtor spouse. By this rationale, because a creditor can reach property that the debtor has legal rights to manage and control, a sound argument can be made that all, or at the very least one-half, of the community property should be reachable by the separate creditors of one spouse.

On the other hand, if the analytic focus is on the *concurrent* feature of community property ownership, an equally sound argument can be made that the community should be shielded, if not deemed exempt altogether, from the reach of certain separate creditors of one spouse.

If the civil law "net community" approach is used, the exact amount of the community share cannot be accurately ascertained until the payment of all community debts and the division of the property is made at the termination of the marital regime. To allow collection of a separate debt against one-half of the community would be to allow a preference to this separate obligation over later community obligations (including support needs of the family). It would also raise unanswered accounting questions relevant to the types of problems discussed in Chapter 7. For example: if a creditor reached one-half of community earnings, would the earnings of the remaining one-half of the community belong entirely to the other spouse? Such issues could possibly be contracted around, but there are no clarifying default rules in the absence of such a contract. Plus, enforceability would be a continuing issue.

There have been some breaks in the traditional reluctance of community property jurisdictions to allow collection of a separate debt, especially an obligation arising from tort, from one-half (but not the whole) of the community property.

- Arizona implies, by how it allows a spouse's premarital creditors to reach the debtor spouse's contribution to the community estate, that the community estate can be conceptualized as nonconcurrent halves for certain purposes.
- California (by statute) and Washington (by case law) adopts a marshaling approach for separate tort judgments. This suggests a policy choice to stress the concurrent aspect of half ownership.
- Louisiana allows a separate property debt to be satisfied from all community property. This

places the stress on the ownership aspect of concurrent ownership. Nevertheless, the law permits a right of reimbursement for the community against the debtor spouse. That right accrues upon the termination of the marital regime, not before.

- Nevada implies that one-half of the community is liable for the premarital debts by stating, in Nev.Rev.Stat. § 123.050, that the community *share* of a married person is not liable for the premarital debts of that person's spouse.
- New Mexico and Wisconsin marshal one-half of the community property only after the separate (and in Wisconsin unclassified "all other") property of a debtor spouse is reached.
- Texas statutory law leaves the order of marshaling to the discretion of the court.
- Washington case law adopts a marshaling approach for the payment of separate tort judgments. The judgment creditor can reach the tortfeasor's separate property and one-half of the community property, as determined on a case-by-case basis. This approach may be modified depending on whether the tortious conduct was intentional or negligent.

For a sociological discussion of the relationship between debt collection, marriage, and bankruptcy, see ELIZABETH WARREN, ET. AL. THE FRAGILE MIDDLE

CLASS (2000). The data is over twenty years old, but the issues are still current.

5. LIABILITY OF SEPARATE PROPERTY

Previously, Spanish civil law authorities proclaimed that any liability incurred during the marriage for the benefit of the community was a community liability. Rebuttal followed for debts incurred by the legal manager (then the husband) for his separate benefit. The wife, not being the legal manager, could sign contracts, but did not have a full right to bind the community by her contracts.

The civil law marshaled the assets of the married couple but then subjected both community and separate property to liability for community contractual debts. The right of reimbursement diminished the distinction between debts and expenses in the sense that payment of a liability from the inappropriate character property gave rise to a right of reimbursement from the property that would otherwise have been legally liable for repaying the debt. Louisiana, with its matrimonial regime approach, remains the most faithful to this traditional civil law model.

Among the U.S. community property states, Louisiana has the most detailed statutes to govern the characterization of obligations (debts) by the marital entity as either community or separate. See Section C, Louisiana below.

Washington formerly used an entity approach that characterized the liability itself as separate or community. Separate property was liable for separate debts and community property was liable for community debts (a term that excluded both premarital debts and separate tort judgments, as discussed above). Today, in Washington, any rigid distinction between these points has been erased by statutes and cases. As applied to separate tort judgment creditors, the entity approach no longer shields all the community property from seizure, as it once did. Instead, a separate tort judgment creditor can reach both the tortfeasor spouse's separate property and one-half of his or her community property, especially in the case of an intentional tort, as discussed below in Section C, Washington below.

Otherwise, most of the U.S. community property states have developed a managerial approach. The basic of this approach is that a creditor should be able to satisfy a debt in default from whatever property a spouse has the *legal right* to manage and control.

In most U.S. community property states, under equal management rules, either spouse acting alone, can manage and control the entirety of the community personal property, as well as their own separate property. Agency principles make separate property liable for contractual debts even if the spouse did not bind his or her separate property with a signature.

To better protect their interests, contract creditors often ask both spouses to voluntarily assume personal liability for a loan by a signature. But absent a signature, there are default methods to hold a spouse's separate property liable. The doctrine of *necessaries of life*, meaning standard of living expenses, applies during marriage. The doctrine of *common necessaries*, meaning basic living expenses, applies in a period of separation.

Additionally, doctrines like the lender's intent test allow a creditor to proactively place a spouse's separate property in priority position in case of default. The lender's intent test is discussed in Chapter 4 and 7.

a. For One Spouse's Individual Debts During Marriage

There is no controversy about the rule that the separate (and in Wisconsin the unclassified "all other") property of each spouse is liable for his or her individual debts.

A separate liability may arise as a matter of civil, contract or tort law; and it may be individual or joint with the other spouse:

Contract liability may occur by reason of the duty of support. Spouses have a duty to support one another during marriage. This is a foundational duty, and in some states (like California) the duty of support may not be waived by premarital contract. Most other provisions imposing liability by virtue of the marital relationship (other than spousal support and community property rules) have been abolished.

Contract liability may arise because of one's own promise (alone, jointly, or as guarantor of the other spouse's promise), by consent or other agreement (including transmutation), or by giving authority to the other spouse, such as by a power of attorney or other specific agency arrangement.

This is understandable enough, but absent a signature how does one spouse become personally liable for a contract debt incurred by the other spouse?

To start with, spouses owe each other a duty of support during marriage, as discussed above.

During marriage, the community is liable for necessaries of life (standard of living expenses), regardless of which spouse incurs the debt.

After a date of separation, the community remains liable for common necessaries (basic living expense, during a period of separation), again regardless of which spouse incurs the debt. Accumulated community property (i.e., savings) is reachable first. If there are no savings, then statutes invoke the duty of support to permit creditors to reach the separate property of the spouse who is most financially able. This happens even if the more financially able spouse did not personally sign the contract, act as an agent, and or personally benefit from the contract, services, or products the contract delivers.

Tort liability, in addition for one's own torts, may be vicarious or derivative. The other spouse may commit a tort that is attributed to the first spouse by virtue of the agency doctrine of respondeat superior or because of ownership, such as with vehicle registration liability. There can also be owner liability derived from community property ownership.

Other obligations such as spousal or child support obligations from a prior union are the responsibility of the spouse who is charged with the obligation. This makes the support obligations satisfiable first from the judgment debtor's separate property, as discussed above in Section B.1.d. above. If the debtor has no separate property when the obligation is due, the community property of the current marriage becomes liable.

b. For Debts Incurred for Necessaries of Life During Marriage

There is still some authority for subjecting the separate property of the manager of the community to liability for acts undertaken as legal manager of the community.

Today, under equal management rules, generally when one spouse obligates the community personal property either the separate property of both spouses is bound, as when both spouses sign a loan contract, or the separate property of neither is bound (as in Arizona).

Three variations reflect how the higher earning spouse, who obtains a benefit as a matter of economics, might also be exposed to greater liability than the other lower earning spouse for standard of living expenses under the necessaries of life doctrine.

The first variation is the ability of a higher earning spouse to bind the property over which he or she would have had control over if not married. Typically, this category of property is the spouse's earnings, as in Texas, or separate property rents, issues, and profits, as in American rule states like California.

The second variation is illustrated by the following Louisiana provision. Under a **"separation of property regime"** spouses are made liable for family expenses not on an equal basis, but **"in proportion to his or her means"** in the language of LSA-C.C. Art. 2373.

c. For Debts Incurred for Common Necessaries After a Date of Separation

A third variation for holding the higher earning spouse liable for certain expenses after a date of separation is the common necessaries doctrine.

Generally, under the common necessaries doctrine, if a spouse signed a contract for basic necessaries but lacked community property or their own separate property to pay the debt, then creditors can reach the separate property of the spouse who did not sign the contract.

If creditors can reach a spouse's property, then practically speaking that spouse is liable for such debts. Liability may be statutorily imposed to further the policy of support or benefit to the community principles.

By rules like these, a higher earning spouse's economic exposure to personal liability, practically speaking, is greater than a lower earning spouse's exposure. This is true during marriage and during any period of separation. Some states specify a limit by statute. This limit turns on the concept of exhaustion of funds: when the community property is marshaled in first position, the separate property of the manager shall be reached only after the community property has been exhausted.

C. INDIVIDUAL STATES

1. ARIZONA

Arizona follows a two-part hybrid approach. Part one incorporates a managerial approach for contracts and acts and omissions taken in furtherance of the community purpose. Part two follows an entity approach for intentional torts.

Ariz.Rev.Stat.Ann. § 25–215(D) permits **"either spouse"** to **"contract debts and otherwise act for the benefit of the community."** In the case of joinder, when liability results, the spouses are sued jointly. Satisfaction comes **"first, from the community property, and second, from the separate property of the spouse contracting the debt or obligation."** Id.

Ariz.Rev.Stat.Ann. § 25–214 requires joinder for **"any transaction for the acquisition, disposition or encumbrance of an interest in real property."**

Otherwise, during the marriage, the separate property of each spouse is liable for his or her own separate debts, but **"shall not be liable for the separate debts or obligations of the other spouse, absent agreement of the property owner to the contrary."** Ariz.Rev.Stat.Ann. § 25–

215(A). This statutory language may block third party creditors from directly reaching a non-debtor spouse's separate property. However, in a property settlement agreement or decree of dissolution, **"[o]n request, the court may impose a lien against the separate property of a spouse to secure payment of debts that the court orders that spouse to pay."** Ariz.Rev.Stat.Ann. § 25–318 Notice.

Arizona does not follow the necessaries of life doctrine.

A property settlement agreement between the spouses or a dissolution decree cannot cancel a debt; for that reason, a spouse can expect to remain liable for whatever contractual obligation may exist between that spouse and a creditor. In a legal separation or dissolution proceeding, each spouse has a statutory right to obtain a copy of the other spouse's credit report to assess what, if any, liability the requesting spouse has to the creditor. Ariz.Rev.Stat.Ann. § 25–318(F).

Prior to the passage of the controlling statute Ariz.Rev.Stat.Ann. § 25–215, in 1973, the entirety of the community property was also exempt from liability for the premarital separate obligations of either spouse. As discussed above, that rule changed with Ariz.Rev.Stat.Ann. § 25–215(B), which was enacted to create a disincentive for avoiding existing obligations to creditors through the voluntary act of marriage. Ariz.Rev.Stat.Ann. § 25–215(B) now provides that **"[t]he community property is liable for premarital separate debts or other**

liabilities of a spouse, incurred after September 1, 1973 but only to the extent of the value of that spouse's contribution to the community property which would have been such spouse's separate property if single."

Schilling v. Embree, 118 Ariz. 236, 575 P.2d 1262 (1977), held that the application of Ariz.Rev.Stat.Ann. § 25–215(B) is limited to debts and liabilities incurred prior to marriage; the rationale being that the phrase **"premarital separate"** modifies both **"debts"** and **"other liabilities."** By this interpretation, the community is not liable for payment of separate liabilities during the marriage but is liable for premarital debts to the extent of the debtor spouse's ***"contribution* to the community property,"** not *share* or *interest* in the community property. (Italics added.) Modification by agreement is covered by Ariz.Rev.Stat.Ann. § 25–215(A)).

Ariz.Rev.Stat.Ann. § 25–215(D) does not distinguish between contract and tort liabilities" **"either spouse may contract debts and otherwise act for the benefit of the community."**

The two types of obligations appear to be treated the same under Arizona case law. *Elia v. Pifer*, 194 Ariz. 74, 977 P.2d 796 (1998), *rev. denied*, for example, affirms that the community is liable for contracts made during marriage, just as it is liable for intentional torts committed by one spouse while performing an activity in furtherance of the community's interest. Nevertheless, the statutory language reflects that Arizona historically has followed Washington law on the question of whether to make the community property liable for the intentional torts of one spouse acting alone without benefit to the community.

The community purpose doctrine, introduced above, holds that if a tort is committed with the intent to benefit the community, the community property can be reached to satisfy the judgment, even if the community does not receive an actual benefit from the wrongful conduct. *Shaw v. Greer*, 67 Ariz. 223, 194 P.2d 430 (1948).

But where the tort is also (i) "a malicious tort" committed by one of the spouses "without knowledge, consent, or ratification of the other" and (ii) does not result in a "benefit to the community" the community property cannot be reached. Id. at 34. In such a case, the tortfeasor's debt becomes the separate obligation of the tortfeasor, and the community is entirely shielded from liability. *Howe v. Haught,* 11 Ariz.App. 98, 462 P.2d 395, 397 (1969). So too is the separate property of the innocent spouse. Ariz.Rev.Stat.Ann. § 25–215(A).

With intentional torts there is a presumption in favor of shielding the community from liability for the delicts of one spouse. A married tortfeasor is presumed to cause malicious or intentional harm while acting outside the community purpose, and thus outside the scope of any managerial authority. The presumption is rebuttable, either with proof that the community benefitted from the tort or that the non-tortfeasor spouse knew about, consented to, or ratified the other spouse's act or omission. Nonintervention while present at the scene of the tort does not per se constitute knowledge, consent, or ratification of the innocent spouse in the tortfeasor's wrongdoing. *Howe* supra at 398. Neither does ignorance. *Selby v. Savard*, 134 Ariz. 222, 655 P.2d 342, 349 (1982), citing *Howe*, supra.

2. CALIFORNIA

The California approach to liability is managerial.

For purposes of the family code, a **"debt"** is **"an obligation incurred by a married person before or during marriage."** A debt can arise from contract, tort, or otherwise. Cal.Fam.Code § 902. Debts are incurred at specific times. For a contract, the debt is incurred when the contract is made; for a tort, at the time the tort occurs; and in other cases, at the time the obligation arises. Cal.Fam.Code § 903.

Statutes and decisional law distinguish between necessaries of life and common necessaries.

The doctrine called "necessaries of life" makes the community liable for **"a debt incurred by either spouse before or during marriage,"** up until a date of separation. Cal.Fam.Code § 910. By this rule, the creditors of one spouse can reach community property for obligations whose purpose is to meet the spouses' basic needs, the family's standard of living expenses, and the educational expenses of minor children. A court has discretion, within the definition of necessaries of life, to include business debts incurred for the purpose of creating income for the family (for example, computers for a community property business).

After a date of separation, the common necessaries doctrine, discussed below, applies.

By statute, a spouse can exempt his or her community property earnings during marriage from the reach of the other spouse's premarital creditors **"so long as** [the shielding spouse's community property earnings] **are held in a deposit account in which the person's spouse has no right of withdrawal and are uncommingled with other property in the *community estate*, except property insignificant in amount."** Cal.Fam.Code § 911 (italics added). The shield automatically drops if the exempt community property earnings are commingled with any other community property funds, or when the account becomes accessible by both spouses. The rationale is one of legal control: once the debtor spouse obtains access to the shielding spouse's account, the debtor spouse gains legal control of the sums on deposit in that account, which in turn exposes sums on deposit in the account to the reach of both spouses' creditors.

A spouse's separate property is liable for debts incurred by that spouse before or during marriage.

By the same rationale, the general rule is that a spouse's separate property is not liable for a debt incurred by the other spouse before or during marriage. Cal.Fam.Code § 913. *Note carefully that this general rule is dwarfed by exceptions.*

Cal.Fam.Code § 914 provides *when* **"a married person is personally liable for the following debts incurred by the person's spouse during marriage."** Cal.Fam.Code § 914(a).

That person is responsible for **"[a] debt incurred for *necessaries of life* of the person's spouse before the date of separation of the spouses."** Cal.Fam.Code § 914(a)(1). An exception for common necessaries appears to make that person also liable for **". . . a debt incurred for *common necessaries of life* of the person's spouse after the date of separation of the spouses."** at Cal.Fam.Code § 914(a)(2). (Italics added.)

Necessaries of life are defined as expenses related to each spouse's statutory obligation to support the other during marriage. Again, such expenses are broadly measured by a standard of living metric that includes basics, amenities, and, depending on the family finances, even luxuries like vacations, club fees, private school tuition, and other lifestyle expenditures.

In a period of separation, the duty of support continues, but in an often radically pared down fashion. The common necessaries doctrine permits each spouse's creditors to reach (i) accumulated community property and (ii) *absent a signature*, the other spouse's post-separation earnings and accumulations (which, after separation, are characterized by statute as the earner's separate property). The spouse who incurs the debt is the supported spouse. The spouse whose income and accumulations are liable to satisfy the debt is the supporting spouse. The common necessaries doctrine refers to basic living expenses: rent, food, utilities, transportation, and possibly basic medical care. To reiterate, standard of living expenses are not covered by the common necessaries doctrine.

Conditions governing any right of reimbursement appear in Cal.Fam.Code § 920.

With respect to tort liability, California modifies the managerial approach with satisfaction of order rules. The community property is liable for a tort judgment and marshaled either in first or second position depending on whether the tort was committed **"while the married person was performing an activity for the benefit of the community."** Unlike in Arizona or Washington, the community is not entirely shielded from one spouse's tort debts; indeed, the community may be finding itself all or partially liable to the injured plaintiff depending on the tortfeasor's separate property resources.

Cal.Fam.Code § 1000 provides in part:

> **"(a) A married person is not liable for any injury or damage caused by the other spouse except in cases where the married person would be liable therefor if the marriage did not exist.**
>
> **(b) The liability of a married person for death or injury to person or property shall be satisfied as follows:**

> **(1) If the liability of the married person is based upon an act or omission which occurred while the married person was performing an activity for the benefit of the community, the liability shall first be satisfied from the community property and second from the separate property of the married person.**
>
> **(2) If the liability of the married person is not based upon an act or omission which occurred while the married person was performing an activity for the benefit of the community, the liability shall first be satisfied from the separate property of the married person and second from the community estate."**

Additionally, the debt allocation provisions of Cal.Fam.Code § 2625 include in the definition of **"separate debts"** contract obligations **"that were not incurred for the benefit of the community."** So, for example, under this provision, the purchase of an airplane during marriage using a joint savings account as collateral was defined as a separate debt when the spouse who incurred the debt did so in anticipation of separation. *Marriage of Mahone*, 123 Cal.App.3d 17, 176 Cal.Rptr. 274 (1981). A contract for attorney fees related to one spouse's criminal defense was assigned to the criminal defendant spouse as a separate debt because the criminal charge "culminated in financial consequences at the time the marriage was coming to an end." *Marriage of Stitt*, 147 Cal.App.3d 579, 195 Cal.Rptr. 172 (1983), cf. *Marriage of Hirsch*, 211 Cal.App.3d 104, 259 Cal.Rptr. 39 (1989). And a contract made after separation by one spouse for the services of a private investigator hired to locate the other spouse was confirmed without offset to the spouse who made the contract *Marriage of Munguia*, 146 Cal.App.3d 853, 195 Cal.Rptr. 199 (1983).

3. IDAHO

The major statutory provision is Idaho Code § 32–912. That provision states a managerial approach: **"Either the husband or wife shall have the right to manage and control the community property, and either may bind the community property by contract, except that neither the husband nor wife may sell, convey or encumber the community real estate unless the other joins in executing the sale agreement, deed or other instrument of conveyance by which the real estate is sold, conveyed or encumbered, . . ."** This language suggests either spouse acting alone can bind the community personal property for secured and unsecured promissory notes or obligations. The Idaho Attorney General issued an advisory statement in 2005 indicating it is unlikely that one spouse acting alone can bind the community property to an unsecured promissory note or loan obligation. OAG 05–1.

The Attorney General's advisory reflects the current rule among the U.S. community property states for community real property, however. The rule is that both spouses shall join in encumbering the community real property. Joinder is required in Idaho, but unlike in California, in Idaho joinder rule is not applied on a document-by-document basis so much as on a transactional basis. Therefore, in a transaction, absent collusion between the creditor and the spouse who incurs the contract debt, if only one spouse signs a promissory note or loan contract but later both spouses sign a deed of trust, then the creditor, opines the Attorney General, should be able to reach the community real property despite the absence of joinder on the loan contract. OAG 05–1, supra. The Attorney General refers to Idaho case law in general but does not cite actual cases.

On the issue of community property real estate, case law often seems inconsistent with the premise that joinder refers to transactions rather than to documents. One possibly inconsistent case involving community property real estate, is *New Phase Invs., LLC v. Jarvis*, 153 Idaho 207, 280 P.3d 710 (2012). There the court held that it is only the nonsigning spouse, not a creditor, who can bring an action to declare a real estate transfer void under Idaho Code § 32–912. The purpose of the provision, the court went on to say, is to benefit the non-signing spouse by providing that spouse with a shield for protecting his, her or their interest in community real property. A default rule that focuses on the transaction rather than on the documents upon which the transaction is built weakens the shield, an issue the Attorney

General did not address. Also contradicting the Attorney General's statement is the holding in *Credit Bureau of Eastern Idaho, Inc. v. Lecheminant*, 149 Idaho 467, 235 P.3d 1188 (2010). There the court ruled that a debt need not be for a community purpose to bind the community. Idaho law needs clarification. Should the default serve as a shield for the creditor or for the non-joining spouse?

Considering the Attorney General's statement, that same statute—Idaho Code § 32–912—may also provide the non-signing spouse with a shield for protecting an interest in community personal property.

Additional clarification would be useful on separate property exemptions as well. Idaho exempts some separate property from liability for certain community obligations. Idaho Code § 32–912, for example, provides that: **"any community obligation incurred by either the husband or the wife without the consent in writing of the other shall not obligate the separate property of the spouse who did not consent."**

The statutory scheme requires the written consent of a person to any community contract which binds his or her separate property. For example, Idaho Code § 32–904 gives **"the wife . . . absolute powers of disposition of her separate property."** Idaho Code 32–903, 23–904, and 32–905 are all gender specific, and this seems a remnant of the male management era. Therefore, one would expect a court to follow precedent and apply the rules in gender-neutral form, especially after *Suter*, supra. But even so, the Idaho Code remains in need of the legislature's attention.

Idaho follows the civil law rule that rents, issues, and profits of separate property are characterized as community for the duration of marriage. But Idaho Code § 32–906 speaks to the case where the separate property owner has transmuted the rents, issues, and profits back to separate property. In such a case, the transmuted property is not exempt from liability. Prepare yourself for three negatives: the rule stated is that neither the separate property nor its income streams **"shall not be liable for the debts of the other member of the community."** *Baruch v. Clark*, 154 Idaho 732, 302 P.3d 357 (2013) and *Credit Bureau of Eastern Idaho*, supra, are Idaho Supreme Court cases on point.

In *Williams v. Paxton*, 98 Idaho 155, 559 P.2d 1123 (1977), applied well accepted principles to allow a creditor to reach a wife's separate property where the creditor had obtained a judgment on a joint promissory note that the spouses contracted during marriage. The creditor was permitted to levy against the wife's separate property regardless of what the purpose of the contract was deemed to be. The court's rationale was that if the act of signing a loan contract during marriage obligates the community, it also personally obligates the signing spouse; therefore, a judgment creditor can execute against the signing spouse's separate property. *Credit Bureau of Eastern Idaho*, supra, makes a similar point.

Community funds that are used to pay off premarital debts are not necessarily reimbursed upon an Idaho divorce, depending on how the court applies Idaho Code § 32–712. The statute allows a court discretion to assign community debts to a higher earning spouse.

If community funds satisfy separate debt and, by doing so, enhance the separate property, a reimbursement may be due the community. See e.g., *Vanwassenhove v. Vanwassenhove*, 134 Idaho 198, 998 P.2d 505 (Ct. App. 2000), ruling that the magistrate erred in denying the community a reimbursement for its principal payments on the husband's separate property farm. But if community funds satisfy separate debt without a corresponding enhancement to the separate property, then a reimbursement is likely not due. See e.g. *Bliss v. Bliss*, 127 Idaho 170, 898 P.2d 1081 (1995) where the court denied a reimbursement to the community for its contributions to paying off the husband's premarital judgment debt. The rationale of the *Bliss*, supra, could be fairly characterized in this way: a debt that does not result in an enhancement of the community estate is not a family expense.

The law is unclear about whether the separate property of one spouse should be exempt from liability for the torts or delicts of the other spouse.

4. LOUISIANA

Louisiana is the most faithful adherent to the community regime concept by how it classifies obligations as separate or community. See LSA-C.C. Art. 2359. **"Community obligation"** is defined in LSA-C.C. Art. 2360 as **"[a]n obligation incurred**

by a spouse during the existence of a community property regime for the common interest of the spouses or for the interest of the other spouse. . . ." Attorney fees and costs in an action for divorce are community obligations prior to the "**the date of a judgment of divorce,**" but not after. LSA-C.C. Art. 2362.1.

Separate obligations are enumerated in LSA-C.C. Art. 2363, which says: "**prior to the establishment of a community property regime, or . . . during the existence of a community property regime though not for the common interest of the spouses or for the interest of the other spouse,**" and after the community terminates. "**An obligation resulting from an intentional wrong or an obligation incurred for the separate property of a spouse is likewise a separate obligation to the extent that it does not benefit both spouses, the family, or the other spouse.**"

Under the above statute, a premarital obligation is characterized as separate because it negatively impacts marital net worth as, for example, when it is repaid with community funds. By comparison, an obligation assumed during marriage—contract or tort—is characterized by whether (and to what extent) its effect is to benefit both spouses, the family, or the other spouse. The concept of conferred benefit is dispositive, here. Not material is the intent of the spouse who incurred the obligation (as in Arizona). Debts incurred after the community regime terminates may be separate obligations on the theory that they can have no impact on both spouses. On the other hand, they may be separate obligations on the theory that they impact on the family or the other spouse.

During the existence of the marital regime a separate obligation may be satisfied from the separate property of the spouse who incurred the obligation and from the community property. LSA-C.C. Art. 2345.

Upon termination of a community property regime, when community property has repaid a separate obligation, the spouse who did not incur the obligation (or heirs) may have a reimbursement claim against the spouse who did incur the obligation. The amount of the reimbursement due is one-half of the amount (if money was used), or one-half the value at the time of use (if things other than money were used). LSA-C.C. Art. 2364.

A spouse who uses separate property **"either during the existence of the community property regime or thereafter to satisfy a community obligation"** is **"entitled to a reimbursement for one-half of the amount or value that the property had at the time it was used."** Effective 2009,." LSA-C.C. Art. 2365. This section further provides that **"The liability of a spouse who owes reimbursement is limited "to the value of his share of all community property after deduction of all community obligations."** If there are no community assets, then no reimbursement is due.

A major exception in Art. 2365 is this. **"If the community obligation was incurred for the ordinary and customary expenses of the marriage, or for the support, maintenance, or education of children of either spouse in keeping with the economic condition of the spouses, the spouse is entitled to reimbursement from the other spouse regardless of the value of that spouse's share of all community property."** In other words, the spouse who pays the expense is entitled to a reimbursement. If there are insufficient community assets to satisfy that debt, then a reimbursement is due from the reimbursing spouse's separate property.

Similarly, a reimbursement is due when a spouse uses separate property to improve the other spouse's separate property. LSA-C.C. Art. 2367.1. Reimbursement is due from the benefitted spouse to the contributing spouse and measured by the amount or value the contributing **"property had at the time it was used."**

The right of reimbursement is heritable.

The provisions quoted above are concerned with the allocation of the burden between the spouses. They do not deal with the rights of creditors. Even so, creditors may intervene and object in the proceeding by which the spouses resolve their rights.

5. NEVADA

Among the few provisions which give guidance in this area is Nev.Rev.Stat § 123.050: **"Neither the**

separate property of a spouse nor the spouses' share of the community property is liable for the debts of the other spouse contracted before the marriage."

There appears to be an exception for **"articles necessary"** in a case where **"a spouse neglects to make adequate provision for the support of his or her spouse."** This statute weighed down by gender specific language until July 2017, when the state legislature enacted gender-neutral language.

6. NEW MEXICO

New Mexico has a relatively complete set of statutory provisions that divide debts into separate and community, and that direct an order of marshaling for satisfying each category of debt.

Generally, a debt incurred during marriage is presumptively a community debt absent proof that the debt falls into one of the categories of separate debts listed in N.M.Stat.Ann. § 40–3–9(A)(1) through (6) (1978).

The statutory provisions for the definition of separate and community debts are set forth as N.M.Stat.Ann. § 40–3–9(A) (1978):

A. "Separate debt" means:

(1) a debt contracted or incurred by a spouse before marriage or after entry of a decree of dissolution of marriage;

(2) [or legal separation]. . . .

(3) **a debt designated as a separate debt of a spouse by a judgment or decree of any court having jurisdiction;**

(4) **a debt contracted by a spouse during marriage which is identified by a spouse to the creditor in writing at the time of its creation as the separate debt of the contracting spouse;**

(5) **a debt which arises from a tort committed by a spouse before marriage or after entry of a decree of dissolution of marriage or a separate tort committed during marriage. . . .**

B. "Community debt" means a debt contracted or incurred by either or both spouses during marriage which is not a separate debt.

Notice N.M.Stat.Ann. § 40–3–9(A)(4) (1978) above. It means that either spouse acting alone can contractually bind the community unless he or she identifies the contract debt to the creditor, at the time the debt is originated, as a separate debt. This essentially is the lender's intent test. This test is used to rebut the presumption of community property as to borrowed proceeds. It rests on the idea that the lender had prior notice that separate property alone would be reachable in the event of default.

New Mexico is a managerial approach state for community debts. But is it one for separate debts as well? How much of the community property can a creditor of an enumerated separate debt reach? Case law answers that (even) a spouse who incurs separate debts is a manager of the community. As a manager that spouse can incur debts that ultimately expose the community property to the reach of creditors. When that happens, however, only one-half (the debtor-spouse's one-half) of the community property is made available. By distinguishing between the debtor spouse's and non-debtor spouse's one-half of the community property, New Mexico shields (exempts) one-half of the community property from the reach a spouse's separate creditors.

In 1997, New Mexico enacted N.M.Stat.Ann. § 40–3–9.1 (1978), a statute specific to gambling debts. It provides that **"[a] gambling debt incurred by a married person as a result of legal gambling is a separate debt of the spouse incurring the debt."**

The New Mexico order of marshaling separate debt is unique among the states in other ways. The next paragraph set forth the marshaling order.

Separate debts are covered under N.M.Stat.Ann. § 40–3–10 (1978).

> **A. The separate debt of a spouse shall be satisfied first from the debtor spouse's separate property, excluding that spouse's interest in property in which each of the spouses owns an undivided equal interest**

as a joint tenant or tenant in common. Should such property be insufficient, then the debt shall be satisfied from the debtor spouse's one-half interest in the community property or in property in which each spouse owns an undivided equal interest as a joint tenant or tenant in common, excluding the residence of the spouses. Should such property be insufficient, then the debt shall be satisfied from the debtor spouse's interest in the residence of the spouses. . . . Neither spouse's interest in community property or separate property shall be liable for the separate debt of the other spouse.

. . .

C. The priorities or exemptions established in this section for the satisfaction of a separate debt must be claimed by either spouse under the procedure set forth in Section 42–10–13 NMSA 1978, or the right to claim such priorities or exemptions is waived as between a spouse and the creditor.

D. This section shall apply only while both spouses are living and shall not apply to the satisfaction of debts after the death of one or both spouses.

During a period of separation, a party may petition that a debt be declared an **"unreasonable debt."** An unreasonable debt becomes a separate debt, payable by the party who incurs the debt. A debt is unreasonable **"if it was incurred by a spouse while the spouse was living apart and the debt did not contribute to the benefit of both spouses or their dependents."** This standard seems to further narrow the already narrow common necessaries doctrine by requiring a benefit to both spouses, not just to the needy spouse, or to their dependents.

Community debts fall under N.M.Stat.Ann. § 40–3–11 (1978).

> **"A. Community debts shall be satisfied first from all community property and all property in which each spouse owns an undivided equal interest as a joint tenant or tenant in common, excluding the residence of the spouses. Should such property be insufficient, community debts shall then be satisfied from the residence of the spouses, except as provided in Section 42–10–9 NMSA 1978. Should such property be insufficient, only the separate property of the spouse who contracted or incurred the debt shall be liable for its satisfaction. If both spouses contracted or incurred the debt, the separate property of both spouses is jointly and severally liable for its satisfaction. . . .**
>
> **C. The priorities or exemptions established in this section for the satisfaction of community debts must be claimed by either spouse under the**

procedure set forth in Section 42–10–13 NMSA 1978 or the right to claim such priorities or exemptions is waived as between a spouse and the creditor.

D. This section shall apply only while both spouses are living and shall not apply to the satisfaction of debts after the death of one or both spouses."

The residence of the spouses (more than the homestead exemption) is not exempt and thus it remains subject to the reach of creditors to satisfy a community debt.

The above statute leaves open the question of how to characterize a tort committed by one spouse during the marriage. The doctrine that decides the character of a tort is the family purpose doctrine. This doctrine turns on whether the tortfeasor's conduct benefitted the community. If the community does not benefit, then the tort judgment creditor can reach the tortfeasor's separate property. *Dell v. Heard*, 532 F.2d 1330 (10th Cir. 1976). For separate torts, the statutes and cases make clear that a spouse who commits a separate tort (intentional or negligent) is individually liable for damages that arise therefrom. The community or separate property assets of the innocent spouse are not liable and therefore cannot be reached by the tort judgment creditor.

If the tortfeasor's conduct benefitted the community, then the tort judgment creditor can reach the community property. As such, the wrongful conduct creates a community liability. The judgment is collectible under the community property provisions set forth above. Those provisions provide that the judgment creditor can seek a judgment lien against the tortfeasor's one-half of the community property. This includes permission for the judgment creditor to reach one-half the income of the non-debtor spouse. *Cent. Adjustment Bureau, Inc. v. Thevenet*, 101 N.M. 612, 686 P.2d 954 (1984).

Additionally, depending on the reach of the state family purpose doctrine, even if a plaintiff only has a cause of action against one spouse, once a judgment is obtained, when the judgment creditor goes to satisfy the judgment, the separate property of both spouses, if any, may be reachable and hence jointly and severally liable. *Dell,* supra.

7. TEXAS

V.T.C.A.Fam.Code § 3.201 provides the basic theme of liability of community property: Property subject to the sole management and control of one spouse is liable for that spouse's marital contract debts.

All the dually managed community property is subject to liability for torts committed during the marriage. So too is property under the sole management of the spouse who incurs the liability.

Here is the text of V.T.C.A.Fam.Code § 3.202:

(a) A spouse's separate property is not subject to liabilities of the other spouse unless both spouses are liable by other rules of law.

(b) Unless both spouses are liable as provided by this subchapter, the community property subject to a spouse's sole management, control, and disposition is not subject to:

(1) any liabilities that the other spouse incurred before marriage; or

(2) any nontortious liabilities that the other spouse incurs during marriage.

(c) The community property subject to a spouse's sole or joint management, control, and disposition is subject to the liabilities incurred by the spouses before or during marriage.

(d) All community property is subject to tortious liability of either spouse incurred during marriage.

Texas couples the managerial approach with marshaling. But order of priority (marshaling) is expressly left to the discretion of the judge by V.T.C.A.Fam.Code § 3.203:

(a) A judge may determine, as deemed just and equitable, the order in which particular separate or community property is subject to execution and sale to satisfy a judgment, if the property subject to liability for a judgment includes any combination of:

(1) a spouse's separate property;

(2) community property subject to a spouse's sole management, control, and disposition;

(3) community property subject to the other spouse's sole management, control, and disposition; and

(4) community property subject to the spouses' joint management, control, and disposition.

(b) In determining the order in which particular property is subject to execution and sale, the judge shall consider the facts surrounding the transaction or occurrence on which the suit is based.

8. WASHINGTON

Wash.Rev.Code § 26.16.200 protects each spouse's separate property from the other's premarital creditors. The statutory basis for that interpretation is a reference in the statute to **"the rent or income of the *separate property* of either . . . ."** (Italics added.) *Haley v. Highland*, 142 Wash.2d 135, 12 P.3d 119, 123–125 (2000).

The same statute does not protect community personal property from the reach of creditors, premarital or marital. Practically, this means that the separate property of the nonliable spouse is not subject to writ or levy for the liable spouse's premarital debt, but any property they acquire during marriage as community property is. See also Wash.Rev.Code § 26.16.010 and 26.16.020.

Despite the above rule, during marriage community property remains more insulated from a creditor's reach if the separate debt is in contract, less insulated if the debt arises from a liquidated (settled) tort claim. The relevant part of the above statute provides **"[t]he earnings and accumulations of the spouse or domestic partner shall be available to the legal process of creditors for the satisfaction of *debts* incurred by such spouse or domestic partner prior to the marriage."** (Italics added.) Wash.Rev.Code § 26.16.020. Debts, as noted above, is a general term that includes contractual liability, liquidated tort liability, and support obligations to a former spouse or to children from a prior union. Id.

Under state statutory and decisional law, community property is generally not available to satisfy the separate debts of either spouse. The following general rule appears at Wash.Rev.Code § 26.16.200: **"Neither person in a marriage or state registered domestic partnership is liable for the debts or liabilities of the other incurred before marriage, or state registered domestic partnership, nor for the separate debts of each other . . ."** See also *Nichols Hills Bank v. McCool*, 104 Wash.2d 78, 701 P.2d 1114 (1985). This rule was enacted in 1881 and modified in 1969.

Three exceptions potentially expose the community property to liability for separate debt.

One, the exception for premarital liabilities that have been are reduced to judgment within three years of the marriage of the parties. Wash.Rev.Code § 26.16.200. Note however that *Caplan v. Sullivan*, 37 Wash.App. 289, 679 P.2d 949 (1984) held that an unliquidated tort claim does not fall into the category of "debts" for purposes of Wash.Rev.Code § 26.16.200, an interpretation affirmed in *Haley*, supra, at 127.

Two, the exception for support obligations to former spouses or children from a prior marriage. *Fisch v. Marler*, 1 Wash.2d 698, 97 P.2d 147 (1939).

Three, the exception for tax liabilities.

Separate debts that are incurred by one spouse during marriage cannot generally be satisfied with the non-debtor spouse's separate property.

But Wash.Rev.Code § 26.16.205, the "necessaries" statute, carves out a huge exception for family expenses: **"The expenses of the family and the education of the children, including stepchildren, are chargeable upon the property of both spouses or both domestic partners, or either of them, and they may be sued jointly or separately."** Scope and timing determine whether an expense is a family expenditure (and thus a community debt) or not (and thus a separate debt). See e.g. *Smith v. Dalton*, 58 Wash.App. 876, 795 P.2d 706 (1990)(ski boat purchased one month before separation was held not to be a family expense, leaving husband's separate property and his one-half of the community property reachable by the seller).

As for torts, Wash.Rev.Code § 26.16.190 exempts the nontortfeasor spouse's separate property from the execution of a separate tort judgment unless there would be joint liability even if the marriage did not exist.

Are separate tort judgment creditors limited to reaching the tortfeasor's separate property? Can they also reach the tortfeasor spouse's one-half of the community property? Is there a marshaling rule? Or as was historically the rule in Washington, is a separate tort creditor barred from executing against community property?

The answer is that creditors are not limited to reaching the tortfeasor's separate property, but they must first execute the judgment against any existing separate property. Only if there is insufficient separate property to satisfy the judgment, can a creditor petition to execute against the tortfeasor spouse's one-half of the community property. *deElche v. Jacobsen*, 95 Wash.2d 237, 622 P.2d 835 (1980) (*en banc*) (Horowitz J., dissenting) lowered the bar for execution of community *personal* property. *Keene v. Edie,* 131 Wash.2d 822, 935 P.2d 588 (1997) lowered it for the execution of community *real property.* Notice the marshaling rule embedded in the decisional law. The rule is that the separate tort judgment creditor must execute against and exhaust the tortfeasor's separate property (if any) before executing against the tortfeasor's one-half of the community property.

What is a separate tort? Here again when it comes to tort liability the community purpose doctrine applies. A separate tort is one that does not benefit the community. A community tort is one that does benefit the community. Prior law exempted all community property from liability for liquidated separate tort claims by defining "community purpose" broadly. But *DeElche*, supra, a split decision, canceled the community property exemption. (New Mexico achieves the same outcome by statute.)

DeElche, supra, involved a married couple that hosted a party on their community property sailboat (a community activity, a community purpose, hosted on a community asset, and paid for with community funds). After the party, one spouse trespassed onto a third person's boat and committed an unlawful act. The tort was deemed a separate tort. The tortfeasor had no separate property with which to satisfy the tort judgment. The creditor sought to reach the tortfeasor's one-half of the community personal property. The previous rule would have shielded all community property from the reach of a separate tort judgment creditor. *deElche* reversed. The rationale was threefold. One, the community is not a legal entity (like a corporation), therefore the spouses, not the entity, incur liability. Two, the spouses have a present and vested interest in community property, as such, the tortfeasor's one-half community property interest should be subject to execution for a judgment debt. Three, it is unfair to immunize tortfeasors or deny remedy to their victims simply because the tortfeasor happens to be married.

Keene, supra, the separate judgment creditor attempted to execute the judgment against the tortfeasor spouse's separate property. When that was insufficient, the creditor attempted to execute against the tortfeasor's community real property. *De Elche*, supra, had canceled the exemption for community personal property. *Keene*, supra, raised the next obvious issue of whether the ruling in *De Elche* extended to community real property. The court ruled it did, citing public policy concerns and the absence of any statutory exemption for community real property from involuntary encumbrances, the Washington Supreme court overruled prior law and expended the rule in *deElche*, supra. *Keene*, supra, at 594–595. *deElche*, supra, is widely cited. There was a dissent in the case; it argued that the legislature, not the courts, should have changed the prior rule.

If community property is reached to satisfy a separate tort judgment, a right to reimbursement in the community typically arises by equitable lien. The purpose of the community lien is to ensure that the innocent spouse receives the same amount of community property he or she would have received had the tortfeasor's one-half of the community property not been used to satisfy the separate tort judgment.

The distinction between community and separate liabilities was historically more important (and more frequently litigated) in Washington than in other community property states. This is because—again historically—most separate debts could not be collected from community property and most community debts could not be collected from separate property. The source of the relative immunity of community property was the judicial interpretation of a statute that subjects community real property to mechanics' liens and materialmen's liens obtained for community debts.

Washington courts have authority to draw the line between community and separate debts. But what serves as a guidepost for where they tend to draw it?

One answer is evidence. There is a rebuttable presumption that a liability incurred by a married person during the continuance of the marriage is a community liability. That presumption can be properly raised on evidence that the debt was incurred during the marriage, either to acquire something, to manage community property, or to benefit the community. Rebuttal is by proof that the expense was directly related to the separate property of the married person who incurred the debt. Alternatively, rebuttal can be made with proof that the liability was incurred by one spouse in the act of making of a nonmutual gift to a third party.

Another answer is the original purpose of the debt. The courts have been liberal in finding community purpose and consequently community liability. Recreational activities, expectation of employment, benefit to a corporation of which the spouse is an officer or director, and even a debt for funds borrowed on the security of separate property have been classified as community debts. Each was shown to have benefitted the community, either directly or indirectly. Therefore, each met the community purpose test.

Intent to benefit the community may of course factor into an analysis of actual benefit, but intent alone is not dispositive. In *Northern Bank & Trust Co. v. Graves*, 79 Wash. 411, 140 P. 328 (1914), a separate obligation was not transformed into a community obligation merely because both spouses signed the promissory note with the intent to benefit the community. The case arose in the male-management era, a time in which the husband was the legal manager of the community property, and the wife had no obligation to sign the promissory note to bind the community. It was decided that by signing the promissory note, husband and (additionally) wife did not create a community debt. Rather they incurred two separate debts, one that obligated husband's separate property and one that obligated wife's separate property.

9. WISCONSIN

Wisconsin adds to the already detailed UMPA provisions to specify which classifications of property are liable for enumerated types of spousal obligations incurred prior to and during marriage.

Family purpose is determined by timing. Wisconsin presumes that an obligation incurred by one spouse during marriage is undertaken for a family purpose, or in the language of Wis. Stat. § 766.55, reproduced below, **"in the interest of the marriage or the family."**

Relevant Wisconsin cases are federal bankruptcy cases. Still, it is useful to bear in mind that a debtor's property interests affected by his or her bankruptcy filing are determined by state law.

In Wisconsin, when an obligation is satisfiable from all "marital property," it is satisfiable from both spouses' community property wages, regardless of which spouse incurred the debt. *In re Passmore*, 156 B.R. 595 (Bkrtcy. E.D. Wis. 1993) raised the issue of whether a prepetition order to garnish the wages of the non-debtor spouse (Mary) was voided by the automatic stay that arose after the debtor spouse (Mary's husband) filed a bankruptcy petition. The court answered in the affirmative and ordered Mary's creditor to return to those of her wages that had been garnished from her after the stay in her husband's case. The reason for including Mary's wages in the automatic stay occasioned by her husband's bankruptcy is that the married bankruptcy debtor, as a Wisconsin domiciliary, owns an undivided interest in all marital property. That undivided interest cannot be partitioned by the creditor. Nor can it be unilaterally severed by the spouse to avoid a creditor. Thus, when the Mary's husband filed a bankruptcy petition, the automatic stay of collection claims against him also barred Mary's creditors from continuing to garnish her (community property) wages.

If a spouse is not also personally liable for the debt, then the property that is not marital property (i.e., all other property) is not reachable. *Smith v. Capital*

One Bank (USA) N.A., 545 B.R. 249 (Bkrtcy. E.D. Wis. 2016) (credit card debt).

Generally, these principles govern contract debt incurred during marriage, but here again there is variation among the states on whether and (if so) how the spouse who does not incur the debt can shield his or her earnings from the reach of certain creditors. Lack of knowledge about the debt has been held insufficient to overcome the Wis. Stat. § 766.55(1) presumption that the debt is in the interest of the marriage or family, at least in the context of a bankruptcy proceeding. *In re Dahle-Fenske*, 525 B.R. 912 (Bkrtcy. E.D. Wis. 2015).

Wis. Stat. § 766.55(2) and (2)(cm), both reproduced below creates an exception from the Wis. Stat. § 766.55(1) presumption that debt incurred during marriage is in the interest of the marriage or the family. That same kind of presumption applies to a tort claim brought during marriage against (only) one spouse.

Wis.Stat. § 766.55 provides in part:

(1) An obligation incurred by a spouse during marriage, including one attributable to an act or omission during marriage, is presumed to be incurred in the interest of the marriage or the family. A statement separately signed by the obligated or incurring spouse at or before the time the obligation is incurred stating that the obligation is or will be incurred in

the interest of the marriage or the family is conclusive evidence that the obligation to which the statement refers is an obligation in the interest of the marriage or family, except that the existence of that statement does not affect any interspousal right or remedy.

(2) After the determination date all of the following apply:

(a) A spouse's obligation to satisfy a duty of support owed to the other spouse or to a child of the marriage may be satisfied only from all marital property and all other property of the obligated spouse.

(b) An obligation incurred by a spouse in the interest of the marriage or the family may be satisfied only from all marital property and all other property of the incurring spouse.

(c) 1. An obligation incurred by a spouse before or during marriage that is attributable to an obligation arising before marriage or to an act or omission occurring before marriage may be satisfied only from property of that spouse that is not marital property and from that part of marital property which would have been the property of that spouse but for the marriage.

(c) 2. An obligation incurred by a spouse before, on or after January 1, 1986, that is attributable to an obligation arising before January 1, 1986, or to an act or omission occurring before January 1, 1986, may be satisfied only from property of that spouse that is not marital property and from that part of marital property which would have been the property of that spouse but for the enactment of this chapter.

(cm) An obligation incurred by a spouse during marriage, resulting from a tort committed by the spouse during marriage, may be satisfied from the property of that spouse that is not marital property and from that spouse's interest in marital property.

(d) Any other obligation incurred by a spouse during marriage, including one attributable to an act or omission during marriage, may be satisfied only from property of that spouse that is not marital property and from that spouse's

interest in marital property, in that order.

(2m) Unless the dissolution decree or any amendment to the decree so provides, no income of a nonincurring spouse is available for satisfaction of an obligation under sub. (2)(b) after entry of the decree. Marital property assigned to each spouse under that decree is available for satisfaction of such an obligation to the extent of the value of the marital property at the date of the decree. If a dissolution decree provides that the nonincurring spouse is responsible for satisfaction of the obligation, the obligation may be satisfied as if both spouses had incurred the obligation.

Wis.Stat. § 766.56(1) provides that a creditor **"shall consider all marital property available under s. 766.55(2)(b)** [reproduced above] **to satisfy the obligation in the same manner that the creditor, in evaluating the creditworthiness of an unmarried credit applicant, considers the property of an unmarried credit applicant available to satisfy the obligation."**

The general rule is that a marital agreement does not adversely affect the interest of a creditor who transacts with a married person, even if that agreement is recorded. Wis.Stat. § 766.56(2)(a) explicitly states that recordation of a martial agreement does not provide actual or constructive notice to third party creditors.

Wis.Stat. § 766.56(2)(b) provides for an adequate notice provision. The statutory section is in the form of a general rule (a marital agreement does not adversely affect the interest of a creditor) and an exception: "**. . . unless the creditor, prior to the time the credit is granted, is furnished a copy of the agreement, statement or decree or has actual knowledge of the adverse provision when the obligation to the creditor is incurred. The notice requirement under this paragraph does not apply to renewals, extensions or modification or the use of an open-end credit plan.**"

PART 4

END OF MARRIAGE

CHAPTER 10

DIVORCE AND DISSOLUTION

A. OVERVIEW

Divorce means to regain one's personal status as a single person. A final court judgment and only a final court judgment terminates a marriage.

Dissolution means to partition community property. The property of a marriage is often divided, most commonly, by a private contract incorporated by the court into its final judgment. When the parties cannot agree on a division, the court steps in to dissolve the community property.

The parties' ability to acquire community property can end by separation, dissolution, a change of domicile, or the death of a spouse. Legal separation terminates the community in all states. Physical separation terminates it in some states. Among the community property states, Texas is alone in permitting informal marriage (sometimes referred to as common law marriage). No community property state permits informal divorce. If parties are validly married, then they must obtain a divorce by final court judgment. See Chapter 5 for more on formal versus informal methods of establishing a date of separation.

Void marriages never come into existence but, in many states, still must be formally annulled. Formally means by a court judgment.

Voidable marriages come into legal existence, but they are subject to annulment or dissolution, at the option of one or both parties.

The equitable putative spouse doctrine addresses property issues that can come up in a void or voidable marriage.

As to the division of community property, most states follow the equal division principle—equal means an arithmetic 50–50. A minority follow the equitable division principle—equitable meaning fair, but not necessarily 50–50.

The rules of division tend to play out when the parties cannot reach a private marriage settlement agreement (a MSA for short).

B. DETAIL

1. ENDING THE COMMUNITY DURING LIFE

The community property system admits to it, by default, a married person who is domiciled within the jurisdiction. However, certain events, enumerated next, can end or significantly alter the way in which the community property rules apply to that married person.

Changing domicile to another state removes a married person or persons (if both spouses change their domicile) from the community property system of their former domicile and includes them in the marital property system of their new domicile. This is so even if the change is from one community property state to another.

Illustration 10.1: H and W are domiciled in California. They move to New Hampshire and establish a domicile there. H and W leave the California community property system and enter the New Hampshire common law marital property system as of the date of the domicile change.

Illustration 10.2: H and W are domiciled in California. They move to Texas and establish a domicile there. H and W leave the California community property system and enter the Texas community property system as of the date of the domicile change.

The transition from one domicile to the next can decide ownership rights from the date of the change in domicile forward. It can also decide management and control rights, duties, and remedies for breach, depending on state law.

Assuming that there is no change in domicile, the following events will end the community's ability to acquire property.

a. Informal (physical) separation when permitted, depending on state law.

b. Legal separation of the spouses.

c. Separation of property regime by court procedure.

d. A property settlement agreement (an MSA).

e. A final judgment of dissolution; or

f. The death of a spouse.

Separation, whether informal or by court process, ends the married person's ability to acquire (although not to hold) community property. In most states, post-separation earnings and accumulations belong to the earning spouse as his or her separate property. For that reason alone, the date of separation can be and often is disputed by the parties in the context of a dissolution. See Chapter 5 for more on date of separation.

An informal date of separation occurs when one or both parties decide that the marriage is over. States have different rules about when an informal period of separation commences as a matter of law. Some states require proof that one of the spouses has moved out of the family residence. Other states admit any evidence that goes toward proving one of the spouses intends to end the marriage and acts in a way consistent with that intent.

Contracts in their various forms can terminate or modify the community estate. A separation agreement is an agreement between the parties pinpointing the date of separation and, thus, each party's ability to acquire and accumulate community property (or not) after that date. Where allowed, a separation agreement may or may not include other important issues relating to property rights, property dissolution, or support awards. Parties who negotiate an enforceable separation agreement must still petition for dissolution and obtain a final judgment of dissolution to legally terminate the marriage and thereby regain their status as a single person.

A regime of separation of property can be created by court order in Louisiana.

A formal legal separation of the spouses generally involves filing a legal separation petition that covers all the elements of a divorce, including the dissolution of property, and the award of spousal support (where necessary). Importantly however, a judgment of legal separation does not restore the parties' legal status to single. When parties are legally separated, they continue to retain their status as married individuals, which means that each is precluded from contracting a subsequent marriage until the court's final judgment on that issue is obtained.

A judgment of dissolution finalizes property issues and restores the parties to single status.

The end of marriage by the death of a spouse is discussed in Chapter 12.

2. ENDING A MARRIAGE BY ANNULMENT, LEGAL SEPARATION, OR DISSOLUTION

There are three general categories of proceedings by which a community (as opposed to a community estate or regime) is terminated. They are annulment, legal separation and dissolution.

a. By Annulment

Certain marriages are void because of a major defect such as bigamy or too close a degree of kinship (incest). A void marriage never comes into legal existence. It never acquires community property.

Other marriages are voidable because of correctable defects that exist at the time of the marriage. A voidable marriage is presumed valid. It can acquire community property. With a voidable marriage, parties have an option to seek annulment or dissolution. In the context of a voidable marriage, annulment voids the marriage whereas dissolution ratifies it and allows dissolution under the state community property laws.

What the parties believe to be community property (or the legal analog for community property) may come into existence during a void or voidable marriage. But this happens at dissolution, by action of the court.

The equitable putative spouse doctrine holds that if one or both parties believed in good faith that their otherwise void or voidable marriage was valid, they may seek a court order to obtain the legal status of putative spouse. For purposes of community property law, once the putative spouse is recognized by a court, the putative spouse has most if not all the rights of a spouse in a valid marriage. Moreover, a putative marriage acquires quasi marital property (a remedial analog to community property). Quasi-marital property is divided as if it were community property. See Chapter 11 for more on quasi-marital property.

b. By Legal Separation

By a separation agreement (in some states) or by legal procedure, the earnings and accumulations of a married person are characterized as their separate property.

After a date of separation, the parties are not yet divorced. Therefore, the parties' obligations to each other to manage and control existing community property continue to exist until a marriage settlement agreement is signed, and in some states until the issuance of a final judgment of dissolution.

A separated person is still married, and as such not eligible to legally contract a subsequent marriage.

Illustration 10.3: H and W sign a separation agreement. Before the final judgement of dissolution, H marries T. The marriage between H and T is void as a matter of law because it is bigamous. T is already married to W when he purports to marry T. Bigamy is not a correctable defect in a marriage. Therefore, H must obtain a final judgment of divorce from W to regain his single status and contract a valid marriage with T.

c. By (Absolute) Divorce

No U.S. state recognizes informal divorce. All divorce is by final court order. Divorce is also referred to as dissolution in contemporary community property systems.

Historically, absolute divorce has proceeded from a status of non-existence (meaning it was not permitted) to separate maintenance, to absolute divorce for fault (adultery, cruelty, desertion, imprisonment, insanity etc.) and eventually to no-fault divorce. The community property states were among the first in the U.S. to adopt no-fault divorce, and all but Louisiana adopted unilateral divorce in the 1970s.

Today, the concept of fault is largely avoidable, if not practically eliminated, as a ground for divorce and in the division of property. Irreconcilable differences, or some variant of that concept, is the main ground for filing a petition for dissolution. So too consent.

Today, additionally, the clear trend is toward unilateral divorce, which simply means that one spouse acting alone can file a petition to end the marriage.

A final judgment returns the parties to their status as unmarried (single) persons.

A judgement of dissolution divides the community property by the equal division rule or by the equitable division rule, depending on the jurisdiction. Equal means fifty-fifty. A minority call for equitable division. Equitable means division in a way the court deems fair.

Parties are of course free to negotiate around property rights, using trades and offsets. If they are successful, they can reduce their dissolution agreement to a writing that will become part of the final judgment of dissolution. But if the parties come to a negotiation impasse, most states require that the court shall step in to carry out the dissolution.

Whether division is equal or equitable, the parties have choice and agency to negotiate a dissolution outcome. In negotiating around community property rights, for example, the stronger negotiation position is to understand that property rights are owned and acquired during marriage, and that they can be traded or offset in the negotiation of a marital property settlement. Thus, it is always useful to bring one's property rights into as clear a focus as one is able prior to sitting down to negotiate.

Likewise, for spousal support. Typically, courts are directed—by statute or case law—"to ignore marital fault and . . . to base any determination solely on the circumstances of the parties, including the duration of their marriage and the ability of the supported spouse to engage in gainful employment." *In re Marriage of Rosan*, 24 Cal.App.3d 885, 892, 101 Cal.Rptr. 295 (1972), now codified. Modernly, most states have mandatory statutory checklists for determining a spousal support award based on need.

3. DISSOLUTION OF PROPERTY

a. The Theoretical Ideal

As a purely theoretical matter, the dissolution of property interests upon divorce would call for each spouse to acknowledge ownership of separate property and of one-half of the community property as to each asset. By acknowledge, I mean disclose, at least categorically speaking.

Some states require what they term a broad categorical statement of disclosure as part of the dissolution paperwork. A categorical statement of disclosure might take the form of an inventory.

The need to inventory property at the end of a marriage is seasoned by reality as well as, in some states, by judicial mandate. In California, the Judicial Council provides a standardized form that parties have the option to use to inventory community and separate assets. The form is offered to assist the parties in reaching a marriage settlement agreement (MSA), but if the parties cannot do so, the form can be used by the court to carry out an asset-by-asset analysis.

After dissolution, co-ownership of each asset is often not desired. After all, the parties are divorcing each other. But co-ownership is also impractical especially if the family has one or two major assets (the house and a car) and much of their remaining wealth is in non-liquid form, like for example life insurance or retirement plans. See Chapter 7 for more on life insurance and retirement related assets.

Ideally, in a divorce action, the parties and the court would be fully informed about and agree to the disposition of all community assets and liabilities. Liabilities would be assigned fairly, with community liabilities assigned in line with the state law, which often considers ability to pay. After the liabilities were addressed, net community assets would be contractually divided (either equally or equitably) by the parties themselves, in a way that best supports each party's aspirations for exiting the marriage.

Ideally, during the negotiation process, no community property interest or asset would be omitted from the categorical inventory. And disclosure would include key details such that no community property interest, asset or even key potential interest would be left undisclosed. The best practices standard of full disclosure (no property secrets) would be followed by both parties.

In a perfect world, cooperative and full disclosure would be the norm. If there were a lapse in disclosure, a legal mechanism would quickly address that lapse. Full disclosure would be the best practice. Disclosure would be understood and upheld as a process by which parties comes to understand what it is they own, owe, and expect to negotiate around for purposes of a marriage settlement agreement.

In a perfect world, there would be no fraud, duress, perjury, pressure or mistake of law or fact. Each party would be represented by a competent attorney who understands and values principles of property and contract law. Negotiations and consequential documents would be in a language understood by the parties. Adequate translation would be available when needed. Negotiations also would be memorialized in a language in which the parties are proficient.

Where necessary, a comprehensive and fair support award would be negotiated. The support award would pay out long enough to meaningfully assist with retraining, and it would be paid on a timely basis.

These would be the barest of the bare parameters of an outcome in a perfect world. An outcome also perfect for how it enhances veracity, fairness, voluntariness and in so doing facilitates the parties' transition from married to single.

Unfortunately, the ideal situation rarely if ever arises, much less exists

A very short list of factors that compromise the ideal are the following:

- *Concealed assets:* Partial disclosures may be a sign of concealed assets. Intentionally or mistakenly concealed or omitted assets take time to discover and investigate.

- *Vagueness:* When information is vague, it may require the parties to readdress issues at a later point during the dissolution or in a subsequent proceeding.

- *Oral agreements:* Generally, oral agreements are not enforceable.

- *Strong arm tactics:* Coercion, fraud, duress, undue influence, misrepresentations, and domestic violence all are actionable harms.

- *Negligence:* Lack of care for the property being dissolved can impair the community estate and result in actionable harm.

- *Unauthorized gifts or transfers:* Unauthorized gifts to third parties may drain the community property estate and thus constitute an actionable harm.

- *Accounting:* The state has an interest in standardizing accounting methods so that like cases are decided similarly. Importantly, parties can do themselves a favor and save on court costs if they understand at the outset that accounting is not "math for math's sake." Rather, courts (or in some states legislatures) decide on whether a proposed accounting method is acceptable for use in dissolution proceedings.

- *Information asymmetries:* To paraphrase multiple philosophers of the late 20th century, knowledge is power.

A process that diverges from the ideal, increases the cost to parties during the legal process and even after a final court judgment is signed. Impasse, time delays, discovery misconduct, and the like have the potential to lead to formal motions for exclusive control of property, discovery, sanctions, adjudicating omitted assets and the like, including domestic violence restraining orders.

A dissolution, ideally, concludes the affairs of an intimate partnership. Default community property laws, in a sense, might be thought of as time tested methods for facilitating the dissolution process. But as with most property related matters, social, cultural, and psychological factors can turn a process that seems straightforward and even fair on paper into a rocky legal road whose many turns exact a high personal and economic cost from one or both parties at a time when they are in a vulnerable financial position.

b. Separate Property

Some states by statute do not grant a court jurisdiction over the separate property of either spouse unless the spouses otherwise consent.

Even in these states, however, courts have discretion to impose an equitable lien on the separate property of either spouse to either effect a division of the community property or a court-approved reimbursement. The lien on separate property is a device to protect and satisfy the community property interest of the spouse who does not own the separate property asset. Most community property states employ the device liberally by how they permit a court to impose an equitable lien upon either spouse's separate property to carry out dissolution of the community property.

There are many reasons to use a lien on one spouse's existing separate property to protect and secure the other spouse's property interest. Texas allows the court to employ an equitable lien to prevent unjust enrichment. See Chapter 7.

c. Community Property

When the issue is how to divide the community property, U.S. community property states differ in their approach, even if they remain consistent in result.

Most state community property codes give little guidance to the family court (and little basis for appeal from its decision). These state require that the division of the community property shall be "equitable" or "substantially equal" or "just." As discussed above, equitable (or just) is not necessarily an arithmetically equal split. Arizona, Idaho, Washington, and Wisconsin are states that describe relevant factors that a court may consider in dividing the community property equitably. The Wisconsin factors are like the mandatory factors used in California to calculate not property interests, but postdissolution spousal support.

Other states require an equal (fifty-fifty) division, even if the parties end up trading or using offsets. The rationale for an equal division approach is that each spouse holds a present and vested one-half interest in each community property asset as of the date of its acquisition during marriage. When the parties *cannot* agree, then the court shall step in. A court can proceed with the division on an asset-by-asset basis, or in some states on an aggregate (hotchpot) basis. Courts also may have discretion to reach an equitable division as to some assets.

Accounting derives, at least in the common law, from equity, and specifically from the law of trusts. Accounting is not a bureaucratic invention imposed by a judicial council, for example, on the parties. The accounting methods discussed in this book are law, either by statute or by judicial holding. Accounting methods protect each party's due process rights; and the normalization of accounting methods through law protects the due process rights of parties in future dissolutions.

4. LEGAL COMPLICATIONS

a. Concealed Assets

Today, with equal management and control, either spouse has the right to manage community property. Consequently, both spouses are legally obligated to the duties that apply to persons in relationships that are adjudged confidential. In the case of marriage, most community property states follow the rule that a confidential relationship arises on the date of marriage as a matter of law. A few find that the confidential relationship starts as early as the engagement.

States allow an exception to the equal division principle when the concealment of assets is proved or even, in some cases, suspected.

If an asset is omitted from the division of the community because it was concealed, the asset is converted from community property to tenancy in common by the divorce of the parties if it comes to light before the judgment. If the property comes to light after the final judgment is signed, then a party may be left only with the option to file a motion for a postdissolution adjudication of the parties' rights in the omitted asset. Statutory limitations apply. See Chapter 5, *Downer v. Bramet*, supra 229 for an example.

A postdissolution set-aside statute serves three goals when it comes to acts of concealment that meet the definition of fraud. One, it erases the line between extrinsic and intrinsic fraud, a historically problematic distinction that has frustrated attempts to correct judgments procured through deception. Two, it expands the definition of fraud to include perjury, duress, undue influence, and even mistakes of law or fact that the innocent party makes because of the other party's deception or misrepresentation. Three, it extends the statute of limitations for claims by adopting the equitable discovery rule: the injured claimant's cause of action accrues when the misconduct was discovered, a point that can occur long after the final dissolution of judgment.

If the time for a postdissolution judgment adjudication has passed, and the time for all appeals has also passed, it may still be possible for a party to move to set aside the dissolution judgment. Such a motion would be granted for fraud related reasons.

A nonmutual gift to or the sale of an asset to a third person may give rise to an allegation of concealment by one spouse against the other.

b. Final Agreement and Final Judgments

Parties can negotiate a marriage settlement agreement to dissolve and dispose of the community estate. Absent such an agreement, the court shall divide the community between them either along equal or equitable lines, depending on state law, as discussed above.

If the parties do reach a negotiated settlement agreement, the interaction of the court varies from state to state and from action to action. It is desirable to allow parties to settle their own differences, whether through lawyers, mediators, or collaborative law specialists. Yet even when parties are represented by counsel, and especially when one or both are not, courts are understandably wary of the specter of collusive or coerced agreements. Judicial wariness has its source in the balancing of competing policies. For example, the policy against fraud is a strong counterweight to the policy in favor of finality, which is to say the policy in favor of reaching final dissolution judgments.

Assuming the permissibility and fairness of a marriage settlement agreement, a further question arises as to the effect of the court decree upon such an agreement. Is the agreement merged in the decree so that it can be enforced by contempt proceedings? Or is it a contract enforceable by a breach of contract action? Who can change the terms of the executed agreement, the court or the parties? Tax and other consequences have flowed from the answers to these questions.

Finally, because a negotiated settlement agreement assigns net community property to the parties, which is to say assets minus liabilities, creditors have a stake in the proceedings.

Every community property state has a long history of protecting the rights of creditors. In part, protection comes in the technicalities of debt assignment and securitization. The smooth functioning of the economy, at the very least, requires that third parties have confidence when transacting with a married person. Consequently, it is imperative that the policy in favor of finality be furthered absent compelling reasons to re-open or set aside a final judgment of dissolution that is tainted by perjury, fraud, or coercion

c. Difficult to Divide Assets

Generally, for purposes of division, assets are to be valued at the time of dissolution.

The equal (or equitable) division principle applies to all assets, even those that are difficult to divide, value or liquidate. Some assets are difficult to divide because they are commingled. Others are difficult to divide because of valuation or liquidation issues; sometimes, for example, with a business, a formal appraisal can be prohibitively expensive, leaving the parties to cite their personal opinions on the value of the business. Other assets can be difficult to divide because of severe fluctuations in market value.

But sometimes it is a breach of fiduciary duty that makes an asset difficult to divide.

When the problem with division is traced to a breach of fiduciary duty, the question of breach must be answered. An impairment of one spouse's undivided interest in a single asset can negatively impair their interest in the entire community property estate. Thus, the fiduciary duty that arises in one transaction might have broader consequences at dissolution. California statutory provisions, for example, connect the dots between the spouses' fiduciary duty in a transaction, a breach of that duty by one spouse that impairs the other spouse's interest in an asset, and the consequences of that impairment on the entire community property estate. See e.g., Cal.Fam.Code § 1101.

Retirement plans may be difficult to disperse for several reasons. They may not be vested. Or, if vested, they may not be matured. They may also pose problems of management. Sometimes they are difficult to value because of other contingencies. If the retirement benefit is community property and both spouses are entitled to participate in its management and control, then it follows that options given to the employee under the retirement plan belong to both spouses. See Chapter 7 for more on retirement assets.

If an employment related annuity is viewed as property, it is an asset for division upon divorce. This is the common approach. On the other hand, the stream of income produced by the annuity can be viewed as the postdissolution income of one party. Support for the other spouse (or the parties' children) may be ordered, based upon that income right. Care must be taken so that the non-employee spouse is not given two bites of the annuity apple. This could happen if the retirement fund is divided in half and the non-employee is given both the non-employee's half of the annuity and a share of what is viewed of as postdissolution income from the employee's half of the annuity.

Federal law requires that a state court issue a "qualified domestic relations order" (a QDRO for short) in order to direct payments from a pension, annuity, profit-sharing, or stock bonus plan, 26

U.S.C.A. § 414(p), ERISA § 206(d)(3). See Chapter 6 and 12.

Some states exempt federal retirement or disability benefits from the reach of community property laws: Arizona and Louisiana are examples.

Among the options which are likely to be found in retirement plans are the following:

- Disability retirement income in lieu of ordinary retirement income. If the employee is entitled, at his or her election, to receive either *community* property *retirement* benefits *or separate* property *disability* benefits, the court may require the employee to apply the higher disability benefits as if they were retirement income to the extent that retirement benefits would have been received. See Chapter 7.

- Lump sum payment or an annuity. Should the spouses be required to select the same plan or could one spouse (typically the non-employee) cash out (take the lump sum payment option as to his or her community property share) and leave the remainder to the employee spouse as an annuity?

- Self or self-and-survivor (or joint) annuity.

- Whether to retire or to stay employed. Occasionally, a court will order a spouse who elects not to retire to pay benefits to his or her ex-spouse as if retirement had occurred. Such an order gives the non-employee spouse an option as to when to receive otherwise deferred income.

d. Conflict of Laws

The marital or separate property may be outside the jurisdiction of the divorce court.

A court may not enter in rem orders affecting the title to realty outside the forum, but it may enter an in personam order which purports to direct a person over whom the court has personal jurisdiction to convey, transfer or take other action with reference to property, especially realty, located outside the forum.

At the other end of the scale is property acquired outside and later brought to the community property forum state. Several states use the concept of quasi-community property to address the issue.

Paradoxes exist.

State and federal constitutions can be invoked. California and Texas, for example, have developed now widely accepted case law and statutory provisions that protect community property rights. But they also have developed accounting rules to help protect the state constitutional right to own separate property during marriage. Other rights that may be implicated by a division of property are state and federal due process and equal protection.

Competing state fiscal protections and mandates also may be implicated, especially in the case where one spouse exits marriage needing public support for self and children while the other spouse exits with (separate property) assets sufficient to comfortably commence life as a newly single person.

e. Separation

In addition to property rights, another theoretical basis for the equal sharing of the income and property acquired during marriage derives from the support obligation that spouses owe each other during marriage.

Often there is a period of psychological and physical separation of spouses prior to the divorce. If the period from date of separation to a dissolution judgment is very short, the termination point for the community is the date of the judgment. But if the physical separation is long, then readjustment of the community property regime is necessary. In a clear majority of states, after a date of separation the earnings and accumulations of a spouse are characterized as their separate property, as discussed in Chapter 5. Absent an agreement, management and control rights and duties will also adjust, depending on the asset and on the context.

The theoretical basis for voluntarily sharing income and gains weakens considerably after a date of separation. Even so, a creditor may be given a statutory right to reach the earnings of the higher earning spouse as to common necessaries (basic living expenses) in the case of the other spouse's default. See Chapter 9.

5. SPOUSAL SUPPORT

Historically, maintenance derived from two concepts: alimony and spousal support. Alimony was analogous to a pension annuity award to a spouse at the end of a marriage. Spousal support is more in the nature of a temporary award intended to enable the supported spouse to retrain or to find gainful employment. Today, spousal support is the more commonly used of the two support options.

A spousal support award obligates the postdissolution (or post-separation) net income of the supporting former spouse for the benefit of the supported former spouse. The supporting former spouse becomes a debtor, the supported former spouse a creditor with a priority claim to the supporting former spouse's postdissolution (or post-separation) net income. This priority claim is typically limited to a certain time; but within that time, it survives the subsequent marriage or death of the supporting former spouse.

The concept of alimony has a complex and gendered history that developed in tandem with the concept of fault. It is important to understand that community property itself is not a form of alimony.

In Louisiana, for example, prior to 1855, a wife who obtained a divorce was not entitled to alimony. When LSA-C.C. Art. 160 passed in 1855, a court had discretion to grant alimony to the wife out of the husband's property (not including his earnings), but the award had to be predicated on proof of the husband's fault in ending the marriage. Those husbands who were deemed without fault were relieved from any alimony obligation. So were those husbands who were at fault and had an income, but who owned no property. In 1916, the same statute was amended to make alimony payable out of the husband's property *and* earnings. In 1926, alimony was conceptualized as a "pension" to the wife that lasted unless and until the wife contracted a subsequent valid marriage; here again, alimony had to be predicated on proof of the husband's fault.

As alimony got culturally and legally delinked from fault, alimony began to be understood as an extension of the spousal support obligation, not as a pension paid out by a guilty male spouse to an innocent female spouse. At first, the support obligation was conceived of as a lifelong one. Today, alimony, now more accurately called postdissolution spousal support, is understood as a temporary award. Its purpose is to assist the supported former spouse, whatever their gender with education, job (re)training, and employment.

A spousal support award is satisfied with the supporting former spouse's individual (postdissolution) property, income, earnings, accumulations, and other forms of wealth. The supported former spouse typically receives monthly payments.

Spousal support obligates individual property rather than community property because it is, by definition, paid after the final judgment of dissolution is signed by a judge—a judgment that also returns both parties to the status of single individuals

In the language of business statements, at dissolution, each soon-to-be-ex-spouse in a community property partnership is given his or her equal (or equitable, depending on the jurisdiction) ownership share in the *assets* that are inventoried on the balance sheet of the partnership at the end of the marriage. These assets represent the amount of income received during the marriage that was not consumed for community expenses. But while *assets* are distributed to the spouses by halves, subject to the rights of secured creditors, a spousal support award consists of the supported ex-spouse's right to the future *net income* of the supporting ex-spouse, even if the supporting spouse remarries.

Spouses do not necessarily exit marriage on an equal financial footing. Therefore, whatever the arguments for or against, the right to petition for postdissolution spousal support exists and continues to be necessary even in a community property system. It is not a right that should be waived lightly, and in some states, it is not a right that even can be waived without legal representation.

Statutory changes have made the spousal support obligation gender neutral. Community property systems recognize the housekeeper as a contributor to the acquisition of community assets during marriage. See Chapter 1. Even so, leaving a marriage with assets must ultimately be distinguished from leaving a marriage with a secure earning capacity.

When a housekeeper spouse contributes to the marital partnership, the community property division recognizes her or his contribution as one that, depending on the circumstances of the marriage, enhanced not just the home but also family wealth. A spousal support award recognizes that the housekeeper spouse, now the former supported spouse, may need assistance to transition back to the formal work economy.

Depending on the state, a spousal support award might also recognize the contribution that the housekeeper spouse made to the employed spouse's human capital during the marriage. Human capital is personal to its holder; it cannot be practicably divided at dissolution. Nevertheless, a spousal support award goes a (very) modest distance in two directions. The first is toward recognizing the former housekeeper spouse's contribution to the house, the home, the care of the children, and the enhancement of the supporting former spouse's career and human capital development. The second is toward assisting the former housekeeper spouse in developing the human capital they now need to support themselves as a single person.

C. INDIVIDUAL STATES

1. ARIZONA

Arizona is a no-fault equitable division state.

Ariz.Rev.Stat.Ann. § 25–318 authorizes, upon dissolution of the marriage or legal separation, an equitable (and therefore not necessarily equal) division the community property. The authorization extends also to property owned by the spouses concurrently with each other.

Fault is not relevant for the division. That said, Arizona is a no-fault state that has adopted legislation to permit covenant marriage as a way for parties to opt out of no-fault divorce. Ending a covenant marriage requires fault-based grounds found at Ariz.Rev.Stat.Ann. § 25–903.

Arizona does not permit the divorce court to award the separate property of one spouse to the other. However, upon request, liens may be imposed on one spouse's separate property for reimbursement or to secure payment of support obligations.

Ariz.Rev.Stat.Ann. § 25–318(E) authorizes liens on separate property or the marital property awarded to either party for:

(1) Any interest or equity the other party has in or to such property.

(2) Community debts that the court has ordered to be paid by the parties.

(3) An allowance for child support spousal maintenance or both.

(4) All actual damages and judgments from conduct that results in criminal conviction of either spouses in which the other spouse or child was the victim.

Provision is specifically made in Ariz.Rev.Stat.Ann. § 25–318(A) for quasi-community property, which is defined as **"property acquired by either spouse outside of this state . . . if the property would have been community property if acquired in this state."**

The key portion of Ariz.Rev.Stat.Ann. § 25–318 is a no-fault provision: **"[i]n a proceeding for dissolution of the marriage, or for legal separation, . . . the court shall assign each spouse's sole and separate property to such spouse. It shall also divide the community, joint tenancy and other property held in common equitably, though not necessarily in kind, without regard to marital misconduct. . . ."**

2. CALIFORNIA

California is an equal division state. However, the Family Law court is a court of law and equity with considerable discretion. Identifying and implementing alternatives to adversarial divorce litigation is and has been a strong legislative policy. Cal.Fam.Code § 2013 states the goal of such a preference as being **"to resolve disputes . . . on an agreed basis without resorting to adversary judicial intervention."**

A negotiated marriage settlement agreement (MSA) is the preferred method for dissolving a community estate. But if the parties reach an impasse, adversarial intervention to obtain judicial help is the next step forward. Parties who own a modest community estate, defined as not exceeding

$50,000, can be submitted by the court for arbitration. Cal.Fam.Code § 2554

California is a no-fault divorce state that also permits unilateral divorce. Cal.Fam.Code § 2335 provides: **"Except as otherwise provided by statute, in a pleading or proceeding for dissolution of marriage or legal separation of the parties, including depositions and discovery proceedings, evidence of specific acts of misconduct is improper and inadmissible."**

Dissolution or legal separation may be based on one of two grounds. **"Irreconcilable differences,"** meaning **"the irremediable breakdown of the marriage",** is one ground. The second is **"[p]ermanent legal incapacity,"** meaning medical or psychiatric proof that **"the spouse was at the time the petition was filed, and remains, permanently lacking the legal capacity to make decisions."** Cal.Fam.Code § 2310 and § 2312. A judgment of nullity is an option for any void or voidable marriage. One main reason to require a judgment of nullity for a void marriage is to provide third parties with notice of the nonexistence of the marriage.

In a private negotiated settlement process, the parties are entitled to use different disclosure standards than those that appear in the Family Code. Typically, in private hearings, parties agree to (summary) disclosure standards that are lower than the standards found in the Family Code. Lower disclosure standards may cause continuing problems in the division of property, especially if the parties have also agreed (as is often the case with arbitration) to waive the right to appeal.

Property agreements are final, absent an expanded definition of fraud found at Cal.Fam.Code § 2122.

Support agreements are modifiable and severable unless the parties specifically agree otherwise. Spousal support is calculated by a mandatory fourteen-point statutory list found at Cal.Fam.Code § 4320.

The court has jurisdiction over community property and quasi-community property; the parties may also request that the court divide any separate property interests held by the parties, in another jurisdiction in joint tenancy or tenancy in common. Cal.Fam.Code § 2660. California has a special community property presumption that applies in a dissolution proceeding to jointly titled assets, as discussed in Chapter 4 and Chapter 6. The intersection between community property and separate property concurrent titles is discussed in Chapter 6.

Valuation is as of the time of trial. Cal.Fam.Code § 2552.

When dissolution involves the rights of a third party who is not a creditor, the concern is with the third party's due process rights (notice and the opportunity to be heard) relative to the dissolution proceeding. This issue is discussed in *Muckle v.*

Superior Court, 102 Cal.App.4th 218, 125 Cal.Rptr.2d 303 (2002).

"During the continuance of the marriage," the spouses' interests in community property are **"present, existing, and equal."** Cal.Fam.Code § 751. At dissolution, Cal.Fam.Code § 2550 restates the equal division principle in cases where parties cannot agree on division for purposes of dissolution. **"Except upon the written agreement of the parties, or on oral stipulation of the parties in open court, or as otherwise provided in this division, in a proceeding for dissolution of marriage or for legal separation of the parties, the court shall, either in its judgment of dissolution of the marriage, in its judgment decreeing the legal separation of the parties, or at a later time if it expressly reserves jurisdiction to make such a property division, *divide the community estate of the parties equally*."** (Italics added.)

Among the numerous statutory exceptions to the general concept of equal division of community property *at dissolution* (as opposed to during the marriage) are the following:

- *Economic circumstances*: The court may award an asset entirely to one party **"[w]here economic circumstances warrant ... on such conditions as the court deems proper to effect a substantially equal division of the community estate."** Cal.Fam.Code § 2601.

- *Deliberate misappropriation*: An additional award or offset is possible if the court determines that one party has **"deliberately misappropriated"** a part of the community estate **"to the exclusion of the interest of the other party in the community estate."** Cal.Fam.Code § 2602.

- *Personal injury claims that arose during the marriage*: Money and property received in settlement of a personal injury claim that arose during the marriage, defined in Cal.Fam.Code § 2603(b) are subject to a mandatory assignment rule at dissolution. Such money and property **"shall be assigned to the party who suffered the injuries unless the court, after taking into account the economic condition and needs of each party, the time that has elapsed since the recovery of the damages or the accrual of the cause of action, and all other facts of the case, determines that the interests of justice require another disposition."** If a court deviates from the mandatory assignment rule, **"at least one-half of the damages shall be assigned to the party who suffered the injuries."** Cal.Fam.Code § 2603(b).

- *A default judgment involving a small estate*: A net community estate of less than five thousand dollars ($5,000) may be awarded entirely to one spouse if the other spouse cannot be located **"through the exercise of**

reasonable diligence." Cal.Fam.Code § 2604.

- *A deferred sale of the family home*: A family home sale may be deferred by a court order that awards, to the custodial parent, temporary exclusive use and possession of the family home. The order can defer sale during the minority of a child or children, or, in the case of an adult dependent with disabilities, if the dependent adult requires continuing support. Cal.Fam.Code § 3800 through § 3808 set forth the basis for a deferred sale of a family home order. A court has authority to consider economic and noneconomic criteria in exercise its discretion. Cal.Fam.Code § 3801 codifies the decision in *Marriage of Stallworth*, 192 Cal.App.3d 742, 237 Cal.Rptr. 829 (1987).

Detailed provisions for the allocation of debts are contained in Cal.Fam.Code § 2620, et seq. The provisions generally correspond to what parties might expect. However, pursuant to Cal.Fam.Code § 2622 **"[t]o the extent that the community debts exceed community and quasi-community assets, the excess debt shall be assigned as the court deems just and equitable, taking into account factors such as the parties' relative ability to pay."** In essence, this provision means two things. One, each party's separate property or future (postdissolution) income may be liable for obligations incurred during marriage. And two, a party who has a greater relative ability to repay creditors can expect to be assigned a greater share of the debt at dissolution.

A special reimbursement statute can be found at Cal.Fam.Code § 2641. This statute returns to the community, with interest, a reimbursement for eligible contributions to the direct costs of an income enhancing education or training of a spouse. The same provision mandatorily assigns **"educational debt"** to the student spouse. The spouses can modify the assignment by agreement. Community contributions to indirect expenses are calculated into a postdissolution spousal support award under Cal.Fam.Code § 4320. This reimbursement is due when the education or training is income enhancing and the spouses were not married long enough to benefit from the education or training. To benefit means to realize the enhanced earnings by using them to acquire property that can be divided at the end of the marriage.

California does not permit the divorce court to award the separate property of one spouse to the other. Nevertheless, liens may be imposed against separate property to secure a reimbursement, or payment of a support obligation. *Fox v. Fox*, 18 Cal.2d 645, 117 P.2d 325 (1941).

California has two community property analogs. *Quasi-community property* and quasi-marital property.

Quasi-community property definitions are found in the California Family Code and in the California Probate Code. The basic theme of each definition is that quasi-community property is property that the parties would have held as California community property had they been domiciled in state when the property was acquired. The definition of quasi-community property given for the purposes of dissolution is found at Cal.Fam.Code § 125; the definition for probate purposes is found at Cal.Prob.Code § 66. See Chapter 4.

For dissolution purposes, quasi-community property is treated as if it were California community property. Cal.Fam.Code § 125 provides: "**'Quasi-community property" means all real or personal property, wherever situated, heretofore or hereafter acquired in any of the following ways:**

(a) By either spouse while domiciled elsewhere which would have been community property if the spouse who acquired the property had been domiciled in this state at the time of its acquisition.

(b) In exchange for real or personal property, wherever situated, which would have been community property if the spouse who acquired the property so exchanged had been domiciled in this state at the time of its acquisition."

Additionally, California, at times and in select provisions, uses the concept of the community estate, which is a broader concept than that of community property. " '**Community estate' includes both the community property and quasi-community property.**" Cal.Fam.Code § 63.

Quasi-marital property appears in the family code. This is property that a person adjudged as a putative spouse can petition the court to divide as if it were community property. Quasi-marital property is defined as "**. . . that property acquired during the union that would have been community or quasi-community property if the union had not been void or voidable, only upon request of a party who is declared a putative spouse under paragraph (1).**" Cal.Fam.Code § 2251(a)(2).

The putative spouse doctrine is discussed in Chapter 12.

If, after all efforts to reach an equal division of the community estate, an asset is omitted, a party can bring a motion for postdissolution adjudication. Personal jurisdiction is required over the defendant because any such judicial action would be wholly independent from the original dissolution proceeding. The defenses of laches and res judicata apply, as do statutory limitations.

The link between property characterization and separation is discussed in Chapter 5.

3. IDAHO

Absent compelling reasons, equal division is the rule in Idaho, which is a no-fault divorce state. In dividing the property, the court weighs factors set out in Idaho Code § 32–712:

"In case of divorce by the decree of a court of competent jurisdiction, the community property and the homestead must be assigned as follows:

1. The community property must be assigned by the court in such proportions as the court, from all the facts of the case and the conditions of the parties, deems just, with due consideration of the following factors:

(a) Unless there are compelling reasons otherwise, there shall be a substantially equal division in value, considering debts, between the spouses.

(b) Factors which may bear upon whether a division shall be equal, or the manner of division, include, but are not limited to:

(1) Duration of the marriage;

(2) Any antenuptial agreement of the parties; provided, however, that the court shall have no authority to amend or rescind any such agreement;

(3) The age, health, occupation, amount and source of income, vocational skills, employability, and liabilities of each spouse;

(4) The needs of each spouse;

(5) Whether the apportionment is in lieu of or in addition to maintenance;

(6) The present and potential earning capability of each party; and

(7) Retirement benefits, including, but not limited to, social security, civil service, military and railroad retirement benefits."

Idaho does not permit the court to award the separate property of one spouse to the other, but liens may be imposed against separate property for reimbursement or to secure payment of support obligations. *Radermacher v. Radermacher*, 61 Idaho 261, 100 P.2d 955 (1940).

Among the community property states, reciprocal duties of (extended) family support were recognized in Idaho Code § 32–1002 up until 2011, when those code sections were repealed. A similar statutory responsibility existed at Idaho Code § 32–1008A for nursing home costs, but that section was also repealed not too long ago.

In *Jones v. State*, 85 Idaho 135, 376 P.2d 361 (1962), where both parents were found unfit for the custody of their children and financially irresponsible, the trial court exercised its discretion and authority in the parents' divorce action to establish a trust of community property to support and educate the children. The trust was subject to continuing supervision of the court.

Idaho allows a homestead to be assigned either from community property or from one spouse's separate property. If assigned from community property, the homestead can be assigned absolutely or for a limited period. Absolute assignments will be factored into the ultimate distribution of the community property. If the homestead is assigned from separate property, the homestead **"must be assigned to the former owner . . . subject to the power of the court to assign it for a limited period to the other spouse."** Idaho Code § 32–712.

4. LOUISIANA

Louisiana is a no-fault equal division of community property state with procedures for a regime of separation of property by which the parties (or one member for cause) agree (or obtain a judgment) that the community regime shall not arise or shall cease to exist. See LSA-C.C. Art. 2370 through Art. 2376. The protective nature of this procedure (the non-voluntary form) can be inferred from the causes for which a judgment of separate property regime can be obtained. A judgment decreeing separation of property is permitted when **"a community property regime is threatened to be diminished by the fraud, fault, neglect, or incompetence of the other spouse, or by the disorder of the affairs of the other spouse . . ."** The judgment **"terminates the regime of community property retroactive to the day of the filing of the petition or motion . . ."**

In Louisiana, divorce is by petition of either spouse.

A separation from bed and board (called a date of separation in other states) must first be obtained before an absolute divorce can be obtained. Proof of separation from bed and board is available for couples who do not want to live together but who want to remain married. Separation from bed and board immediately terminates the community regime and entitles the parties to move for division of the community property, but it does not allow the parties to validly remarry. Each spouse retains the status of married rather than a single person.

A divorce shall be granted if the spouses have been living apart for a statutory time period of either 180 days if there are no minor children of the marriage (or 365 days if there are) (LSA-C.C. Art. 103.1), or because of adultery or conviction of a felony and sentence to death or imprisonment at hard labor. LSA-C.C. Art. 103. Obviously, proof that the statutory period was met requires establishing a clear date of separation.

Covenant marriage is available in Louisiana. In a covenant marriage, the grounds for separation from bed and board are found at LSA-R.S. Art. 9:307. Those grounds are adultery; conviction of a felony and sentence to death or imprisonment at hard labor; abandonment; physical or sexual abuse of the spouse seeking the divorce or of a child of one of the spouses; living apart for extended period of times without reconciliation. In a covenant marriage, a prerequisite to a divorce or to a separation from bed and board is that the parties must seek counseling.

5. NEVADA

Nevada is a no-fault equal division of community property state.

In awarding alimony and adjudicating property rights, the divorce court **"shall, to the extent practicable, make an equal disposition of community property,"** but the court is also given discretion to make a **"just"** disposition **"if the court finds a compelling reason to do so and sets forth in writing the reasons for making the unequal disposition."** Nev.Rev.Stat. § 125.150(1)(b). Cases point to financial misconduct as a compelling reason for an unequal division. Retirement benefits are discussed in § 125.150(c).

Nevada once had a national reputation for a relaxed attitude toward divorce, primarily because of its six-week residency requirement for establishing domicile. Nev.Rev.Stat. § 125.020. The state grants divorces upon grounds of incompatibility, living apart for one year, or insanity. Nev.Rev.Stat. § 125.010.

The court has jurisdiction over and power to divide property placed in joint tenancy. Nev.Rev.Stat. § 125.150(2). This statute was amended in 2013.

A limited power over separate property as a source for alimony is given in Nev.Rev.Stat. § 125.150, the relevant portion of which reads:

"In granting a divorce, the court may also set apart such portion of the separate property of either spouse for the other spouse's support, the wife's separate property for the husband's support or the separate property of either spouse for the support of their children as is deemed just and equitable."

6. NEW MEXICO

New Mexico is a no-fault equal division state.

The division of property is governed by N.M.Stat.Ann. § 40–4–7 B.(3)(a) and (4)(1978), which also gives the divorce court power to order alimony in a single sum or in installments out of a spouse's separate property. An additional provision says the divorce court to **"may set apart out of the property or income of the respective parties such portion for the maintenance and education of: (a) their unemancipated minor children as may seem just and proper; or (b) their children until the children's graduation from high school, if the children are emancipated only by age, are under nineteen and are attending high school. . . ."** The statute, which also covers guardianship in N.M.Stat.Ann 40–4–7 C. does not specifically permit an unequal division of the community property upon divorce, and precedent appears to require equal division of the community property, *Michelson v. Michelson*, 86 N.M. 107, 520 P.2d 263 (1974).

New Mexico has two statutory procedures for ending the community. (N.M.Stat.Ann. § 40–4–1 A.

and B. **"A. incompatibility between the parties to the marriage; or B. the marriage is void, voidable or invalid."**

The second is division of property without a dissolution of marriage (N.M.Stat.Ann. § 40–4–3 (1978).

Incompatibility is defined in N.M.Stat.Ann. § 40–4–2 (1978): **"Incompatibility exists between the parties when, because of discord or conflict of personalities there exists no expectation of reconciliation."** This standard can be used to establish date of separation.

7. TEXAS

Texas is a no-fault equal division state. V.T.C.A.Fam.Code § 6.001. Even so, cruelty, adultery, conviction of a felony, abandonment, living apart without cohabitation for at least three years, and confinement in a mental hospital are all grounds for divorce, even if seldom used. Fraud, duress, or force in inducing a person to marry, concealed divorce, and conducting a marriage ceremony within the 72-hour waiting period following the issuance of the marriage license are all grounds for an annulment. V.T.C.A.Fam.Code §§ 6.002 through 6.110.

Additionally, to facilitate the legal process, a court, on the parties' or on its own motion, may refer a suit for dissolution or mediation; or the parties may agree to a collaborative law process. V.T.C.A.Fam.Code §§ 6.602.

A court may not order spousal support that remains, depending on the circumstances, in effect five, seven, or ten **"years after the date of the order."** V.T.C.A.Fam.Code § 8.054(1). Five years support is permitted if the spouses were married less than 10 years but not more than 20 years. Seven years support is permitted if the spouses were married to each other for at least 20 years but not more than 30 years. And ten years is permitted if the spouses were married for thirty years or more.

Once eligibility for spousal support is established, a court V.T.C.A.Fam.Code § 8.054(2) says that a court **"*shall* limit the duration of a maintenance order to the *shortest reasonable period* that allows the spouse seeking maintenance to earn sufficient income to provide for the spouse's *minimum reasonable needs*, ..."** (Italics added.) A court can make exceptions for a disabled spouse, a spouse who has custodianship of an infant or young child, or another **"compelling impediment to earning sufficient income to provide for the spouse's minimum reasonable needs."**

There are exceptions for a disabled spouse, and for a spouse who will care for infant or disabled children, but even these exceptions are limited in duration. The flexibility lost by the three-year limitation on spousal support is partly recaptured (when there are assets as opposed to earning power) by allowing the divorce court to divide the quasi-community property and community property as **"the court deems just and right, having due regard for the rights of each party and any children of the marriage."**

V.T.C.A.Fam.Code § 7.001. The duration of spousal support appears to be one of the most litigated sections in the Texas Family Code.

Texas has further reduced the chance of spousal support because it does not permit the court to divest either spouse of the title to separate real estate. The code section for this proposition (V.T.C.A.Fam.Code § 3.63 was repealed, but precedent may continue to hold. *Cameron v. Cameron*, 641 S.W.2d 210 (Tex. 1992) extends the rule to separate personalty, though the case has some negative treatment. Plus, the Texas Constitution protects the right to own separate property during marriage.

Liens may be imposed against separate property to secure a reimbursement or payment of support obligations. Moreover, the statutory protection of separate property from divorce obligations has been weakened by cases permitting the court to award one spouse a homestead for life in the separate property of the other spouse, and authorizing subjection of the income, rents, or revenues of the separate real estate to the support of the other spouse or to the education and support of the children. *Hedtke v. Hedtke*, 112 Tex. 404, 248 S.W. 21 (1923). *Burney v. Burney*, 225 S.W.3d 208 (Tex.App. 2006) and *Motley v. Motley*, 390 S.W.3d 689 (2012) are related cases. The homestead is recognized in the state constitution.

The community property system is modifiable by contract. Parties have the right to enter into a property settlement agreement that provides for extended or conditional spousal support payments that replicate something akin to long term alimony.

8. WASHINGTON

Washington is a no-fault state that mandates a **"just and equitable"** division. Wash.Rev.Code § 26.09.080 factors for the court's consideration are set forth as follows:

> **"In a proceeding for dissolution of the marriage or domestic partnership, legal separation ... the court shall, without regard to marital misconduct, make such disposition of the property and the liabilities of the parties, either community or separate, as shall appear just and equitable after considering all relevant factors including, but not limited to:**
>
> **(1) The nature and extent of the community property;**
>
> **(2) The nature and extent of the separate property;**
>
> **(3) The duration of the marriage or domestic partnership; and**
>
> **(4) The economic circumstances of each spouse or domestic partner at the time the division of property is to become effective, including the desirability of awarding the family home or the right to live therein for reasonable periods to a spouse or domestic partner with whom the children reside the majority of the time."**

Washington grants a no-fault dissolution of marriage or legal separation upon a finding that the marriage is irretrievably broken. Wash.Rev.Code § 26.09.030. A petitioner must be a Washington resident, a member of the armed forces stationed in Washington, or married to someone who fits one of the above two categories. The parties to a marriage may enter into a separation contract to dispose of any property owned by both or either of them under Wash.Rev.Code § 26.09.070. This same provision authorizes the recording and publishing of notice of such a contract.

9. WISCONSIN

Wisconsin is a no-fault equal division state, but the court has discretion to divide the property equitably, as discussed below.

In Wisconsin, a court may grant a judgment of divorce or legal separation only upon finding that a marriage is **"irretrievably broken."** Wis.Stat. § 767.35 and § 767.315(1).

The court shall divide the property of the parties. **"Upon every judgment of annulment, divorce or legal separation, or in rendering a judgment in an action [for property division], the court shall divide the property of the parties.** Wis.Stat. § 767.61(1) (effective 2021).

Wis.Stat. § 767.61(2) (effective 2021) identifies property that is not subject to this mandate.

Wis.Stat. § 767.61(3) (effective 2021) as to the property enumerated in (a) and (m) below:

"The court shall presume that all property not described in sub 2(a) is to be divided equally between the parties, but may alter this distribution without regard to marital misconduct after considering all of the following: . . . .

(a) The length of the marriage.

(b) The property brought to the marriage by each party.

(c) Whether one of the parties has substantial assets not subject to division by the court.

(d) The contribution of each party to the marriage, giving appropriate economic value to each party's contribution in homemaking and child care services.

(e) The age and physical and emotional health of the parties.

(f) The contribution by one party to the education, training or increased earning power of the other.

(g) The earning capacity of each party, including educational background, training, employment skills, work experience, length of absence from the job market, custodial responsibilities for children and the time and expense necessary to acquire sufficient education or training to enable the party to become self-supporting at a standard of living reasonably comparable to that enjoyed during the marriage.

(h) The desirability of awarding the family home or the right to live therein for a reasonable period to the party having physical placement for the greater period of time.

(i) The amount and duration of an order . . . granting maintenance payments to either party, any order for periodic family support payments . . . and whether the property division is in lieu of such payments.

(j) Other economic circumstances of each party, including pension benefits, vested or unvested, and future interests.

(k) The tax consequences to each party.

(*l*) Any written agreement made by the parties before or during the marriage concerning any arrangement for property distribution; such agreements shall be binding upon the court except that no such agreement shall be binding where the terms of the agreement are inequitable as to either party. The court shall presume any such agreement to be equitable as to both parties.

(m) Such other factors as the court may in each individual case determine to be relevant."

(Italics added.)

Disclosure of **"all assets owned in full or in part by either party separately or by the parties jointly"** is required. See Wis.Stat. § 767.127(1).

The discovery of concealed property after entry of a judgment dividing the spouses' property is dealt with by imposition of a constructive trust. Wis.Stat. § 767.127(5) provides: **"Failure to disclose; constructive trust. If a party intentionally or negligently fails to disclose information required . . . and as a result any asset with a *fair market value of $500* or more is omitted from the final distribution of property, the party aggrieved by the nondisclosure may at any time petition the court granting the annulment, divorce or legal separation to declare the creation of a constructive trust as to all undisclosed assets, for the benefit of the parties and their minor or dependent children, if any, with the party in whose name the assets are held declared the constructive trustee. The trust shall include such terms and conditions as the court may determine. The court shall grant the petition upon a finding of a failure to disclose assets as required. . . ."** (Italics added.)

CHAPTER 11

DEATH

A. OVERVIEW

When a marriage ends by the death of a spouse, the community's ability to acquire property ends. At that point, the decedent spouse's probate estate comes into existence. The term probate estate is used here to indicate the assets of a decedent that are subject to the scheme of distribution under state probate administration laws.

1. THE DECEDENT'S ESTATE

The probate estate includes the property owned by the decedent at death. Excluded from the probate estate are assets that do not belong to the decedent and assets which are disposed of by other means, such as by right of survivorship or by inter vivos gift.

Alternatives to probate administration include joint tenancy (which passes to the surviving joint tenant), the trust, and life insurance (each of which would pass to the designated beneficiary or beneficiaries). These alternatives are discussed in previous chapters.

State probate law determines how a decedent's estate is distributed.

The assets of the decedent's probate estate are consumed to pay debts or distributed.

The order of payment is as follows.

- Taxes are paid first.
- Expenses and debts of administration are paid second.
- The set aside of homestead property, exempt property, the elective share of the spouse (in a common law state), and any family allowance to the surviving spouse or dependent children or both are paid.
- Beneficiaries designated by a valid will (which includes codicils) or those indicated as substitute beneficiaries in cases involving lapse, renunciation, or other circumstances affecting the distribution of testate estates receive their gifts.
- Heirs (intestate takers) or those indicated as substitutes for heirs (in cases involving renunciation or other circumstances affecting the devolution of intestate estates) take their statutory share of any property that is disposed of through the state intestacy statute.

If there are no beneficiaries or heirs, the decedent's property escheats to the state.

In some states, family protections are or may be paid before the debts of creditors are paid. See for example Texas, discussed below.

Only those assets that are left over after the exhaustion of the preceding categories pass to subsequent categories. Thus, a decedent's spouse or children or both may exhaust a small probate estate by taking exempt property or a family allowance. A person could die with assets insufficient to pay all creditors and nothing would pass to his or her will beneficiaries. A valid will that effectively disposes of the entire estate to will beneficiaries who are not also intestate heirs could deprive the intestate heirs of any inheritance.

Uniform Probate Code 1969 (the UPC for short) or the amended UPC (1989 and 1990) has been adopted by eighteen states. Some of these states have adopted the UPC in its entirety. Others have adopted the UPC with significant modifications.

Of the U.S. community property states, Arizona (adopted 1973), Idaho (adopted 1971), and New Mexico (adopted 1975) have adopted versions of the revised UPC (1989 or 1990). California imports individual sections of the UPC for certain issues. Details about the UPC, original or revised, are outside the scope of this Nutshell.

2. COMMUNITY PROPERTY VARIATIONS

In a community property state, the death of a married person terminates the community and the community character of property.

A note on terminology: A decedent spouse's community property share is "former community property" rather than community property. Nevertheless, for efficiency of expression, here, former community property is called community property.

For a person who is married at their death, only the separate property of the decedent and his or her one-half of the community property should fall in the probate estate.

If property in joint title form was determined to be community property, then probate administration (and liability for taxes, expenses of administration, and debts) necessarily follows upon the death of one of the owners. If the property is truly joint tenancy with the right of survivorship, community property with the right of survivorship, or (as in Wisconsin) survivorship marital property, that titled asset passes by right of survivorship. Survivorship property is nonprobate and, therefore, not included in the decedent's probate estate.

Liability of a probate estate for debts usually follows the same rules as the liability of the community for debts during the marriage. However, some states impose a greater liability upon the community half of a decedent for his or her separate debts.

The right of the surviving spouse to family allowance is a family protection. It is a continuation of the obligation of support during marriage owed by one spouse to the other. The family allowance also alleviates economic difficulties caused by the termination of the marriage by death. The concept of exempt property and homestead is discussed in

Chapter 6. The homestead idea has been adopted in one form or another by almost all the states.

In addition to third party creditors, a married person may die leaving the surviving spouse as a creditor. The basis for a surviving spouse's claim can be a tort judgment, a community property impairment claim, a pro rata share of a separate property asset, a claim for reimbursement of community funds used to make capital improvements to the separate property of the decedent, or any other reimbursement allowed by state law.

The net probate estate is what remains after payment of taxes, administration expenses, debts and family support priority items are satisfied. The net probate estate is distributed in accordance with the effective provisions of the decedent's last will (including any codicils). Assuming that the character of the property has been determined to be community, there are two areas where litigation tends to occur:

a. Provisions made by the decedent's will are less generous to the surviving spouse than are the intestacy statutes.

b. The decedent attempts to dispose of more than he or she is entitled to dispose of by will or attempts to impose conditions or restrictions upon the share that the surviving spouse is entitled to receive outright and in kind.

B. DETAIL

1. PROBATE ADMINISTRATION OF COMMUNITY PROPERTY

Administration of the estate of a decedent (loosely called "probate" after the proof of a will) is the process by which a personal representative (executor or administrator) is appointed by the local court to gather the assets of the decedent, to pay taxes, administration expenses and debts, and to distribute the estate to the decedent's will beneficiaries or heirs. The probate process is also used to prove or clear title to assets. Probate administration provides a legal forum in which the community or separate character of property can be determined. Probate administration has not been popular with the ultimate takers of the probate estate because of the length of processing time and the possibility of estate shrinkage, the latter being caused largely by administration expenses, including attorney fees.

Some states, including California, attempt to alleviate the problem of overly long processing times. Those states either allow summary probate estate proceedings or else hold that probate is not necessary under certain circumstances. Cal.Prob.Code § 13000 et seq. Texas and Washington were leaders in this movement with the concept of the independent executor who qualified with, and reported a list of assets to, the probate court, but then operated informally, meaning independent of probate court supervision. The UPC allows both formal and informal probate administration.

Each combination has advantages. If the community property is entirely included in the probate administration, proof of title and collection of debts are simplified. If only the decedent's half of the community is included, the equal ownership of each spouse is recognized. If probate administration is completely avoided, there are savings in time and cost for the surviving spouse, but less protection for the creditors and will beneficiaries.

a. Administration of Community Property

The functions of the personal representative duplicate some, but not all, of the functions of the manager of community property.

Many of the community property states have not, and some still do not, require probate administration of the community property, especially when the decedent's half of the community property passes by intestacy to the surviving spouse.

b. Present Rules for the Administration of Community Property

The UPC permits less formal probate procedures when simplicity, rather than protection, appears appropriate.

The trend is to define small probate estates by statute to allow for informal probate in those cases.

High net worth estates will almost always require probate, even if only to wrap-up stray assets not covered by trusts and non-probate transfers.

2. FORCED ELECTIONS AND FAMILY PROTECTIONS

In the U.S. community property states, a decedent spouse cannot disinherit the surviving spouse of community property. This is because community property is owned by the spouses in halves. Nevertheless, the decedent can posthumously put financial pressure on the surviving spouse to decide whether to take under or against the decedent's will.

a. Taking Under the Decedent's Will

A forced election scenario happens when the decedent spouse purports to use a will to devise the surviving spouse's share of the community property in exchange for substitute provisions. If the surviving spouse acquiesces to the substitution(s), then he or she takes in accordance with the deceased spouse's will. If not, the surviving spouse must formally renounce the will and take the decedent's property under the state intestacy laws.

Most community property states declare that the surviving spouse is entitled to one-half of each asset, outright and in kind. Therefore, the testator forces the surviving spouse to an election when the testator manifests the clear intent to devise either the entire interest in a community asset (or, in some states, more than one-half of the aggregate community wealth) to a nonspousal beneficiary in exchange for other devises made in the will to the surviving spouse. A state may look to the total aggregate amount received by the surviving spouse before declaring that the survivor is forced to elect.

Another way to force an election is for the testator to put limitations on property that belongs to the surviving spouse. This happens, for example, if surviving spouse's community one-half is placed into an irrevocable trust (usually paired with the testator's half of the community for more efficient management of the whole). Indeed, the forced election has been used consensually in estate tax planning. Some of the tax importance has been reduced by the federal estate tax unlimited marital deduction and upward changing values of the unified credit.

If forced to an election, the surviving spouse may either take the property that would transfer by the will to him or her (thus electing to allow his or her share of the community property to pass in accordance with the deceased spouse's will) or retain his or her share of the property and relinquish all inconsistent gifts under the decedent spouse's will.

What is an inconsistent gift?

Courts often indulge in the presumption that the testator intended to dispose only a portion of the property which he or she owned, i.e., his or her one-half of the community, if the asset is community property. A bequest of "my automobile" is often construed as "my community property interest in our automobile." A bequest of "one-half of my estate to my brother, the other half to my wife" may be construed to give the brother one fourth of the community property since the decedent had the right to dispose of only the decedent's one-half of the community estate.

If this presumption is not raised or if the language of the will is too clearly indicative of an unmistakable intention to dispose of property which was not entirely the decedent's own, then the decedent spouse's will may be deemed to force the surviving spouse to an election.

b. Taking Against the Decedent's Will

Theoretically, the vested nature of the community property interest protects the surviving spouse from disinheritance. Even so, family protections are an important part of any community property system.

If the decedent's will does not make adequate provision for the surviving spouse, he or she also may assert the right to take a specified fraction of the estate, or additional assets up to that fraction of the estate. When this protection is invoked, the surviving spouse is said to take *against* the provisions of the will. (The UPC permits the surviving spouse to take a share of an "augmented estate," meaning an estate defined by the UPC for the purpose of supporting the surviving spouse.)

3. INTESTACY STATUTES

Succession statutes apply when a decedent dies intestate. A person dies intestate in any one of the following situations.

- The person dies without a valid will.
- The person dies with a valid will that disposes of only part of the decedent's property.

- The person dies with a will that disposes of all the decedent's property, but the will is (only) partly valid.

State intestacy statutes mandate how an intestate estate will be distributed.

In community property states, when a married decedent dies intestate, (only) one-half of the community property but all the separate property descends through the state intestacy statute. In all community property states except Arizona, different disposition schemes exist for community as opposed to separate property.

In a community property state, the surviving spouse owns one-half of the community property. The decedent has the right to dispose of his or her one-half by will, as discussed above. If the decedent dies intestate, only one-half of the community property (the decedent's one-half) descends by intestate succession. Some of the variations are as follows:

- In California, Idaho, Nevada, New Mexico and Washington, the decedent's community property passes to the surviving spouse regardless of the number of issue of the decedent.

- In Wisconsin, the surviving spouse shares community property with the issue of the decedent who are not also the issue of the surviving spouse.

- Louisiana retains *legitime*, a modified forced heirship system originating in Roman law.

> Legitime in Louisiana prevents a decedent from disinheriting children who are younger than 23 years of age or disabled. The legitime cannot be reduced by the surviving spouse's claim to an intestate share.

Separate property of the decedent is subjected to a different and usually more complicated distribution scheme, except in Arizona and Wisconsin. The disposition scheme for separate property normally requires that the surviving spouse share with the deceased spouse's descendants, collateral heirs, or ancestors, as mandated by statute. The rationale behind the intestacy statute governing separate property distribution is to provide for the surviving spouse while also recognizing those of the decedent's intestate heirs who are not also the heirs-apparent of the surviving spouse.

Illustration 10.1: B and C are married. B dies intestate (without a valid will) survived by children who are also C's children. B and C own community property valued at $100,000. B owns no separate property. After accounting for taxes, debts, family allowances, and support obligations, C would take B's one-half of the community property by intestate succession. Thus, C, who already owns $50,000 of the community property, succeeds to B's $50,000 of community property. B and C's children take $0.

Illustration 10.2: B and C are married. B dies intestate (without a valid will) survived by children who are not also C's children. B and C own community property valued at $100,000, and B owns separate property valued at $100,000. After accounting for taxes, debts, family allowances, and support obligations, the most likely distribution is as follows. C takes B's one-half of the former community property by intestate succession, as in Illustration 10.1 above. B's children are entitled to B's separate property in proportional shares, as mandated by the state intestacy statute.

4. INDIVIDUAL RETIREMENT ACCOUNT ASSETS

Individual retirement account assets (IRA assets for short) are tax deferred or protected accounts, as discussed in Chapter 7. IRA assets are disposed of by a pay on death (POD) designation in a beneficiary form on file with the IRA institution. Because IRA assets do not pass by will, they are categorized as nonprobate assets.

The IRS has many different rules for a married IRA asset owner depending on whether the IRA owner names a spousal beneficiary or a nonspousal beneficiary. The rules are complex and outside the scope of the Nutshell. Even so, one major distinction concerning minimum distribution calculations bears noting here.

If the married IRA asset owner dies on or after the required minimum distribution date (after the age of 74 in 2024), and names a spouse who is more than 10 years younger than the IRA owner as the sole beneficiary of an IRA asset, the IRS allows the spousal beneficiary to use his or her own life expectancy (recalculated every year) for determining the minimum distribution required. Life expectancy numbers are found in the Uniform Lifetime Table, IRS Publication 590–B, which is updated from year to year.

If, on the other hand, the married IRA asset owner dies on or after the required minimum distribution date, and names a nonspousal beneficiary, IRS rules lock in an initial time-certain period for calculating minimum distributions. This time is reduced by one for each year following.

For taxpayers who have accumulated significant balances in IRA assets in the form of tax deferred and protected accounts, federal estate tax and state tax liabilities may become an issue in any number of situations.

- If the taxpayer dies without a surviving spouse, no marital deduction is available on the taxpayer's death.
- If the taxpayer dies with a surviving spouse, but the marriage was subject to a premarital agreement that affected or eliminated the marital deduction in whole or part, then federal and state estate tax may be due.
- If the federal estate tax exemption is too low to cancel out federal estate tax liability on an estate, then federal and state estate tax may be due.
- If the IRS audits the deceased spouse's estate and concludes that more federal estate taxes are owed, then federal and state tax estate may be due.

States can eliminate a state tax by repealing the tax altogether, as Arizona does. Or impose a stand-alone tax, as Washington does.

States can lower the estate tax by raising exemptions. In these states, a state estate tax is imposed only if the decedent's estate is taxable under federal estate tax law. The policy aim is to impose estate taxes on decedent's who leave substantial estates upon death.

C. INDIVIDUAL STATES

1. ARIZONA

Arizona has adopted and revised the UPC in 1973, which an update in 1990.

Ariz.Rev.Stat.Ann. § 14–2101 provides that **"[a]ny part of a decedent's estate not effectively disposed of by will passes by intestate succession to the decedent's heirs. . . ."**

The decedent's estate is made up of his or her separate property *and* his or her one-half vested interest in the community property.

Ariz.Rev.Stat.Ann. § 14–2102 clarifies that only the decedent's one-half of the community property passes by will or intestate succession. The surviving spouse retains his or her one-half vested share.

Ariz.Rev.Stat.Ann. § 14–2102 provides for the following intestate distribution:

> **"The following part of the intestate estate, as to both separate property and the**

one-half of community property that belongs to the decedent, passes to the surviving spouse:

1. **If there is no surviving issue or if there are surviving issue all of whom are issue of the surviving spouse also, the entire intestate estate.**

2. **If there are surviving issue one or more of whom are not issue of the surviving spouse, one-half of the intestate separate property and no interest in the one-half of the community property that belonged to the decedent."**

Formerly, under Arizona law a surviving spouse had rights to the decedent spouse's entire *intestate* estate only if the decedent died without issue.

Today, Ariz.Rev.Stat.Ann. § 14–2102 gives the surviving spouse the entire **"intestate estate"** if the decedent dies without issue, or if the decedent dies survived by issue who are also issue of the surviving spouse. The idea here is that children of the decedent and the surviving spouse remain the natural bounty of the surviving spouse, and therefore retain rights as the intestate heirs of the surviving spouse. The **"intestate estate"** only breaks down into its **"separate property and community property"** components when the surviving issue of the decedent are not also the issue of the surviving spouse (i.e., when the issue of the decedent are not also the birth or adopted children of the surviving spouse). But even then, all the decedent's community property descends to the surviving spouse; only the decedent's separate property is subject to division between the surviving spouse and those of the decedent's issue who are not also issue of the surviving spouse.

Arizona repealed the estate tax in 2006. Ariz.Rev.Stat.Ann. §§ 42–4001 through 42–4008 were repealed by Laws 2006, Ch. 262, § 3.

2. CALIFORNIA

California has not adopted the Uniform Probate Code because it has its own probate code.

Cal.Prob.Code § 28(a) through (c) expressly converts into California community property, for purposes of the California Probate Code the following. **"[P]roperty *acquired* during marriage while domiciled in the state, . . . all personal property wherever situated and all real property situated in this state . . . *acquired* during the marriage by a married person while domiciled elsewhere, that is community property, or a substantially equivalent type of marital property, under the laws of the place where the acquiring spouse was domiciled at the time of its acquisition."** And all property acquired **"in exchange"** for the above property. So, for example, if a decedent owns Texas or Louisiana community property, for purposes of the probate proceeding, that property is characterized as California community property upon the domiciled spouse's death.

The need for a probate-specific quasi-community property concept arose from the situation in which persons retired, after working in a common law state, then moved to California. In the common law state, the surviving spouse would have had a statutory elective share right against a will that did not provide for her or him. A similar right does not exist in California because of the community property system.

Thus, for the retired couple who did not engage in the labor force while domiciled in California (they were no longer working, their assets had been acquired in another state, and any capital gains of separate property were themselves separate property under California law), the surviving spouse of a retiree could lose the alternative legal protections against disinheritance that he or she would have enjoyed in a common law state. He or she also would be unable to claim the existence of community property. To rectify the situation, the California legislature created a new character of property called "quasi-community property," and deemed that it would descend, upon intestacy, in the same manner as community property.

Cal.Prob.Code § 66 defines quasi-community very broadly for purposes of probate:

> **" 'Quasi-community property' means the following property, other than community property as defined in Section 28:**
>
> **(a) All personal property wherever situated, and all [California] real**

> **property . . . acquired by a decedent while domiciled elsewhere that would have been the community property of the decedent and the surviving spouse if the decedent had been domiciled in [California] at the time of its acquisition.**
>
> **(b) All personal property wherever situated, and all [California] real property . . . acquired in exchange for real or personal property, wherever situated, that would have been the community property of the decedent and the surviving spouse if the decedent had been domiciled in this state at the time the property so exchanged was acquired."**

Cal.Prob.Code § 6402.5 provides special intestacy rules for ancestral property, defined as former property (separate, community, and quasi-community) of a predeceased spouse if the surviving spouse (the present decedent) dies intestate after 1984 without (a subsequent) spouse or issue surviving. The provision deals only with property governed by the intestacy statute. The historical source of the property covered by this statute is unique in the sense that it is (i) the ancestral property of the present decedent's predeceased spouse (ii) that passed to the present decedent when his or her former spouse died within a certain period (15 years for realty, 5 years for personalty). If the present decedent dies without a surviving spouse or issue of his or her own, then the statute provides that the ancestral property shall descend to certain of the decedent's predeceased spouse's relatives (issue, parents, or issue of parents) rather than to relatives of the present decedent. Ancestral property provisions do not often come into play, since they apply only to property that falls into the present decedent's intestate estate. For that reason, estate planning that brings the property into the decedent's probate estate or passes the property by a nonprobate method will nullify the application of this ancestral property statute in all cases.

Cal.Prob.Code § 6401 provides that the intestate share of a surviving spouse consists of the decedent's one-half of community property, as defined in Cal.Prob.Code § 28; the decedent's one-half of quasi-community property, as defined in Cal.Prob.Code § 66; and a portion of the decedent's separate property which varies depending upon the relationship of other surviving kindred of the decedent (who are the takers of the balance of the decedent's estate under Cal.Prob.Code § 6401(c)).

Cal.Prob.Code § 6401(c), provides that:

- The surviving spouse inherits **"the entire intestate [separate property] estate"** if the decedent left no surviving issue, parent, sibling, or issue of a deceased sibling. Cal.Prob.Code § 6401(c)(1).
- The surviving spouse inherits **"one-half of the intestate [separate property] estate"** if the decedent is survived by only one child,

or the issue of a deceased child; or if the decedent is not survived by issue but is survived by a parent or parents, or their issue (siblings), or the issue of either of them (stepsiblings of the decedent). Cal.Prob.Code 6401(c)(2).

- The surviving spouse inherits **"one-third of the intestate [separate property] estate"** if the decedent is survived by more than one child living; or one child living and the issue of one or more deceased children; or the issue of two or more deceased children. Cal.Prob.Code 6401(c)(3).
- § 6402.5 ancestral property is exempt from the reach of this statute.

California has provisions for small estate set asides, homestead exemptions, family protections, support provisions, and many other provisions designed to protect the surviving spouse.

California prohibits the imposition of tax on transfers made by reason of death (see Cal.Rev. & T. 13301) unless the taxpayer is also liable for federal estate tax. If so, then the California estate tax is **"equal to the portion, if any, of the maximum allowable amount of the credit for state death taxes, allowable under the applicable federal estate tax law, which is attributable to property located in the State of California."** Cal.Rev. & T. § 13302. State tax liability cannot exceed federal estate tax liability.

3. IDAHO

Idaho has adopted and revised the UPC in 1971.

"As to community property," Idaho Code § 15–2–102(b) provides that **"the one-half of community property which belongs to the decedent passes to the surviving spouse."**

The surviving spouse takes all the community property, and all the separate property of the decedent if it has a value of less than $50,000 after the homestead exemption.

As to separate property, Idaho Code § 15–2–102(a) provides that if the decedent leaves neither surviving issue nor parents, the surviving spouse is entitled to all of the separate property intestate estate of the decedent. If the decedent leaves surviving issue (children, grandchildren, or more remote lineal descendants), the surviving spouse is entitled to one-half of the separate property intestate estate; the surviving issue share the other one-half. If the decedent leaves no surviving issue but is survived by parents, then the surviving spouse takes one-half of the separate property intestate estate; the decedent's parent or parents share the other one-half.

Idaho grants a surviving spouse the right to take a forced share of the estate augmented by any quasi-community property. See Idaho Code § 15–2–202 and § 15–2–203. Quasi-community property is described and distributed in language almost identical to the California definition. All quasi-community property is subject to the debts of decedent.

Idaho Code 14–403(1), the Estate and Transfer Reform Act of 1988 provided: **"[a] tax in the amount equal to the federal credit is imposed on the transfer of the taxable estate of every resident."** This section was repealed on July 1, 2020

4. LOUISIANA

Louisiana has not adopted the UPC.

Louisiana's civil law heritage shows strongly in the provisions for administration and distribution of a decedent's estate. To give just one example, Louisiana permits the legitime, a Roman law action meant to protect the decedent's heirs against lifetime donations (gifts) that were made by the decedent with the intent to deprive his descendants of their (forced) heirship.

Louisiana recognizes two types of succession, by valid will and by intestacy statute.

In the case of intestate succession, Louisiana divides intestate heirs into classes, called "orders." While the surviving spouse has a primary status in other community property states, in Louisiana the class of the decedent's descendants has primacy over the class of parents and siblings, which in turn has primacy over the surviving spouse.

The surviving spouse—defined as a spouse who is not juridically separated from the decedent—succeeds to the decedent's share of community property only if there are no descendants, parents, siblings, or descendants from siblings. Otherwise, the surviving spouse takes by a right of usufruct. LSA-

C.C. Arts. 888, 889 and 890. Usufruct gives the surviving spouse, as usufructuary, the right to use the property for a certain period. A usufructuary is not an outright owner of the property. Usufruct is discussed in Chapter 1 and Chapter 4.

Separate property succession devolves in accordance with LSA-C.C. Art. 894. That article reads: **"if the deceased leaves neither descendants, nor parents, nor brothers, sisters, or descendants from them, his spouse not juridically separate from him shall succeed to his separate property to the exclusion of other."**

As noted above, Louisiana recognizes the concept of forced heirship and therefore allows for legitime. The institution of forced heirship has undergone changes in Louisiana, but still today the state prohibits a property owner from disinheriting certain descendants, as discussed below. The traditional common law gave a decedent full legal rein to intentionally disinherit descendants, collaterals, ancestors, and even the surviving spouse. Therefore, there is no equivalent to the legitime in the common law.

As incorporated into the 1974 Louisiana Constitution, Art. XII, § 5 on October 21, 1995, legitime currently only applies to certain descendants. By this constitutional amendment, the legislature has a duty to provide a law for forced heirship as it applies to descendants who are **"23 years of age or younger . . . or . . . any age who, because of mental incapacity or physical**

infirmity, are incapable of taking care of their persons or administering their estates."

A testator can affect the legitime by a subsequent marriage or remarriage. *Succession of Becker*, 660 So.2d 61 (La.App. 1995).

Louisiana recognizes the marital portion, a concept that was incorporated into Louisiana law in 1808. The marital portion appears to be a benefit that the law obligates the decedent's estate to provide to a surviving spouse under certain conditions. The time for a surviving spouse to make a claim for the marital portion is upon the death of the other spouse. The surviving spouse's marital portion is "irrespective of the rights of heirs, forced or otherwise, and of the legatees . . . [and it] is demandable in a testate, as well as in an intestate succession." *Malone v. Cannon*, 41 So.2d 837, 839 (La. 1949).

LSA-C.C. Art. 2432 articulates the need for and scope of the marital portion: **"When a spouse dies rich in comparison with the surviving spouse, the surviving spouse is entitled to claim the marital portion from the succession of the deceased spouse."** A long line of cases makes the point that, as between individual spouses "rich" is a relative term. And LSA-C.C. Art. 2433 provides that a **"marital portion is an incident of any matrimonial regime."** The marital portion **"may be claimed by the surviving spouse, even if separated from the deceased. . . ."** The marital portion also may be claimed if the deceased spouse disinherited the surviving spouse by will.

LSA-C.C. Art. 2434 sets forth the quantum of the marital portion, often referred to in case after case as the "marital fourth." (Why the marital portion equals one-fourth relates to the legitime action, which would set aside three-fourths of a succession for the forced heir(s).) This statute provides that **"the marital portion is one-fourth of the succession in ownership if the deceased died without children, the same fraction in usufruct for life if he is survived by three or fewer children. In no event, however, shall the amount of the marital portion exceed one million dollars."** Recall, as noted above, that children are in the primary class of descendants, but they take subject to the surviving spouse's marital portion. Revision Comments 1979.

The surviving spouse is receiving the marital portion (or marital fourth) in usufruct, rather than in outright ownership. For that reason, she (or he) is subject to the rights and duties of a usufructuary. Even so, the spouse is not otherwise required to post a security.

Whether usufruct is terminated by the surviving spouse's remarriage seems an often-litigated issue. Generally, a surviving spouse's remarriage terminates the right to a marital portion by usufruct unless the decedent has provided otherwise in a valid will provision. Nonmarital cohabitation ("living in open concubinage" as some of the cases put it) long has been held not to terminate the surviving spouse's right to a marital portion by usufruct. See e.g. *Benoit v. Benoit*, 379 So.2d 270 (La.App. 1979), *Kelley v.*

Kelley, 198 La. 338, 3 So. 641 (1941), *Moore v. Moore*, 20 La.Ann. 159 (1868), *Succession of Viaud*, 11 La.Ann. 297 (1856), footnoted and discussed in KATHRYN VENTURATOS LORIO, SUCCESSIONS AND DONATIONS (2009) at § 2.16. Nonmarital cohabitation is discussed in Chapter 11.

"A legacy left by the deceased to the surviving spouse and payments due to him as a result of death are deducted from the marital portion." LSA-C.C. Art. 2435.

A periodic allowance for the maintenance of the surviving spouse is also allowable, but it is dependent upon the right to, and subtracted from, the marital portion (or marital fourth) as finally fixed. LSA-C.C. Art. 2437.

Louisiana imposes an estate tax, but for taxpayers whose death occurs after 1992. The Louisiana inheritance tax statute previously exempted from the calculation **"the total amount or value of the inheritance, legacy, donation or gift made in contemplation of death to a surviving spouse of a decedent . . ."** LRS 47:2402, as amended by 1987 La. Acts, No. 236. The exemption, however, was repealed effective Jan 1., 2010.

The legal usufruct of a surviving spouse also may be exempt from taxation. *Succession of Marsal*, 42 So. 778 (La. 1907).

5. NEVADA

Nevada has not adopted the UPC.

Nevada's intestacy statutes (similar to California) pass the decedent's one-half of the community property to the surviving spouse (Nev.Rev.Stat. § 135.060).

Nev.Rev.Stat. § 134.040 divides the decedent's separate property between the surviving spouse and the decedent's issue. If the decedent dies survived by a spouse and one child (or **"the lawful issue"** of one child), the division of separate property is one-half to the surviving spouse and one-half to the child. If the decedent dies survived by a spouse and more than one child living, or a child and **"the lawful issue"** of one or more deceased children, then the separate property estate goes one-third to the surviving spouse and two-thirds to the decedent's children or their issue.

Nev.Rev.Stat. § 132.055 excludes (one presumes unadopted) stepchildren and foster children from the definition of child; thus stepchildren, foster children, step-grandchildren, foster grandchildren, and so on are not **"lawful issue"** for purposes of Nev.Rev.Stat. § 134.040.

If the decedent dies leaving no issue, Nev.Rev.Stat. § 134.050 divides the decedent's separate property between the surviving spouse and the decedent's parents equally, or the survivor of them. If neither parent survives the decedent, the property goes to the decedent's siblings or their issue by right of representation. If no member of the immediate family (i.e., no parent, sibling, nephew, or niece) survives the decedent, then the surviving spouse takes all the separate property over more distantly related heirs.

Nevada imposes a tax on the transfer of a taxable estate of resident and nonresident decedents. Nev.Rev.Stat. § 375A.100. For residents and nonresidents, tax is calculated **"in the amount of the maximum credit allowable against the federal estate tax for the payment of state death taxes on all."** Nev.Rev.Stat. § 375A.100.1 and § 100.2.

For resident decedents, property included in the calculation is real estate, tangible personal property located in the state, and intangible personal property in or outside the state but otherwise subject to the jurisdiction of the state at the time of the owner's death. Nev.Rev.Stat. § 375A.100.1(a) and (b).

For nonresident decedents, property included in the calculation is real estate, tangible personal property located in the state, and intangible personal property. Intangible personal property includes any stock of a Nevada corporation and any interest in a Nevada business, a federal corporation, or national bank that has its place of business or does a major part of its business in Nevada. Personal bank deposits are excepted unless they are used in connection with a Nevada business. Nev.Rev.Stat. § 375A.100.2(a) and (b).

6. NEW MEXICO

New Mexico adopted and revised the UPC in 1975, effective July 1, 1976.

N.M.Stat.Ann. § 45–2–102 (1978) transfers to the surviving spouse the decedent's **"one-half of the community property as to which the decedent could have exercised the power of testamentary disposition."**

The separate property intestate estate is divided one-fourth to the surviving spouse and three fourths to the surviving issue of the decedent. If there are no surviving issue, N.M.Stat.Ann. § 45–2–102 (1978) transfers the entire separate property intestate estate of the decedent to his or her surviving spouse.

All the community property is subject to the payment of community debts. N.M.Stat. Ann. § 45–2–807(b)(1978) also provides: **"The deceased spouse's separate debts and funeral expenses and the charge and expenses of administration are to be satisfied first from his separate property, excluding property held in joint tenancy. Should such property be insufficient, then the deceased spouse's undivided one-half interest in the community property shall be liable."**

N.M.Stat.Ann. § 45–2–804 (1978), revised in 2012, automatically revokes probate and nonprobate transfers in the event of a divorce. If applicable, property otherwise titled in joint tenancy could properly find its way into the decedent's probate estate. This is part of the UPC.

New Mexico imposes an estate tax in an amount equal to the federal credit on **"the transfer of the net estate of every resident."** See N.M.Stat.Ann. § 7–7–3.A (1978). The net estate is the taxable estate as defined by I.R.C. § 2051.

7. TEXAS

Texas has not adopted the UPC.

On January 1, 2014, the Texas Probate Code, which had been in effect since 1956, was repealed and replaced by the Texas Estates Code (2013 Tex. Sess.Law Serv.Ch. 1136 (H.B. 2912) (VERNON'S), effective January 1, 2014. See Conversion Chart—Probate Code to Estates Code is a helpful chart prepared by the Professor Gerry W. Beyer blog.

The Texas Probate Code had distinguished between personalty and realty. Its replacement, the Texas Estates Code, makes substantive changes in Texas law that may alter where the distinction had previously been drawn.

Texas originated two concepts that affect the passage of property at death (in addition to lifetime implications). The first is the concept of the independent executor. The second is the concept of the homestead right, as discussed in Chapter 1, Chapter 4, and Chapter 6 .

The independent executor concept emphasized the non-intervention of the Probate Court after the qualification of the personal representative. V.T.C.S.Estates Code § 453.002 exempted the community property estate from administration; it was repealed, effective January 1, 2014, but no change was made to the language: **"If a spouse dies intestate and the community property passes to the surviving spouse, no administration of the community property is necessary. . . ."** The idea is that the community intestate estate of a decedent passes entirely to the surviving spouse if the decedent leaves no living descendants, or if the decedent's surviving issue are also issue of the surviving spouse. V.T.C.S. Probate Code § 45. The disposition is subject to payment of the debts, but the use of **"shall"** suggests that a creditor cannot force an administration.

The concepts of the homestead right and exempt personal property originated in Texas. Although designed primarily to protect a family farm or home, and certain minimum amounts of clothing, furnishings and work equipment from execution of creditors, the protection has been extended after the death of a spouse or parent. The extension is logical because otherwise death would terminate legal protection given to family members when they may most need it. The exemption from creditors has also been applied as an exemption when a decedent dies with a valid will. Thus, in Texas, as in many jurisdictions, the spouse or the children of the decedent claim their homestead and other family protections before creditors can reach the decedent's property. A family allowance may also be ordered paid, as a preferred item from the decedent's estate, again prior to creditors.

Texas labels the estate tax an inheritance tax. V.C.T.A. § 211.051(a) imposed **"[a] tax equal to the amount of the federal credit imposed on the transfer at death of the property of every resident."** This includes property that passes by devise. Real property, tangible personal property, and intangible personal property wherever located including notes, bonds, stock certificates and interests proved by other evidence all fall within the category of property that is subject to the state inheritance tax. Id. Homestead property is not subject to state inheritance tax.

Note: V.C.T.A.§ 211.051 was repealed by S.B. No. 752 effective Sept. 1, 2015, but the changes do not affect tax liability accruing before the repeal date. **V.T.C.A. Estates Code 124.001(1). "The former law is continued in effect for the collection of taxes due and for civil and criminal enforcement of the liabilities for those taxes." V.T.C.A. Estates Code 124.001(3).**

8. WASHINGTON

Washington has not adopted the UPC.

Washington subjects both halves of the community property to probate administration when either spouse dies. This allows a continuing control of community debts and payment from the probate estate.

Wash.Rev.Code § 11.02.070 provides that upon the death of a decedent, **"a one-half share of the community property shall be confirmed to the**

surviving spouse or the surviving domestic partner." The balance of the section makes clear, however, that it is a net one-half of the community *after* the **"payment of obligations and debts of the community, the award in lieu of homestead, the allowance for family support, and any other matter for which the community property would be responsible or liable if the decedent were living."**

If the decedent dies wholly or partially intestate, the surviving spouse or domestic partner, in addition to having his or her one-half of the community property confirmed in him or her, receives the decedent's one-half of the community property by succession.

As to the net separate property estate, Wash.Rev.Code § 11.04.015 gives the surviving spouse one-half if the decedent was survived by issue Those issue take the other half of the separate property. If the decedent is not survived by issue, the spouse takes three fourths of the net separate property estate and the immediate family (parents if both are alive, surviving parent if one is alive, or issue of the parents by right of representation if neither parent survives the decedent) take the other fourth. If the decedent is not survived by issue or parent or sibling, the surviving spouse takes all the net separate property estate.

Wash.Rev.Code § 11.04.095 provides a special rule for certain types of ancestral property. It comes into play when a surviving spouse or surviving domestic partner who received all or substantially all the property of his or her previously deceased spouse or domestic partner (during the joint lifetime or at the death of the first spouse or domestic partner to die) dies without a will or an heir. In that case, if the covered property would otherwise escheat, the property of the second to die passes by intestacy to the surviving issue of the first to die. See California.

As in California, the Washington ancestral property provision applies only to the intestate estate, and thus is easily avoided by use of a will, trust, or nonprobate transfer.

Although during the continuation of the community Washington separate property is not liable for community debts and Washington community property is not liable for separate debts, different rules apply to timely filed creditors' claims in the probate estate. The community debts are paid from the total community, producing a net community estate; then, the separate claims against the decedent are asserted against his or her half of that net community estate.

Wash.Rev.Code § 26.16.120 authorizes spouses or domestic partners to make a contract which disposes of the community property upon the death of the first of them. This survivorship contract does not have to be executed with the formalities of a will. It is a contract, meaning (absent a specific provision to the contrary) that one spouse, acting alone, ordinarily cannot terminate or revoke the parties' agreement (as one could with a joint tenancy or a will, respectively). See Chapter 2.

Washington imposes an estate tax by Wash.Rev.Code § 83.100.040(1), which was revised in 2013, effective Jan. 1, 2014. The statute reads: **"A tax in an amount computed as provided in this section is imposed on every transfer of property located in Washington."**

Subject to applicable exemptions, the estate tax due is computed by reference to a table found in Wash.Rev.Code § 83.100.040(2)(a). The estate tax is calculated on estate valuations that proceed in increments of $1,000,000. Tax rates are progressive, and they range from 10% to 20%. So, for example, estates under $1,000,000 pay a $0 **"initial tax amount"** plus a **"tax rate %"** of 10%. Id. Estates between $1,000,000 and $2,000,000 pay a $100,000 initial tax amount plus a tax rate percentage of 14%. Id. The statutory table provides initial tax amounts and tax rate percentages for estates up to $9,000,000 and over, which pay a $1,490,000 initial tax amount plus a tax rate percentage of 20%. Id.

Unlike the estate taxes of the other community property states, the Washington estate tax is a stand-alone estate tax. As such the Washington estate tax is **"independent of any federal estate tax obligation and is not affected by termination of the federal estate tax."** Wash.Rev.Code § 83.100.040(3).

9. WISCONSIN

Wisconsin adopted the revised UPC in 1998.

Wisconsin revised its probate administration and intestate and testate succession laws, effective January 1, 1986, the same time that it became a community property state.

The intestate share of a surviving spouse of a Wisconsin domiciliary who dies after 1985 consists of the following:

1. The deceased spouse's entire intestate estate if no issue survive or if the surviving issue are all issue of the decedent and the surviving spouse; or

2. One-half of the deceased spouse's property other than marital property and other than deferred marital property (defined below) if there are any surviving issue who are not also issue of the surviving spouse.

Wisconsin law permits each spouse to will his or her portion of each item of marital property and his or her nonmarital (i.e., individual and unclassified) property, subject to the surviving spouse's elective rights.

Only the decedent's one-half of marital property is subject to probate administration. Survivorship marital property, like joint tenancy, belongs by operation of law to the survivor; therefore, survivorship marital property is not subject to administration, nor does it pass by will.

Wis.Stat. § 766.58(3)(f) permits spouses to enter a marital property agreement containing provisions that act as a will substitute to transfer property without probate administration:

> **"Providing that upon the death of either spouse any of either or both spouses' property, including after-acquired property, passes without probate to a designated person, trust or other entity by nontestamentary disposition. If a marital property agreement provides for the nontestamentary disposition of property, without probate, at the death of the 2nd spouse, at any time after the death of the first spouse the surviving spouse may amend the marital property agreement with regard to property to be disposed of at his or her death unless the marital property agreement expressly provides otherwise and except to the extent property is held in a trust expressly established under the marital property agreement."**

To afford surviving spouses some additional economic protection (to cover Wisconsin's legal transition from a separate property title state to a community property state), an elective right (rather than the automatic property interest envisioned by the UMPA) is provided to a surviving spouse. By this right the surviving spouse may elect to receive up to one-half of certain nonmarital property called "deferred marital property" in the deceased spouse's probate estate. Deferred marital property is property acquired during marriage that would have been marital (community) property had the marital property law applied when the property was acquired. This provision is designed to sunset.

A surviving spouse may also elect to receive up to one-half of the value of the "augmented marital (community) property estate." The augmented marital property estate (a concept borrowed from the UPC) consists of certain nonprobate transfers effected on or after April 4, 1984 (the date on which the Governor signed the law). Those nonprobate transfers must be of deferred marital property to third parties, and they can include certain trusts, joint tenancies and life insurance. The amount elected by the surviving spouse is reduced by amounts transferred by the decedent to the surviving spouse. The surviving spouse is eligible to collect the amount remaining after deferred marital property is transferred. See Wis.Stat. § 861.03 to § 861.17.

Unlike the other community property states, Wisconsin makes clear at the outset that its purpose in imposing an estate tax is to obtain a benefit for the state, and thus laws governing the estate tax are **"to be liberally construed to effect this purpose."** Wis.Stat. § 72.005. The amount of the state estate tax is **"the maximum credit allowable upon the United States estate tax . . . ."** Moreover, **"[a]n estate tax is imposed upon the transfer of all property that is subject to a federal estate tax and that has a taxable situs in [the] state."** Wis.Stat. § 72.02.

PART 5

SPECIAL PROBLEMS

CHAPTER 12
NONMARITAL RELATIONSHIPS

A. OVERVIEW

1. GENERAL OUTLINE

I find it difficult to settle on a title for this chapter mostly because the term to describe those who choose not to marry their intimate partners has become a bit of a contested terrain.

I have used the term "nonmarriage" in this and other editions of this Nutshell to signify intention. I use the term nonmarriage to refer to couples who intentionally do not formalize their intimate partnership by obtaining a marriage certificate or an RDP registration. This term has been used in the law review literature, but most often without definition.

Other than the definition stated in the first paragraph above, the term "nonmarriage" can apply as an umbrella term to couples who intended to marry and went through the motions of getting legally married, but subsequently discovered that they were not legally married due to a flaw in the formalization process. If the couple correct the flaw and marry, they become married. If they do not correct the flaw, but continue to cohabitate, they remain single people in an intimate relationship who are living together.

By the terms "nonmarriage" and "nonmarital relationships" what I want most to communicate is the fluidity that can exist between a relationship that is legally documented as a marriage and one that is not.

Drawing the line between who is married and who is by choice or circumstance not married (single) is a different question than the one of who has the legal right to contract a formal marriage, a topic discussed below.

Here are useful terms.

Formal marriage: A marriage is both a private contract and a public institution. A marriage is valid when it is formally contracted in accordance with state law. With respect to property issues, a valid marriage brings the parties clearly within the community property system.

Void marriage: When a marriage is *void* the parties fall outside of the community property system should they break up and need to divide property.

Voidable marriage: When a marriage is *voidable*, that marriage is presumed valid unless it is challenged in court. During life, a party in a voidable marriage may opt to terminate the marriage by divorce or annulment. Annulment voids the marriage, which cuts off use of the community property system. Divorce validates the marriage, which allows the parties access to the community property system for property division and support petitions. Upon the death of a spouse, a voidable marriage becomes valid.

Putative marriage: A void marriage that one or both parties believed was valid can be adjudged a putative marriage. What is required is a claimant's proof that that they had a good faith belief in the validity of a marriage that turned out to be void. Putative spouse status justifies amelioration under the equitable putative spouse doctrine, which some states have codified. Often the remedy is to allow the putative spouse access to the state marital property laws for purposes of dissolution.

Registered domestic partners (RDPs for short) are parties who formalize their relationship under the state Registered Domestic Partnership laws (RDP law for short), not under the state marriage laws. In some jurisdictions, RDPs who register their relationship with the state have all the rights and responsibilities of marriage. In other jurisdictions, RDP rights and duties are more limited than those of spouses. If so, some but not all the remedies in this chapter may apply.

Nonmarried cohabitants are single persons who have intentionally chosen not to marry, and who live together in an intimate relationship. In terms of property, they are nonmarried partners in the sense that they are joint venturers who are not married to each other. They work together to pay bills, acquire property, and do other things that married couples do, but their ventures fall outside of the community property system. There is no law mandating that nonmarried partners be allowed to use laws that are maintained for validly married persons. That said, nonmarried parties can and do borrow from community property law and from stress-tested community property workouts to divide any property they may acquire together or to assess liability at the end of a relationship. Often their agreements are informal, but sometimes they formalize their agreements—not the relationship itself—into what are called cohabitation agreements. See Chapter 2 for more on cohabitation agreements.

Some states allow nonmarried cohabitants to prove changed circumstances to allow them entrance into the community property system as an equitable remedy. Washington, for example, employs what it calls the committed intimate relationship doctrine. Other states allow this benefit on the theory that the parties have a marriage-like relationship. California, the state where I teach, does not have such an option out of what I theorize is a concern for forced marriage. My untested hypothesis is that the California model reserves a designated choice, which I call nonmarriage, for parties who want to live together without formalizing their relationship.

Informal marriage (sometimes called a common law marriage) is not allowed except in one of the nine community property states, Texas. An informal marriage comes into existence when statutory requirements are met. Often the requirements are more than just living together. If the informal marriage is called into question or if the parties decide that they want written proof of marriage, they can either enter a formal marriage or else go to court to confirm their informal marriage. If they choose the latter option, and if they are successful in court, then the court judgement will confirm that their marriage exists and that, by application of the relation back doctrine, it commenced upon the date that it came into existence.

Formally married spouses intend to marry.

Informally married spouses intend to marry.

Nonmarried partners intend to remain single, which is to say not to marry.

2. FORMAL LEGAL RELATIONSHIPS: SPOUSES AND REGISTERED DOMESTIC PARTNERS

A valid, or lawful marriage, is a solemnized marriage that is licensed in accordance with the state's internal law. U.S. states recognize as valid a marriage performed in another state. Thus, a marriage that is contracted validly in one state will be recognized as valid in another state.

For example, among the community property states, only Texas allows for the creation of an unlicensed (informal or so-called common law) marriage, as just discussed. Once an informal marriage is contracted in Texas under Texas law, it is valid for all purposes. Moreover, if the spouses move to another state, their marriage also will be recognized by their new home state as valid for all purposes. The spouses may have difficulties of proof as they go through their daily lives, and these might send them to court for a written judgement that proves their marriage, but their marriage is nevertheless eligible for full faith and credit protection.

Same-sex marriage is licensable in every U.S. state. The Fourteenth Amendment protects fundamental liberties, and the right to marry is such a liberty. The right to marry is protected for each one of us by the U.S. Constitution. *Obergefell v. Hodges*, 576 U.S. 644 (2015), which holds that a state is required to license a marriage between two people of the same sex and to recognize marriage between two people of the same sex when their marriage is lawfully licensed and performed out-of-state. And *U.S. v. Windsor*, 133 U.S. 2675 (2013) holds that a same-sex spouse is included within the definition of "spouse" as that term is used in federal statutes. In *Windsor*, supra, when Edith Windsor succeeded to her deceased spouse Thea Spyer's estate, Windsor sought a tax exemption under the U.S. Internal Revenue Code as Spyer's surviving spouse. Windsor was first barred from claiming the exemption, but through her advocacy in the U.S. Supreme Court ruling, she was granted surviving spouse status.

Pre-*Obergefell*, supra, as noted above, every U.S. community property state except New Mexico and Washington banned same-sex marriage by state constitution. Over time as these bans were lifted, a patchwork of state laws remained in place. This patchwork created foundational human rights problems with respect to the institution of marriage and its corollary, the institution of divorce.

States with constitutional provisions that banned same-sex marriage did not recognize same-sex marriages contracted in another state—now illegal post *Obergefell*, supra. Also, pre-*Obergefell*, validly married same-sex couples who subsequently moved to a state with a same-sex marriage ban could not petition for divorce in the courts of their new domicile. Today, same-sex marriage is legal. Given the political times we live in, however, it is important to protect fundamental rights.

Against the backdrop of *Obergefell*, supra, marriage remains a state law procedure, as does divorce. Different U.S. community property states allow for different relationship options.

All states permit licensed marriage.

As explained above, only Texas permits informal marriage.

Likewise, as to divorce, all states require a final judgment of dissolution. The final judgment of dissolution serves many functions. For a valid marriage, the judgment ends the marriage and returns the partners to the status of single individuals. For a voidable marriage, the judgment validates the marriage, thus allowing the divorcing parties to use the state's community property laws. For a void marriage, an annulment judgment gives third parties and especially creditors notice that the marriage was void.

No state permits informal divorce.

At the time this Nutshell goes to press, California, Nevada, and Washington have registered domestic partnership (or RDP for short) legislation that gives RDPs the exact same rights and obligations as married persons. Wisconsin has limited domestic partnership legislation—the limitation was due to the state's same-sex marriage ban. Arizona, Idaho, Louisiana, New Mexico, and Texas either have no RDP legislation or they are developing it. In the states that permit RDPs, the parties must register their relationship with the state. Once registered, if they break up, they must formally terminate the RDP according to state law. Termination requirements are found within the parameters the statute that authorizes the RDP in the first place.

Equitable corrections are available.

A person who believed they were validly married but later discovers they were not can petition for putative spouse status. Upon proof that the petitioner had a good faith belief in the validity of the marriage, the court will allow that person, now formally deemed a putative spouse by the court, to use the state community property system to divide property of the partnership. That property is called *quasi marital property*, not community property since the parties are not validly married. Quasi-marital property is property that would have been community property had the parties been validly married.

A person who knows they have not registered their relationship with the state but who lives together with an intimate partner is a *nonmarried cohabitant*. Nonmarried cohabitants cannot acquire community property. Instead, they must use the general civil law to settle property matters when they break up.

Washington has crafted what it refers to as the *committed intimate relationship doctrine*. This doctrine allows a nonmarried cohabitants to petition for the legal right to use the state community property system when they break up or when one of the partners passes away. To me, the equitable relationship doctrine seems a sort of delayed marriage option. It permits one of two people who choose not to marry, to later change their mind due to changed circumstances. The change does not come through a wedding. It comes through a petition from a court requesting that the nonmarried cohabitancy be treated, for equitable reasons, as if it had been a valid marriage. Success means access to state marital property laws that are reserved for married people.

California takes a sharply different view than Washington by maintaining nonmarriage as a distinct option for intimate partners. The state employs the putative *spouse* doctrine, but since nonmarried persons know they are not married, they cannot prove a good faith belief in the validity of a marriage. Therefore, what they are left with are the general laws available to single (nonmarried) persons and to business partners. This is general civil law, not the state family code or family law.

3. VOID, VOIDABLE, AND PUTATIVE MARRIAGES

A valid marriage comes into existence by documents filed with the state. The marriage starts with a license that bears the seal of the state and the signatures of the parties. Eventually, once the marriage is solemnized and witnessed, the license becomes a marriage certificate, which also bears the state seal. By contracting a valid marriage, the parties give the courts of the state the power to dissolve their marriage.

A void marriage never comes into legal existence. It is void ab initio (Latin for from the start). Typically, what makes the marriage void is the violation of statutes that bar plural marriage (bigamy or polygamy) and marriage between consanguineous relatives that are too closely related to each other by blood.

A voidable marriage comes into legal existence, but it can be challenged later. The marriage might be challenged because of a defect in legal formalities, or an adjudged lack of consent on the part of one of the parties to the marriage. Annulment is the judicial procedure that leaves a court judgment declaring a marriage void. A void marriage will not acquire community property. But a voidable marriage can acquire community property during the time it is presumed valid. Because a voidable marriage is presumptively valid until it is declared annulled the petitioner is permitted access to the community property system by right, for certain periods.

Divorce and dissolution end a valid marriage. Community property rules are made with validly married parties in mind.

A putative marriage is one for which at least one of the parties has a good faith belief in the validity of the marriage. The putative spouse chose to marry, but later discovered that their marriage was void. A typical putative spouse case might arise if one of the spouses is still married when they contract a subsequent marriage. The subsequent marriage is void because it is bigamous.

The putative spouse doctrine permits a putative spouse to access state marital property rules to facilitate property dissolution between the parties. General civil code rules do not facilitate dissolution. Hence there is often a good financial reason for a putative spouse to seek access to a state's community property system.

Non-property reasons also can make it important to be adjudged a putative spouse. For example, if the defect in the marriage is due to bigamy, a person who is adjudged a putative spouse will be released from criminal liability related to circumstances arising therefrom.

However, once a person has inquiry notice of the defect in their marriage, that person may lose eligibility to claim putative spouse status.

An unlicensed (so-called common law) spouse and a putative spouse do not share the same legal status. A spouse who is in an unlicensed (common law) marriage, only in a state that allows informal marriages to be contracted within its boundaries, is validly married despite not possessing a formal marriage certificate.

A person who is in a void marriage is a single person. That person possesses a marriage certificate, but the certificate has no legal effect.

A spouse who is in a voidable marriage is presumptively married and therefore does not need the putative spouse doctrine. But, if there is a breakup, one or both persons must choose to dissolve the marriage or to annul it. If annulment is chosen, the putative spouse doctrine might assist in dissolving property acquired during the relationship.

Not all states accept the putative spouse doctrine. Certainly not all states have codified the doctrine. In those that have codified the doctrine, courts vacillate between understanding the putative spouse as an actor who must demonstrate a good faith belief that their marriage was *valid* versus one who must demonstrate a good faith belief that their marriage was *lawful*. This is perhaps too fine a distinction in most cases, but it is sometimes one upon which property rights can rest

Finally, states can enact a putative spouse provision to recognize quasi-marital property rights. But not all states will go the next step and allow the putative spouse the right to petition for post break-up spousal support.

4. NONMARRIED COHABITANTS

States take different approaches to the rights of nonmarried cohabitants, as discussed above.

As a legal matter, a nonmarried cohabitant is a person who lives with a sexual partner without a marriage certificate or an RDP registration certificate. Otherwise nonmarried cohabitants are a family. They live together. They work as joint venturers. They may parent children. They may care for companion animals. They manage jobs, commutes, family expenses, bank accounts, investment accounts, and so on as partners who are emotionally committed to each other. They may own or lease their family residence. They may share the same last name. Their children may believe they are married. They might even hold themselves out as married. But in a state that does not recognize informal marriage, even doing all the above will not result in a valid marriage.

Still to the nonmarried partners, it does not matter that the state has not licensed their union. Their choice, whether due to circumstance or belief, was and is to forego licensure, certification, registration, or any other legal formality associated with a formal marriage. We might say that these parties have a social marriage, but not a legal one. This is not a criticism of the parties' choices; rather, it is a statement of fact: the parties have chosen to remain single in terms of their personal legal status, even though they are intimate partners.

In terms of property law, the general rule is that a nonmarried cohabitant does not, simply by living with their partner, acquire rights in the accumulations of their partner during the continuance of the relationship. Nor is that person entitled to petition for support when the relationship ends.

On one side of the spectrum is Washington, which through its committed intimate relationship doctrine, gives the court discretion to equitably grant nonmarried cohabitants access to the community property system on a case-by-case basis.

On the opposite side of the spectrum is Louisiana, which does not grant a nonmarried petitioner access to the default marital regime laws. Neither does Louisiana lean toward enforcing agreements made in the context of an adult domestic relationship.

In the middle ground is California, which enforces pooling contracts—including implied and tacit contracts—between nonmarried cohabitants. In California, when nonmarital cohabitants break up, they can settle their property issues by reference to a formal or informal property contract, or even to a tacit property contract. If the state enforces the parties' contract, it does so, but not by changing the parties' legal personal status. The parties remain single persons, not married persons, and thus general contract law applies. This approach deters the creation of a backdoor to marriage.

Historically, the meretricious relationship doctrine was the reason for skepticism about enforcing pooling agreements or property contracts between nonmarried cohabitants. When courts began to acknowledge that, yes, the parties in an intimate partnership are sexual partners, the doctrine of unjust enrichment came into play with its identification of conferred and received benefits. The doctrine of quantum meruit also came into play with its focus on uncompensated labor.

Today, the meretricious relationship doctrine as applied to nonmarried partners is mostly dead letter.

Instead, cohabitants rely on theories of contract and equitable contract defenses (part performance and equitable estoppel), quantum meruit, or unjust enrichment. Contracts can be written, express, implied, tacit. Presumptions about beneficial ownership can raise questions of conferred benefits that require reimbursement to prevent unjust enrichment. Court orders for reimbursements secured by equitable liens, trusts, partnership, quasi-partnership, joint ventures, and even remedies like the resulting and constructive trust. Each of these theories has been successfully relied on to divide property at the end of a nonmarital relationship.

Creditors of nonmarried cohabitants must likewise look to general law rather than to family law (community property) to protect their property rights.

B. DETAIL

1. THE PUTATIVE SPOUSE AND THE DIVISION OF PROPERTY

Historically, a person whose marriage was void from the start or ultimately declared void had no clear recourse for arguing that their claims should be addressed from within the community property system. The person could make an equitable appeal to a court, but the court was under no duty to apply community property rules. States today trend toward adopting equitable principles to assist persons who believed they were legally married, but later discovered they were not.

The judicial doctrine used to do equity is the putative spouse doctrine. The putative spouse doctrine allows a court, upon proof of a party's good faith belief in the lawfulness of their otherwise invalid marriage, to order that community property principles be used to dissolve the property of the union. The label putative spouse indicates that the party has been adjudged eligible to access default family law rules otherwise reserved for married persons. This system may have its own name, like in California where it is called the "quasi-marital property system."

California has codified the putative spouse doctrine, as well as the concept of quasi-marital property. In California, a person who has been formally adjudged a putative spouse can opt to address property-related issues under the family code or under general codes, such as the civil code or the partnership code. The family code recognizes community property, and it incorporates elements of the other codes to facilitate property division for parties going through marital dissolution. The civil code or the partnership code, by contrast, deal with the claims of arm's length transactors and nonmarital business partners.

In the event of a breakup, the putative spouse doctrine permits an innocent spouse to access default dissolution rules. The spouses are both alive, so the court can hear testimony and make credibility determinations.

In the event of death, there may be multiple survivors, one of whom is a lawful spouse and the other a putative spouse. Where there is only one survivor, the putative spouse doctrine protects a survivor as it would a lawful spouse. Where there are two or more survivors, courts are divided on how the quasi-marital property system should operate among them. Sometimes courts award a share to one (preferred) claimant, and the remainder to the other claimant or claimants.

In cases where there are two claimants in the form of a lawful spouse and a putative spouse, Louisiana and California judges have solomonically divided the property between the survivors, awarding one-half to the lawful spouse as community property and the other one-half to the putative spouse as quasi-marital property.

Not surprisingly, given a long history of immigration in both California and Texas, the two most populous community property states, there are more than a few cases that arise when, for example, a person cannot or does not obtain a final divorce from a spouse in their country of origin.

The following examples underscore the potential legal difficulties that can arise when there are multiple claimants, each with a reasonable doctrinal basis for asserting their claim to the decedent's property.

Illustration 11.1: H lawfully marries Wife 1 (W1), but ineffectively divorces her. H subsequently ceremonially marries Wife 2 (W2). W2 has no knowledge of the valid H-W1 marriage. In this scenario, W1 is H's lawful spouse, but W2 believes in good faith belief that the H-W2 marriage is valid.

Assume that the asset under discussion is H's salary during the continuance of the relationship with W2. What are W1's and W2's possible claims to H's salary? H is legally separated from W1. His earnings in most states would be his separate property relative to W1. For that reason, W1 might have no claims to H's earnings regardless of the presence of W2. But H is not married to W2. Relative to her, W2, H's earnings are his individual property. W2 is not entitled to a share H's earnings unless and until (i) she legally marries H after he finalizes his divorce to W1 or (ii) she goes to court to get a judgment confirming her status as H's putative spouse. If W2 succeeds on the putative spouse claim, she can claim one-half H's salary as quasi-marital property.

Illustration 11.2: Same facts as in Illustration 11.1 above except that H is not separated from W1. Assume H and W2 ceremonially "marry" before a religious officiant prior to a date of separation between H and W1.

As H's legal spouse, W1 is entitled to a one-half community property share of H's earnings. Additionally, if W2 is adjudged a putative spouse relative to H, W2 has an argument for reaching one-half of H's earnings. Depending on W2's circumstances, she may believe that a ceremonial marriage before a religious officiant is all that is necessary to formalize a marriage. If so, this will raise the issue of whether the putative spouse good faith belief standard is an objective or subjective one.

Illustration 11.3: Same facts as Illustration 11.2 except that H dies while living with W2. W1 has a claim to H's estate based on the existence of the valid H-W1 marriage on the date of H's death. W2 has a claim to H's estate if she can obtain status as a putative spouse.

What about H?

In Illustration 11.1, W1 is H's lawful spouse because H never obtained a final divorce decree. Here, H might seek putative spouse status to shield him from criminal liability for bigamy, and perhaps from liability for fraud on W2 and W1.

In Illustration 11.2, W1 is H's lawful spouse because the H-W1 marriage is still in existence when H ceremonially marries H2. H and W1 have not separated, much less obtained a final divorce decree. In this case, H has no basis for putative spouse status. H knows he is married to W1 at the time that he ceremonially marries W2. And while he might not face criminal liability for bigamy, he might be subject to liability for fraud on W2 and W1.

In Illustration 11.3, H has predeceased W1 and W2. This leaves it for the court to divide H's estate, as is often the case, between two innocent parties.

In sum, Illustration 11.1 and 11.2 are more difficult cases than Illustration 11.3. This is simply because H is still alive, and he might have his own reasons for being adjudged a putative spouse relative to W2.

Additionally, the picture gets more complicated if all three of the parties are employed or have earnings. Is W2 entitled to a share of W1's earnings through H? Is W1 entitled to a share of W2's earnings through H? Is H entitled to a part of W1's earnings and a part of W2's earnings? For example, if H earns less than either W1 or W2, and he is deemed a putative spouse, does that status entitle him to a share of W1 earnings, as her legal spouse, and W2's earnings, as her putative spouse?

One would think not, as to do so could be thought of permitting a form of bigamy. Nevertheless, it seems important to note that these permutated problems can arise.

2. NONMARRIED COHABITANTS

There are several theories of general law available to a nonmarried cohabitant.

Washington relies on the *committed intimate relationship doctrine* (discussed above and below in Section C. Washington) to grant nonmarital partners access to the community property system on a case-by-case basis. The concern with the Washington approach is that it may lead to a de facto form of unlicensed marriage in a state that does not permit unlicensed marriage by statute. Another concern, especially where the petition is contested, is about forced marriage. Nonmarried partners are persons who have chosen a legal status of single. Therefore, the argument goes, unless both partners consent to be married it is legally problematic to retroactively treat those persons as if they had a status of married.

Considering these theoretical problems, nonmarried cohabitants can expect and perhaps should plan to use general law theories in addition to any other theories they may employ.

General legal theories available to nonmarried cohabitants are:

a. Implied Contract

What follows is a simplified discussion of contracts options.

A contract case claims expectancy losses. What could the plaintiff have expected to gain if the defendant had performed on the contract?

In the case of a nonmarital break-up, an alleged failure of performance can be established in multiple ways depending on the asset in question or the support promised. Had the contract been written and signed, absent liquidated damages, the claimant could assess defendant's promises to perform or refrain from performing relative to specifically itemized assets. The measure of damages would be the loss to the plaintiff of the value of the defendant's performance. Related claims of loss could be alleged as consequential damages. Consideration would be required to support the enforceability of such a contract.

But where the contract is not written, details and expectations are left vague. A contract between nonmarried partners can relate to a period, or to a specific asset or assets, or to tracing earnings to purchases. It can also relate to post-breakup support. Each of these points might be a basis for a claim of loss of value due to nonperformance.

Pooling agreements can raise a host of issues, some of which have to do with multiple party bank accounts law, discussed in Chapter 4, Chapter 6, and Chapter 7. Parties during the relationship tend to demonstrate the existence and possibly the terms of a partnership or joint venture, throughout the cohabitancy period, by their conduct. As for the pooling agreement, the conduct required to prove it is that both parties do in fact pool their earnings or bank deposits. Bank accounts are not governed as investment accounts, but rather as deposit accounts.

Contract defenses might be by proof of large discrepancies in the parties' actual respective cash contributions to their shared household. Specialized tracing, like that discussed in Chapter 7, can help identify beneficial ownership to sums on deposit in a pooled bank account.

Illustration 11.4: Assume a case where unmarried cohabitants tacitly agree that one cohabitant will take care of home and children while the other develops a professional career. The parties want to lower childcare costs, enhance their co-parenting, and help the higher earning partner advance in her profession. To prevail on an implied contract theory, the contract claimant would need to prove the existence of the contract. Writing fragments (if any), discussions and conduct might go toward this proof. To prevail on a tacit contract theory, proof of conduct would show that the parties were carrying out a contract despite it not having been reduced to writing.

General law makes consideration a contract formality. Meretricious consideration is illegal. Therefore, a contract supported by meretricious consideration fails. A caveat is necessary here: when the consideration for a contract involves or can be interpreted to involve support *solely* in exchange for sex it will fall into the category of meretricious consideration as a matter of law. What makes the meretricious doctrine dead letter in this context is that the parties are living their lives together while having a sexual relationship. Sex is not the sole reason, if it even is a reason, for their contract.

b. Quasi-Contract

When nonmarried cohabitants lack a written contract or evidence upon which to base a claim, or if consideration to support the contract is lacking, the claimant must look to other potential legal remedies.

Restatement (Second) of Contracts § 344 says that judicial remedies serve to protect reasonable expectation, reliance, or restitutionary interests of the promisee. Thus, the theories discussed next all fall generally within the rubric of restitutionary remedies.

Quasi-contract is a restitution-based claim. Quasi-contract attempts to disgorge from defendant the value of what the plaintiff expended for defendant's benefit. For the quantum meruit theory the claimant must prove that the parties intended to compensate the laboring partner for identifiable services. Thus, here the problem for a claimant who is ending a cohabitancy is defining the limits of the claim itself.

Restitution today is complex, but here is some textbook advice about the essence of the restitution claim that restores the defendant—rather than the plaintiff—to their rightful position. Thomas, Levine, and Young note the potentially large swath of gray area when they say this about restitution.

> "It is an attractive remedy for a plaintiff who does not need a future order and believes the wrong is better measured by the defendant's profit than its loss. The remedy of restitution is almost self-evident to lawyers and clients; but attorneys must learn to frame their claims using the applicable standards of the courts."[1]

Illustration 11.5: Assume a case where the parties tacitly agree that one cohabitant will leave a high paying job to work, without pay, as an assistant in the other party's start-up business. The work is completed, a break-up ensues, and the party who conferred the labor as an assistant is not paid. The unpaid party brings a quasi-contract theory to define the total value of uncompensated labor. The suit

---

[1] REMEDIES: PUBLIC AND PRIVATE 7th Ed. (Tracy A. Thomas, David I. Levine, David J. Jung eds.) p. 587.

seeks restitution to prevent unjust enrichment of the defendant. As restitution the court would order the defendant to be disgorged the amount of the benefit conferred by the laboring partner on the start-up business. This measure may disappoint the claimant since it is not based on what the assisting cohabitant gave up in terms of pay, but rather on the value of the services conferred on the start-up.

c. Expectancy Interest (the Benefit of the Bargain) versus Restitutionary Interest (Preventing Unjust Enrichment)

Lon Fuller defined the claimant's expectancy interest as the parties' "interest in having the *benefit of his bargain* by being put in as good a position as he would have been in had the contract been performed."[2] This definition has had long legs over nearly a century.

Restatement (Second) of Contracts § 347 measures the expectancy interest by:

(a) The loss of the value to the claimant of the other party's performance, caused by its deficiency, plus.

(b) Any other loss, including incidental or consequential loss, caused by the breach, less.

---

[2] Lon Fuller & William Perdue, *The Reliance Interest in Contract Damages*, 46 YALE L.J. 52 (1936), cited in REMEDIES: PUBLIC AND PRIVATE 7th Ed. (Tracy A. Thomas, David I. Levine, David J. Jung eds. 2023) p. 485.

(c) Any cost or other loss that he has avoided by not having to perform.

The claimant's reliance interest is "his interest in being *reimbursed for loss* caused by reliance on the contract by being put in as good a position as he would have been in had the contract not been made."[3]

Expectancy—an interest in the benefit of the bargain—versus reliance—reimbursement for loss caused by reliance on the bargain—often overlap.

Where the measure of the expectancy under the contract is greater than the reliance upon it, Thomas, Levine, and Jung advise that the award should provide the claimant with the full benefit of the advantage that was expected.[4]

Claims for lengthy periods of service may be cut short by statutes of limitation. If so, it is possible, in a cohabitancy case, that only the final few years of the cohabitancy might be eligible to serve as the basis for an implied contract claim.

d. Quantum Meruit

For the quantum meruit theory the claimant must prove that the parties intended to compensate him or her (in his or her specific role as laboring partner). Here the claim is not to disgorge excess profits or contributions to purchase. Here the claim is far more specifically for payment for identifiable services rendered.

---

3 Id.

4 Id.

e. Partnership

Partnership is yet another theory that allows a nonmarried person to seek compensation in the context of a breakup. A formal partnership agreement is useful but not necessary to pursuing such a claim. The partnership can be equal or unequal. It can duplicate many of the features of community property.

Generally, courts uphold partnership agreements if a business (or real property) is involved, and there is adequate proof of an agreement to partner on the project.

Occasionally, a court embraces approximately the same principles, but more loosely, by calling the agreement a *joint venture*. Joint ventures might be more transaction specific. Partnerships go more toward the whole of the business. A pooling agreement, as discussed above, can be evidence of a partnership to maintain a household and a joint venture to buy a house or a car.

f. Form of Title

None of the community property states authorizes the common law tenancy by the entirety title, or TBE. To create a TBE requires five unities (time, title, interest, possession, and marriage); if the fifth unity is broken, the title defaults to the common law TIC. See Chapter 6 for more on concurrent titles.

As to title forms, the general rule is that form of title controls ownership. A title in one partner's name alone is that partner's individual property. Both cohabitating partners own a concurrent title.

All community property states permit the tenancy in common (TIC) title form.

All community property states except Louisiana permit the joint tenancy (JTWROS) title form.

No community property states allow nonmarried persons to access the community property system *by default*. Therefore, only a married person can own community property or hold a community property (CP) title form. Likewise, only a married person can hold the community property with the right of survivorship (CPWROS) title form.

The form of holding title is less important in civil law countries; and it can be shown to fail to reflect the parties' understanding about ownership of the titled asset. Nevertheless, for single persons, the general rule holds. The person whose name is on the title is presumed to be the beneficial owner of the property absent clear and convincing evidence to the contrary.

If the parties have contributed equally to the purchase of property, either joint tenancy (JTWROS) or a tenancy in common (TIC) in equal shares will accurately reflect their intentions as to ownership.

If the contributions by the parties are unequal, only a tenancy in common (TIC) can be divided into pro rata shares based on the parties' respective purchase contributions. Here the TIC title deed is being used as a contract between the parties, with respective contributions to purchase the contract terms.

Labor (sweat equity) is typically not considered a contribution to purchase, but it may be considered a conferred benefit, as in Texas. A conferred benefit should be reimbursed upon proof that the lack of reimbursement will unjustly enrich the party upon whom the benefit was conferred. Uncompensated labor can be the basis of a quasi-contract claim, a quantum meruit claim, or an unjust enrichment claim.

g. Constructive Trust

One remedy for unjust enrichment is called the constructive trust. Restatement (Third) of Restitution § 55 Constructive Trust.

A constructive trust is not a private trust, it is a legal remedy imposed by the court regardless of the intentions of the parties.

With a private trust, the legal title holder must eventually return the trust property (corpus and appreciation) to the trust beneficiary; plus, state law, at the very least, will impose a range of duties on the trustee.

With a constructive trust, the court orders the record title owner or possessor of property (as trustee or legal title holder) to carry out the one and only duty that person has as trustee, namely, to transfer title of the asset to the constructive trust beneficiary. Just as the "constructive trustee" is no trustee of a trust, the "constructive beneficiary" is no beneficiary of a trust. Rather the beneficiary is a party (sometimes called an equitable owner) who was wrongly taken out of title and possession by the other party. The constructive trust remedy addresses the legal claim that the property fell into the wrong hands without the consent of the true owner. Restatement (Third) of Restitution and Unjust Enrichment § 1 cmt. b (2011).

An ineffective transaction can be caused by multiple circumstances. Four common scenarios are identified by the Restatement (Third) of Restitution and Unjust Enrichment § 1 cmt. b (2011) and quoting the Restatement (Third) of Restitution:

- The claimant confers *unrequested* benefits without obtaining the recipient's agreement to pay for them.
- An attempted contractual exchange miscarries after partial performance.
- The defendant acquires benefits by wrongful interference with the claimant's rights.

The term unrequested benefits in the first bullet point does not refer to inter vivos gifts. It refers to a gratuitous transfer induced by mistake, fraud, or undue influence that confers a benefit on the recipient. What distinguishes the gift from the wrongful gratuitous transfer (the conferred benefit) is a lack of donative intent upon delivery of the property. Furthermore, whereas the recipient of an unrestricted gift has an unconditional legal right to retain the property, the recipient of a wrongfully induced gratuitous transfer does not have a right to retain the property, or if they do that right is conditional and restricted.

h. Resulting Trust

A resulting trust arises from the presumed intentions of the parties.

Illustration 11.5: Assume a case where unmarried cohabitants purchase a house. One party, Alpha, delivers the down payment. The other party, Beta, obtains a purchase money loan from Bank, signs a deed of trust naming Bank as trustee for sale, and takes title in Beta's name alone. Here, Alpha supplied part of the purchase price by gratuitous transfer, yet beneficial title was initially taken in Beta's name alone. After closing the loan, Beta has a duty to change the title to reflect Alpha's contribution to purchase. Failing that duty, Alpha can petition for a reimbursement from Beta for these reasons.

One, Alpha delivered the funds to Beta without donative intent, hence Alpha's delivery was not an inter vivos gift, but rather a conferred benefit.

Two, Alpha's gratuitous transfer conferred a benefit on Beta that, if not reimbursed, would unjustly enrich Beta.

Three, until Beta changes the deed to reflect the fact of concurrent title, Beta must hold the property for the benefit of Alpha and Beta.

Four, the fact that the title is not accurate puts third parties who might purchase the property on the retail real estate market at risk of litigation—i.e., the title might be good, but it will not be marketable until it reflects that there are two beneficial owners of the property, Alpha and Beta.

Upon proof, Alpha's ownership interest will be confirmed by a court judgment that raises a resulting trust on Beta. Hence, the remedy here is that Beta is holding the property in resulting trust until the title gets changed.

Does a resulting trust negatively impact the mortgage company's rights? Not immediately, especially since the loan is secured by the property itself.

i. Equitable Lien

An equitable lien helps secure a loan.

Here the restitutionary theory is that buying property together gives rise to a reasonable expectation of shared ownership as to the asset purchased.

Between married persons, separate property business accounting methods might be understood as necessary to identify whether an equitable lien is necessary to prevent unjust enrichment of the business; if it is, then the equitable lien allows excess profits to be disgorged from the separate property business and paid over to the community. See Chapter 7 for more on separate property business accounting. Likewise, between married persons, unwritten pro tanto ownership interests can be understood as an equitable lien remedy that serves the purpose of disgorging the record title holder from the amount the conferring estate has paid to release the record title holder's loan principal indebtedness. See Chapter 7 for more on credit acquisition accounting.

But what happens when the parties are unmarried in a state that does not provide access to its marital property statutes to unmarried persons? The short answer is that unmarried persons get what they asked for: the chance to use general law to resolve their disputes. But can unmarried cohabitants use the accounting methods developed for married persons under a state's community property laws? Yes, and I cover this in point below.

If these actions can be understood generally as disgorgement remedies, then the answer is yes. The marriage license is the contract that allows access to the state's community property laws. For married people, the accounting methods are law. But for nonmarried people the accounting methods can be thought of more as negotiating points based on arithmetic that has been stress-tested by marital dissolution cases. That arithmetic is available to all litigants as part of our common legal knowledge.

j. General Equitable Principles

The courts of equity have long exercised powers to correct legal imbalances. The rise in non-marital relationships puts greater demands on systems of law and equity for correction of inequalities at break-up or the death of one of the parties.

There is a growing body of law review literature on the rights of unmarried or nonmarried partners. One point that much of this literature misses is that the claims set forth above are legal claims, not moral claims. At this point in time, it is not only socially acceptable to live with an intimate partner, it might also be financially advisable to do so. This is the test-drive for marriage theory. To get morally outraged that nonmarried people cannot be treated like married people is perhaps an extreme position, especially if in the same article there is a hearty condemnation of marriage as a thoroughly sexist institution.

Another point that emerging literature tends to miss is that there is no need to reinvent wheels that work. The wheel is not difficult to grasp as a concept. But, in this context, a wheel may require more legal analysis than a counterpart community property default rule, which is an existing wheel that works to facilitate dissolution. Even partners with contracts can consciously uncouple. Not all conscious uncouplers are wealthy, and so it might matter to one or both how the property gets divided, and whether it can be divided equitably.

Here is the key takeaway for every couple, married or not. Marital property laws facilitate dissolution between intimate partners, general laws do not.

Therefore, all things being equal, litigation to split up the holdings and debts of nonmarital partners will likely be more drawn out (and expensive) than litigation to split up the holdings of married partners. This is not to say that married people are more rational or that their divorces are always inexpensive. Even a fast skip through divorce literature and cases will illustrate that the default rules, although theoretically made of stainless steel, can be chipped away at as if they were an old clay pot. Parties can and do use divorce as an analog for therapy. Those parties who do are usually unusually wealthy.

C. INDIVIDUAL STATES

1. ARIZONA

Arizona did not repeal its state constitutional ban on same-sex marriage. However, that ban is unenforceable under the ruling in *Obergefell*, supra, which legalized same-sex marriage nationwide.

Arizona does not permit informal marriages but does formally recognize by statutes such marriages validly contracted in any jurisdiction that allows them. Ariz.Rev.Stat.Ann. § 25–111 and § 25–112. Arizona does not recognize informal divorce, therefore, informally married spouses must still obtain a formal divorce to terminate their marriage, as is the case in all states.

Bigamous marriages are void and illegal upon proof that a person knowingly married another person in a manner that would be valid but for the defendant's ongoing marriage. *State v. Guadagni*, 218 Ariz. 1, 178 P.3d 473 (2008). Only marriages that are void or voidable may be annulled. Valid marriages are dissolved. Nevertheless, the granting of a dissolution does not preclude the granting of a valid decree of annulment under *Hodges v. Hodges*, 118 Ariz. 572, 578 P.2d 1001 (Ct.App. 1978) and *Medlin v. Medlin*, 194 Ariz. 306, 981 P.2d 1087 (Ct.App. 1999).

Additionally, a voidable marriage that is annulled *does* acquire community property. This is because a voidable marriage is presumed valid until and unless it is annulled. *Hammett v. Hammet*, 247 Ariz. 556, 453 P.3d 1145 (Ct.App. 2019) explained why this is. "The community property statute, A.R.S. 25–211, does not distinguish between community property acquired during a marriage that is later dissolved and community property acquired during a marriage that is subsequently annulled." Moreover, the court pointed to A.R.S. 25–211(b), which clearly states that annulment does not alter the status of community property. It says, **"a petition for dissolution of marriage, legal separation or annulment does not alter the status of *preexisting community property.*"** The phrase preexisting community property implies that this section applies most squarely to a voidable marriage.

Here is yet another gray area in the nonmarriage to marriage spectrum. Under the civil law, a void marriage is not valid, but a voidable marriage is valid at least until it is annulled. During the period of presumed validity, a voidable marriage nevertheless can result in community property acquisitions and debt. If the parties later divorce, they confirm the marriage as valid. If the parties annul, they dispute the validity of the marriage, and even though they do this, they may still have preexisting community property acquisitions and debt to dissolve.

If a marriage is clearly void, the spouse who in good faith believed in the validity of the marriage could petition for putative spouse status. Arizona acknowledged the putative spouse doctrine in *Stevens v. Anderson*, 75 Ariz. 331, 256 P.2d 712 (1953), but does not appear to have scrutinized it at the appellate level.

Clarifying the law on this point could be helpful.

The general rule is that if parties are not lawfully married, they cannot predicate property rights on marital status. *Cross v. Cross*, 381 P.2d 573 (1963). They can, however, seek recovery on theories of partnership or contract.

2. CALIFORNIA

California Proposition 8 implemented a state constitutional ban on same-sex marriage with the words "only marriage between a man and a woman is valid or recognized in California." Proposition 8 was later overturned in the *Hollingsworth v. Perry*, 570 U.S. 693 (2013). The tapes in that case were only recently unsealed. Additionally, the ban is unenforceable under the ruling in *Obergefell*, supra, which legalized same-sex marriage nationwide.

Consent, license, and solemnization make for a valid marriage in California. Consent refers to mental competence to agree to marriage. Solemnization refers to the witnessing of the marriage ceremony by third parties. A license, once recorded, refers to the marriage certificate bearing the state seal that serves as proof of a valid marriage. The failure to record a marriage license will not invalidate an otherwise valid marriage; but neither will a marriage license turn an otherwise void or voidable marriage into a valid one.

A void marriage is one that is bigamous, polygamous, or between relatives of a certain degree of kinship. One type of bigamy is potentially excusable. It occurs when a spouse has been missing for a long time.—Cal.Fam.Code. § 2210, newly amended and effective as of Jan 1. 2019, says this. **"The spouse of either party was living and the marriage with that spouse was then in force and that spouse (1) was absent and not known to the party commencing the proceeding to be living for a period of five successive years immediately preceding the subsequent marriage for which the judgment of nullity is sought or (2) was generally reputed or believed by the party commencing the proceeding to be dead at the time the subsequent marriage was contracted."**

The mere absence of a spouse does not raise a presumption of death. Instead, there is case law that suspends the first marriage (between spouse 1 and 2) once the second marriage (between spouse 2 and 3) is contracted. After the date of suspension, either spouse 1 or spouse 2 can opt to annul or dissolve the first marriage. Dissolution is discussed in Chapter 10.

A voidable marriage is one with a defect that vitiates consent. A voidable marriage is presumed valid unless and until one of the parties (or both), during life, seek an annulment. Upon the death of one party to the union, a voidable marriage becomes valid.

California has codified the putative spouse doctrine. Cal.Fam.Code § 2251, updated on Jan 1, 2016, provides as follows. **"If a determination is made that a marriage is void or voidable and the court finds that either party or both parties believed in good faith that the marriage was valid, the court shall (1) Declare the party or parties, *who believed in good faith that the marriage was valid*, to have the status of a putative spouse."** (Italics added.)

If division of property is an issue, a putative spouse can claim his or her share of "quasi-marital property" which is defined as **"that property acquired during the union that would have been community property or quasi-community property if the union had not been void or voidable, *only upon request of a party who is declared a putative spouse under paragraph (1)*."** (Italics added).

In California, a person who is declared a putative spouse can also petition for spousal support rights unlike in Nevada, as discussed below.

A recent line of cases holds that a putative spouse is one who has a subjective good faith belief in the validity of an otherwise void or voidable marriage.

That line starts with *Ceja v. Rudolph & Sletten, Inc.*, 56 Cal. 4th 1113, 158 Cal.Rptr.3d 21, 302 P.3d 211 (2013). Subjective means from the perspective of the individual who is petitioning for putative spouse status.

Cal.Fam.Code § 297 et seq. brings registered domestic partners (RDPs) completely into the community property system. Cal. Fam.Code 297 defines the term domestic partners. **"Domestic partners are two adults who have chosen to share one another's lives in an intimate and committed relationship of mutual caring."**

Proposed and yet unsigned amendments to (AB 2924) would raise the statutory age at which a person can file for a marriage license or an RDP license to eighteen. At present a person who is under eighteen years old can file for a marriage license or for RDP status with parental consent or proof of emancipation.

The difference between this idea and the Washington committed relationship doctrine is that a couple who meets this definition must also file a Declaration of Domestic Partnership with the Secretary of State for the relationship to be recognized as an RDP. Thus, RDP status is formal in the sense that benefits derived from it are granted by the state of California upon filing the proper documents with the state.

In California, RDPs have all the benefits of legal marriage. This is important to keep in mind for matters of property acquisition and division.

Cal.Fam.Code § 297. **"Registered Domestic Partners shall have the same rights, protections, and benefits, and shall be subject to the same responsibilities, obligations, and duties under law, whether they derive from statutes, administrative regulations, court rules, government policies, common law, or any other provisions or sources of law, as granted to and imposed upon spouses."**

Under this same provision, an RDP has the same rights and obligations and the same access to California community property law as a spouse. An RDP must be terminated before a subsequent RDP relationship, or a formal marriage, can be contracted.

Over decades, case law has come to define nonmarital cohabitants as two adults who choose to share their lives with each other in an intimate and committed sexual relationship. Nonmarried partners conduct their relationship outside the scope of the Family Code, and under the Civil Code. Their property and support issues (if any) are governed by the general laws discussed in Sections A and B above. However, the California Domestic Violence Prevention Act (DVPA) does apply to nonmarried cohabitants. So does most of the state's multiple parties accounts law (CAMPAL). However, the CAMPAL special community property presumption for sums on deposit in an account does not apply to nonmarried partners. The DVPA and CAMPAL are discussed in Chapter 7.

California is the place that made contracts between nonmarried cohabitants, known as *Marvin* contracts, famous. *Marvin v. Marvin*, 18 Cal.3d 660, 134 Cal.Rptr. 815, 557 P.2d. 106 (1976) continues to be a leading case on the issue of nonmarital cohabitant's breakup remedies. There, the California Supreme Court considered, as a general matter, the appropriateness of enforcing an implied pooling (sharing) contract for which the alleged consideration was housekeeping. It also considered, again as a general matter, the appropriateness of "rehabilitation," meaning post-breakup financial support.

The trial court dismissed the claimant's contract claims as to certain assets (like a Los Angeles mansion) for lack of consideration, but it awarded her $104,000 of "rehabilitation" on general equitable principles conditional on proof that the claimant had supported her celebrity partner in the development of his career.

Appeals were ultimately taken to the California Supreme Court. As to contract enforceability, the state supreme court held that implied or tacit pooling contracts between nonmarital partners are enforceable upon proof of (i) the terms of the contract (ii) valid consideration for the contract, and (iii) breach. There is extensive case law on what constitutes sufficient consideration to support a *Marvin* contract.

As to the "rehabilitation award," the trial court's grant of post-breakup support was ultimately reversed on the rationale that the nonmarried cohabitants, not having been married, were not eligible to access the community property system for purposes of seeking spousal support. The consideration that loomed large was the state's policy to generally disallow opening a back door to the recognition of informal (unlicensed) marriage. Also relevant was that the defendant was already in a valid marriage when he established a nonmarital relationship with the plaintiff.

A later case, *Byrne v. Laura*, 52 Cal.App.4th 1054, 1063, Cal. Rptr. 2d 908 (Cal.App.Ct. 1st Dist. 1997) extended *Marvin*, supra, to an oral agreement for lifetime post-breakup support brought against a decedent nonmarital partner's estate.

A *Marvin* claim can be consolidated by the parties or by the court with an existing family law case, as for example when nonmarital cohabitants marry and then eventually dissolve their marriage. But in the end, a *Marvin* claim is a civil action, not a family court action. The doctrine of estoppel (the cohabitants live together) precludes application of the statute of frauds as a defense. See *Marvin*, supra, and *Byrne*, supra. Different statutes of limitation apply depending on the claims, as indicated in the state Civil Code. And the *Marvin* contract does not implicate the state Labor Code. *Whorton v. Dillingham*, 202 Cal. App.3d 447, 248 Cal.Rptr. 405 (Cal.App.Ct. 4th Dist. 1988)

Just as nonmarried cohabitants are outside of the Family Code, persons who have a sexual relationship but who do not cohabitate with each other fall outside of the holding in *Marvin*, supra, rule. See e.g., *Bergen v. Wood*, 14 CalApp.4th 854, 18 Cal. Rptr. 2d 75 (2nd Dist. 1988), which held that intimate partners who do not cohabitate are barred by law from bringing *Marvin* contract claims.

California does not permit informal marriage but will recognize as valid such a marriage lawfully contracted in another jurisdiction. California does not recognize informal divorce—no state does.

3. IDAHO

Idaho did not repeal its state constitutional ban on same-sex marriage. But that ban is unenforceable under the ruling in *Obergefell*, supra, which legalized same-sex marriage nationwide.

Idaho recognizes marriage as a civil contract, but no longer permits informal marriages after January 1, 1996. The change is non-retroactive. Prior to January 1, 1996, cohabitation alone could give rise to presumption of an informal marriage. Such a marriage arose from the parties' mutual and non-licensed assumption of marital rights, duties, or obligations.

After January 1, 1996, the operative statute became Idaho Code § 32–201. It reads: **"Consent alone will not constitute marriage; it must be followed by the issuance of a license and a solemnization as authorized and provide by law."**

Related to marriage equality issues, this statute became and remains controversial, because it remains red flagged. Idaho, like Navada, amended its state constitution to prevent same-sex couples from marrying and to bar state recognition of same-sex marriages validly performed in another state. *Latta v. Otter*, 771 F.3d 456 (2014).

Idaho recognizes as valid a common law marriage lawfully contracted outside of Idaho.

Idaho never did and does not now recognize informal divorce. However, there are some questions on this issue raised by Idaho Code § 32–208. This code provision releases a party from a contract to marry if they are unaware that the other party is unchaste or if the other party participates in unchaste conduct alone. Release from a contract to marry seems, at least to me, quite different than release from a state-recognized marriage contract. Case law does not help define key terms. The only point of information that contextualizes this statute, which is still very much on the books, is that it was originally enacted by the state legislature in 1887 and amended in 1909 and again in 1919.

Idaho has not adopted the putative spouse doctrine. But Idaho Code § 5–311 permits a person who can make the case for being a putative spouse under general doctrine to sue for wrongful death. *Reichert v. Sunshine Mining Co.*, 95 Idaho 647, 516 P.2d 704 (1973) provides more information on why this statute become significant in Idaho legal history.

4. LOUISIANA

Louisiana had a state constitutional ban on same-sex marriage and other marriage-like relationships, which probably means the recognition of same-sex marriages validly contracted in another state.

Louisiana did not repeal its state constitutional ban on same-sex marriage. But that ban is unenforceable under the ruling in *Obergefell*, supra, which legalized same-sex marriage nationwide.

LSA-C.C. Art. 86. **"Marriage is a legal relationship between a man and a woman that is created by civil contract. The relationship and the contract are subject to special rules prescribed by law."** This statute remains on the books, but on its face, it violates federal constitutional and statutory law.

Covenant marriage (after premarital counseling and upon the execution of a declaration of intent) is permitted in the state. LSA-R.S 9:272 defines the term. **"A covenant is a marriage entered into by one male and one female who understand and agree that the marriage between them is a lifelong relationship. . . . Only when there has been a complete and total breach of the marital covenant commitment may the non-breaching party seek a declaration that the marriage is no longer legally recognized. . . . A covenant marriage may not be dissolved, rescinded, or otherwise terminated by the mutual consent of the spouses."**

Grounds for terminating a covenant marriage are found at LSA-R.S. 9:307.

LSA-R.S. 40:62 **"Any person born in Louisiana who has sustained sex reassignment or corrective surgery which has changed the anatomical structure of the sex of the**

individual to that of a sex other than that which appears on the original birth certificate of the individual, may petition a court of competent jurisdiction as provided in this Section to obtain a new certificate of birth."

Equal protection issues may arise because of the statute's silence on how to deal with a pre-operative marriage document that would reveal the person's pre-operative sex. Until the statutory gap is addressed probably with a clarified statute, transgender petitioners who were or are currently married, as compared to petitioners who have never been married, are at risk of receiving disparate treatment under Louisiana law. Additionally, LSA-R.S. 40.62 contains no direction for how it reconciles with LSA-C.C. Art. 86, which was found unconstitutional in *A.M.C. v. Caldwell*, 239 So. 3d 948 (2018).

Louisiana codified the putative spouse doctrine which it adopted from the civil law. LSA-C.C. Art. 96 provides: **"An absolutely null marriage nevertheless produces civil effects in favor of a party who contracted it in good faith for as long as that party remains in good faith."** The phrase civil effects here means that the putative spouse can gain access to the matrimonial regime for purposes of addressing property issues A recent modification to this same Article appears in its second sentence. **"When the cause of the nullity is one party's prior undissolved marriage, the civil effects continue in favor of the other party, regardless of whether the latter remains in good faith,**

until the marriage is pronounced null or the latter party contracts a valid marriage."

The rationale for this modification, according to the Revision Comments, is that in such a situation:

> "The party whose prior undissolved marriage is the cause of nullity is the one who has the dispositive power to rectify the nullity (by divorcing his former spouse and remarrying his present one). The other party cannot do so. Accordingly, the second sentence of this Article permits the spouse who has acted in good faith and whose prior marriage was not the cause of the nullity to enjoy the civil effects of marriage even after he ceases to be in good faith. This additional period ends when the party benefitted by it contracts a valid marriage (whether with the other party to the null union or with a third party), or when the nullity of the bigamous marriage is judicially recognized, whichever occurs first." Revision Comments 1984.

In a putative spouse situation, (LSA-C.C. Art. 2336) extends protections to the children of the union.

Contracts between nonmarried cohabitants (Louisiana cases use obsolete terms like "concubinage," "concubine," and "paramour") can be unenforceable as against public policy depending on the facts of the case. LSA-C.C. Art. 2030 provides as follows. **"A contract is absolutely null when it violates a rule of public order, as when the**

object of a contract is illicit or immoral. A contract that is absolutely null may not be confirmed." Equitable lien and quantum meruit claims are denied on similar policy grounds.

In *Schwegmann v. Schwegmann*, 441 So. 2d 316, 324 (La. App. 1983) writ denied sub nom. *Blackledge v. Schwegmann*, 443 So. 2d 1122 (La. 1984), after her nonmarried cohabitant had a stroke, the plaintiff sued her cohabitant, his children, and his multiple corporate business entities to enforce an oral agreement, an implied agreement, equitable liens, quantum meruit for uncompensated domestic services (cooking, cleaning, chauffeuring, child care, assisting the defendant after his stroke), and quantum meruit for uncompensated business services as a business advisor, a political assistant, and a business confidant. The court called the 12-year relationship a concubinage. The court called the plaintiff a concubine, which the court explained was a woman who occupies position, performs duties, and assumes responsibilities of the wife, without title and privileges flowing from legal marriage. Id. The court called the man a paramour, which the court defined as a man with whom a concubine lives. Id. The court then dismissed claims related to what the court referred to throughout as the concubinage, but it allowed the uncompensated business services claim on the ground that those claims might not be related to the relationship (the so-called concubinage. (Eventually, the court denied the business claim too.)

The rationale for the dismissal of the contract claims was that they were void for public policy. The rationale on the dismissal of the equitable lien and quantum meruit claims was that "nonmarried cohabitation does not give rise to property rights analogous to or like those of married couples," and that "concubines have no implied contract or equitable liens that afford them any rights in the property of their paramours." Id. The court said, of its policy, that "although Victorian, the values sought to be protected by the formulation of those legal concepts are imperative if we are to maintain our civilized society." Id.

5. NEVADA

Nevada is one of the states that banned same sex marriage by state constitutional amendment, but the state then became the first state to remove the same-sex marriage ban from its constitution by voter referendum.

Couples over a certain age can solemnize their relationship under the Nevada Domestic Partnership Act. Nev.Rev.Stat. § 122A.010 appears to parallel the California legislation in extending the rights and liabilities of marriage to RDPs. RDPs must be formally terminated.

Hay v. Hay, 100 Nev. 196, 199, 678 P.2d 672, 674 (1984) quoted *Marvin,* 18 Cal.3d 660, 134 Cal.Rptr. 815, 557 P.2d. 106 (1976), to expressly hold that *Marvin* contracts are enforceable in Nevada.

The Nevada Supreme Court, in *Williams v. Williams* 120 Nev. 559, 97 P.3d 1124 (2004), adopted the putative spouse doctrine in annulment proceedings for purposes of property division, but rejected the doctrine as a basis of awarding equitable spousal support. The rationale was that Nevada's annulment statutes do not provide for an award of support upon annulment. The court also stated in dicta that although a bigamous marriage is void under the plain meaning of Nev.Rev.Stat. § 125.290, an annulment proceeding is nonetheless necessary to legally sever the relationship. Id. at 564. *Marriage of Seaton*, 200 Cal.App. 4th 800, 807–08, 133 Cal.Rptr. 3d 50, 56 (2011) discussed *Williams* in a case involving a spouse who entered a void marriage in Nevada and subsequently married a different person in California.

6. NEW MEXICO

New Mexico early on recognized same-sex marriage. New Mexico did not ban same sex marriage in its state constitution.

New Mexico has not recognized the putative spouse doctrine by statute. However, courts have ruled in favor of the rights of spouses in an invalid marriage. See e.g., *Estate of Lamb*, 99 N.M. 157, 655 P.2d 1001 (1982), and *Prince v. Freeman*, 45 N.M. 143, 112 P.2d 821 (N.M. 1941).

7. TEXAS

Texas banned same-sex marriage and other marriage-like relationships by voter referendum in 2005. It also enacted a statutory license prohibition for persons of the same gender who sought to marry. V.T.C.A.Tex.Fam.Code § 2.001. Neither is constitutional after *Obergefell*, supra, which legalized same-sex marriage nationwide.

Recently Texas revised much of its code to replace gendered terms (man and woman) with gender neutral terms (spouses), but in some places, gendered terms were left unaddressed. Whether this oversight was an unintentional error, or an intentional political move is unclear at this time.

However, even post-*Obergefell*, supra, Texas case law continues to frustrate the rights of transgender persons. By case law, gender assignment at birth, not gender at the time of the marriage, determines marriage validity and how a person's gender gets named on their own marriage certificate. *Littleton v. Prange*, 9 S.W.3d 223 (1999), *rev. denied, rehearing of petition for review overruled, cert. denied* 121 S.Ct. 174, 531 U.S. 872 (2000), raised the issue and explained its rationale as to marriage validity. Despite inclusive changes in the law, obstacles other than being misgendered on that person's own marriage certificate remain. For example, a person who swears a gender different than the one assigned at birth can be charged with false swearing. V.T.C.A.Tex.Fam.Code § 2.004(c) and Op.Att'y Gen. No. M–1277 (1972).

Texas recognizes informal, or common-law, marriage for different-sex partners upon proof offered in a **"judicial, administrative, or other proceeding"** by the party claiming the validity of the marriage. V.T.C.A.Fam.Code § 2.401. It is unclear how and in what way *Obergefell*, supra, implicates the Texas rules on informal marriage, which uses gender specific husband and wife language.

To establish an informal marriage, three elements must be established. One, the partners agreed to be married. Two, the partners lived together in Texas as spouses. And three, the partners held themselves out as married to each other.

Each case of claimed common-law marriage is determined on its own facts. *Joplin v. Borusheski*, 244 S.W. 3d 607 (2008). The burden of proof is by a preponderance of the evidence. *Small v. McMaster*, 352 S.W.3d 280 (2011), petition for review filed.

A conditional agreement made by the parties to live together for a trial period does not constitute a valid informal marriage. The precedent here is a line of cases interpreting element one (the agreement element) to require a present, unconditional, and unqualified, bilateral agreement between the parties *to be married*. See e.g., *Schwingle v. Keifer*, 105 Tex. 609, 153 S.W. 1132 (1913), *Texas Employers' Ins. Ass'n v. Borum*, 834 S.W.2d 395 (1992), *Nguyen v. Nguyen,* 355 S.W. 3d 82 (2011).

Additionally, an agreement to be spouses must be followed by cohabitation *as spouses*. The idea being that the parties' conduct must give them a public reputation of being married, not just one of being engaged, cohabitating, or in a trial period of cohabitation. *Smith v. Deneve*, 285 S.W.3d 904 (2009). *Grigsby v. Reib*, 105 Tex. 597, 153 S.W. 1124 (1913)—a rather interesting case—ruled that cohabitation as spouses need not be continuous, once the three elements for establishing the informal marriage are met.

An informal marriage may be declared and registered under V.T.C.A.Fam.Code § 2.401. Bigamy is a criminal offense in Texas, and an unterminated common-law marriage can form the basis for a bigamy prosecution. *Melton v. State*, 71 Tex. Crim. 130, 158 S.W. 550 (1913). Common-law divorce is unknown to Texas law; once an informal marriage is a contracted, however, it must be dissolved in the same way as a licensed marriage. In *Claveria v. Claveria's Estate*, 597 S.W.2d 434 (1980), the court recognized common-law divorce, but this decision and the rationale of common-law divorce were reversed on appeal in *Claveria's Estate v. Claveria*, 615 S.W.2d 164 (1981).

Where two marriages are alleged, the most recent marriage is presumptively valid against each marriage that precedes it, unless the party who asserts the validity of an earlier marriage proves otherwise. *Nguyen v. Nguyen*, 355 S.W.3d 82 (2011). If a court finds an earlier marriage valid as against a later in time marriage, Texas protects the good faith later-in-time putative spouse through an equitable doctrine that entitles the putative spouse to one half of the product of the joint efforts acquired while believing in good faith that a marriage existed. The courts have not been consistent with terminology. Some cases have declared the share to be community; others have stated the shares to be the separate property of each party. The lesson here is that putative spouse status will not necessarily support a community of property in Texas—no matter what it is ultimately called—as it does in California.

Nonmarried cohabitants, even if they live together, are not spouses, and thus they lack the right to avail themselves of the benefits of the community property system. Their remedies against each other rest in legal theories applicable to non-married persons such as agreements for contract, quantum meruit, and partnership or joint venture claims when there have been contributions of labor or capital to the life shared together.

8. WASHINGTON

Washington did not ban same-sex marriage in its state constitution, but it did pass legislation, which defined marriage in gendered (man and woman) terms. That legislation was repealed in 2012.

Washington recognizes marriage as a **"civil contract between two persons . . . ."** Additionally, Washington passed broad registered domestic partnership legislation in the pre-*Obergefell*, supra, era to protect the right of same-sex couples to formalize their intimate relationship. Wash.Rev.Code § 26.16.030. During life, if the parties decide to split up, they must formally end their RDP.

By tradition and by precedent, as in *Brenchley's Estate*, 96 Wash. 223, 164 P. 913 (1917), as well as by the logic applied to equitable relationships (discussed next), Washington protects the rights of the putative spouse, at least as to property obtained during the putative marriage. The state also allows the putative spouse to petition for spousal support.

Rather than create a parallel community property system, the equitable relationship doctrine admits the successful claimant to the Washington community property system.

A mid-twentieth century case, *Creasman v. Boyle,* 31 Wash.2d 345,196 P.2d 835 (1948), denied nonmarried cohabitants access to the state community property system. This left the couple to resolve their property rights by contract, business partnership, trust, or constructive trust theories.

Creasman was overruled in *Matter of Marriage of Lindsey,* 101 Wash.2d 299, 678 P.2d 328 (1984), which held that courts must " 'examine the [parties'] relationship and the property accumulations and make a just and equitable disposition of the property.' " Id. at 307. The label meretricious relationship to refer to these family relationships is insultingly inexact. Meretricious has negative connotations pointing to sex being exchanged for value.

To move away from negative connotations, Washington uses the term *committed intimate relationship doctrine*. The proof required to show the existence of a committed intimate relationship is straightforward: some courts simply ask was the relationship in question marriage-like? It is not necessary to establish a specific underlying contract, a business relationship, a joint venture, or a wrongdoing that necessitates a constructive or resulting trust to establish the existence of a marriage-like relationship.

An marriage-like relationship is defined as one that is stable and built on the intention to pool and share resources (and by implication) acquisitions. See e.g. *Marriage of Pennington*, 142 Wash.2d 592, 14 P.3d 764 (2000). By this rationale (but not the outcome) any two parties domiciled in the state who can (but nevertheless choose not to) marry can invoke the protections of *Lindsey*. *Vasquez v. Hawthorne*, 141 Wash.2d 1025, 11 P.3d 825 (2000).

9. WISCONSIN

Wisconsin had a state constitutional ban on same-sex marriage. The ban was overturned by a federal court in 2014.

Limited domestic partnership legislation exists in Wisconsin, as Wisconsin was one of the states that banned same sex marriage by state constitutional amendment. RDPs in Wisconsin did not have access to Wisconsin marital property statutes but now do as Wis.Stat. § 770.001 was repealed on April 1, 2018.

In 1922—long before Wisconsin's adoption of UMPA—Wisconsin allowed recovery on an implied contract theory in a case involving a putative spouse. The putative widow believed in good faith that she was validly married while the purported "husband" knew that the marriage was invalid. See *Estate of Fox*, 178 Wis. 369, 190 N.W. 90 (1922). Today, under Wis.Stat. § 765.24, if there is an impediment to a lawful marriage, once the impediment is removed, the parties can have their marriage recognized as lawful.

The Wisconsin Supreme Court has held that nonmarried cohabitants may raise claims based on unjust enrichment following the termination of their relationship. The claim accrues when one party attempts to retain an unreasonable amount of the property acquired through the efforts of both. See *Watts v. Watts*, 137 Wis.2d 506, 405 N.W.2d 303 (1987) and *Lawlis v. Thompson*, 137 Wis.2d 490, 405 N.W.2d 317 (1987).

Wis.Stat. § 766.01 does not subject the spouses to marital property rules unless both are domiciled in the state.

CHAPTER 13

FEDERAL PROBLEMS

A. FEDERAL SUPREMACY

1. OVERVIEW OF THE FEDERAL SYSTEM

The U.S. federal system contemplates a full body of state laws in each state and a superimposed network of federal laws.

The federal laws are generally not all encompassing. Instead, federal laws envision fuller interpretation by use of the various state laws. For example, bankruptcy is federal law, but state law determines which property is not subject to execution.

Most of the fields with which this Nutshell is concerned—property interests, creditors' rights, marriage, divorce, and probate administration—are almost entirely a matter of state law with very little federal intrusion. Whenever federal law and state law conflict, however, the federal law (if constitutional) is given priority under the supremacy clause, Constitution of the United States, article VI, clause 2.

If a state law is considered destructive of the spirit and purpose of federal legislation, the federal legislature or courts can reject it. For example, *Free v. Bland*, 369 U.S. 663, 82 S.Ct. 1089, 8 L.Ed.2d 180 (1962) asserted federal supremacy in the form of ownership of U.S. Series E and F Savings Bonds. As a matter of federal law, the "or" form of ownership established a survivorship between the parties (similar to joint tenancy); but Texas provisions (the local law) purported to declare the "or" form of bond ownership to be community property (without a survivorship feature). In this instance, the state (local) law was required to yield to the federal law.

An analytic approach to constitutional interaction of federal and state laws is as follows.

Constitutionality. What power granted to the federal government authorizes the statute? Is the federal statute prohibited by any constitutional provision? Is the federal law otherwise unconstitutional?

Few federal statutes are deemed to be in excess of the constitutional power to enact laws which are necessary and proper to carry out the enumerated federal powers. There is a remote possibility that a statute might be deemed to attempt to take property without due process. If so, the statute would violate the 5th Amendment to the U.S. Constitution.

Pre-emption. Does the federal statute purport to preempt the field or does it defer to state law? Federal laws may preempt a field, but not all federal laws necessarily do so.

Federal interests. Does the state law do major damage to clear and substantial federal interests? Some state laws are inconvenient to the federal law without being damaging to federal interests. See for example *Poe v. Seaborn*, 282 U.S. 101, 51 S.Ct. 58, 75 L.Ed. 239 (1930), the U.S. Supreme Court required the modification of the federal tax laws in order to eliminate the advantage otherwise available only in community property states.

2. FEDERAL PRE-EMPTION AND FEDERAL INTERESTS

Wissner v. Wissner, 338 U.S. 655, 70 S.Ct. 398, 94 L.Ed. 424 (1950) is the doctrinal ancestor of current cases dealing with the interaction of state and federal law. In that case, a National Service Life Insurance on the life of a deceased California serviceman who was domiciled in California was held exempt from the state community property laws. Evidence for pre-emption was found in Federal Employee's Group Life Insurance Act (FEGLI for short) statements that the insured "shall have the right to designate" and change the beneficiary at all times and that payments of proceeds "shall be exempt from the claims of creditors, and shall not be liable to attachment, levy or seizure by or under any legal or equitable process whatever, either before or after receipt by the beneficiary." *Wissner*, supra, is discussed in Chapter 7.

Hisquierdo v. Hisquierdo, 439 U.S. 572, 99 S.Ct. 802, 59 L.Ed.2d 1 (1979) and *McCarty v. McCarty*, 453 U.S. 210, 101 S.Ct. 2728, 69 L.Ed.2d 589 (1981) are decisions of the U.S. Supreme Court that concern the application of state community property laws to federal retirement plans, and specifically to military retirement plans.

Hisquierdo, supra, continues to be relied upon. The case dealt with the federal Railroad Retirement Act (the RRA for short), a federal law that the U.S.

Supreme Court wrote "resembles both a private pension program and a social welfare plan". *Hisquierdo*, supra at 573. The case involved a married worker's railroad retirement benefits, earned during marriage while domiciled in California and covered by the RRA. The legal question was whether the covered benefits were divisible at dissolution, and if so, whether an offsetting award to the non-employee spouse would defeat the purpose of the RRA. The U.S. Supreme Court held that RRA covered benefits are not community property subject to division upon divorce. Consequently, an offsetting award to the non-employee spouse would defeat (damage rather than merely inconvenience) the purpose of the RRA.

In its rationale, *Hisquierdo*, supra, summarized the federal pre-emption doctrine, as enforced by the Supremacy Clause, as follows. The subjects of domestic relations and probate administration belong to the laws of the individual states rather than to the laws of the federal government. State laws must do major damage to clear and substantial federal interests before the supremacy clause of the federal constitution will override the state law. The tests applied are whether the asserted right conflicts with the express terms of federal law and whether its consequences sufficiently injure the objectives of the federal program to require nonrecognition. *Hisquierdo*, supra, classified as preempting language a provision in the RRA against attachment or anticipation of a specified beneficiary's interest.

McCarty, supra, was reversed by FUSFSPA, 10 U.S.C.A. § 1408, The FUSFSPA provision accomplishes two federal goals. One, it removes disposable military retirement pay from the federal pre-emption found to exist in *McCarty*. Two, it permits courts to determine the divisibility of disposable military retirement pay according to laws of the jurisdiction. Retired disposable pay means the total monthly retired pay a member is entitled to less overpayments, forfeitures, disability elections, and annuity elections for a spouse or former spouse, as enumerated in FUSFSPA § 1408(a)(4)(A). For more on Military Retirement and Disability Payments under FUSFSPA see Chapter 7.

See also *In re Marriage of Howell*, 238 Ariz. 407, 408, 361 P.3d 936, 937 (2015). The veteran former spouse petitioned for certiorari.

The possibility of federal pre-emption remains in other areas. For example, one legal question in need of clarification is how federal and state laws on educational loan liabilities might interact.

B. STATE CONSTITUTIONAL PROVISIONS

1. OVERVIEW: FEDERAL AND STATE CONSTITUTIONS

Areas in which community property problems tend to arise under the U.S. Constitution include:

- Supremacy clause problems.
- Fourteenth Amendment problems involving either the due process or the equal protection

provisions of the Constitution of the U.S. as applied to the state.

- Privileges and immunities problems which arise primarily between domiciliaries and non-domiciliaries of the state.

Each of the community property states also has its own constitution. The contested areas under state constitutions tend to be:

- Clauses that are identical to the U.S. Constitution.
- Clauses that protect the right to own separate property during marriage.
- Equal rights provisions. In the absence of such a provision, states can still protect equal rights by application of the equal protection provision of the federal constitution, New Mexico has added such a provision to its constitution.
- Retroactive applications of substantive rule changes.

Suter v. Suter, 97 Idaho 461, 546 P.2d 1169 (1976), for example, declared unconstitutional a sex-based distinction that appeared in a provision for the character of property acquired while a couple is separated. A prior Idaho case, *Reed v. Reed*, 404 U.S. 71, 92 S.Ct. 251, 30 L.Ed.2d 225 (1971), had invalidated on the same grounds an Idaho statute that preferred males in the appointment of administrators of decedents' estates. Bans on same-sex marriage provisions, which remain on the books in several U.S. community property states, have been nullified by the U.S. Supreme Court in *Obergefell*, supra. One possibly sees echoes of this in state definitional statutes, such as in Texas, where a husband and wife continue to be defined by gender for some limited purposes. This most likely is an oversight on the Texas legislature's part. Other statues in a similar situation have recently been amended to be gender neutral and gender inclusive.

Pre-*Obergefell*, supra, the U.S. community property states took different approaches to same-sex marriage. Washington, California, and New Mexico permitted same-sex marriage; Idaho, Louisiana, Nevada, Texas, and Wisconsin passed state constitutional amendments banning same-sex marriage. The state patchwork created significant human rights problems with respect to the institution of marriage and of divorce. States that banned same-sex marriage did not recognize marriages between same-sex spouses even if they were validly established in another state—a practice *Obergefell*, supra, now bars. One little analyzed aspect of the pre-*Obergefell* legal patchwork is that same-sex couples who validly married in one state but subsequently changed their domicile to a state that banned same-sex marriage could not divorce in their new domicile. Today, the previous legal patchwork uniformly resolves in favor of equal protection rights for same-sex marriage and equal protection rights for its institutional corollary, same-sex divorce.

Against the backdrop of *Obergefell*, supra, marriage remains a state law procedure, as does divorce. Different U.S. community property states allow for different relationship options. All U.S. community property states permit licensed marriage. Among those community property states, only Texas today permits informal marriage. Likewise, as to divorce, all states require a final judgment of dissolution to terminate a *valid* marriage, whether licensed or unlicensed. No state, including no community property state, permits informal divorce.

At the time this Nutshell goes to press, California, Nevada, and Washington have registered domestic partnership (RDP for short) legislation that gives RDPs the same rights and obligations as married persons. Wisconsin has limited domestic partnership legislation—the limitation was due to the state's constitutional amendment banning same-sex marriage. Arizona, Idaho, Louisiana, New Mexico, and Texas have no domestic partnership legislation. States that permit RDPS, require a formal start to the RDP, at which point the relationship becomes "registered" with the state. And, because of the formal registration, an RDP must be formally terminated in accordance with the legal parameters of the statute that authorized it.

2. STATE CONSTITUTIONAL DEFINITIONS OF SEPARATE PROPERTY

California, Nevada, and Texas have state constitutional provisions that define separate property. These constitutional provisions are sometimes considered anemic adoptions of the ganancial system by how they serve as a limitation on legislative powers to do away with a erode the state's system of community property laws.

The character of rents, issues, and profits obtained during marriage. Separate property rents, issues, and profits receive different treatment, during marriage, depending on state law. See Chapters 2, 4, and 7.

There was a time when California, Nevada, and Texas used the same constitutional language for rents, issues, and profits. Subsequent amendments have changed the wording of all three constitutions. But even when the wording was identical, different interpretations arose.

The major difference in interpretation was whether the income from separate property should be characterized, during marriage, as community or as separate property. During the early statehood era California held, in *George v. Ransom*, 15 Cal. 322 (1860), that the income from separate property remains separate property during the marriage. Two decades later, Nevada indicated by dictum in *Lake v. Lake*, 18 Nev. 361, 382–84, 4 P. 711, 722–23 (1884) as modified by *Johnson*, supra that it would follow the California (American rule) approach.

Texas held in *Arnold v. Leonard*, 114 Tex. 535, 273 S.W. 799 (1925) that separate property income received during marriage is community in character. Additionally, both Texas and California have held that statutes attempting to transmute, *by operation of law*, rents, issues, and profits of separate property received during marriage are unconstitutional.

In *George*, supra, the California court based its decision upon what it called the fixed meaning in the common law of the term separate property. Whereas in *Arnold*, supra, the Texas court viewed the omission of the term rents, issues and profits from its constitutional definition of separate property as an indication that separate property rents, issues, and profits were not included within that definition. The Texas court went on to say that because of the state constitutional definition the legislature could neither enlarge nor diminish a spouse's separate property.

Commentators have questioned whether the California court, because it used a common law analysis in reaching its result, was less true to the ganancial system than the Texas court, which relied on the civil law tradition. Some commentators have called the California rule a mistake precisely because it veers away from the civil law approach.

Perhaps the better way to understand community property rules that adhere or veer from the parent system, however, are that they represent policy choices, not mistakes. Each state arrives at its own policy decisions independent of the others. Hence, one could say that a mistake, as such, only occurs when the rule is inconsistent with or counter to the state's own policy.

The California approach today, sometimes called the American rule approach, is widely followed. However, even in those states that do not follow the so-called American rule, there can be a drifting toward California law in certain areas. There are ways to stop the drift, however. In 2013, Texas voters rejected a proposal to amend the Texas Constitution in favor of adopting the American rule approach.

3. RETROACTIVE CHANGES IN COMMUNITY PROPERTY LAWS

a. Retroactivity

Changes in community property laws can affect vested property rights. This happens when standards get raised, as in for example when a writing requirement is added where there was not one before.

There can be an initial ambiguity about how to define the concept of retroactivity when applying changes in community property laws. The ambiguity is over legal transitions.

A statute may have an effective date that is determined as a general rule to apply to all statutes in the state. Or it might include a date for a particular statute or set of statutes. This happens, for example, with emergency legislation. Sometimes there is a discrete or introductory statute that specifically addresses the retroactivity issue for purposes of its application.

The effective date of a statute can be prospective as to some operative event, but retroactive as to some other operative event. This type of legislative change may dictate what operative event should serve as the line between retroactive and prospective operation.

The date of the marriage itself, for example, might be the date that designates if the statute is applicable to the case.

Sometimes a question arises as to whether the legislature intended the statute to operate prospectively or retroactively. The intention may be express, implied, or inferred. As a general matter, if, after considering all pertinent factors, the court is unable to determine the legislative intent, the statute will be presumed (and preferred) to operate prospectively, not retroactively.

Even more generally, a guiding principle is that constitutional questions are avoided by rules of statutory construction or of general property law, absent statutory language to the contrary. The presumption here is that retroactive application is not intended unless it is specifically stated in the language of the statute itself.

In California, *Spreckels v. Spreckels*, 116 Cal. 339, 48 P. 228 (1897), imposed a constitutional prohibition upon retroactive changes. The case questioned an 1891 legislative amendment that required a wife's consent to any gift of community personal property made by the husband to a third party. The amendment was held constitutionally inapplicable to property acquired before the effective date, the rationale being that each spouse had a one-half vested right in community property, and, therefore, it was beyond the power of the legislature to deprive a spouse of his or her vested right without due process of law.

Yet another example comes from the passage of codes.

California passed a comprehensive Family Code in 1992, effective 1994. The California Family Code abrogates much of the prior code law as a general matter. Nevertheless, there remains a considerable body of applicable case law despite the adoption and amendment of the state codes.

Texas repealed it Probate Code and replaced it with an Estates Code. So complex was the renumbering that one had to, at least conditionally, consult conversion charts to track transitions from the former code to the new code.

Tax laws can be instructive as well. Several community property states have in the past few years repealed inheritance tax codes.

b. Vested Rights

Often, the inquiry over the quality of a right revolves around a determination of whether the right is vested. Cases tend to start the analysis with the proposition that the interest being changed was (or was not) a property right; from there the analysis moves to whether the right is vested, contingent, or a mere expectancy.

Amendments that seek to change in any manner the vested rights of the spouses between themselves cause an enlargement of the share of one spouse at the expense of the other spouse. Therefore, as to property already acquired during marriage, one spouse may be deprived of a potentially vested property right by the retroactive application of a newly enacted statute. If the deprivation is without due process or without compensation, or if it denies one party the equal protection of law, there is a basis for arguing that the legislation has been applied in an unconstitutional manner. It is also remotely possible in some cases to argue that the legislation impairs the obligation of the marriage contract.

Constitutional objections are sometimes avoided by deciding that the interest is not a vested right, or that the legal approach does not affect or directly impact a vested right. Thus, the attribute of the community property law that is being changed (such as the application of an evidentiary presumption) can be declared to be merely an incident to a right rather than a right itself. In this case, adopting a special community property presumption that goes into effect on a certain date becomes understood to start the conciliation proceeding only, not to affect a vested property right.

Historically, the constitutional analysis focused on asking whether there was any impairment of a vested right. Modernly, a more nuanced analysis prevails. Even if there is an impairment, the analysis goes a step further to ask (i) how much of an impairment (ii) of how important a right (iii) and for how important a reason. The emphasis, for constitutional purposes, therefore, is on the due of due process. Is the change under consideration sufficiently necessary to the public welfare to justify the impairment?

In determining the value of the change, the factors to be considered include "the significance of the state interest served by the law, the importance of the retroactive application of the law to the effectuation of that interest, the extent of reliance upon the former law, the legitimacy of that reliance, the extent of actions taken on the basis of that reliance, and the extent to which the retroactive application of the new law would disrupt those actions," *Marriage of Bouquet*, 16 Cal.3d 583, 592, 128 Cal.Rptr. 427, 432, 546 P.2d 1371, 1376 (1976).

Finally, there can be reasons to make a statute retroactive.

If the basis of a change in a default law is in furtherance of a compelling social policy, then only retroactive application will bring about the change for all spouses.

Prospective-only application, by contrast, delays the implementation and uniformity of the changes, leaving some spouses protected and some not due to their presumed reliance on the old law.

Another complexity with prospective-only legislation is that new legal transitions arise with each legislative change. As a result, administrative difficulties tend to increase, and the default system of community property laws tends to become more complex.

c. Texas Due Course

Texas has interpreted its constitution as imposing limits upon the extent to which a divorce court can assign the separate real property of one spouse to the nonowning spouse upon divorce.

In *Eggemeyer v. Eggemeyer*, 554 S.W.2d 137 (Tex.1977), the Texas Supreme Court prohibited such a transfer on the basis that it was contrary to two constitutional provisions—the definition of separate property in Tex. Const. Art. XVI, § 15 and the due course provision of Tex. Const. Art. I, § 19. The Texas due course provision, it turns out, is almost identical to the due process provisions of the federal and other state constitutions. Moreover, the Texas due course provision was deemed to require not only procedural, but also substantive, due course. Id.

Finally, *Eggemeyer*, supra, applies as much to personal property as it does to real property. And it applies to each spouse's one-half share of the community property as well as to any separate property. Thus, it is not inconceivable that *Eggemeyer*, supra, could be applied to declare unconstitutional provisions for the division of property upon divorce if those provisions tend to divide property equitably between the parties to the marriage without rigid conformity to previous ownership or character.

C. CONFLICT OF LAWS

1. CHOICE OF LAW

The federal system permits diversity so that each state can decide whether it will have a community property system and what attributes that community property system will have. A price of the federal system is that the laws of various states can conflict, meaning they can reach opposing conclusions depending upon which system of law is chosen.

To resolve conflicts of laws, courts seek to use one or more contacts. The method of choice of law is often to seek the jurisdiction with the most significant contacts with the subject matter of the litigation. Among the significant contacts are the forum, domicile, location of realty, and place where a tort occurred.

a. Forum

The forum is the jurisdiction which contains the court in which a lawsuit is filed.

A state could declare that it intends to apply its own law to all situations regardless of the domicile and location of the parties and persons who come before it. In addition to constitutional and jurisdictional problems, this would make the applicable law almost entirely the choice of the plaintiff since the choice of forum is made by the plaintiff.

The easiest law for the forum court to apply is its own law. In many instances, a choice of law problem is ignored because the existence of a contradictory system is not called by the parties to the attention of the court. For example, if a couple who own community property are divorced in a non-community property state, the divorce court might ignore community property problems because one or both parties and their attorneys have failed to point out the conflict. When this happens, one spouse may be adversely affected, relative to the other spouse, in terms of property division.

Similarly, the presumption that the law of another jurisdiction is the same as the law of the forum puts the burden of proving the different law upon the person who asserts that there is a difference.

Finally, the total law of the forum includes both its internal law and its choice of law provisions. Therefore, it is imprecise to say that the forum court is applying its own law *or* the law of another state. The internal law of another state may be applied through the choice of laws law of the forum.

b. Domicile

Domicile is the most important criterion in determining the application of community property law.

The validity of the marriage itself is tested by the law of the place where it is executed, but the domicile of the parties may nevertheless declare the marriage invalid if the marriage is contrary to a strong policy of the domicile.

Domicile is the legal status of citizenship and residency in a state.

Generally, domicile results from a combination of physical presence in the state, and the intent to remain (or at least not to leave) the state. Generally, a person's legal domicile is the state in which the person resides. But residence and domicile are not identical terms. A residence can be a permanent or a temporary address, but a domicile is the individual's permanent, legal address.

In the male-management era, which ended for all community property states in the mid-1970s, the (now rejected) rule was that the husband's domicile determined the wife's domicile unless the wife was justified in establishing a separate domicile for herself.

The current rule, from the mid-1970s forward is that each person in a marriage establishes a domicile. Any person, married or not, has (only) one domicile at a time. Spouses typically share the same domicile as a practical matter. But today it is also possible for persons who are married to each other to establish different domiciles, and a person's domicile can change during marriage. Objective facts determine a person's domicile: personal residence, family residence, place of employment, voter registration, vehicle registration, and any other fact tending to show that the party has a present intent to permanently reside in the state. Once domicile is established, it remains the same until it is reestablished elsewhere.

Sometimes a person is present in the state but not domiciled there. Some examples follow. A military person who is stationed in a community property state may be physically present in the state but not domiciled there. A college student can be a physical resident of a state without being domiciled there.

Likewise, a person housed in a federal prison may have a permanent legal residence in another state.

If spouses are domiciled in different states, the marriage will be governed by the state with the most significant relationship to the spouses and the property at issue.

Definitions of community property laws are based upon the domicile of the parties at the time that property is acquired. Generally, all property acquired during marriage while domiciled in the state is community property under the laws of that state. Thus, if a married couple change their domicile from one community property state to another, they may acquire different categories of community property. When this happens, the married persons may own State A community property—governed by State A's community property rules—and State B community property—governed by State B's community property rules.

If the community is terminated by dissolution, the domicile of one or both parties is the proper jurisdiction for the dissolution action.

If the community is terminated by death, the domicile of the decedent is the proper jurisdiction as to personal property to administer the probate estate, to judge the validity and effect of any will, and to apply its intestacy rules.

Jurisdiction over a defendant is usually most easily obtained at the defendant's domicile. The defendant's domicile is frequently also the forum.

c. Situs

Realty, the classic immovable, is generally governed by the law of its situs, or location.

Further, the concept of quasi-community property is a labeling device. It does not give the court of one state jurisdiction over property in another state.

For the above reason, ancillary probate administrations are necessary in the estate of a decedent who dies owning property in states other than the domiciliary state. The choice of laws law of the situs state, like that of the forum, may look to the domiciliary state law to determine the character of property.

d. Place Where Tort Committed

The choice of law rule for torts generally looks to the law at the place where the tort was committed, the lex loci delicti.

For the above reason, if community property state domiciliaries are tortiously injured in a non-community property state, the law of the place of the tort appears to be the proper law to apply.

Several conflicts of laws could arise. For example, if the community property domiciliary rules make the non-injured spouse a necessary party to the tort action and the non-community property site of the accident requires only the injured spouse be named as a party, a question may arise as to whether the non-injured spouse is a necessary party to the action.

2. MOVING TO A COMMUNITY PROPERTY STATE

a. Multistate Problems

There are several ways in which the laws of more than one state may be involved in deciding which law to apply to determine the character of property.

Married couples may move to, from, or between community property states, own property, or become involved in a tort in a state other than the state of domicile.

There is seldom community property unless and until a married couple has both married and established domicile in a community property state. Just as there is no community prior to marriage, there is no community without domicile.

Minor exceptions do exist. For example, a couple can marry with the plan to establish a new domicile in a community property state soon after the wedding. But if that same couple ends up residing in a community property state for work, with no intention to establish a domicile in that state, then they will not acquire community property under the state's rules, practically speaking.

b. Retiring in a Community Property State

The Sun Belt of the U.S. historically has drawn retirees from colder parts of the country. Several of the Sun Belt states (Arizona, California, Nevada, New Mexico, and Texas) are community property states. The flow of married couples into community property states is therefore not an isolated phenomenon.

Upon the death of a primary wage-earning spouse, the different approaches of community and non-community property states can leave a gap in coverage for the immigrant surviving spouse. The spousal protection statutes of a separate property state (forced share dower substitutes, for example) will not be part of the law of a community property state.

In this case, the surviving spouse's protection, if any, must come from the decedent's estate plan. This is because the couple, having moved to the state to retire, not to work, will not have earned income in the community property state.

c. Privileges and Immunities Problems

The first attempt by California to define quasi-community used entry into the state as the trigger for changing the character of an immigrant couple's out-of-state property. That attempt was held unconstitutional in *Estate of Thornton*, 1 Cal.2d 1, 33 P.2d 1 (1934), where the court ruled that the use of entry into the state as a trigger for characterizing property within the community property system is a deprivation of property without due process and a denial of the privileges and immunities of those who move to California. The result is that establishing a domicile in a community property state is not enough, without more, to bring the party or parties' property into the community property system of the person's new domicile.

Thornton, supra, is now superseded by a quasi-community property statute. That statute names the filing of a petition in a California court (not mere entry into the state) as the event that gives a California court authority to characterize out-of-state property within the California community property system.

Addison v. Addison, 62 Cal.2d 558, 43 Cal.Rptr. 97, 399 P.2d 897 (1965) upheld the application of California's quasi-community property statute in the dissolution situation.

Addison, supra, distinguished *Thornton*, supra, on the ground that the statute with which the former case dealt attempted to alter property rights because and by virtue of the married couple reestablishing domicile in California. The new statute, on the other hand, only comes into force when the party or parties file a petition for dissolution in a California court. By filing a petition in a California court, parties who were not originally married in California give their consent to use the state's community property system to label any property that they acquired in the state where they previously resided.

d. The Concept of Quasi-Community Property

Wisconsin and UMPA 1983 use the quasi-community property concept as a major transitional provision for domiciliaries who were married and owned property on the effective date of the community property law. Wisconsin uses the concept of deferred marital property, which is known as property that would have been marital property if it had been acquired after the determination date.

Quasi-community property statutes, where enacted, can apply in divorce actions to property acquired during marriage. They can also apply in death situations. In the latter, the concept applies only to the decedent's property that would have been community property had it been acquired in the new domicile. The surviving spouse's property is not treated as quasi-community property.

e. Emigration from a Community Property State

Some of the community property states have attempted to adjust for those who emigrate from a separate property state. But, practically speaking, separate property states do not make a similar adjustment to accommodate the interests of those who emigrate from a community property state into a separate property state.

Community property remains community property when a married person changes domicile to a separate property state. The problem of adapting a separate property system to community property is like converting meters into inches without using fractions or decimals: The result is only approximate. Thus, the typical, and most correct, separate property state treatment of existing community property is to consider it as a form of the common law tenancy in common, giving equal shares to each party. This eliminates some of the attributes of community property such as management and control rights and duties, just as whole number usage eliminates fractions or decimals in a metric conversion.

The Uniform Disposition of Community Property Rights at Death Act (the UDCPRDA for short) is designed to protect the rights of surviving spouses in community property states. But, interestingly, the list of adopters are separate property states. Not a single community property state, to date, as adopted the UDCPRDA.

As discussed above, a party may ignore community property aspects of the case. But whereas a party is free to ignore whether they are adversely affected (or not) by the strategies they undertake, an attorney is not. An attorney who does not pursue zealously the client's right to community property may face both professional discipline and malpractice claims.

Whenever spouses from a community property state migrate to a non-community property state, those spouses bring with them the protections of the community property system under which they acquired property during their marriage. If their marriage ends, their (non-community property system) attorneys too often neglect the community property ramifications of their client's divorce or estate. By ignoring the community property era of a marriage's existence, attorneys in non-community property states overlook (or even abandon) the significant advantages that their clients (and their families) gained while domiciled under their former community property regime.

D. THE INTERNAL REVENUE SERVICE

The Internal Revenue Service maintains an online resource to assist I.R.S. employees with community property issues.

E. A CONCLUDING THOUGHT

The whole of a community property system is far greater than the sum of its parts.

The joke among lawyers who are unfamiliar with community property law is that it is easy, just divide in half.

The joke under-imagines the risk of dismissing community property as an area of law unworthy of social or philosophical analysis. A community property system is a default property system, it is true. It assists with facilitating dissolution. But it is also a powerful financial tool for intimate partners who want to manage and plan for their own and their family's future.

Ultimately, a community property system is a public institution for assigning property rights during marriage. Fairness, choice, agreement, financial accountability, financial disclosure, stewardship—these are principles that any community property system develops to cast light on legal issues that can arise between intimate partners.

Given that many people enter marriage, I believe it is important to make the study of marital property principles a core part of legal education. However, as we enter a future dominated by artificial intelligence, the law school curriculum becomes less exacting in the upper division, when a marital property course would be taught. As a result, it is becoming increasingly necessary for individuals to underscore for their attorneys how important the dissolution process can be for moving forward with life. I write this book for those individuals and for their attorneys.

INDEX

References are to Pages